Mongolia and Northeast Asian Security

This book assesses Mongolia's position in the security calculus of Northeast Asia and presents the policy outlooks of major powers vis-a-vis the region, including the United States, Japan, China, Russia, and India.

Ground-breaking and modernistic in its approach, the book treats the often marginalised and landlocked small power state of Mongolia as a critical regional actor, particularly with regards to managing ties with encircling major powers Russia and China and assist in engaging the nuclear state of North Korea through dialogue mechanisms. This compilation of chapters by distinguished scholars explores Mongolia in the Northeast Asian geographical space within the context of three major themes: nuclear proliferation, environmental security, and socio-economic and civilisational conflicts. The book provides a multidisciplinary and multinational approach to Mongolia's role in the region's strategic landscape. It moves the regional security discussion beyond major power politics, North Korea's denuclearisation, and the impasse on the Korean Peninsula to discuss and analyse other underappreciated challenges facing the region.

Considering Mongolia's role in achieving peace and stability in the neighbourhood, the book will be a valuable resource for researchers and readers in International Relations, Political Science, and Asian Studies.

Alicia J. Campi is Vice President of The Mongolia Society and SAIS/Johns Hopkins University, USA. Dr. Campi is a China/Mongolian specialist and a former U.S. State Department Foreign Service Officer of 14 years who served in Asian posts (Singapore, Taiwan, Japan, and Mongolia) and the U.S. Mission to the United Nations in New York.

Jagannath P. Panda is Research Fellow and Coordinator at Manohar Parikkar Institute for Defence Studies and Analyses (MP-IDSA), New Delhi, India. Dr. Panda is in charge of the East Asia Centre at the MP-IDSA, and responsible for the track-II and track 1.5 dialogue with think-tanks in China, Taiwan, Japan, and Korea.

Routledge Studies on Think Asia
Edited by Jagannath P. Panda
Institute for Defence Studies and Analyses, India

This series addresses the current strategic complexities of Asia and forecasts how these current complexities will shape Asia's future. Bringing together empirical and conceptual analysis, the series examines critical aspects of Asian politics, with a particular focus on the current security and strategic complexities. The series includes academic studies from universities, research institutes and think-tanks and policy oriented studies. Focusing on security and strategic analysis on Asia's current and future trajectory, this series welcomes submissions on relationship patterns (bilateral, trilateral, and multilateral) in Indo-Pacific, regional and subregional institutions and mechanisms, corridors and connectivity, maritime security, infrastructure politics, trade and economic models and critical frontiers (boundaries, borders, bordering provinces) that are crucial to Asia's future.

Japan's Evolving Security Policy
Militarisation within a Pacifist Tradition
Kyoko Hatakeyama

India and the Arab Unrest
Challenges, Dilemmas and Engagements
Prashanta Kumar Pradhan

The Future of the Korean Peninsula
Korea 2032 and Beyond
Edited by Mason Richey, Jagannath P. Panda and David A. Tizzard

Mongolia and Northeast Asian Security
Nuclear Proliferation, Environment, and Civilisational Confrontations
Edited by Alicia J. Campi and Jagannath P. Panda

Asian Geopolitics and the US-China Rivalry
Edited by Felix Heiduk

URL: https://www.routledge.com/Routledge-Studies-on-Think-Asia/book-series/TA

Mongolia and Northeast Asian Security

Nuclear Proliferation, Environment, and Civilisational Confrontations

Edited by Alicia J. Campi and Jagannath P. Panda

LONDON AND NEW YORK

First published 2022
by Routledge
2 Park Square, Milton Park, Abingdon, Oxon OX14 4RN

and by Routledge
605 Third Avenue, New York, NY 10158

Routledge is an imprint of the Taylor & Francis Group, an informa business

© 2022 selection and editorial matter, Alicia J. Campi and Jagannath P. Panda; individual chapters, the contributors

The right of Alicia J. Campi and Jagannath P. Panda to be identified as the authors of the editorial material, and of the authors for their individual chapters, has been asserted in accordance with sections 77 and 78 of the Copyright, Designs and Patents Act 1988.

All rights reserved. No part of this book may be reprinted or reproduced or utilised in any form or by any electronic, mechanical, or other means, now known or hereafter invented, including photocopying and recording, or in any information storage or retrieval system, without permission in writing from the publishers.

Trademark notice: Product or corporate names may be trademarks or registered trademarks, and are used only for identification and explanation without intent to infringe.

British Library Cataloguing-in-Publication Data
A catalogue record for this book is available from the British Library

Library of Congress Cataloging-in-Publication Data
Names: Campi, Alicia J., editor. | Panda, Jagannath P., editor.
Title: Mongolia and Northeast Asian security : nuclear proliferation, environment, and civilisational confrontations / edited by Alicia J. Campi and Jagannath P. Panda.
Description: London ; New York, NY : Routledge, Taylor & Francis Group, 2022. | Series: Routledge Studies on Think Asia | Includes bibliographical references and index.
Identifiers: LCCN 2021008575 (print) | LCCN 2021008576 (ebook) | ISBN 9780367700638 (hardback) | ISBN 9780367709495 (paperback) | ISBN 9781003148630 (ebook)
Subjects: LCSH: National security–East Asia. | National security–Mongolia. | Mongolia–Strategic aspects. | East Asia–Military relations–Mongolia. | Mongolia–Military relations–East Asia.
Classification: LCC UA832.5 .M645 2022 (print) | LCC UA832.5 (ebook) | DDC 355/.03305173–dc23
LC record available at https://lccn.loc.gov/2021008575
LC ebook record available at https://lccn.loc.gov/2021008576

ISBN: 978-0-367-70063-8 (hbk)
ISBN: 978-0-367-70949-5 (pbk)
ISBN: 978-1-003-14863-0 (ebk)

DOI: 10.4324/9781003148630

Typeset in Times New Roman
by MPS Limited, Dehradun

For John Gombojab Hangin

Contents

Editors ix
List of contributors xi
List of abbreviations xvi

Introduction: The Northeast Asian security calculus 1
ALICIA J. CAMPI AND JAGANNATH P. PANDA

PART I
Major powers, Mongolia, and Northeast Asian security 7

1 An examination of the Trump administration's National Security Strategy in the Indo-Pacific: Where is Northeast Asia? 9
   ALICIA J. CAMPI

2 China's foreign policy in Northeast Asia and implications for Mongolia 30
   DENNY ROY

3 Russia in Northeast Asia: strengthening security through cooperation 47
   ELENA BOYKOVA

4 Why Northeast Asian regional economic integration is important for Mongolia 76
   NANJIN DORJSUREN

5 Japan's foreign policy security mechanisms in the Asia-Pacific and Northeast Asia 85
   FUJIMAKI HIROYUKI AND TSEDENDAMBA BATBAYAR

6 India, Mongolia, and Northeast Asia: between geography and the geopolitical realities 103
MAHIMA N. DUGGAL AND JAGANNATH P. PANDA

PART II
Nuclear challenges in Northeast Asia 139

7 The relationship of United States-Japan-Mongolia democratic trilateralism to the Indo-Pacific strategy and Korean Peninsular discussions 141
ALICIA J. CAMPI

8 Why Asia should lead a global push to eliminate nuclear weapons—the role for Mongolia 162
MICHAEL ANDREGG

9 Nuclear non-proliferation in Northeast Asia and Mongolia's policy 178
JARGALSAIKHAN ENKHSAIKHAN

10 The changing regional dynamics in Northeast Asia: Russia's North Korean conundrum and the case of Mongolia 199
NIVEDITA KAPOOR

PART III
Socio-economic, environmental, and civilisational challenges in Northeast Asia 217

11 Environmental security issues in Northeast Asia and cooperation among Russia, China, and Mongolia 219
ELENA BOYKOVA

12 Asia and beyond: organised environmental crime 237
LYNN RHODES

13 When Toynbee's "fossilized" or "arrested" societies are reborn as peripheral states: the cases of Israel, Mongolia, Korea, and Japan 255
JOSEPH DREW

Index 273

Editors

Dr. Alicia J. Campi is Vice President of The Mongolia Society and SAIS/Johns Hopkins University, USA. Dr. Alicia Campi is a China/Mongolian specialist and a former U.S. State Department Foreign Service Officer of 14 years who served in Asian posts (Singapore, Taiwan, Japan, and Mongolia) and the U.S. Mission to the United Nations in New York. Since 2013, she has been a research fellow at the Edwin O. Reischauer Center for East Asian Studies at SAIS/Johns Hopkins University and adjunct professor teaching on Northeast Asia. She is a lecturer on Mongolia and Northeast Asia for the State Department's Foreign Service Institute, and regularly writes commentaries on China's minority and peripheral relations for various research institutions, including The Jamestown Foundation and East West Center. A fluent Chinese speaker, she received her A.B. in East Asian History from Smith College in 1971 and obtained an M.A. in East Asian Studies with a concentration in Mongolian Studies from Harvard University in 1973. She received a Ph.D. in Mongolian Studies with a minor in Chinese in 1987 from Indiana University. In July 2004, she was awarded the "Friendship" Medal by Mongolian President N. Bagabandi and in 2011 received the "Polar Star" (Mongolia's highest medal) from President Ts. Elbegdorj for her contribution to bilateral relations. In September 2007, she was awarded an honorary doctorate from the National University of Mongolia. Dr. Campi has published over 120 articles and book chapters on contemporary Chinese, Mongolian, and Central Asian issues. She advises business clients on Mongolian investment issues, particularly in the mining sector, and is an expert witness on Mongolian political asylum and human rights cases. Her book, *The Impact of China and Russia on U.S.-Mongolian Political Relations in the 20th Century,* was published in 2009, and her latest book, *Mongolian Foreign Policy: Navigating a Changing World,* was published in 2019. She was president of the Mongolia Society for 12 years and now serves as its vice president.

Dr. Jagannath P. Panda is Research Fellow and Coordinator at Manohar Parikkar Institute for Defence Studies and Analyses (MP-IDSA), New Delhi, India. Dr. Panda is in charge of the East Asia Centre at the MP-IDSA, and responsible for the track-II and track 1.5 dialogue with think-tanks in China, Taiwan, Japan, and Korea. He is also the series editor for

x *Editors*

Routledge Studies on Think Asia. Dr. Panda is the author of several key texts like *India-China Relations: Politics of Resources, Identity and Authority in a Multipolar World Order* (Routledge: 2017); and *China's Path to Power: Party, Military and the Politics of State Transition* (Pentagon Press: 2010). He is the editor of the volume, *India-Taiwan Relations in Asia and Beyond: The Future* (Pentagon Press, 2016). Dr. Panda also has a number of other books to his credit as an editor. Most recently, he has published an edited volume *Scaling India-Japan Cooperation in Indo-Pacific and Beyond 2025: Connectivity, Corridors and Contours* (KW Publishing Ltd. 2019), and *The Korean Peninsula and Indo-Pacific Power Politics: Status Security at Stake* (Routledge, 2020). He is also the co-editor of the just released volume, *Chinese Politics and Foreign Policy under Xi Jinping: The Future Political Trajectory* (Routledge, 2020).

Contributors

Dr. Michael Andregg, University of St. Thomas in Minnesota, USA. Dr. Andregg earned a Ph.D. in behaviour genetics (1977) from the University of California, Davis after completing a triple-major B.S. in genetics, zoology, and physical anthropology (1973). Dr. Andregg's study of global armed conflict and genocide resulted in his book, *On the Causes of War*, which won the International Peace Writing Award in 1999. He taught undergraduate and graduate courses as an adjunct professor at the University of Minnesota for 35 years, with brief stints at Macalester and Gustavus Adolphus Colleges. He also joined the Justice and Peace Studies faculty at the University of St. Thomas in 1993 until 2017. Dr. Andregg has lectured in South Korea and Japan on sustainable development, weapons of mass destruction, and causes of wars, at Romania's National Intelligence Academy, and at many European conferences on intelligence reform and human survival issues. He still lectures at the National Intelligence University, Army Command and General Staff College, and the Naval Postgraduate School. In 1982, Dr. Andregg founded an educational, non-profit organization called Ground Zero Minnesota, which produced over 50 public television programs and sponsored about 5,000 educational programs in schools, churches, and civic groups on issues of peace, justice, and implications of weapons of mass destruction.

Dr. Ambassador Tsedendamba Batbayar is Director of the Institute of Oriental and International Studies of the Mongolian Academy of Sciences, Ulaanbaatar, Mongolia. Dr. Batbayar obtained his Ph.D. from Leningrad State University and pursued both a diplomatic and research career. He served in the Ministry of Foreign Affairs in Tokyo and Beijing, and was Mongolia's ambassador to Cuba 2015–2019. In between his diplomatic postings, he was a researcher at the Woodrow Wilson Center in Washington DC and director of the East Asia Institute in the Mongolian Academy of Sciences. Dr. Batbayar has authored several articles on Mongolian Twentieth Century topics and published two books on this subject.

Dr. Elena Boykova is a senior researcher, Institute for Oriental Studies, Russian Academy of Sciences. She specializes in Modern History and cultural development of Mongolia, Russian-Mongolian relations, Mongolia's foreign policy, problems of security in North-East Asia. She graduated from the Moscow State Institute of International Relations (MGIMO), Ministry of Foreign Affairs. She holds Ph.D. (Hist.) from the Institute for Oriental Studies, RAS. She is the author of three books, more than 100 articles in Russian, Mongolian, English, and Japanese, editor-in-chief of more than 10 books. She is a member of the International Association for Mongol Studies, of the Permanent International Altaistic Conference (PIAC), of the Mongolia Society (USA), of the China-Mongolia-Russia Think Tank "China-Mongolia-Russia Economic Corridor," and a member of the Presidium of the Russian Society of Mongolists. Dr. Boykova received the Polar Star Decoration (highest award for non-Mongol citizen) in 2016 and an Honorary Doctorate Degree from the Institute of International Affairs of the Mongolian Academy of Sciences in 2018.

Mr. Nanjin Dorjsuren is Director of the Mongolian Institute of Northeast Asian Security and Strategy (MINASS), Ulaanbaatar, Mongolia. He obtained his Bachelor's in International Relations from Mongolian National University, Master's in China studies in Zhejiang University, China, and Master's in Public Policy in Ritsumeikan University, Japan. At the Institute of Strategic Studies of Mongolia, he served as study group leader of Northeast Asian Security studies, and coordinated and supervised research projects and international conferences, such as the annual Ulaanbaatar Dialogue. He is a specialist on national security and DPRK issues.

Dr. Joseph Drew is Editor of *Comparative Civilizations Review*, International Society for the Comparative Study of Civilizations since 1995. He received an M.A., Ph.D. (1975) in Sociology from The New School and a B.A. in Sociology and M.S. J. in Journalism from Columbia University. He has been a professor at the University of Maryland University College since 1995 and visiting professor, DeVry University since 2005. He was also on the faculty in the Community College Leadership Doctoral Program, Morgan State University from 2015–2018. Dr. Drew was president of the University of Northern Virginia 2004–2008; president of the Anglo-American University of Prague in the Czech Republic 2001–2004; executive director of the Potomac Regional Education Partnership in Washington DC from 1999–2002; dean of Business and Social Science at Shepherd University in West Virginia USA 2000–2001; vice president for Academic and External Affairs at Southeastern University in Washington DC 1997–2000; and professor of Political Science, University of the District of Columbia USA 1978–1997.

Ms. Mahima N. Duggal is Research Associate at the Centre for Air Power Studies, New Delhi, India. She is also an Associate Research Fellow at the Institute for Security and Development Policy (ISDP) and an Editorial Assistant to the series Editor of the *Routledge Studies on Think Asia*. Her research interests are focused on Indo-Pacific affairs, with a focus on South Asian dynamics covering India-China Relations, India and its neighbourhood region, and the middle power dynamics. Ms. Duggal graduated at the top of her class with an M.A. (distinction) in International Security from the University of Warwick. She also holds a Bachelor's degree in International Relations from the University of London and a Bachelor's in Communication with a double major in Journalism and Public Relations from the University of Newcastle, Australia. She has been widely published in outlets such as *World in One News* (WION), *Eurasia Review*, *9DashLine*, Institute for Peace and Conflict Studies (IPCS), Human Rights Law Network, and Institute for Security and Development Policy.

Ambassador Jargalsaikhan Enkhsaikhan is President of the Blue Banner Foundation, Ulaanbaatar, Mongolia. Ambassador Jargalsaikhan Enkhsaikhan is an international lawyer and diplomat who served at the Ministry of Foreign Affairs of Mongolia for 35 years, including as ambassador in Austria and the International Atomic Energy Agency (2008–2012) and at the United Nations New York (1996–2003). From 1993–1996, he served as the foreign policy and legal advisor to the first democratically elected president of Mongolia and later as the executive secretary of the Mongolian National Security Council. In 2013–2014, he served as Ambassador-at-Large in charge of disarmament issues, especially on nuclear-related threat issues. A graduate of Moscow State Institute for International Relations, where he also received his PhD in International Law, his legal experience includes such issues as promotion of peace, democratic governance, human rights, gender equality, and providing international legal advice on property, family, civil and criminal, and commercial arbitration-related issues. After his retirement in 2014, Ambassador Enkhsaikhan served as chairman of Blue Banner, a Mongolian NGO dedicated to promoting the goals of nuclear non-proliferation and Mongolia's nuclear-weapon-free status. He has contributed nearly 110 articles in Mongolian, English, and other languages on international relations, non-proliferation and regional security, as well as organised many regional meetings aimed at promoting peace, stability, international cooperation, environmental protection, and good governance.

Dr. Fujimaki Hiroyuki is Associate Professor at the Department of Political Science, Tokai University, Japan. Dr. Fujimaki has an expertise in International Relations and regionalism in Northeast Asia. He studied regionalism in Eurasia and Russian energy policy at Webster University

(U.S.), Tokai University (Japan), and the Institute of World Economy and International Relations (IMEMO) in the Russian Academy of Sciences. Presently, he is an assistant researcher and part-time lecturer at Strategic Peace and International Affairs Research Institute, Tokai University. His books include *Regional Security Governance in Central Asia* (2015), *The United States and International Order* (2013), and *Creating East Asian Community* (2006).

Dr. Nivedita Kapoor is Junior Fellow for the Strategic Studies Program, Observer Research Foundation since May 2019. Her research interests lie in the field of Russian foreign policy, with a particular focus on Moscow's approach towards Asia. As part of her work at ORF, she tracks Russian foreign and domestic policy—and Eurasian strategic affairs. Kapoor began her career as a journalist working with the Free Press Journal, DNA and Press Trust of India. She was awarded her Ph.D. in 2020 from the School of International Studies, Jawaharlal Nehru University, New Delhi focusing on her thesis on Russia-China Relations in East Asia. She completed both her MPhil in Russian Studies (2015) as well as Master's Degree in International Relations from JNU (2010) and has a Bachelor's Degree in Journalism and Mass Communication (2008) from Devi Ahilya University, Indore, India. She has published over ten articles in journals and online magazines and contributed chapters to two upcoming edited volumes (on post-Soviet Eurasia and East Asia).

Ms. Lynn Rhodes is President of the International Society for the Comparative Study of Civilizations, California USA. Ms. Rhodes is the former chief of California State Parks Law Enforcement Division. She is an international consultant on environmental protection, land use, and strategic planning. She is also the president of the International Society for the Comparative Study of Civilizations (ISCSC) and trustee of the Anza Borrego Foundation. Ms. Rhodes serves on the Environmental Crimes Committee of the International Association of Chiefs of Police. A graduate of the FBI National Academy, she is a published author and consults nationally and internationally on several subjects including natural and cultural resource protection, land-use design and planning, trends in environmental law, and trends in law enforcement including effects on society and civili sation. Ms. Rhodes serves as a formal advisor for Protected Area Management in Mongolia and as an environmental consultant for Zhongnan University, Wuhan, China. She is an honorary professor of Soochow University, Suzhou, China.

Dr. Denny Roy, East-West Center Honolulu, Hawaii. Dr. Roy is one of the leading American specialists on Northeast Asian and Asia Pacific political and security issues, particularly those involving China. He received his Ph.D. in Political Science at the University of Chicago. Dr. Roy has written on Chinese foreign policy, the North Korean nuclear weapons crisis, China-Japan relations, and China-Taiwan relations. His interests include not only traditional military-strategic matters and foreign policy, but also international relations theory and human rights politics. Before joining the East-West Center Honolulu in 2007, Dr. Roy worked at the Asia-Pacific Center for Security Studies in Honolulu for seven years. From 1998–2000, Dr. Roy was a faculty member in the National Security Affairs Department at the Naval Postgraduate School in Monterey, California. From 1995 to 1998, he was a research fellow with the Strategic and Defence Studies Centre at the Australian National University in Canberra and in 1997 was attached to the Singapore Armed Forces Training Institute. From 1990 to 1995, Dr. Roy held faculty appointments in the Political Science Departments of the National University of Singapore and Brigham Young University, teaching courses on international relations and Asian politics. He is conversant in Mandarin Chinese and Korean. Dr. Roy is a co-editor of *The North Korea Crisis and Regional Responses* (2015); *Return of the Dragon: Rising China and Regional Security* (2013); *The Pacific War and its Political Legacies* (2009); *Taiwan: A Political History* (2003); and *China's Foreign Relations* (1998). Dr. Roy also is a co-author, editor, and writer for scholarly journals such as *International Security, Survival, Asian Survey, Security Dialogue, Contemporary Southeast Asia, Armed Forces and Society*, and *Issues and Studies.*

Abbreviations

ABM	Anti-Ballistic Missile treaty
ADB	Asian Development Bank
ADMM+	ASEAN Defense Minister's Meeting-Plus
AEP	Act East Policy
AIIB	Asian Infrastructure Investment Bank
AJI	Australia-Japan-India trilateral
APEC	Asia-Pacific Economic Cooperation
APHA	Asian Political History Association
APLN	Asia-Pacific Leadership Network for Nuclear Non-Proliferation and Disarmament
ARF	ASEAN Regional Forum
ASEAN	Association of Southeast Asian Nations
ASG	Northeast Asian Super Grid
BRI	Belt and Road Initiative
BRICS	Brazil, Russia, India, China and South Africa
CBM	Confidence-Building Measure
CCP	Chinese Communist Party
CFC	Chlorofluorocarbon
CMREC	China-Mongolia-Russia Economic Corridor
CTBT	Comprehensive Nuclear Test Ban Treaty
CVID	Complete, Verifiable and Irreversible Dismantlement
DEFRA	Department for Environment, Food and Rural Affairs
DIPA	Dauria International Protected Area
DMZ	Demilitarised Zone
DPRK	Democratic People's Republic of Korea (North Korea)
EAEU	Eurasian Economic Union
EAS	East Asian Summit
EEF	Eastern Economic Forum
EPA	Economic Partnership Agreement
EPA	Environmental Protection Agency
ERINA	Economic Research Institute of Northeast Asia
EU	European Union
EWS	Early Warning System

FDI	Foreign Direct Investment
FEFD	Far Eastern Federal District
FOIP	Free and Open Indo-Pacific
FTA	Free Trade Agreement
GDAP	Guidance for Development for Alliances and Partnerships
GDP	Gross Domestic Product
GPF	Global Peace Foundation
GPPAC	Global Partnership to Prevent Armed Conflict
HA/DR	Humanitarian Assistance and Disaster Response
HPP	Hydroelectric Power Plant
IACP	International Association of Chiefs of Police
IAEA	International Atomic Energy Agency
IC	Intelligence Community
ICBM	Inter-Continental Ballistic Missile
IEA	International Energy Agency
INF	Intermediate-Range Nuclear Forces treaty
ISCSC	International Society for Comparative Study of Civilizations
IT	Information Technology
ITEC	India's Technical and Economic Cooperation programme
IUCN	International Union for Conservation of Nature
JAI	Japan-America-India trilateral
JICA	Japan International Cooperation Agency
KOICA	Korea International Cooperation Agency
LAC	Line of Actual Control
LEP	Look East Policy
LLDC	International Think Tank for Landlocked Developing Countries
MAD	Mutual Assured Destruction
MDA	Maritime Domain Awareness
MFN	Most Favoured Nation
MINASS	Mongolian Institute of Northeast Asian Security and Strategy
MOFA	Ministry of Foreign Affairs
MOU	Memorandum of Understanding
NAM	Non-Aligned Movement
NATO	North Atlantic Treaty Organization
NDPG	National Defense Program Guidelines
NDS	National Defense Strategy
NEA	Northeast Asia
NEA-NWFZ	Northeast Asian Nuclear Weapons Free Zone
NEAPC	Northeast Asia Plus Community of Responsibility-sharing
NEASPC	Northeast Asian Sub-regional Program for Environmental Cooperation
NGO	Non-Governmental Organisation
NIS	National Intelligence Strategy

NNWS	Non-Nuclear Weapon State
NPT	Non-Proliferation Treaty
NSP	New Southern Policy
NSS	National Security Strategy
NUM	National University of Mongolia
NWFZ	Nuclear Weapons Free Zones
NWS	Nuclear Weapon State
ODA	Official Development Assistance
PKO	Peace-Keeping Operation
PLA	People's Liberation Army
PPE	Personal Protective Equipment
PRC	People's Republic of China
QUAD	Quadrilateral Security Dialogue among United States, Japan, India, Australia
RCEP	Regional Comprehensive Economic Partnership
RECNA	Research Center for Nuclear Weapons Abolition
ROC	Republic of China (on Taiwan)
ROK	Republic of Korea (South Korea)
SCO	Shanghai Cooperation Organisation
SCRI	Supply Chain Resilience Initiative
SDG	Sustainable Development Goal
SEZ	Special Economic Zone
SIRPA	School of International Relations and Public Administration
SLBM	Submarine-Launched Ballistic Missile
SPNA	Special Protected Natural Areas
SPT	Six Party Talks
START	Strategic Arms Reduction Treaty
TAC	Treaty of Amity and Cooperation in Southeast Asia
TCS	Trilateral Cooperation Secretariat
THAAD	Terminal High Altitude Area Defence system
TICAD	Tokyo International Conference on African Development
TPP	Trans Pacific Partnership
UBD	Ulaanbaatar Dialogue on Northeast Asia Security
UBTZ	Ulaanbaatar Railway
UN	United Nations
UNDC	United Nations Disarmament Commission
UNEP	United Nations Environment Programme
UNESCAP	United Nations Economic and Social Commission for Asia Pacific
UNESCO	United Nations Educational, Scientific and Cultural Organization
UNGA	United Nations General Assembly
UNODC	United Nations Office on Drugs and Crime
UNSC	United Nations Security Council

US	United States
USAID	United States Agency for International Development
WHO	World Health Organization
WMD	Weapons of Mass Destruction
WTO	World Trade Organization
WWF	World Wildlife Fund

Introduction

The Northeast Asian security calculus

Alicia J. Campi and Jagannath P. Panda

This book is devoted to assessing the impact of the little recognised state of Mongolia on the security situation of Northeast Asia. While there has been much analysis of the security challenges posed by nuclearisation and instability on the Korean Peninsula and the resulting security policies of major powers active in the region such as the United States (US), Japan, China, Russia, and India, this book breaks new ground in exploring how the previously marginalised, landlocked Mongolian nation in the Twenty-first century has been able to leverage its good relations with the Democratic People's Republic of Korea (DPRK) and its two superpower neighbours of China and Russia to assist in opening dialogue mechanisms and in pursuing other tension-reducing policies throughout the Northeast Asian region. Mongolia's nuclear non-proliferation, "Third Neighbor," and trilateral balancing policies have raised its image globally and indicated that it intends to play a much larger role within its geographical space in order to maximise development of its vast energy mineral resources.

This unique collection of chapters from eminent scholars from all over the world also moves beyond the focus on the complications of the power struggle among the major players to shape political and economic events on the peninsula and throughout the Northeast Asian territory. It illuminates other specific, very relevant subsets of challenges that are impacting the relationships of those powers with Northeast Asian nations and impeding the creation of a stable regional security infrastructure. Thus, the authors explore the themes of nuclear proliferation, environmental crime, and ideological and civilisational conflicts in a key region of the globe which still suffers negative effects from the Cold War. This book will expand the national security focus in Northeast Asia beyond nuclear issues and reunification of the Koreas to other serious and at times underappreciated challenges, which must be addressed if peace in the region can be obtained.

The multidisciplinary and multinational approach of the volume brings a new and much-needed perspective to the field of Northeast Asian and Eurasian security studies since for the first time it will place a spotlight on the under-appreciated role of Mongolia. Mongolia is now an influential player in Asian regional politics and national security planning, because of

DOI: 10.4324/9781003148630-101

its geographical transit corridor position between China and Russia, its unique status as a new democratic and free market economy that emerged from the Cold War era in a troubled region, and because of its long-standing, trusted relations with the DPRK which allow it to assist major powers in peaceful negotiations on nuclear proliferation and Korean Peninsula stability issues. Its potential contribution to de-escalating tension has grown larger particularly during the Trump and Xi era, when the leaders of these two superpowers have evidenced a renewed commitment to regional stability as they pursue their own agendas in the Indo-Pacific.

Until the present, examination of Northeast Asia's strategic landscape has been dominated by the issue of North Korean denuclearisation. While the collected authors do not dispute this reality, they present logical and persuasive new material from additional perspectives to analyse the motivations and policies of the large and small states that are active in Northeast Asia and explain why denuclearisation is more even more complex. Thus, the all-important topic of nuclear proliferation is evaluated side by side with regional environmental, ideological, and civilisational themes in order to explain why this area of the world, while comparatively economically rich, lacks the security architecture, transit links, and ideological consensus to overcome the continuing Korean Peninsula impasse and develop much-needed connectivity to assure greater and more equitable economic growth. This approach moves the book's discussion beyond the typical "Great Game" political analysis of much contemporary Northeast Asian national security analysis. Also, it is an explanation of why cooperative conditions for resource cooperation among Northeast Asian countries in the area of energy security and economic development to date have not been able to overcome political rivalry or to reduce regional tension. This volume delineates the strategy behind Mongolia's efforts, in coordination with the major critical actors, to create cooperative mechanisms and more receptive conditions to achieve a more stable geopolitical environment for all states.

The origin for the book stems from a September 2019 international conference in Ulaanbaatar, Mongolia entitled "Challenges Confronting Asia Today: Nuclear Proliferation, Environment, Economic, Civilisational," which Dr. Campi organised on behalf of Clarewood University in Virginia USA and was sponsored by the Asia Politics and History Association, Blue Banner Foundation, International Society for the Comparative Study of Civilizations, and The Mongolia Society. About one-third of the chapters are derived from previously unpublished papers presented at this conference. They and the other additional contributions by eminent international scholars in the field of international relations have been combined into a cohesive whole to present a variety of different approaches in exploring today's national security challenges in the Northeast Asian region. These contributors utilise primary material sources across a broad spectrum, which enhances its value for researchers, graduate students, scholars, and policymakers. They draw attention to the historical legacy issues which have lingered in the region since the end of the Cold War and blocked the construction of regional security and economic architecture. Throughout the book, particular emphasis is placed on the role of major powers in both safeguarding the shaky peace and perpetuating tension throughout it. Contrast is drawn to the example of Mongolia as an ex-Soviet satellite that was cut off from its neighbourhood during the Cold War and then became a functioning successful democracy after 1990 with ambitions to play a greater role in Northeast Asia for its own national security interests.

The book is divided into three sections which present the main arguments explored by the contributors: I) Major Powers, Mongolia, and Northeast Asian Security, II) Nuclear Challenges in Northeast Asia, III) Socio-Economic, Environmental, and Civilisational Challenges in Northeast Asia. Section I consists of six chapters that analyse the foreign policy and national security strategies of the major powers in the region and of Mongolia in order to reveal the power rivalry which grips the Korean Peninsula and interstate relations. Chapter 1, "An examination of the Trump administration's National Security Strategy in the Indo-Pacific—Where is Northeast Asia?," by Dr. Campi recounts the history of the Indo-Pacific policy for different US administrations and explains the differences and special features of the policy during the Trump presidency. It provides specific examples of how Northeast Asia and Mongolia have assumed a special importance within the global national security strategy of the US in the "America First" era. In Chapter 2, "China's foreign policy in Northeast Asia and implications for Mongolia," Dr. Denny Roy discusses the Chinese foreign policy agenda in Northeast Asia which permits Beijing to aspire to a higher level of influence over the region. This growing trend has different ramifications and poses serious long-term risks for each of China's neighbours, especially Mongolia.

In the chapter on "Russia in Northeast Asia: strengthening security through cooperation," Dr. Elena Boykova explains that Russia's close relationship with this region is largely due to the fact that the Russian Far East is of great geopolitical and geostrategic importance, and the comprehensive development of a new economy being created there now is a national priority for Russia. Moscow is building on its centuries-long political and military relations with the various nations in the Northeast Asian region and moving beyond its previous constant rivalry with China to develop commonalities of economic partnership with Northeast Asian states, especially China. The Mongolian view of its place in Northeast Asia is addressed by N. Dorjsuren in his chapter on "Why Northeast Asian regional economic integration is important for Mongolia." This chapter focuses on three main areas: 1) the strategic motivations behind the main principles of Mongolian foreign policy towards Northeast Asia; 2) the kind of challenges Northeast Asian integration mechanisms are facing, especially the China-Mongolia-Russia Economic Corridor and its implications for Northeast Asian economic integration; and 3) the strategic advantages and disadvantages Mongolia has in its region in regard to regional security.

4   *Alicia J. Campi and Jagannath P. Panda*

This section concludes with two chapters articulating the specific viewpoints of Japan and India. The chapter on "Japan's foreign policy security mechanisms in the Asia Pacific and Northeast Asia," co-authored by Dr. Ts. Batbayar and Dr. Fujimaki Hiroyuki, delineates how the importance of the Japan-US alliance and the effects of the rise of China have influenced Japanese reaction to developing new security architecture in the region. They also address the significance of Japan's "Free and Open Indo-Pacific" policy and the potentialities and dangers in a fully functioning Quad (US-Japan-India-Australia) relationship in the future. The final chapter in this section is "India, Mongolia, and Northeast Asia: between geography and the geopolitical realities" by Mahima N. Duggal and Jagannath P. Panda. This study examines the impact on the Asian region of an Indian foreign policy that has become increasingly proactive as a middle power. The authors draw attention to the historical ties between India and Mongolia and the shared values within their foreign policies and joint economic projects, especially since 2015. They believe that the true potential of India-Mongolia ties still remains unrealised in India's strategic imagination, but there are potential areas of new cooperation in relation to North Korea and establishing peace and stability on the Korean Peninsula.

Section II explores Northeast Asia and the denuclearisation dialogue. Special attention is paid to recent bilateral discussions between the US and North Korea that have broadened into multi-party negotiations through the assistance of Mongolia. Dr. Campi's chapter on "The relationship of United States-Japan-Mongolia democratic trilateralism to the Indo-Pacific strategy and Korean Peninsular discussions" reveals how these three countries have developed a special relationship within the context of growing trilateral arrangements found in the Asian region and spurred by a Mongolian initiative to find a new mechanism to balance its geographical relationship with China and Russia. This special democratic trilateralism relationship among the US, Japan, and Mongolia is a new institutional framework which is a product of the Indo-Pacific strategies of the US and Japan and their search for a more efficacious way to seek peace and denuclearisation in Northeast Asia. The chapter "Why Asia should lead a global push to eliminate nuclear weapons—The role for Mongolia" by Dr. Michael Andregg reviews various political and technological issues that are impacting the denuclearisation roadmap and define the security environment. He explicates reasons why Northeast Asia is especially well-positioned to lead a global push to eliminate, or greatly reduce, nuclear weapons inventories worldwide, and why Mongolia could provide the catalyst for that effort.

Other authors illustrate the role of Mongolia in facilitating mutual exchange and cooperation with North Korea and bridging the Sino-Russian-US strategic competition that blocks aspects of current denuclearisation negotiations. Dr. J. Enkhsaikhan, Mongolia's leading expert on nuclear non-proliferation and national security, discusses the nuclear weapons threat in Northeast Asia in his chapter on "Nuclear non-proliferation in Northeast Asia and Mongolia's policy." He presents information on various organisations now working on the civil society and academic levels to address the issue of denuclearising the Korean Peninsula and establishing a Northeast Asian nuclear-weapons free zone. The section concludes with Dr. Nivedita Kapoor's chapter on "The changing regional dynamics in Northeast Asia: Russia's North Korean conundrum and the case of Mongolia," which examines the success and limitations of Russia's policy towards North Korea within the broader paradigm of its position in Northeast Asia. In this context, it analyses Russia-Mongolia relations to trace their evolution and examine possibilities and challenges regarding engagement on North Korea.

Section III focuses on economic resource competition and geostrategic rivalry among the neighbouring countries in Northeast Asia, where conflict rather than cooperation is stirred by growing resource and environmental insecurity in the critical space of Northeast Asia. It also contains unique perspectives from a civilisational overview that impact on the national security of Mongolia and the major powers as they interact throughout Northeast Asia. The chapter by Dr. Elena Boykova on "Environmental security issues in Northeast Asia and cooperation among Russia, China, and Mongolia" utilises Russian and Mongolian source materials to analyse problems facing the region and progress on solutions. Cooperation at the national and regional levels and bilateral and multilateral agreements on environmental issues are discussed with special focus on the problems of environmental safety that have regional impact.

Lynn Rhodes' "Asia and beyond: organised environmental crime" is an interesting exploration of organised, transnational, transboundary crimes against the environment in Asia, including Mongolia, that have serious repercussions affecting society, legal development, economies, biodiversity, human rights, and civilisation. Organised transnational networks, particularly in Asia, are involved in exploitation of natural resources, wildlife poaching and trade, illegal and unregulated fishing, and illegal exploitation of and trafficking in minerals. Ms. Rhodes illustrates that the transnational nature of environmental crimes and increasing involvement of organised criminal groups, along with varying degrees of government capacities, is impacting enhanced law enforcement and coordinated enforcement action across boundaries.

This section and our book concludes with a theoretical analysis by Dr. Joseph Drew in "When Toynbee's "fossilized" or "arrested" societies are reborn as peripheral states: the cases of Israel, Mongolia, Korea, and Japan." He reconsiders how Arnold Toynbee, the founder of the comparative study of civilisations, dismissed certain societies as "fossilized" only to have them reappear on the world stage after disappearing for centuries. Particular attention is paid to the contemporary, no-longer-dead but now alive civilisations in Mongolia, Korea, Japan, and Israel.

In sum, this book aims to review the present and future national security challenges in Northeast Asia for the major powers and the nations of the region. It presents varied analysis from multidisciplinary and multi-ethnic approaches. The overriding theme that emerges is that the small but vibrant nation of Mongolia is likely to play an important, even pivotal, role in the overall growth and development of Northeast Asia, as well as towards building regional security architecture and greater stability. It is hoped that this collection of chapters will contribute to greater understanding about the plans of modern Mongolia, a landlocked country of vast energy mineral resources within a dynamic Eurasian continent, to raise its image globally so that it is able to play a much larger role within its geographical space and determine its own fate.

Part I
Major powers, Mongolia, and Northeast Asian security

1 An examination of the Trump administration's National Security Strategy in the Indo-Pacific
Where is Northeast Asia?

Alicia J. Campi

In the United States, it has been said that "President Obama talked of pivoting to Asia. Donald Trump made Asia pivot to America."[1] US President Donald J. Trump first outlined his vision for a free and open Indo-Pacific at the Asia-Pacific Economic Cooperation (APEC) CEO Summit in Vietnam in mid-November 2017.[2] Only a few weeks later, his National Security Council issued "A New National Security Strategy for a New Era"[3] on December 18, 2017. This document reflected President Trump's often uttered belief that putting America first is the primary duty of his government and the foundation for effective United States leadership in the world. It also pledged to expand "defense and security cooperation with India, a Major Defense Partner of the United States, and support India's growing relationships throughout the region."[4] The publication of the "National Intelligence Strategy 2019"[5] in January 2019 further revealed strong evidence that the Trump Administration's view of the world, especially the Indo-Pacific and its several sub-sections, is both a continuum and a significant change from previous decades.

It was understandable that this new policy strategy and implementation first came as a shock to many domestic and foreign observers.[6] During the Trump years, led by the US' engagement with the North Korean problem, Northeast Asian affairs has risen to new prominence within the American national security apparatus. However, this phenomenon is less obvious and the question remains why? This chapter will not only examine the US Indo-Pacific national security policy in general, but also consider how the new strategy has impacted its approach to the Northeast Asian region and the states within it.

National Security Strategy of 2017 and the National Intelligence Strategy of 2019

The publication of the National Security Strategy (NSS) is a research study required by law in which the NSS explains to the American people, US allies and partners, and federal agencies how the President intends to put his national security vision into practice. The NSSs in the past did not connect

DOI: 10.4324/9781003148630-1

national objectives to the tasks and resources necessary to accomplish specific goals, and the Trump Administration's NSS followed this pattern of describing key strategic challenges and 117 priority tasks within a "broad assessment of the international strategic context in which the United States is operating, as well as an articulation of an Administration's underlying philosophy for advancing US interests."[7] Yet, some "could infer from the NSS that the Trump Administration regards homeland security, economic growth, and national security as more fundamentally interrelated than its predecessors have argued, and that at times, the United States must cooperate with those states with which it also competes."[8]

However, one of the biggest departures in 2017 from previous NSS documents was the placement of emphasis by the US policymaking establishment on the Indo-Pacific region above Europe and the Middle East. This was the first mention of the term "Indo-Pacific" in any NSS, although the President George W. Bush's 2002 NSS referred to the Indian Ocean sea lanes. This Trump Indo-Pacific framework was rationalised by analysts, who often evoked images of a new Cold War, as motivated by China's greater assertiveness throughout the region.[9] The 2017 NSS did not carve out a section on NEA specifically, so one might say the Trump Administration had downgraded the NEA region. However, this can be explained as pulling back the US' focus to a macro or continental level rather than just a regional one.

To better understand Washington's view of the NEA region and Korean denuclearisation, we must turn to the NSS' enumeration of the four vital, national interests—called four pillars—that form the backbone of this strategy:

1. **Protect the homeland**, the American people and the American way of life
2. **Promote American prosperity**
3. **Preserve peace through strength**
4. **Advance American influence**

The NSS and its four themes are guided by what the White House called a return to *principled realism*, a strategy that is realist in content and focused on global competition. It acknowledged the central role of power in world affairs, affirmed that sovereign states are the best hope for a peaceful world, and clearly defined US national interests. It is principled because it is grounded in the principle that promoting American values is key to spreading peace and prosperity around the globe. The goal always is to protect American vital national interests by addressing key challenges and trends that affect American standing in the world. Some of these major challenges outlined are:

- Revisionist powers (meaning China and Russia) that use technology, propaganda and coercion to shape a world antithetical to US interests and values;

- Regional dictators who spread terror, threaten their neighbours and pursue weapons of mass destruction;
- Jihadist terrorists that foment hatred to incite violence and transnational criminal organisations that bring drugs into American communities.

Four major pillars of 2017 NSS

1. Protect the Homeland: The 2017 NSS explains that President Trump's fundamental responsibility is to protect the American people, the homeland, and the American way of life. It declares that the US will strengthen control of the borders and reform the US immigration system in order to protect the homeland and restore the sovereignty of the borders. The greatest transnational threats are defined as "Jihadist terrorists, using barbaric cruelty to commit murder, repression, and slavery, and virtual networks to exploit vulnerable populations and inspire and direct plots," and "Transnational criminal organizations, tearing apart our communities with drugs and violence and weakening our allies and partners by corrupting democratic institutions." The Strategy is to target threats at their sources before they ever reach US borders. Among the measures to be utilised to accomplish this are to redouble efforts to protect critical infrastructure and digital networks, because new technology and new adversaries create new vulnerabilities, and to deploy a layered missile defence system to defend the nation against missile attacks.
2. Promote American Prosperity: This is defined as a strong economy that protects the American people, supports the American way of life and sustains American power. The Trump Administration promises to rejuvenate the American economy for the benefit of American workers and companies because it is necessary to restore American national power. The NSS declares that the US will no longer tolerate chronic trade abuses and will pursue free, fair, and reciprocal economic relationships. It states that to succeed in Twenty-first century geopolitical competition, the US must lead in research, technology and innovation and protect the US national security innovation base from those who would steal intellectual property. Thus, the US will use its energy dominance to ensure international markets remain open and that the benefits of diversification and energy access promote economic and national security.
3. Preserve Peace Through Strength: This pillar derives from the belief that a strengthened and rejuvenated US will ensure peace and deter hostility. Thus, the Trump Administration promises to rebuild the US' military strength by using all of the tools of statecraft in a new era of strategic competition—diplomatic, information, military and economic. It specifically mentions strengthening space and cyber capabilities. The NSS notes that American allies and partners are important to magnify US

power and protect shared interests, but it proclaims that the Trump Administration expects them to take greater responsibility for addressing common threats in order to ensure the balance of power remains in favour of the US in the key regions of the world, which are the Indo-Pacific, Europe, and the Middle East.

4. Advance American Influence: Since the Trump Administration saw the US as a force for good throughout its history, it pledged to continue to advance American interests and benefit humanity by enhancing US influence overseas to protect the American people and promote American prosperity. However, the 2017 NSS noted that the US' diplomatic and development efforts must achieve better outcomes in bilateral, multilateral and in the information realm to protect national interests, find new economic opportunities for the nation's citizens and challenge any competitors. Therefore, the US seeks partnerships with like-minded states to promote free market economies, private sector growth, political stability, and peace. This NSS pledges to champion American values—including the rule of law and individual rights—that promote strong, stable, prosperous, and sovereign states. It stated that the Trump Administration's "America First" foreign policy "celebrates America's influence in the world as a positive force that can help set the conditions for peace, prosperity, and the development of successful societies." A final point was that the administration was seeking to incentivise foreign policy reforms by using diplomacy and assistance to encourage other countries to make choices that improve governance, rule of law, and sustainable development.[10]

2019 National Intelligence Strategy

The 2019 National Intelligence Strategy (NIS) is designed as a four-year blueprint to communicate and advance the mission of the US intelligence community (IC) and align it with diverse national strategies, including the NSS. It describes seven mission objectives that cover a broad range of regional and functional topics facing the IC and are prioritised through the National Intelligence Priorities Framework.

The first three mission objectives address foundational missions of the IC and are not regional in focus: 1) *Strategic Intelligence* addresses issues of enduring national security interest. 2) *Anticipatory Intelligence* addresses new and emerging trends, changing conditions and underappreciated developments. 3) *Current Operations Intelligence* supports planned and ongoing operations. The next four mission objectives address specific, topical missions of the IC and cover specific regional issues, such as conflict areas. 4) *Cyber Threat Intelligence* addresses state and non-state actors engaged in malicious cyber activities. 5) *Counterterrorism* addresses state and non-state actors engaged in terrorism. 6) *Counterproliferation* addresses state and non-state actors engaged in the proliferation of weapons of mass destruction and their means of delivery. 7) *Counterintelligence and Security* addresses threats from foreign intelligence entities and insiders.[11]

In this document, NEA and the Indo-Pacific are not mentioned at all, and North Korea and Russia are not cited by name under any of the mission objectives. North Korea is only referenced as part of the "Strategic Environment" section wherein the US sees opportunities to work with China "on issues of mutual concern, such as North Korean aggression and continued pursuit of nuclear and ballistic missile technology."[12]

US Priority Actions in the Indo-Pacific

The 2017 NSS states that the Priority Actions of the US will be launched in three sectors:

1. *Political:* Declaring that no Indo-Pacific nation is excluded, it promises that the US will redouble its commitment to established alliances and partnerships, while deepening relationships with partners "that share respect for sovereignty, fair and reciprocal trade, and the rule of law." Thus, the US will reinforce its commitment to freedom of the seas and the peaceful resolution of territorial and maritime disputes in accordance with international law. It will work with allies and partners to achieve complete, verifiable, and irreversible denuclearisation on the Korean peninsula and preserve the non-proliferation regime in NEA.
2. *Economic:* There is a strong commitment to the present open maritime system in the South China Sea. Therefore, the US will encourage regional cooperation to maintain free and open seaways, transparent infrastructure financing practices, unimpeded commerce and the peaceful resolution of disputes. The Trump Administration's policy was based on a bilateral rather than multilateral trade agenda through seeking bilateral trade agreements on a fair and reciprocal basis with equal and reliable access for American exports. The NSS promised to work with partners to build a network of states dedicated to free markets and strengthen cooperation with allies to construct high-quality infrastructure. Joining Australia and New Zealand, the US pledged to shore up fragile partner states in the Pacific Islands region to reduce their vulnerability to economic fluctuations and natural disasters.
3. *Military and security:* In this sector the 2017 NSS is similar to previous administrations' NSS statements, but with a renewed emphasis on maritime security issues. It states that the US will maintain a forward military presence capable of deterring and, if necessary, defeating any adversary. It calls for strengthening long-standing military relationships and encouraging the development of a strong defence network with allies and partners. It specifically mentions cooperation on missile defence with Japan and South Korea to move towards an area defence capability. This NSS asserts that the US remains ready to respond with

overwhelming force to North Korean aggression and will improve options to compel denuclearisation of the peninsula. The Trump Administration also promises to improve law enforcement, defence and intelligence cooperation with Southeast Asian partners to address what it calls "the growing terrorist threat."

The 2017 NSS also mentions that the US will maintain strong ties with Taiwan in accordance with its "One China" policy, including its commitments under the Taiwan Relations Act to provide for Taiwan's legitimate defence needs and deter coercion. It promises to expand defence and security cooperation with India, which it calls a "Major US Defence Partner," and support India's growing relationships throughout the region. Finally, this NSS states that the US will re-energise its alliances with the Philippines and Thailand and strengthen its partnerships with Singapore, Vietnam, Indonesia, and Malaysia to help them become cooperative maritime partners.

Reaction to Trump's Indo-Pacific policy

The above-mentioned two national security documents were the foundation blueprint of the Trump presidency for conducting its foreign relations. One of the key takeaways of the 2017 NSS' overall strategy was that the American security establishment was focused on the Indo-Pacific, as opposed to what in the past was called "Asia-Pacific". This is because the National Security Council believed that a geopolitical competition between free and repressive visions of world order is taking place in the Indo-Pacific region, which is defined as stretching from the west coast of India to the west coast of the United States.

Reaction by many security specialists to the Trump Administration's foreign policy strategy as outlined in the 2017 NSS and 2019 NIS often was strongly negative, since they maintained that the US-created international system erected at the end of World War II and somewhat modified in the post-Cold War era had resulted in global prosperity and relative peace and so was too valuable to dismantle.[13] Some observers did not fully comprehend what the Trump Administration's change of focus and rhetoric meant for US security policy and so simply remained hostile. We can see three distinct camps of national security critics. The dismissive, consistently negative pundits were represented by Professor Melvyn Leffler, who wrote in *Foreign Affairs* that the new strategy was "delusional".[14] Another such voice was Steven Metz at the US Army War College Strategic Studies Institute, who complained that

> Under Trump's direction, the approach to the world that served the United States well for decades has crumbled, but there is no discernible replacement. The primary reason for that is Trump's attitude toward statecraft, particularly his failure to follow time-tested principles of strategy.[15]

The second camp consists of openly hostile analysts who maintained that the principle goals of recent American administrations actually have not radically changed, but rather the philosophy and methods of American power moved from Obama's liberal hegemony and interdependence in a world where "power is shifting below and beyond the nation-state"[16] to Trump's "America First" 'ultra-nationalism'. For example, Pierre Gerlain at the Université Paris Ouest, Nanterre, France, wrote that "the word 'chaos' appears in many contexts to describe the Trump administration," but he dismissed the 2017 NSS as "a typical neoconservative text, which could have been released by the George W. Bush team."[17]

British scholar Oliver Turner asserts that President Trump's "hyper-nationalist, coercive America First strategy" maintains the hub-and-spokes bilateral character of US foreign relations with its allies but in a more extractive, transactional way—all with the goal of maintaining US superiority as a global power. The Obama strategy of a dense web of US-Asian connections of economic, financial, and security relationships and agreements built on the established international framework was replaced by Trump's aggressive approach, which he termed "bullying other nations to achieve his administration's America-First goals."[18] Yet, this author believes that in the Trump era the dense web of relationships became even denser in bilateral, trilateral, and even quadrilateral ways as global platforms and multilateral institutional mechanisms were de-emphasised. Turner does agree that a different view of the Indo-Pacific emerged during the Trump years. He suggests that the "Indo-Pacific" phraseology popularly in use by the Trump Administration indicated that the US saw the Pacific and Indian Oceans, including such strategic waterways as the Straits of Malacca, as "a 'joined-up' strategy to counter the perceived 'China threat'" posed by the global engagement represented by Beijing-led international institutions such as the Asian Infrastructure Investment Bank (AIIB) and Belt and Road Initiative (BRI)."[19]

A 2020 Brookings study on Trump policy in the Indo-Pacific by Lindsey Ford, who served in the Department of Defense during the Obama administration, asserted that there was little new substance in the Trump Administration's initiatives and maintained that they are just a reframing of ideas first endorsed by the George W. Bush and Barack Obama administrations.[20] Although Ford claimed at times that the differences in Trump policy can be attributed to typical shifts in Republican and Democratic administrations, most of her analysis concluded that US policy in the Indo-Pacific regardless of the president actually has been the same for decades. Her commentary was much more focused on Southeast Asia and did not mention Russia, North Korea or stabilisation of the Korean peninsula. However, the increase in US friction with China was attributed more to China's own efforts to reshape the regional order than the confrontation style of President Trump and so suggested this trend would outlive his presidency.

The third school of thought about the Trump security framework is revealed in the slow evolution of generally positive analysis found at the

Heritage Foundation, considered a bastion of neo-conservativism. It offers the caveat that the challenge of adjusting to the change in leadership style at the White House has caused significant uncertainty, even by allies, over how the US would implement the goals of the 2017 NSS: "There was confusion over the distinctions between the new strategy and the previous Administration's concept of a 'pivot to Asia.'"[21] The Heritage Foundation did recognise that the Trump administration considered that in this region India is now the "most consequential" of security partners.

Another more positive view of the Trump administration's Indo-Pacific policy was evidenced in the East West Center 2019 *Policy Studies* series monograph of Dr. Kaewkamol Karen Pitakdumrongkit of Nanyang Technological University, Singapore. She stated that

> While Washington has relied on the term 'Indo-Pacific' to conceptualize the region and formulate its foreign policies, the Trump administration's use of the term has departed from previous eras....The policy was formulated based on an assumption that China and the United States are locked in a power contestation.[22]

She equated this change with its perception that the Indo-Pacific zone is where America's economic future lies, because it will be a very populous, dynamic, and lucrative market for US business. Pitakdumrongkit believes that despite Trump's insistence that American allies and partners do more burden sharing, many nations in the region, such as Japan, India, and Australia, had positive reactions to the new Indo-Pacific policy. Some of the foreign officials she personally interviewed in 2018 "were delighted to learn that the United States sees the importance of small- and medium-sized actors and multilateral institutions shaping regional governance architectures."[23] Many Asian policymakers had doubts as to how the US would implement its trade, investment and infrastructure plans to advance economic cooperation and promote stability, and they usually opposed Washington's bilateral approach to foreign policy. Nonetheless, she concluded that "although more articulation is needed, the U.S. Indo-Pacific strategy in its current form, with America's continued engagement with regional players and multilateral institutions, is to some degree reassuring to Indo-Pacific actors."[24]

The elevation of the role of India as a leading global power and a stronger strategic and defence partner in US security calculus particularly was pointed out by Alyssa Ayres in the Council on Foreign Relations' blog, *Asia Unbound*: "one lesser-discussed area worth further attention is the more prominent place given to India and the Indo-Pacific region in U.S. national security."[25] She believes the 2017 NSS characterised the region in terms reminiscent of the Cold War: "A geopolitical competition between free and repressive visions of world order is taking place in the Indo-Pacific region... [which] represents the most populous and economically dynamic part of the world."[26] In her analysis the "allies and partners" of the US, especially South Korea, Japan, Australia, and New Zealand, were the centrepieces of the new American strategy and the focus on India within the larger Indo-Pacific framework boosted India's place in terms of overall American policymaking.

In comparison, in the 2015 NSS of President Obama, India as a "key center of influence" was mentioned in relationship to South and Central Asia, but within the existing regional security architecture: "We support India's role as a regional provider of security and its expanded participation in critical regional institutions. We see a strategic convergence with India's Act East policy and our continued implementation of the rebalance to Asia and the Pacific."[27] While the tone of the 2015 NSS towards India indicated the US was "primed to unlock the potential of our relationship with India,"[28] in the end the implementation was less positive.

Many observers saw a new tone of hostility towards China throughout the Trump Administration's national security strategy. Trump's pessimistic view of the efficacy of the US-China relationship was "a clear departure from the Obama administration, making reference to China as a challenger to American power, influence, and interests, as well as a threat to American security and prosperity."[29] Although the 2017 NSS calls for cooperation with China, it states that China is using economic inducements and penalties, influence operations and implied military threats to persuade other nations towards the Chinese political and security agenda. The Trump foreign policy viewpoint was that China's infrastructure investments and trade strategies reinforced Chinese geopolitical aspirations, and Chinese efforts to build and militarise outposts in the South China Sea endangered the free flow of trade, threatened the sovereignty of other nations in the Indo-Pacific, undermined regional stability, and were designed to limit US access to the region.

Pointed criticism of China was emphasised in New Delhi at the Raisina Dialogue on January 25, 2018 when Admiral Harry Harris said that, "The reality is that China is a disruptive transitional force in the Indo-Pacific; they are the owner of the trust deficit in the region."[30] His statement has been interpreted as illustrating "the scope of Washington's terminological pivot from the Obama-era "Asia-Pacific" to Trump's "Indo-Pacific", and of US growing concern that other Asian countries' closer commercial and investment relations with China would strategically impinge on Washington's interests.

Some analysts have asserted that the 2017 NSS reflected reduced American interest in Asian regional affairs in favour of focusing on the Quad relationship among US, Japan, India, and Australia that always was seen by Beijing as a containment strategy. However, during the Trump Administration, in some ways the US was more active in the Asian region than in previous decades. The 2017 NSS stated that the Trump Administration believes that allies of the US are critical to responding to mutual threats such as North Korea and preserving mutual interests in the Indo-Pacific region. This statement contradicts the general impression in domestic and foreign policy circles that Trump's "America First" world view devalued longstanding key American partners in favour of isolationism.[31] Although the US abandoned the Trans Pacific Partnership (TPP),[32] which was considered to be the centrepiece of President Barack Obama's strategic pivot to Asia, US Secretary of State Mike Pompeo in late July 2018 announced that "Our Indo-Pacific vision excludes no nation. We seek to work with anyone to promote a free and open Indo-Pacific."[33] He mentioned three new Trump initiatives: 1) Digital Connectivity and Cybersecurity Partnership that started with a $25 million initial investment to improve partner countries' digital connectivity and expand opportunities for US technology exports. 2) Asia EDGE (Enhancing Development and Growth through Energy) of nearly $50 million invested in 2018 to help Indo-Pacific partners to import, produce, move, store, and deploy their energy resources. 3) Infrastructure Transaction and Assistance Network with nearly $30 million to boost development by establishing a new interagency body to coordinate, strengthen and share US tools for project scouting, financing, and technical assistance. This Network also established a new Indo-Pacific Transaction Advisory Fund to help partners' access private legal and financial advisory services. A few weeks later at the ASEAN Regional Forum Secretary Pompeo announced that the US intended to provide nearly $300 million of security assistance for nations in the Indo-Pacific region, which was based upon the assumption that its Indo-Pacific strategy was the cornerstone of American national security. These monies were slated "to improve security relationships across the region," with projects in Bangladesh, Indonesia, Mongolia, Nepal, the Pacific Islands, the Philippines, Sri Lanka, and Vietnam.[34]

Where is Northeast Asia in US policy?

When the Trump Administration developed the 2017 NSS as well as the 2019 NIS, NEA as a region was not singled out, but key nations within this region, allies such as Japan and South Korea and competitors China and Russia, were important elements. This was the same formula used in the Obama 2015 NSS. Remembering that the 2017 NSS was written prior to the June 11, 2018 Trump-Kim Singapore summit, the 2017 NSS is very DPRK-centric in its calculations by strongly emphasising the threat from North Korean rapid acceleration of its cyber, nuclear, and ballistic missile programmes. The document asserted that North Korea's pursuit of these weapons poses a global threat that requires a global response and that a nuclear-armed North Korea could lead to the proliferation of the world's most destructive weapons across the Indo-Pacific region. Furthermore, it warned that continued provocations by North Korea would prompt neighbouring countries and the US to further strengthen security bonds and take additional measures to protect themselves. This statement foreshadowed the closer US-Japanese relationship that emerged in the Trump years to manage the North Korean situation.

Nevertheless, the US' interest in quadrilateral cooperation in the Indo-Pacific inevitably led to the perception that there was a reduction of support in the US-Japan-ROK trilateral alliance. Like the Trump Administration's questioning of the balance and efficiency of the traditional NATO alliance structure, the Trump White House questioned whether or not retaining the division of East Asia into its North and South parts was the best way to protect freedom of navigation and promote fairer trade and investment practices in response to the rise of China and the regional instability generated by the DPRK. For decades, many experts have claimed that the ROK and Japan shared common values with the US,[35] but years of failure to permanently resolve historical issues amongst NEA nations and the continuing lack of progress in denuclearisation and unification talks for the Korean peninsula stoked questions about the efficacy of the US-ROK-Japan trilateral approach. Domestic discord within all three nations has sapped the synergies within the partnership and made it increasingly difficult to work in harmony and claim that the relationship is up to the challenges of the Twenty-first century. The Trump Administration's decision to strengthen the quadrangle of Australia, India, Japan, and the US indicated that it was elevating Japan's role in the greater region, while signalling that it would approach the DPRK-ROK situation from a narrower context by blocking China, Russia, and Japan from direct talks.

There can be no American national security policy towards NEA that is divorced from prioritising Korean peninsula issues, especially denuclearisation. Since the disappointing breakup of the February 2019 Vietnam Summit and the subsequent year of no progress despite the June 30, 2019 demilitarised zone handshake of President Trump and Kim Jong Un, the Trump Administration was pressured domestically by both hardliners and conciliators regarding its North Korean denuclearisation strategy. Many hard-line strategists looked at Korean peninsula denuclearisation mainly from the larger perspective of America's over-arching Indo-Pacific interests. James Carafano, writing for the Heritage Foundation, advocated pursuing a policy of projecting American strength by not ceding space in Asia:

> The goal is simple. Beijing has to respect America as a formidable Asian power—and concede that the United States is not going anywhere. And what the United States does there must be part of an overall strategy to stabilize key regions of the world and ensure the freedom of the commons (air, sea, space and cyberspace) that benefits the United States and all nations.[36]

He believes the US has two core interests in relation to North Korea: prevent a war in NEA and protect the US homeland against nuclear blackmail or attack by the DPRK. Yet, Carafano acknowledged that it was not clear if the Trump Administration's pressure campaign—a mixture of nuclear and conventional deterrence, missile defence and heavy sanctioning together with opening a diplomatic track offering to normalise relations in exchange for denuclearisation—would succeed.

President Trump's efforts to reach out to Kim Jong-un were not supported by his former National Security adviser John Bolton, who advocated for a more militaristic, hard-line approach: "The fact is that we wasted a lot of time with Trump's failed diplomacy with North Korea. Rogue states need time to perfect their nuclear capabilities, their ballistic missile capabilities. That's what Kim Jong Un was doing."[37] While Bolton, Secretary of State Pompeo, and others in the US government in 2018–2020 advocated a multipronged strategy towards the denuclearisation of the Korean peninsula in order to stabilise both NEA and the Indo-Pacific, there were voices, on the right as well as the left, that increasingly grew concerned that the President's hard-line push for DPRK denuclearisation and dismantling would result in grave miscalculations on both sides and potentially slip into war.

For example, in early May 2019 Harry Kazianis, director of Korean Studies at the Center for the National Interest, called for a return to the gradual step-by-step approach as the "only way" for Washington to strike a denuclearisation deal with Pyongyang: "Donald Trump today tweeting out about increasing tariffs and things of that nature, he needs to be a little careful because his North Korea policy could blow up in his face."[38] However, President Trump was not interested in the step-by-step, concession-for-concession approach. Even after North Korea resumed missile testing and the break-down of working level talks in Stockholm in 2019, he still did not publicly return to denunciatory and personally hostile language towards Chairman Kim.

Victor Cha, Korea Chair for the Center for Strategic and International Studies, was not as critical but still pessimistic about the Trump DPRK policy,

> ...we are left with the question of who benefits from a pause in the diplomacy. We may believe that time is on our side because of the continued bite of the sanctions, but the North may believe their continued production of weapons, materials, and missile designs puts added pressure on the United States. In either case, President Trump may be realizing the limits of his "bromance" diplomacy with North Korea.[39]

Some observers believed that talks between the two sides stalled over an inability to reconcile North Korea's demands for relief from punishing sanctions and US demands for North Korea to denuclearise.[40] The stalemate might have been related to the North Koreans holding back to watch the outcome of the long process surrounding the impeachment of President Trump and the 2020 presidential campaign and Trump's subsequent loss of interest in pursuing negotiations with Kim during the COVID-19 crisis in his 2020 re-election year.[41] In December 2019 Stephen Biegun became Deputy Secretary of State. Biegun had been Secretary Pompeo's US Special Representative for North Korea since August 2018 and thus was the chief

American negotiator on all US policy on North Korea.[42] Nevertheless, the administration continued with a strong DPRK sanction regime because President Trump stated that he was in no hurry to strike a deal. So, although Biegun's elevation to a senior State Department position was interpreted as part of a plan to prioritise the North Korean issue, these negotiations remained sidetracked until the end of the Trump presidency.

A final hindrance to a more definitive US strategic policy towards NEA is the continuing lack of definition of this region. Does it embrace China and its corollaries, Hong Kong, and Taiwan? What about Russia and Mongolia? Or is NEA still the old academic definition of the Koreas and Japan? Answering this question is crucial in order to conceive of a security strategy. With no firm answer accepted by the parties in the region and the US, equivocation can only be overcome by developing policy on the micro level, country by country, or the macro level of East Asia, Eurasia, or the Indo-Pacific.

Mongolia within the Trump Indo-Pacific strategy for Northeast Asia

This author previously has written that "a major part of Mongolia's soft power foreign relations strategy is to see where it can find space to establish new regional institutional frameworks to promote transportation and communication formulas" beneficial to itself and its NEA neighbours so that Mongolia is viewed as more than a buffer nation.[43] Mongolia had been shut out of all six rounds of the Six Party Talks that were organised to negotiate the dismantling of North Korea's nuclear programme and then dormant since 2009. To strengthen its overall ability to secure constructive participation in any future political or economic integration process, Mongolia revised its National Security Concept of 2010 to give greater attention to the Asia-Pacific region, especially NEA and Central Asia. The Mongolian government noted that the situation in its home region was delicate because of historical and territorial disputes and conflicted circumstances on the Korean peninsula which disrupted regional integration efforts and had a negative impact on long-term stability:

> As an integral part of Northeast Asia, Mongolia prioritizes these regional concerns. It remains one of our top foreign policy objectives to not only develop and strengthen ties with our neighbours, but also to constructively contribute our share to the common well-being and security of the region.[44]

In 2013, out of conviction that there must be progress on North-South Korean peninsula issues in order to improve Mongolian and overall regional security, Mongolia launched the idea for an "Ulaanbaatar Dialogue on Northeast Asian Security" (UBD). Its purpose was to propose various NEA regional framework security strategies and examine the role of economic and environmental factors in promoting NEA regional cooperation and trust. Comparing this mechanism to the Helsinki dialogue of Cold War days, Mongolia's President Tsakhia Elbegdorj proclaimed that because it wished to facilitate a peaceful solution on the Korean peninsula through dialogue, "Mongolia is willing to open up new gateways for the issues at standstill."[45]

While originally not enthusiastically embraced by the US and other Six Party governments, the UBD proceeded in a systematic fashion and slowly garnered international support when foreign policymakers saw that the North Koreans usually attended. Since its inaugural meeting in June 2014 in Ulaanbaatar, the UBD has established a proven record of success in attracting the participation of North Korean diplomats/researchers as well as those from the Six Party countries, India, and Europe. The DPRK diplomats often were willing to meet with American, Japanese, and South Korean delegates for sideline discussions. One of the attractions of this forum was that it not only discusses NEA regional framework security strategies but also the roles of economic, energy, disaster management, and environmental factors in promoting regional cooperation and confidence building.

While the Obama government was cool towards the UBD process and meticulously avoided any official presence at the UBD forums even as observers, Trump Administration officials recognised that there were distinct advantages to Mongols playing the role of non-judgmental active facilitator for international talks. Mongolia found space to continue its policy of cooperation, and understood that in this way it could raise its image with Washington policymakers. It sees its position as reinforcing the idea of Mongolia as a problem solver in Asia and as a non-nuclear weapon state positioned to act as a possible peacemaker: "While neighboring countries, China, Japan and South Korea are seeking deterrence, Mongolia may become an integral part of stabilizing the Korean Peninsula with its small country diplomacy."[46]

One of the major positive developments that emerged from Mongolia's offering to be a bridge to the North Koreans was that the Trump Administration became open to finding concrete ways to strengthen the bilateral economic relationship. US Embassy to Mongolia Chargé d'Affaires Manuel Micaller emphasised American support of Mongolia:

> It is a statement of the United States' strong, long-term commitment to the bilateral relationship and a recognition of the leading role Mongolia can play in ensuring a rules-based order in the Indo-Pacific region and beyond based on our shared values of promoting peace, protecting human rights, and ensuring the political and economic sovereignty of all nations.[47]

The US government considered Mongolia as an "emerging partner" and as a country with which it could cooperate to achieve a "shared vision of rules-based order in the Indo-Pacific."[48]

The Trump foreign policy era began in January 2017 with bilateral relations defined by a Comprehensive Partnership agreement dating from 2004. US-Mongolian foreign relations advanced to an Expanded Comprehensive Partnership in 2018 and then to a Strategic Partnership in 2019, which was signed during the state visit of President Khaltmaa Battulga to Washington. In the text of the Strategic Partnership agreement, US affirmation of Mongolia's constructive role in the Indo-Pacific clearly was expressed by the shared desire to:

> Cooperate in promoting national security and stability across the Indo-Pacific region so that all nations, secure in their sovereignty, are able pursue economic growth consistent with international law and principles of fair competition; Deepen national security and law-enforcement ties through collaboration on bilateral and multilateral security, judicial, and law-enforcement efforts in the region and to strengthen cooperation in multilateral engagements such as peacekeeping, humanitarian assistance, and disaster preparedness and relief operations.[49]

James Carafano[50] has suggested that the US pursues five specific national security policies which fit into the national security strategic principles of President Trump and the greater US foreign policymaking establishment. It is possible to apply these to NEA, and it is evident that within the region only the country of Mongolia consistently comes to mind as the nation to facilitate these policies:

1. *Recognise that the US cannot do everything alone. It needs strong alliances and strategic partnerships in the region on a cost-sharing basis. It must seek partners not in the usual sense and cooperate with small states.* It is obvious that Mongolia is the sole friendly nation in the NEA region that can be an example of a small state promoting democracy and free enterprise and a strategically important one to promote peaceful negotiations among its larger neighbours since it has friendly relations with all of them.
2. *Build and strengthen the "Free and Open Indo-Pacific" architecture, not by replacing ASEAN or trying to set up a Pacific NATO, but supporting new security mechanisms such as the Quad.* This argument is justification for supporting Mongolia's UBD to eventually jumpstart or even replace the stalled Six Party Talks on the Korean peninsula. Mongolia has garnered agreement from all six parties to participate in this new negotiation forum and keep this new mechanism going despite financial constraints and periods of heightened tension.
3. *Promote economic freedom by encouraging economic liberalisation in the region across all sectors—goods, services and investment.* This could be done bilaterally if not multilaterally through a TPP by prioritising the US-Japan relationship and relations with Taiwan, but the US should be

looking for other partners. The ongoing crisis in Hong Kong has shown the limitations of trying to maintain economic liberal principles without the underpinning of strong democratic values and political systems. Democratic Mongolia's interest in promoting its image as a neutral peacemaker in its region has led it to volunteer its capital of Ulaanbaatar as a negotiating safe space like Geneva and Vienna. Certainly, the strong desire of Mongolian policymakers to enlarge the trade relationship with the US so it can be a "Third Neighbour" balance to the monopoly of its economy by its two geographical neighbours is a goal that meshes well with the American objective of reducing Chinese and Russian economic influence in NEA and all of Eurasia.

4. *Forge "very special relationships" in the Indo-Pacific region.* India, Taiwan, and Australia come to mind. Although the US has several bilateral long-term ally relationships with NEA nations, this has not brought military and political stability to the region. The only remaining country that could possibly be such a non-ally special friend is Mongolia. This fact was recognised by Secretary of State Pompeo when he thanked Mongolia for supporting the "uneasy process of denuclearization of the Korean Peninsula" in September 2019.[51]

5. *Make American military presence felt by doing more than developing better means to move limited forces quickly to where they are required* (Secretary of Defense Jim Mattis called this plan, "Dynamic Force Deployment"). There is strong support in the Pentagon for the Trump Administration's military build-up, but there is no real chance, barring a major military incident, of any additional American military deployment in the Indo-Pacific. Negotiations with both South Korea and Japan on reducing the numbers of American troops stationed on their territories begun under the Trump Administration likely will be affirmed by the new Biden Administration. Still to be discovered is the effectiveness of dynamic force deployment on thwarting any projections of power by Russia and China, and the effect of the altered deployment process on military equipment, manpower, and readiness.

Although Mongolian law precludes the establishment of foreign bases on its soil, the US with $18 million of funding provided by Secretary of Defense Donald Rumsfeld in 2005, assisted Mongolia's Ministry of Defence in upgrading its Five Hills military base into an effective international peacekeeping training centre.[52] Today, the Mongolian Armed Forces at this centre host the annual Khaan Quest multinational exercise co-sponsored by US Indo-Pacific Command. Khaan Quest 2019[53] was the seventeenth iteration in a continuing series of exercises designed to promote regional peace and security (the 2020 round was cancelled because of COVID-19). One can postulate that in the future Mongolian and other international peacekeepers could be deployed from this site for duty on the Korean peninsula or other regional border hot spots to reduce tension on the Korean DMZ.

Conclusion

The national security strategy of the Trump Administration was re-oriented towards the Indo-Pacific. This trend did not originate with President Trump, but expanded and accelerated a tendency that was evident in US policymaking circles since the end of the Cold War with the rise of China and then India. As the US has turned its attention more and more towards the Asia-Pacific and away from longstanding conflicts in Europe, the Middle East and South Asia, the trend has been interpreted both as a competitive response to the economic and military rise of China and a de-emphasising of globalism.

The George W. Bush and Obama administrations initiated the Asia pivot strategy while promoting the strengthening of the existing multilateral, interdependent institutional framework. In the Trump era of "America First" policies, the Asia pivot was extended to embrace a larger geography that includes Eurasian and South Asian nations with a definite maritime focus. Among the special features of the Trump Indo-Pacific strategy were: 1) Reliance on bilateral, trilateral, and quadrilateral relationships over larger multinational groupings and organisations. 2) Outreach to smaller nations that could serve as bridges to larger, less friendly nations and be counter examples to Chinese policies in the region. 3) Strengthen economic, more transactional, relations with all nations, large or small, allies or competitors.

Within the Trump Indo-Pacific strategy, there was not a strong NEA integrative focus. However, because very developed and successful economies as well as militarily hostile nations exist within this sub-region, there was intense interest in applying the new strategy to individual states throughout the area. This led Trump policymakers to be open to Mongolian initiatives to play a more active role in various thorny NEA problems including denuclearisation of the Korean peninsula, economic development and peacemaking. There is no reason to assume that this trend will be changed by the incoming Biden foreign policy team.

Notes

1 James Jay Carafano, "America's Next 5 Moves in the Indo-Pacific Region," Heritage Foundation, April 9, 2019, at https://www.heritage.org/asia/commentary/americas-next-5-moves-the-indo-pacific-region (accessed November 12, 2020).
2 "Remarks by President Trump at APEC CEO Summit," November 10, 2017, at https://www.whitehouse.gov/briefings-statements/remarks-president-trump-apec-ceo-summit-da-nang-vietnam/ (accessed May 22, 2020).
3 "The National Security Strategy of the United States," December 2017, at https://www.whitehouse.gov/wp-content/uploads/2017/12/NSS-Final-12-18-2017-0905.pdf (accessed May 22, 2020).
4 Ibid., p. 47.
5 "The National Intelligence Strategy of the United States of America 2019," at https://www.dni.gov/files/ODNI/documents/National_Intelligence_Strategy_2019.pdf (accessed May 23, 2020).
6 Jacob Heilbrunn, "Has Trump Altered the Course of American Foreign Policy?" *The National Interest*, February 14, 2020, at https://nationalinterest.org/feature/

has-trump-altered-course-american-foreign-policy-124101 (accessed May 23, 2020); Adam Garfinkle, "The Real Problem with the Trump Foreign Policy," Foreign Policy Research Institute, September 17, 2019, at https://www.fpri.org/article/2019/09/the-real-problem-with-the-trump-foreign-policy/ (accessed May 23, 2020); Matthew Hill and Steven Hurst, "The Trump presidency: continuity and change in US foreign policy," *Global Affairs*, 6, 2020, Issue 1, at https://www.tandfonline.com/doi/full/10.1080/23340460.2020.1726788 (accessed May 23, 2020).
7 Kathleen J. McInnis, "The 2017 National Security Strategy: Issues for Congress," *CRS Insight*, December 19, 2017, (IN10842), p. 2, at https://fas.org/sgp/crs/natsec/IN10842.pdf (accessed May 25, 2020).
8 Ibid., p. 2.
9 Kori Schake, "America Faces the Stakes and Style of a Cold War in Asia," in Iskander Rehman, "Policy Roundtable: Are the United States and China in a New Cold War?," *Texas National Security Review*, May 15, 2018, at https://tnsr.org/roundtable/policy-roundtable-are-the-united-states-and-china-in-a-new-cold-war/#_ftnref13 (accessed May 24, 2020); Cary Huang, "Trump Versus China: Is This the Dawn of a New Cold War?," *South China Morning Post*, February 18, 2018, at http://www.scmp.com/week-asia/geopolitics/article/2133344/trump-versus-china-dawn-second-cold-war (accessed May 24, 2020).
10 It sought to continue to do this through the Millennium Challenge Corporation, which selects countries that are committed to reform and then monitors and evaluates their projects.
11 "National Intelligence Strategy," p. 7.
12 Ibid., p. 4.
13 The belief by many analysts is that a return to Obama-era engagement with Asian allies will be the long-term strategy post-Trump. See "Breaking the Mould: Trump's China Policy," Institute for Security and Development Policy, *Focus Asia*, February 2018, at https://isdp.eu/content/uploads/2018/02/Trump-China-FA.pdf (accessed May 26, 2020).
14 Melvyn P. Leffler, "Trump's Delusional National Security Strategy. How the Administration Ignores What Made America Great," *Foreign Affairs*, December 21, 2017 reprinted in International Information Center For Balkan Studies-Cibal, *Occasional papers*, 405, April 9, 2018, at https://cibal.eu/occasional-papers/6882-occasional-papers-volume-405-2018-trump-s-delusional-national-security-strategy-how-the-administration-ignores-what-made-america-great (accessed May 25, 2020).
15 Steven Metz, "How to Fix the Flaws in Trump's Approach to U.S. National Security," *World Politics Review*, July 12, 2019, at https://www.worldpoliticsreview.com/articles/28027/how-to-fix-the-flaws-in-trump-s-approach-to-u-s-national-security (accessed May 26, 2020).
16 "National Security Strategy 2015," February 6, 2015, p. 4, at https://nssarchive.us/national-security-strategy-2015/ (accessed May 26, 2020).
17 Pierre Guerlain, "US Foreign Policy of Chaos under Trump: the Wrecker and the Puppeteers" [«La politique étrangère du chaos sous Trump: le casseur et les marionnettistes»], *Review LISA e-journal*, 16 (2), 2018, para. 18, at https://journals.openedition.org/lisa/10208 (accessed May 25, 2020).
18 Oliver Turner, "The growing importance of the Indo-Pacific in the Trump administration's foreign policy strategy," London School of Economics US Centre, March 20, 2020, at https://blogs.lse.ac.uk/usappblog/2020/03/20/the-growing-importance-of-the-indo-pacific-in-the-trump-administrations-foreign-policy-strategy/ (accessed May 25, 2020).
19 Ibid.

20 According to Professor Ford, US interests were centred within a broader Indo-Pacific region and re-focused on multilateral cooperation around large regional democracies, highlighted by the administration's emphasis on a U.S.-Japan-Australia-India quadrilateral dialogue (known as "the Quad"): "Beyond 'the Quad' and 'the Indo-Pacific,' the administration's rhetorical emphasis on regional security networks and shared principles were consistent with longstanding U.S. policy in the region." See Lindsey Ford, "The Trump Administration and the 'Free and Open Indo-Pacific," Brookings, May 2020, p. 2, at https://www.brookings.edu/wp-content/uploads/2020/05/fp_20200505_free_open_indo_pacific.pdf (accessed June 4, 2020).
21 James Carafano, Luke Coffey, Nile Gardiner, Walter Lohman, Terry Miller and Thomas Spoehr, "Preparing the U.S. National Security Strategy for 2020 and Beyond," Heritage Foundation, May 23, 2019, at https://www.heritage.org/defense/report/preparing-the-us-national-security-strategy-2020-and-beyond (accessed May 25, 2020).
22 Kaewkamol Karen Pitakdumrongkit, "The Impact of the Trump Administration's Indo-Pacific Strategy on Regional Economic Governance," East-West Center, Honolulu, *Policy Studies*, 79, 2019, p. 6, at https://www.eastwestcenter.org/system/tdf/private/ewc_policy_studies_79_web.pdf?file=1&type=node&id=37123 (accessed June 4, 2020).
23 Ibid., pp. 12–13.
24 Ibid., p. 14.
25 Alyssa Ayres, "More Prominence for India and the Indo-Pacific in the U.S. National Security Strategy," Council on Foreign Relations, *Asia Unbound*, December 19, 2017, at https://www.cfr.org/blog/more-prominence-india-and-indo-pacific-us-national-security-strategy (accessed May 25, 2020). See her comparison of various NSSs in the Bush and Obama eras as to their views on India.
26 Ibid.
27 "National Security Strategy 2015," p. 25.
28 Ibid., cover letter signed by President Barack Obama, p. 1.
29 "Breaking the Mould."
30 Pepe Escobar, "'Quad' version of Belt and Road feels like a South China Sea Watch," *Asia Times*, February 24, 2018.
31 Deb Riechmann, "Trump's 'America first' policy to key in on foreign shores," *apnews.com*, February 2, 2019, at https://apnews.com/72008d8d52774fd3a1f6910c6333d120 (accessed June 3, 2020).
32 James McBride and Andrew Chatzky, "What Is the Trans-Pacific Partnership (TPP)?" *Backgrounder*, Council on Foreign Relations, at https://www.cfr.org/backgrounder/what-trans-pacific-partnership-tpp (accessed June 2, 2020).
33 Secretary of State Mike Pompeo, "America's Indo-Pacific Economic Vision," Indo-Pacific Business Forum, U.S. Chamber of Commerce, Washington, DC, July 30, 2018, at https://www.state.gov/remarks-on-americas-indo-pacific-economic-vision/ (accessed November 12, 2020).
34 As part of this strategy, the US and its Indo-Pacific partners would develop coastal radar-enhanced maritime domain awareness (MDA) with manned and unmanned aerial systems, maritime platforms for rapid deployment of HA/DR efforts, and increased information sharing mechanisms to link security and defence institutions at the operational level. See State Department Spokesperson Heather Nauert, quoted by Anwar Iqbal, "US sets up security assistance fund to counter China," *Dawn*, August 5, 2018, at https://www.dawn.com/news/1425055 (accessed November 12, 2020).

28 *Alicia J. Campi*

35 Frank Jannuzi, "Out of Tune: Japan-ROK Tension and U.S. Interests in Northeast Asia," National Bureau of Asian Research, October 9, 2019, at https://www.nbr.org/publication/out-of-tune-japan-rok-tension-and-u-s-interests-in-northeast-asia/ (accessed May 27, 2020).
36 Carafano, "America's Next 5 Moves."
37 Bolton was quoted from an interview on CNBC. See Zachary Halaschak, "'We wasted a lot of time': John Bolton says North Korea is 'more dangerous now'," *The Washington Examiner*, October 14, 2020, at https://www.msn.com/en-us/news/world/we-wasted-a-lot-of-time-john-bolton-says-north-korea-is-more-dangerous-now/ar-BB1a1o0Z (accessed November 12, 2020).
38 Harry Kazianis told CNBC's "Squawk Box Asia" on May 6, 2019. See Shirley Tay, "Trump's China threats could cause his North Korea policy to 'blow up in his face'," *CNBC*, May 6, 2019, at https://www.cnbc.com/2019/05/06/trump-china-tariffs-north-korea-policy-might-blow-up-in-his-face.html (accessed May 27, 2020).
39 Victor Cha, "U.S. Policy Toward North Korea After the Second Summit," CSIS, March 28, 2019, at https://beyondparallel.csis.org/u-s-policy-toward-north-korea-after-the-second-summit/ (accessed June 1, 2020).
40 Kylie Atwood and Vivian Salama, "Trump tells advisers he doesn't want another summit with North Korea's Kim before the election," *CNN*, February 10, 2020, at https://www.cnn.com/2020/02/10/politics/trump-north-korea-thaw/index.html (accessed May 28, 2020).
41 See Atwood and Salama, p. 1: "CNN on Monday quoted two sources familiar with the matter as saying that Trump, frustrated at the lack of progress, had told top foreign policy advisers he does not want another summit with Kim before the U.S. presidential election in November."
42 Stephen Biegun, Department of State website, at https://www.state.gov/biographies/stephen-biegun/ (accessed May 28, 2020).
43 Alicia J. Campi, "Mongolian foreign relations under 25 years of democracy," in Te-Kuang Chang and Angelin Chang (eds), *Routledge Handbook of Asia in World Politics*, Taylor and Francis, London and New York, 2018, p. 82.
44 Government of Mongolia, Brochure on the Ulaanbaatar Dialogue on Northeast Asia Security, December 2015, at http://www.mfa.gov.mn/wp-content/uploads/2015/12/Ulaanbaatar-Dialogue.pdf (accessed June 1, 2020).
45 Ts. Elbegdorj, "Every Man and Woman Can Live a Free a Peaceful Life," Speech at Opening Session of the VII Ministerial Conference of the Community of Democracies, Ministry of Foreign Affairs, April 29, 2013, at http://www.mfa.gov.mn/wp-content/uploads/2015/12/Ulaanbaatar-Dialogue.pdf (accessed June 1, 2020).
46 Bolor Lkhaajav, "Mongolia's Small Country Diplomacy and North Korea," *thediplomat*.com, September 29, 2016, at https://thediplomat.com/2016/09/mongolias-small-country-diplomacy-and-north-korea/ (accessed November 12, 2020).
47 Manuel Micaller, "Remarks by Chargé d'Affaires, a.i. Manuel P. Micaller at the AmCham Rollout of the 2018 Mongolia Investment Climate Statement," September 28, 2018, at https://mn.usembassy.gov/2018-cda-remarks-amcham-ics-rollout/ (accessed June 3, 2020).
48 Congressional Research Service, "Mongolia", *In Focus*, July 1, 2019, at https://fas.org/sgp/crs/row/IF10926.pdf (accessed June 5, 2020).
49 Department of State, "Declaration on the Strategic Partnership between the United States of America and Mongolia July 31, 2019," at https://www.state.gov/declaration-on-the-strategic-partnership-between-the-united-states-of-america-and-mongolia/ (accessed June 3, 2020).
50 Carafano, "America's Next 5 Moves."

51 During a meeting with Mongolian Prime Minister Khürelsükh in Washington, DC. See "Prime Minister Receives Secretary Pompeo," Mongolian Ministry of Foreign Affairs, September 20, 2019, at http://www.mfa.gov.mn/?p=47924&lang=en (accessed June 6, 2020).
52 Donna Miles, "Rumsfeld's Mongolia Visit Focuses on Peacekeeping Operations, American Forces Press Service, United States Department of Defense, October 22, 2005, at https://archive.defense.gov/news/newsarticle.aspx?id=17992 (accessed June 6, 2020).
53 Approximately 220 US personnel and 900 Mongolian soldiers participated in Khaan Quest 2019, along with approximately 750 personnel from Australia, Bangladesh, Benin, Cambodia, Canada, China, Croatia, El Salvador, Fiji, Indonesia, Israel, Japan, Jordan, Malaysia, Moldova, Nepal, New Zealand, Peru, Philippines, Qatar, Rwanda, Singapore, South Korea, Sri Lanka, Togo, United Kingdom, Uruguay, Vietnam and Zambia. Scott Schmidt, "30 nations arrive in Mongolia for peacekeeping exercise, Defense Visual Information Distribution Service," June 10, 2019, at https://www.dvidshub.net/news/326331/30-nations-arrive-mongolia-peacekeeping-exercise (accessed June 6, 2020).

2 China's foreign policy in Northeast Asia and implications for Mongolia

Denny Roy

Chinese foreign policy in Northeast Asia features an agenda that is expanding as China's growing relative power enables Beijing to aspire to a higher level of influence over the region. This has different ramifications for each of China's neighbours. For Ulaanbaatar, the combination of China's power and intentions poses serious long-term risks for an independent Mongolia.

Beijing's policy is understandable as a collection of efforts to support four general Chinese objectives. The *first* objective is for China to attain enough influence over neighbouring governments to dissuade them from pursuing policies or taking postures that the Chinese assess as threatening to China. Beijing would aspire to prevent other regional states, for example, from hosting strong and unfriendly foreign military forces or from closely partnering with a hostile great power. China is permanently opposed to eliminating the post-war restrictions on Japan's military forces and their rules of engagement. Beijing watches closely and strongly condemns any steps in this direction. Clearly, China would keep Japan militarily weak, if possible. The case of Japan is one where Beijing has been unsuccessful in dissuading an objectionable security policy decision by a neighbouring government.

The Chinese government has been more successful in the case of the Terminal High Altitude Area Defence system (THAAD) in South Korea (ROK). With North Korea improving its missile capabilities, the United States government pressed its ally Seoul to deploy THAAD, which is designed to shoot down incoming missiles. Claiming that THAAD's powerful radar could detect missile launches inside China and thereby help the US negate China's nuclear second-strike capability, China opposed the deployment. When in 2016 Seoul decided to install THAAD, Beijing retaliated with a partial economic embargo against South Korea. After a year of this pressure, Seoul announced it had reached a settlement with Beijing; bilateral trade would return to normal, and Seoul promised not to deploy additional THAAD launchers as previously planned as well as not join a larger US-Japan regional missile defence network. This was a win for China on the larger issue of preventing movement towards a multilateral US-led regional alliance, or "Asian NATO," that Beijing fears would be an anti-China coalition.[1]

DOI: 10.4324/9781003148630-2

The *second* foreign policy objective of the People's Republic of China (PRC) is ensuring that China is at the centre of regional economic arrangements. This is the optimal way to ensure that China has the best possible opportunity to continue its rapid economic development, sustain its prosperity, ensure access to essential imports as well as foreign markets, and successfully make the transition from middle-income to high-income country. Strengthening China's regional economic leadership position also increases Beijing's capacity to use economic leverage to force other governments to comply with Chinese preferences on political and strategic issues. Thus, Beijing is supportive of a Regional Comprehensive Economic Partnership (RCEP)[2] because China is the largest economy in the group and will have a dominant role in setting its agenda.[3]

The Belt and Road Initiative (BRI) also is a concrete manifestation of the Chinese goal of shaping regional economic arrangements to China's maximum benefit. BRI projects enable China to be the architect of an international trade infrastructure network, the first principle of which is to make China's penetration and domination of the global economy more extensive and more efficient. The actual economic benefit to Chinese citizens of many of the projects to improve cross-border infrastructure is questionable, which leads to the suspicion that in some cases the real objective of the Chinese leadership is to create symbolic political connections between China and its neighbours.[4]

The response of other Northeast Asian countries to the BRI is best characterised as ambivalent. A major emphasis of the BRI is development of Chinese links with Central Asia, a region that Moscow sees as traditionally within the Russian sphere of influence. China's "New Silk Road" and Russia's Eurasia Economic Union are direct competitors and a potential source of bilateral tension. Japan cooperates with China in selected infrastructure projects, but generally sees the BRI as part of a larger Chinese political project to replace the liberal international order with one centred on Chinese preferences.[5] Under the Abe government, Japan publicly professed lukewarm support for the BRI in order to help maintain constructive relations with China, but hoped to steer Beijing towards pre-existing norms and institutions not created by China.[6] It is likely that Abe's successor, at least in the short term, will continue this policy.

However, Seoul is an easier sell than Tokyo. South Korean President Moon Jae-in has said his country wants to participate in the BRI despite foreseeable problems. China-built infrastructure such as natural gas pipelines offers South Korea a way to strengthen its commercial connections with the Eurasian landmass given that North Korea's geographic position effectually isolates South Korea from the rest of the continent.[7] Any connections that traverse either Chinese or North Korean territory, however, will create serious vulnerabilities for the ROK, as both China and North Korea have in the past tried to use economic leverage to extort political concessions from Seoul. Moon's New Southern Policy,[8] which intends to strengthen South Korean economic connections with Southeast Asia, reflects persistent South Korean anxiety over the possibility of being dominated by large neighbours such as China.[9]

North Korea appears eager for more Chinese investment in infrastructure building, but in a departure from the general Chinese enthusiasm for signing up most of the rest of the world to the BRI, Beijing is hesitant towards North Korea. This stems from concerns about reinforcing negative international perceptions that the Chinese are sanctions-breakers, that the BRI has low standards, and that it serves mainly to trap other countries into dependence on China.[10]

Strengthening economic connections with Taiwan has been a major part of China's strategy to convince the island to submit voluntarily to becoming a province of the PRC. Cross-Strait economic interdependence deepened in the first years of the Ma Ying-jeou presidency (2008–2016), but stalled with a public backlash among the Taiwanese population that coalesced into the 2014 Sunflower Movement. This movement, motivated by fear that China was using trade and investment to build political leverage over Taiwan, succeeded in derailing a planned Cross-Strait Agreement on Trade in Services, which halted further major steps in China-Taiwan economic integration. Since 2016, the anti-unification Democratic Progress Party has controlled Taiwan, frustrating Beijing's plans to use economics to achieve desired political outcomes.

In the area of energy supplies, China seeks to guarantee its own energy security through a web of bilateral agreements that reduce China's reliance on global organisations such as the International Energy Agency (IEA). IEA-promoted initiatives are at variance with China's discomfort with the notion of relying on the open international market and with Beijing's desire that China should be the hub of any regional energy regime. China has welcomed Northeast Asian countries to join an alternative, Chinese-led energy governance structure within the BRI, but these countries have largely resisted, preferring a regional multilateral regime.[11]

The *third* PRC foreign policy objective is satisfying Chinese irredentism. The ruling Chinese Communist Party (CCP) has set the recovery of what the Chinese consider stolen or lost territories as one of the main criteria for judging the CCP's worthiness to rule China. Xi's regime, in particular, has said the reunification of China is a prerequisite for achieving the "China dream" of national power and wealth.[12]

As a rule, national territorial disputes are among the most volatile and intractable problems in international relations. In China's case, the situation is more difficult and potentially more dangerous than usual for three reasons. First, China's territorial claims cover a huge area on China's periphery—so large an area as to generate suspicion that China is using irredentism as a cover to simply carve out for itself a zone of domination on its immediate periphery and thus indicating an expansionist tendency.[13] Second, China's claims to disputed territory have increased over time, including China's reassertion of ownership over part of the East China Sea claimed by Japan.[14] This tendency fuels worries that Beijing might invent new "historical" claims over additional territory as China grows stronger. Third, China has pursued its irredentist agenda comparatively aggressively, threatening war against Taiwan and periodically employing deadly force in the South China Seas and on the Sino-Indian border. This Chinese objective makes Taiwan arguably the most dangerous flashpoint in Northeast Asia. While the Korean Peninsula crisis is equally long and intractable, the military standoff there is relatively stable. However, Taiwan must manage an intensifying clash between waning Taiwanese interest in unification to China with a growing Chinese desire to resort to settling such issues by relying on military superiority.

A *fourth* Chinese objective is pushing out the strategic leadership and influence of the US from the region. Xi's government has sent mixed signals, with Xi seemingly calling for an immediate end to US influence in Asia, while other Chinese analysts have argued that China is not trying to topple American regional leadership.[15] Nevertheless, it is beyond question that China eventually wants to displace the US as the strategically dominant country in Northeast Asia. Even if the Chinese might have found US regional involvement useful in some instances, such as in deterring possible North Korean adventurism or calming Chinese paranoia about resurgent Japanese militarism, the Chinese clearly see the US and Chinese overall strategic agendas as mostly incompatible. The consistent Chinese allegation that the US aims to "contain" China reveals a belief that China cannot achieve its goals within a regional order presided over by Washington.[16]

Under Xi, Beijing has characterised US involvement in the region as disruptive, has tried to intimidate and insult regional countries into reducing their security cooperation with Washington, and has attacked America's worthiness of global leadership.[17] From Beijing's perspective, the ideal Northeast Asia would have the following six major characteristics:

1. China would have the leading role in making policy decisions for economic frameworks and arrangements that involve two or more regional governments, so as to ensure that China's economic needs are met.
2. The US would be a major trading nation in the region, but would have little or no military role or activity, somewhat like the European Union's current relationship with Northeast Asia. Furthermore, the US would not use its economic and diplomatic leverage contrary to China's wishes in regional political questions, such as in the imposition of economic sanctions as punishment for misbehaviour.
3. Regional countries would accept China's claims over disputed land and maritime borders. The governments of neighbouring countries would agree to the principle that criticising the Chinese government, the CCP, or CCP leaders is an unlawful intrusion into China's internal affairs.

China also would desire that all neighbouring states allow Chinese media, diplomats and United Front organisations to purvey a positive image of China within their countries.
4. Japan would be a major source of foreign direct investment (FDI) and technology transfer for China, but would maintain only weak military forces with no power projection capability and would foreswear permanently any interest in developing or deploying nuclear weapons. Tokyo would adopt a position of maximum contrition for Japan's aggression during the World War II era and would condemn assiduously or suppress any statements that China would consider militarist or revisionist.
5. The Koreas would remain divided. North Korea would supply China with exports without restrictions arising from distrust of Chinese influence, would be willing to bargain away its nuclear missile capability, would cease using military tensions to extort concessions from South Korea, and would undertake Chinese-style economic reforms. Meanwhile, South Korea, no longer allied with the US or hosting American military forces, would be a strong economic partner for China and agreeable to accommodating Chinese strategic sensibilities.
6. Taiwan would unify politically with China, becoming a province of the PRC, and no longer able to acquire military equipment from any other foreign nations.

China-Mongolia relations in the modern era

In medieval times, Mongolia controlled the largest empire in human history. However, Mongolia's national security during the modern era has been chronically uncertain. A quick review of recent history bears this out. Mongolia was part of the (then Manchu-led) Chinese empire when the Qing Dynasty collapsed in 1911. The Bogd Khaan, Mongolia's chief religious leader, took the opportunity to declare Mongolia an independent country, and so Mongolia became a theocratic monarchy. Its borders were similar to the area encompassed by today's Mongolian Republic. At that time, its aspiration to annex the Chinese province of Inner Mongolia to the south proved insufficiently strong.

The successor government to the Qing Dynasty in China, the Beiyang government of the newly established Republic of China (ROC or Nationalist China), continued to claim Mongolia as Chinese territory. In 1919, Chinese troops led by warlord General Xu Shuzheng occupied Mongolia, imprisoned the Bogd Khaan, and nominally restored Chinese rule. Chinese control was brief. In 1921, a multi-national mercenary army commanded by the ethnic Baltic German anti-Bolshevik, White Russian warlord Roman von Ungern-Sternberg expelled Chinese forces from Mongolia's capital and restored the Bogd Khaan monarchy. A few months later, however, Bolshevik Russia organised an army of Russian and pro-Russian Mongolian troops that seized control of Mongolia and established a communist government aligned with Russia in a July revolution.

Soviet Russia was content to leave Mongolia as client state rather than annex it, because Moscow wanted to avoid antagonising China, which still considered Mongolia to be Chinese territory. The Russians also saw Mongolia as a useful buffer between Russia and China, keeping Chinese forces far from most of southern Russia.[18] Nationalist China never completely gave up its desire to rule Mongolia. At the Yalta Conference in February 1945, Moscow insisted that Mongolia remain independent after the war. In August, under Soviet pressure, the ROC agreed to acknowledge Mongolia's independence, if supported by the results of a referendum and if the Soviets pledged to stop supporting the CCP insurgency and the Uyghur independence movement on Chinese territory. That referendum took place in October 1945, with the questionable official result of 100 per cent voting in favour of independence.

In discussions with Stalin in July 1945, ROC representative T.V. Soong asked Stalin to recognise Mongolia "as an integral part of China." Soong explained, "We cannot tell our people that we are giving up any part of our territory" without the result that "our position as a government will be badly shaken before our people." Stalin countered with his own worry, that "Outer Mongolia has a geographic position from where one can overthrow the Soviet Union position in the Far East."[19] He particularly mentioned the danger of an adversary using Mongolia as a base from which to cut off access to Siberia, so he refused to accommodate the Chinese request.

Exiled to Taiwan after defeat on the mainland by communist forces in 1949, the ROC, nevertheless, continued to hold the China seat in the United Nations and to claim Mongolia as part of its territory. A CCP-led government took over mainland China and immediately the two communist nations of Mongolia and the PRC recognised each other. The ROC government accused the Soviet Union of violating its part of the bargain by continuing to support the CCP and advocating for international official diplomatic recognition of Mongolian independence. In 1955, the ROC used its veto power in the United Nations Security Council to deny Mongolia's entry into the United Nations General Assembly, but under protest in 1961 finally assented, pressured by the US government. The constitution used today by the ROC on Taiwan continues to define Mongolia as part of China.

During the 1950s, the CCP in Beijing continued to pester the Soviets to change their position and support Mongolia returning to Chinese control.[20] In subsequent decades, PRC leaders privately continued to regard Mongolia as a rightful part of China, which was lost due to Soviet manipulation.[21] Up to the mid-1960s, the PRC had economic influence in Mongolia through the supply of thousands of Chinese workers who assisted in the construction of industrial infrastructure and through the transit revenue Mongolia derived from its railroad linking China and Siberian Russia. China tried to use that leverage to pry Mongolia away from Moscow.

Ulaanbaatar sided with the Soviets during the Sino-Soviet split, and in 1966, Mongolia and the Soviet Union signed a mutual assistance treaty that committed them to using "all means, including military, to safeguard the security and independence of both countries."[22] As a Soviet satellite, Mongolia was a threat to the PRC as the Soviets based missiles and 100,000 troops there. Moscow used Mongolia against China just as Stalin had said he feared another government would use Mongolia against Russia.

That changed, however, in 1990. The collapse of the Soviet empire sparked a peaceful democratic revolution in Mongolia. The communist party government resigned to make way for the implementation of a multi-party political system and market-oriented economic reforms. Ulaanbaatar saw the end of the Cold War as an opportunity to improve Mongolia's national security. Previously, Mongolian forces were on call to defend the Soviet Bloc, fight alongside Russian troops, and defend against a Chinese invasion. Mongolia's new post-Cold War posture was "rational" (i.e., policy was no longer dictated by communist ideology or pressure from Moscow), non-aligned, called no other state an enemy, hosted no foreign troops (the withdrawal of Russian forces was completed in 1992), and defined national self-defence as the Mongolian military's only mission. The country reduced its number of soldiers by several thousand.[23] Such steps alleviated the danger of the PRC seeing Mongolia as a staging area for a military attack against the Chinese homeland.

Both the 1994 Foreign Policy Concept and the 1994 National Security Concept confirmed by the Mongolian Parliament emphasised the principle of maintaining cordial relations with both Russia and China. Since Mongolia had been closely aligned with the USSR during the Cold War, moving to a "balanced" relationship required Ulaanbaatar to measurably reduce its cooperation with Russia and significantly increase its engagement with China. Chinese Premier Li Peng visited Ulaanbaatar in 1994 and signed a bilateral Treaty of Friendship and Cooperation that outwardly solved all of Mongolia's problems with China, since Beijing recognised Mongolia's sovereignty and territorial integrity and pledged non-interference in Mongolia's internal affairs. Nevertheless, Mongols became increasingly worried in the 2000s that growing economic dependence on China was compromising Mongolia's security.

Post-Cold War Mongolian security strategy was a combination of balanced and friendly relations with the two big neighbours plus the "third neighbour" (discussed below) effort to establish links with other states and regional institutions. The apparent assumption was that a wide array of foreign relationships would help deter either China or Russia from trying to impose unwanted influence. Scholars have compared this approach to the survival strategy practised by small and middle powers in Southeast Asia, when their governments neither explicitly identified any particular country as an enemy nor unambiguously sided with any other strong state. Rather, they welcomed all strong states to become involved in regional affairs in the hope that the resulting web of overlapping and interlocking interests would dis-incentivise aggressive or domineering behaviour by any particular strong state. This has been called an enmeshment strategy.[24]

Since 2000, Mongolia has added an additional element to the enmeshment strategy so as to balance China's growing power. While continuing to maintain friendly relations with Beijing, Mongolia re-established military relations with Russia, increased its security cooperation with the US and sought military cooperation with other states and international institutions worldwide. The revised 2010 National Security Concept and 2011 Foreign Policy Concept reflected this change.[25] As a result, while post-Cold War Mongolia is no longer a military threat to China as a base for Soviet forces, its political liberalisation has created new irritants to China, both strategic and ideological.

Chinese objectives and Mongolia

In several respects, an independent Mongolia clashes with Chinese interests. Mongols generally are not fond of China, which works against the Chinese foreign policy objective of eliminating unfriendly policies or postures among neighbours. Mongols are well aware that China has a long history of colonial designs on Mongolia. In 2017, 90 per cent of Mongols had a favourable opinion of Russia and 82 per cent a favourable opinion of the US, while for China the numbers were 43 per cent favourable and 53 per cent unfavourable.[26] Even Chinese official media acknowledge that in recent years "incidents of violence and robbery targeting Chinese frequently happened in Mongolia. Negative news on Chinese workers in Mongolia appeared on local media from time to time."[27]

Antipathy towards China increased in Mongolian society in the 1990s as uncensored media began associating Chinese influence with crime, corruption of politicians and officials, reckless environmental practices, and alleged interest in overthrowing the Mongolian government.[28] Such attitudes continued to grow, and politicians often pandered to these sentiments.[29] During the 2017 Mongolian presidential election campaign, eventual winner Khaltmaa Battulga attempted to tar his opponent Miyegombo Enkhbold with the epithet of *erliiz*, meaning a person of mixed Chinese-Mongolian heritage. Battulga also reinforced the message with his slogan "a Mongol will win," implying he should secure victory because he was the only purely Mongolian candidate.[30] Such attacks led both rival candidates Enkhbold and Sainkhuu Ganbaatar to publish their genealogies in attempts to dispel the accusation they had Chinese ancestry.[31]

Fears of Chinese carpetbagging led Mongolia in 2006 to amend its regulations so that only a Mongolian citizen could obtain a licence for extracting minerals. Many Chinese companies managed to circumvent that regulation by operating through Mongolian middlemen. As with many other countries, Chinese migrant workers in Mongolia also are a source of bilateral tension. The number of Chinese workers has risen steadily in recent years despite Mongolian unemployment being as high as 10 per cent. Pressure from local labour groups led the Mongolian parliament in 2018 to consider a law that would cap legal immigrants from China at 30 per year,[32] but this change was not approved.

Mongolia's "third neighbour" policy of seeking ties with other developed countries to counter-balance Chinese power directly challenges China's goal of reducing US' influence in the region and especially in a country on China's border. The policy was associated closely with the US because US Secretary of State James Baker visited Mongolia in 1990 and suggested that the Mongols view the US as a "third neighbour." John Tkacik has written, "The concept electrified Mongolians, who had never dared think of themselves as anything but real estate over which Russians and Chinese had fought for centuries."[33] The United States is now one of several major nations other than China and Russia that have substantial relationships with Mongolia. In fact, in 2019 the US became the fifth country to forge a strategic partnership agreement with Ulaanbaatar, following Russia (2004), Japan (2010), China (2014), and India (2014).

It is official American policy "to ensure the United States remains a preferred partner over geographical neighbours Russia and China and to give Mongolia greater latitude to chart an independent foreign and security policy."[34] From the Chinese point of view, such a policy intends to directly thwart China's objectives, which are to establish pre-eminent Chinese influence over Mongolia and to make certain that it is never so "independent" as to disregard Beijing's wishes. Another US goal is "promoting democratic values and human rights" jointly with Mongolia.[35] To China, this looks like another aspect of the US' campaign to overthrow the CCP, in this instance by supporting a multi-party democracy on China's northern border.

Concrete US security cooperation with Mongolia has been enough to attract China's attention. Mongolia is a "NATO partner country," although the bar for this designation is low—the countries in Central Asia that were former Soviet republics, for example, also are NATO partners, despite the fact that some are authoritarian governments that do not always support NATO operations. Mongolia contributed forces to the American-led coalitions fighting in Iraq and Afghanistan. The Mongolian military hosts an annual peacekeeping exercise with the US Indo-Pacific Command called Khaan Quest, and US military educational institutions are open to Mongolian military personnel. The US Department of Defense "Indo-Pacific Strategy Report" of 2019 classes Mongolia as one of the regional democracies that "are reliable, capable, and natural partners of the United States." Specifically, the report praises Mongolia for its contributions to United Nations peacekeeping operations and to the Allied coalition fighting in Afghanistan, and for supporting the US' vision of "a free and open Indo-Pacific."[36]

As another example of striving for equidistance contrary to Chinese wishes, Mongolia has observer status in the Shanghai Cooperation Organization

(SCO). However, it resists Chinese pressure to become a full member because of Western perceptions of the SCO as a Chinese-led quasi-alliance.[37] Further, Mongolian nationalism remains a threat to China's irredentist agenda. It not only precludes Mongolia from voluntarily re-joining the Chinese empire, it creates political discontent in the PRC province of Inner Mongolia and emboldens other ethnic minority regions of China to oppose rule by Beijing. Chinese tend to believe in a nexus between non-Han nationalism and separatism. Thus, they see the revived Mongolian reverence for the nation's founder Genghis Khan, pan-Mongolism, and Tibetan separatism as mutually reinforcing.[38]

Mongolia is a divided nation. The existence of an independent Mongolia complicates China's management of the four million Mongolians who live in China's Inner Mongolia Autonomous Region, directly south and east of Mongolia. Although there are more Mongolians in Inner Mongolia than in independent Mongolia, the prospect of Inner Mongolia ever breaking away from Chinese rule seems foreclosed by the fact that ethnic Han Chinese outnumber Mongols in Inner Mongolia six to one. Large numbers of Han Chinese have relocated to Inner Mongolia under CCP government incentive programmes, which are part of a deliberate effort to dilute Mongolian nationalism. In 2014, the government of one county in Inner Mongolia began offering cash payments and subsidised services to married couples of whom one member was ethnic Han and the other was an ethnic minority, with the obvious expectation that many of the children of such marriages will self-identify as Han.[39]

Another, more recent, Chinese attempt to quash Mongolian nationalism in China illustrates how an independent Mongolia makes the Chinese task harder. In August 2020, the Chinese government announced it would severely curtail the use of Mongolian as the language of instruction in schools in Inner Mongolia, shifting to more use of Mandarin. The result was an education "strike", with over 300,000 Inner Mongolian schoolchildren refusing to attend school, and scenes of massed policemen attempting to prevent parents from withdrawing their children from school. The 300 employees of the government-controlled television and radio stations in the province reportedly signed a petition threatening to quit if authorities attempted to punish the parents of striking students. Chinese police, nevertheless, began arresting and prosecuting organisers of the strike.[40]

Not surprisingly, Mongolians across the border joined the protests against the Chinese government. An estimated 100 protestors appeared on Sukhbaatar Square in front of Mongolia's Government Palace to mark the visit of PRC Foreign Minister Wang Yi to Ulaanbaatar in September 2020. Although there was no public indication that Wang's hosts raised the issue with him,[41] former Mongolian president Tsakhia Elbegdorj wrote a letter addressed to Xi criticising the new Chinese policy as an "atrocity".[42] The Chinese official press retorted that "Elbegdorj's letter has been returned as the remarks in the letter were considered wrong."[43] The entire incident has attracted negative attention for the CCP from the international press.

The Chinese can expect an independent Mongolia will always draw attention to and criticise Chinese attempts to erase ethnic Mongolian identity, embarrassing China externally and emboldening activists inside China.

China's future danger to Mongolia

In the long term, China poses a severe security risk to Mongolia. This risk will increase to the extent that China's economic, technological, and military capabilities relative to Mongolia grow, but even more pertinent is the increase of China's power relative to Russia's and, to a lesser degree, relative to the US'.

China already has an important basis for attempting to constrain Mongolia's freedom of independent action: critical monopoly over Mongolia's economy. The Chinese bought over 90 per cent of Mongolia's exports in 2018.[44] The key transportation node for landlocked Mongolia's access to foreign trade goes through the Chinese port of Tianjin via a railroad from Mongolia into Chinese territory. Mongolia needs Chinese investment and technical expertise for infrastructure development, particularly in the mining industry. In 1990, China's economic influence in Mongolia was far behind Russia's,[45] but China's foreign direct investment (FDI) in Mongolia rose steadily through the 1990s and early 2000s. By 2010, China accounted for over half of the FDI from all foreign countries.[46] The official amount of Chinese investment is understated because many Chinese firms use Mongolian front companies. Researcher Jeffrey Reeves has noted that "Chinese firms determine, through their investments, which portion of the Mongolian economy will grow and, indirectly, which will shrink."[47]

Ulaanbaatar is dependent on loans from China to pay its debts to other countries. While trade with China is profitable, it simultaneously deepens the Mongols' sense of being exploited by the Chinese. Mongolia mainly exports irreplaceable minerals such as copper and coal to China while getting cheap consumer goods in return. The overdependency on trade with China inhibits the development of certain Mongolian industries.[48] Yet, China seeks even deeper penetration. Beijing has been urging Mongolia to open itself more fully to Chinese banks and to work out a bilateral free trade agreement. In 2016, Mongolia, Russia, and China jointly announced their intention to develop a China-Mongolia-Russia Economic Corridor. The proposed effort would enhance transportation links across Mongolia's northern and southern borders, with the potential benefit to Mongolia of making a higher volume of exports at faster transportation speed feasible. Many Mongolian businessmen are supportive of the idea.[49]

Greater linkage, however, brings to Mongolia the usual risks. The additional investment would increase Mongolia's already very high external debt (nearly 200 per cent of GDP),[50] raising the possibility of Mongolia falling victim to the "debt trap," wherein a country's permanent inability to pay off its debts leaves it vulnerable to a creditor government demanding political concessions. The resulting increase in Chinese direct investment could stifle the development of Mongolian domestic industries and bring in more Chinese workers. In addition, any increases in profits dependent on transit goods through China could be subject to a future Chinese cutoff for political or other reasons.

Beijing already has amply demonstrated its willingness to exploit its economic leverage to coerce Ulaanbaatar into compliance with Chinese political demands. For example, the Chinese leadership remains very concerned about Mongolia's relationship to the Dalai Lama. Most Mongolians adhere to a form of Tibetan Buddhism. Mongolia's own Bogd Khaan was the third-highest figure in Tibetan Buddhism, subordinate only to the Dalai Lama and the Panchen Lama. The Dalai Lama, therefore, is a popular and revered figure. Beijing, on the other hand, considers the Dalai Lama to be a separatist and enemy of the CCP and demands that foreign governments accord him no respect or legitimacy.

The Dalai Lama has made nine visits to Mongolia since 1990, and Chinese reaction often has been fierce. When Ulaanbaatar hosted him in 2002, China retaliated by closing its border with Mongolia, which cut rail access to the port of Tianjin for two days. In 2016, when the Mongolian government allowed the Dalai Lama to visit at the request of a Mongolian Buddhist organisation, Beijing fruitlessly demanded that the visit be cancelled. The Chinese punishment was to call off important negotiations about Chinese loans and investment. Afterwards, Mongolian leaders promised never to host the Dalai Lama again, and the Chinese Foreign Minister stated, "We hope that Mongolia has taken this lesson to heart."[51]

Xi Jinping publicly has affirmed that "China respects Mongolian independence and integrity" and added that "Both nations should give mutual firm support to each other in core issues concerning sovereignty, security and territorial integrity."[52] In consistently pushing for mutual respect for "sovereignty", Beijing implicitly has conditioned China's promise not to encroach on Mongolian territory on the guarantee that Ulaanbaatar will not support "separatists" such as the Dalai Lama. This puts the Mongolian government in a squeeze between Chinese expectations and the demands of Mongolian citizens who consider the Dalai Lama their spiritual leader.

Conclusion

Besides economic coercion, an even stronger Chinese attempt to impose control over Mongolia—by forcible annexation—cannot be ruled out in the future. Mongolia's current situation is a historical anomaly. It has vast territory, valuable natural resources, and a population (3 million) far too small to defend the country against either of its strong neighbours. Mongolia is rich in mineral wealth, including copper, coal, and uranium. China remains heavily reliant on coal, is a net importer of copper, and needs foreign supplies of uranium to fulfil its plans for expanding the use of nuclear power. The Chinese general public thinks Mongolia should be part of China.[53] In Chinese hands, Mongolia would provide strategic depth insulating the capital Beijing, which is only 560 kilometres from the Chinese-Mongolian border. The absence of Chinese control creates a vulnerability. The Soviet-Mongol army entered China through eastern Mongolia towards the end of World War II, and this region saw frequent Soviet military manoeuvres during the Cold War. Furthermore, an independent Mongolia interferes with Chinese control over the PRC province of Inner Mongolia by acting as a beacon of Mongolian nationalism and a critic of Chinese attempts to assimilate ethnic Mongols in China.

A desire to avoid antagonising Moscow has stayed China's hand up to now, but the efficacy of that consideration could fade, if China continues its relatively rapid growth in economic and military power. In the future, the disparity in leverage between China and Russia may be so large, and an elder brother-younger brother relationship so well established, that Beijing could feel emboldened to seize Mongolia with the expectation that, even if unhappy, the Russian government would acquiescence without the relationship suffering irreparable damage.

In addition to this strategic problem, Chinese analysts see Mongolia's relationship with the US as an ideological threat to China. In their view, Washington intends to use Mongolia to foment competition and disunity between China and Russia and also as a base for promulgating democracy into the region.[54] Mongolia's relationship with the US creates a security concern for China without guaranteeing Mongolia's safety against determined Chinese encroachment. How much material assistance the US would be willing to offer a seriously threatened Mongolia is highly questionable. Washington recently abandoned its Kurdish allies in Syria and took no military action in response to Russia's forcible annexation of Crimea and occupation of eastern Ukraine. That the US would go to war against either Russia or China to rescue Mongolia is almost inconceivable, given the geographic circumstances and the relatively superficial US interest in Mongolia's fate. The increase in Chinese capabilities, along with the correspondingly expansive Chinese aspiration to make Northeast Asia amenable to Beijing's agenda, creates a danger to Mongolia that is exceeded only by the danger faced by Taiwan.

Notes

1 "Russia engages with China on THAAD," *People's Daily*, August 12, 2016, at http://en.people.cn/n3/2016/0812/c90000-9099132.html (accessed September 30, 2020).
2 A proposed free trade agreement in the Asia-Pacific region between the 10 member-states of ASEAN, namely Brunei, Cambodia, Indonesia, Laos, Malaysia, Myanmar, the Philippines, Singapore, Thailand, and Vietnam, and five of their FTA partners—Australia, China, Japan, New Zealand, and South Korea. The 15 negotiating countries account for 30 per cent of the world's population and just under 30 per cent of the global GDP. See "India stays away from RCEP talks in

Bali," *Nikkei Asian Review*, Jakarta, February 4, 2020, at https://asia.nikkei.com/Economy/Trade/India-stays-away-from-RCEP-talks-in-Bali (accessed October 10, 2020).
3 Peter A. Petri and Michael Plummer, "China could help stop the freefall in global economic cooperation," Brookings Institution, July 16, 2020, at https://www.brookings.edu/blog/order-from-chaos/2020/07/16/china-could-help-stop-the-freefall-in-global-economic-cooperation/ (accessed September 15, 2020).
4 Ankur Shah and Vivek Pisharody, "BRI Draws Skepticism in China's Northeast," *Reconnecting Asia*, November 8, 2019, at https://reconnectingasia.csis.org/analysis/entries/bri-draws-skepticism-china-northeast/ (accessed September 22, 2020).
5 Kai Neagle, "Why Is China's Belt and Road Initiative Being Questioned by Japan and India?," *E-International Relations*, London, May 2, 2020, at https://www.e-ir.info/2020/05/02/why-is-chinas-belt-and-road-initiative-being-questioned-by-japan-and-india/ (accessed September 14, 2020).
6 Andrea A. Fischetti and Antoine Roth, "Japan's Belt & Road Ambivalence," *Tokyo Review*, May 14, 2019, at https://www.tokyoreview.net/2019/05/sino-japanese-review-japans-bri-ambivalence/ (accessed September 29, 2020).
7 Sungku Jang, "Should South Korea Participate in China's Belt and Road?," *The National Interest*, January 6, 2019, at https://nationalinterest.org/blog/buzz/should-south-korea-participate-chinas-belt-and-road-40732 (accessed September 18, 2020).
8 The New Southern Policy targets Southeast Asian and India for increased tourism, cultural exchanges, trade, and cooperation in counter-terrorism and cyber and maritime security. Sungil Kwak, "A View from South Korea," ASAN Forum, January 7, 2020, at http://www.theasanforum.org/a-view-from-south-korea-3/ (accessed October 14, 2020).
9 Balbina Y. Huang, "Northeast Asian Perspectives on China's Belt Road Initiative: The View from South Korea," *East Asia*, 36, 2019, pp. 129–150.
10 Nyshka Chandran, "North Korea's Kim appears to have a big goal: Winning Belt and Road investments from Beijing," *CNBC*, January 11, 2019, at https://www.cnbc.com/2019/01/11/what-north-korea-really-wants-from-china-is-membership-in-the-belt-and-road.html (accessed September 19, 2020).
11 Gaye Cristofferson, "The Asian Super Grid in Northeast Asia and China's Belt and Road Initiative," *Stiftung Wissenschaft und Politik*, Berlin, October 2018, at https://www.swp-berlin.org/fileadmin/contents/products/projekt_papiere/Christoffersen_BC-AS_2018_Northeast_Asian_Supergrid_13.pdf (accessed October 3, 2020).
12 Lu Hui, "Xi says 'China must be, will be reunified' as key anniversary marked," *Xinhua*, January 2, 2019, at http://www.xinhuanet.com/english/2019-01/02/c_137714898.htm (accessed September 13, 2020).
13 Denny Roy, "Assertive China: Irredentism or Expansionism?," *Survival*, 61 (1), 2019, pp. 51–74.
14 "Tensions in the South China Sea," *Global Conflict Tracker*, Council on Foreign Relations, September 24, 2020, at https://www.cfr.org/global-conflict-tracker/conflict/tensions-east-china-sea (accessed September 17, 2020).
15 Teddy Ng, "Xi calls for 'Asian people to uphold Asia's security' as he aims to sideline US," *South China Morning Post*, May 21, 2014, at https://www.scmp.com/article/1517256/xi-calls-asian-people-uphold-asias-security-he-aims-shut-out-us (accessed September 26, 2020); Wang Dong, "Is China Trying to Push the U.S. out of East Asia?," *China Quarterly of International Strategic Studies*, 1 (1), pp. 59–84.
16 "World voices condemn US' containment mind-set of new cold war," *Global Times*, August 5, 2020, at https://www.globaltimes.cn/content/1196814.shtml (accessed September 14, 2020).

44 Denny Roy

17 Zhu Dongyang and Yang Tianmu, "Manila's dangerous, futile game of involving outsiders in regional row," *Global Times*, April 4, 2016, at https://www.globaltimes.cn/content/977030.shtml (accessed September 23, 2020); Chen Qingqing and Liu Xin, "Australia gets 'slap to the face' as global community welcomes China-sponsored resolution on COVID-19," *Global Times*, May 19, 2020, at https://www.globaltimes.cn/content/1188817.shtml (accessed September 23, 2020); Hua Xia, "Commentary: Absurd remarks reflect typical US hypocrisy," *Xinhua*, September 29, 2020, at http://www.xinhuanet.com/english/2019-08/08/c_138293893.htm (accessed September 24, 2020).
18 Elena Boikova, "Aspects of Soviet-Mongolian relations, 1929–39," in Kotkin, Stephen and Bruce A. Elleman (eds), *Mongolia in the 20th Century: Landlocked Cosmopolitan*, M.E. Sharpe, New York, 1999, p. 118.
19 David Wolff, "Record of a Meeting between T.V. Soong and Stalin," July 2, 1945, *History and Public Policy Program Digital Archive, Victor Hoo Collection*, box 6, folder 9, Hoover Institution Archives, at http://digitalarchive.wilsoncenter.org/document/122505 (accessed October 2, 2020).
20 Sergey S. Radchenko, "The Soviets' Best Friend in Asia: The Mongolian Dimension of the Sino-Soviet Split," Working Paper No. 42, p. 5, Woodrow Wilson Center for International Scholars, Washington, DC, November 2003, at https://www.wilsoncenter.org/sites/default/files/media/documents/publication/ACF4CA.pdf (accessed October 1, 2020).
21 Sergey Radchenko, "The Truth About Mongolia's Independence 70 Years Ago," *The Diplomat*, October 22, 2015, at https://thediplomat.com/2015/10/the-truth-about-mongolias-independence-70-years-ago/ (accessed October 1, 2020).
22 Government of the USSR, *Soviet-Mongolian relations (1921–1966)*, Government Printing House, Moscow, 1966, p. 321.
23 "Mongolian Defense White Paper 1997/1998," Ministry of Defense of Mongolia, Ulaanbaatar, February 1998, at https://www.files.ethz.ch/isn/157120/Mongolia_Eng-1998.pdf (accessed September 17, 2020).
24 Evelyn Goh, "Great power and hierarchy order in Southeast Asia: analyzing regional security strategies," *International Security*, 32 (3), 2007, pp. 121–126.
25 Jeffrey Reeves, "Mongolia's evolving security strategy: omni-enmeshment and balance of influence," *The Pacific Review*, 25 (5), 2012, p. 600.
26 "Pre-Presidential Election National Survey of Mongolian Public Opinion," International Republican Institute, Washington, DC, 2017, at https://www.iri.org/sites/default/files/wysiwyg/iri_mongolia_poll_-_may_2017_.pdf (accessed September 13, 2020).
27 Zhang Dan, "Reporter's diary: Mongolians taking different view of China after arrival of BRI," *Global Times*, July 16, 2019, at https://www.globaltimes.cn/content/1158078.shtml (accessed September 15, 2020).
28 Morris Rossabi, *Modern Mongolia: From Khans to Commissars to Capitalists*, University of California Press, Berkeley, CA, 2005, pp. 237–239.
29 See Alicia Campi, *Mongolia's Foreign Policy, Navigating a Changing World*, Lynne Rienner Publishers, Denver, 2019, pp. 88–89; Franck Billé, *Sinophobia: Anxiety, Violence, and the Making of Mongolian Identity*, University of Hawaii Press, Honolulu, October 31, 2014.
30 Sharad K. Soni, "Mongolia's new president is Mongolia first and China last," *East Asia Forum*, August 11, 2017, at https://www.eastasiaforum.org/2017/08/11/mongolias-new-president-is-mongolia-first-and-china-last/ (accessed September 18, 2020).
31 Agence France-Presse, "Anti-China sentiment and centuries-old hostilities take centre stage in Mongolian election campaign," *South China Morning Post*, June

24, 2017, at https://www.scmp.com/news/asia/east-asia/article/2099822/anti-china-sentiment-and-centuries-old-hostilities-take-centre (accessed September 29, 2020).
32 Terrence Edwards, "Mongolia lawmakers to consider strict immigration cap," *Reuters*, February 6, 2018, at https://www.reuters.com/article/us-mongolia-workers/mongolia-lawmakers-to-consider-strict-immigration-cap-idUSKBN1FR0KO (accessed September 19, 2020).
33 John Tkacik, "Mongolia's Democratic Identity," Heritage Foundation, June 21, 2005, at https://www.heritage.org/asia/commentary/mongolias-democratic-identity (accessed September 14, 2020).
34 Quote from the Department of State's "Congressional Budget Justification for Foreign Operations, FY2019," in Thomas Lum and Ben Dolven, "Mongolia," *In Focus*, Congressional Research Service, Washington, DC, July 1, 2019, p. 1, at https://fas.org/sgp/crs/row/IF10926.pdf (accessed September 24, 2020).
35 United States Department of State, "Declaration on the Strategic Partnership between the United States of America and Mongolia," July 31, 2019, at https://www.state.gov/declaration-on-the-strategic-partnership-between-the-united-states-of-america-and-mongolia/ (accessed September 28, 2020).
36 United States Department of Defense, "Indo-Pacific Strategy Report," June 1, 2019, p. 33, at https://media.defense.gov/2019/jul/01/2002152311/-1/-1/1/department-of-defense-indo-pacific-strategy-report-2019.pdf (accessed September 28, 2020).
37 Maria Siow, "US-China tensions: why Mongolia is in the middle of a new cold war," *South China Morning Post*, August 15, 2020, at https://www.scmp.com/week-asia/politics/article/3097419/us-china-tensions-why-mongolias-middle-new-cold-war (accessed September 30, 2020).
38 Wang Peiran, "Mongolia's Delicate Balancing Act," *China Security*, 5 (2), 2009, p. 23.
39 Jonathan Kaiman, "Chinese authorities offer cash to promote interethnic marriages," *The Guardian*, September 2, 2014, at https://www.theguardian.com/world/2014/sep/02/chinese-authorties-cash-inter-ethnic-marriages-uighur-minority (accessed September 19, 2020).
40 Christian Shepherd and Emma Zhou, "Authorities Quash Inner Mongolia Protests," *Financial Times*, September 9, 2020, at https://www.ft.com/content/c035c3d7-0f96-4e23-b892-2666bc110e20 (accessed October 14, 2020).
41 Anand Tumurtogoo and David Stanway, "Mongolians protest visit of China diplomat as language dispute simmers," *Reuters*, September 15, 2020, at https://www.reuters.com/article/us-mongolia-china-protests/mongolians-protest-visit-of-china-diplomat-as-language-dispute-simmers-idUSKBN2661SO (accessed September 14, 2020).
42 Ts. Elbegdorj, *@elbegdorj*, Twitter, September 29, 2020, 12:54 am, at https://twitter.com/elbegdorj/status/1310895813132869633 (accessed September 30, 2020).
43 "Chinese ambassador rejects former Mongolian president's remarks on bilingual education," *Global Times*, September 27, 2020, at https://www.globaltimes.cn/content/1202190.shtml (accessed September 30, 2020).
44 "Mongolia," *World Integrated Trade Solution*, World Bank, at https://wits.worldbank.org/CountryProfile/en/Country/MNG/Year/LTST/TradeFlow/Export/Partner/all/ (accessed October 14, 2020).
45 In 1989 Mongolia's trade volume with China was only $24 million, while by 2000, it had jumped to over $300 million. See Campi, *Mongolia's Foreign Policy*, p. 84. In 1992 trade volume with Russia was $400 million, while in 2001 it had fallen to $250 million. See Tsedendamba Batbayar, *Mongolia's Foreign Policy in the 1990s*, Institute for Strategic Studies, Ulaanbaatar, 2002, pp. 100, 122.

46 Foreign Investment and Foreign Trade Agency, Mongolia, "FDI in Mongolia," *investmongolia*, 2011, at http://www.investmongolia.com/fiftanew/contents.php?id=1&sId=2&lang=Eng (accessed September 22, 2020).
47 Reeves, "Mongolia's evolving security strategy," p. 593.
48 Andy Eskenazi, "Between a Rock and a Hard Place: Mongolia's Economic Dependence on China with a Focus on the Mining Industry," *Synergy*, July 24, 2020, at https://utsynergyjournal.org/2020/07/24/between-a-rock-and-a-hard-place-mongolias-economic-dependence-on-china-with-a-focus-on-the-mining-industry/ (accessed October 14, 2020).
49 Antonia Graceffo, "Mongolia and the Belt and Road Initiative: The Prospects for the China-Mongolia-Russia Economic Corridor," *China Brief*, July 15, 2020, Jamestown Foundation, at https://jamestown.org/program/mongolia-and-the-belt-and-road-initiative-the-prospects-for-the-china-mongolia-russia-economic-corridor/ (accessed October 1, 2020).
50 "Fitch Affirms Mongolia at 'B'; Outlook Stable," *Fitch Ratings*, May 28, 2020, at https://www.fitchratings.com/research/sovereigns/fitch-affirms-mongolia-at-b-outlook-stable-28-05-2020 (accessed October 14, 2020).
51 Christian Shepherd, "China says hopes Mongolia learned lesson after Dalai Lama visit," *Reuters*, January 24, 2017, at https://www.reuters.com/article/us-china-mongolia-dalailama/china-says-hopes-mongolia-learned-lesson-after-dalai-lama-visit-idUSKBN158197 (accessed September 24, 2020).
52 Teddy Ng, "Xi says China respects Mongolia's independence, but stresses joint development," *South China Morning Post*, August 23, 2014, at https://www.scmp.com/news/china/article/1579609/take-ride-our-express-train-xi-jinping-tells-mongolia (accessed September 17, 2020).
53 Wang, ibid., p. 23.
54 Fan Lijun, "US-Mongolia relations lack healthy balance," *Global Times*, August 11, 2019, at https://www.globaltimes.cn/content/1161082.shtml (accessed September 15, 2020).

3 Russia in Northeast Asia: strengthening security through cooperation

Elena Boykova

Introduction

At the turn of the Twentieth and Twenty-first centuries, the Asia-Pacific region and its northeastern part assumed a special place in world politics. In a constantly changing world, the key role of Northeast Asia (NEA) in the Asian region remains unchanged. This is largely due to the fact that the regional players include China, Russia, Japan, United States, South Korea, Mongolia, and North Korea. The first three countries are key actors in the international arena, and their interests in the region intersect. At the same time, unresolved traditional regional problems persist in NEA; new ones appear and become aggravated; mutual intertwining occurs. All of this serves as a serious challenge to peace and stability in the region and dictates the need for constant concern to strengthen security by the states. One cannot but take into account the fact that confrontation and the struggle for influence between the US and China are escalating in the region which cannot but affect the general situation in NEA.

NEA occupies a special place in Russia's foreign policy. The Foreign Policy Concept of the Russian Federation (2016) states that:

> Russia views strengthening its positions in the Asia-Pacific Region and stepping up relations with its States as a foreign policy area of strategic importance, which is attributable to Russia belonging to this vibrant geo-political region. Russia is interested in participating proactively in the integration processes in Asia-Pacific, using the possibilities it offers to implement socioeconomic development programmes in Russia's Siberia and Far East, and creating an inclusive, open, transparent and equitable collective security and cooperation architecture in Asia-Pacific.[1]

The region of the Russian Far East is of great geopolitical and geostrategic importance for Russia. The area of the region is more than 6.9 million sq. km, or about 42 per cent of the territory of the Russian Federation. The economic development of the Far East is influenced by such factors as good

DOI: 10.4324/9781003148630-3

supply of natural resources and an advantageous transport and geographical position associated with the direct access to the Asia-Pacific Region. The region also has an access to two oceans—the Pacific and the Arctic, and borders with NEA countries China, Mongolia, Japan, DPRK, and the United States.

The region has huge natural resource potential with reserves of coal, iron ores, gold, silver, platinum, copper, and polymetallic ores. Woodlands occupy about 30 per cent of the total forest area in Russia. The main problems are harsh, even sometimes extreme climatic conditions, and remoteness from central Russian regions, all of which results in economic and infrastructural isolation from most developed Russian markets. In 2000, an administrative formation was created in the Far East known as the Far Eastern Federal District (FEFD). The District is one of the most important geostrategic regions of Russia because it has the potential to attract capital and large commodity flows, but where the levels of socio-economic development of the population is highly differentiated.[2]

Serious challenges that need to be addressed include a difficult demographic and social situation, underdeveloped transport infrastructure, low degree of natural resources development and disparities in the industrial development of territories. The growth of industrial production in the FEFD in 2019 was 6 per cent, which was higher than the average Russian growth rate of 2.4 per cent.[3] The eastern regions of Russia, located at a considerable distance from the industrially developed sections of central Russia, the Ural-Volga region, and the south of Siberia, represent areas of sharp decline in population and noticeable shortage of labour resources. Although having the largest territory among the other federal districts, the FEFD is the least populated one. A little more than 40 per cent of the country's territory is home to only 5.5 per cent of its population. According to preliminary estimates, the FEFD resident population as of January 1, 2020 amounted to 8,167,400 people.[4] In 2019, the population decreased by 21,300 people. The population decline was due to both natural decline (9,300 people or 44 per cent of the total decline) and migration loss (12,000 people or 56 per cent) continues.

Nonetheless, comprehensive development of the Far East is a national priority for Russia in the entire Twenty-first century. A new economy is being created in the region with large, medium-sized, and small businesses provided with tax incentives and administrative preferences, soft loans and the support of state development institutions. The importance of the Russian leadership to the development of the Far Eastern territories is evidenced by the following figures: since 2015, more than 40 laws have been adopted that are aimed at stimulating investment activity and improving the social sphere. Twenty territories of advanced development and five free ports have been created. Thanks to this, the implementation of over 1,780 investment projects worth 3.8 trillion roubles has begun and more than 230 new enterprises have been created. The state has provided targeted infrastructure and financial support to investors with more than 70,000 people receiving land free of charge, building dwellings, and creating farms on their "Far East hectare".[5]

In September 2020, the Russian government approved the National Programme for the Development of the Far East. The main goals of the programme are to accelerate the development of the regional economy, improve the demographic situation, stop the migration outflow and improve the quality of life of people in the Far East.[6] The programme is planned to be implemented in three stages: from 2020 to 2024, from 2025 to 2030, and from 2031 to 2035. For Russia the expansion of interaction with the states of Northeast Asia acquires special significance.

Russia's relations with key actors in Northeast Asia

The Eastern Economic Forum (EEF) was established by President Putin in a decree dated May 19, 2015. Its purpose is to promote the development of the economy of the Russian Far East by stimulating foreign investment, as well as expanding international economic cooperation in the Asia-Pacific region. Every year the leaders of the countries of the Asia-Pacific region, including the elite of Russian and international business, heads of government bodies, foreign officials, scientists and experts, gather in Vladivostok to discuss global economic issues.[7] The Forum is a platform where those who are ready to cooperate with Russia, work in the Russian Far East, launch new production facilities and develop existing ones, create jobs, build roads, residential buildings, and social facilities, meet and exchange views. Within the framework of the EEF, Russia carries out economic cooperation with 17 countries—China, Japan, ROK, Australia, New Zealand, Mongolia, Vietnam, and others. About 32 per cent of direct foreign investment in Russia since 2014 has come to the Far Eastern regions.[8]

The Forum in Vladivostok has become a leading platform aimed at developing multilateral cooperation and international cooperation. The role played by the forum in the development of regional cooperation in NEA is evidenced by the fact that in different years it was attended by the leaders of the NEA states. In 2019, the V (Fifth) Forum hosted over 8,500 participants from 65 countries. Compared to the First Forum, its representation has more than doubled, which is convincing evidence of the growing interest in the Russian Far East and in the possibilities of cooperation in this region.[9]

Russia-China relations

The year 2019 marked the 70th anniversary of the establishment of diplomatic relations between Russia/USSR and the PRC. Today, Russian-Chinese relations demonstrate an example of good-neighbourly coexistence and mutually beneficial cooperation. Relations between the two are stable, not subject to outside influence and have enormous potential prospects. The USSR became the first foreign state to recognise of the People's Republic of China (PRC) on October 2, 1949. In the early 1990s, after the collapse of the USSR, improvement in Russian-Chinese relations began, which led to the establishment of a strategic partnership. The nature of their relationship largely depends on common economic, political, and security interests, and both countries adhere to the principle of multipolarity in international relations. At present, China is Russia's most powerful partner in Northeast Asia. Deepening relations with China is a priority for Russian foreign policy. Bilateral relations formally are defined in the Treaty on Good Neighborliness, Friendship, and Cooperation between the Russian Federation and the PRC of July 16, 2001.[10] Relations are characterised by a strong legal base, extensive organisational structure and active connections at all levels. Currently, bilateral relations are governed by more than 300 intergovernmental treaties and agreements that cover almost all areas of cooperation.

In 2005, the State Duma of the Russian Federation and the PRC National People's Congress ratified an additional agreement on the Russian-Chinese state border on its eastern part[11] wherein Russia ceded a small territory. The problem of the disputed islands of Tarabarov and Bolshoi Ussuriisky arose in 1964. The agreement of 2005 defines the borderline in two sections (in the area of Bolshoi Island in the upper reaches of the Argun River of the Chita Region and in the area of the Tarabarov and Bolshoi Ussuriisky Islands at the confluence of the Amur and Ussuri rivers near Khabarovsk). Minister of Foreign Affairs Sergey Lavrov noted that the solution of the issue with China in no way was a precedent for discussing territorial disputes with Japan.[12]

Bilateral relations have developed significantly under Vladimir Putin and Xi Jinping. Chinese analysts describe this as "a one-of-a-kind relationship", highlighting the intentions of Russia and China to consolidate and deepen strategic and comprehensive partnerships in the long term.[13] The fact that President Putin pays attention to relations between Russia and China is evidenced by the fact that since 2000 he has visited China 16 times, and President Xi has visited Russia on several occasions. Russia was the first country Xi visited as PRC chairman or head of state in March 2013. In addition to mutual visits, the leaders of Russia and China meet at the annual summits of the Shanghai Cooperation Organisation (SCO) and BRICS (Brazil, Russia, India, China, and South Africa).

In September 2018, Xi participated for the first time in the IV Eastern Economic Forum in Vladivostok. In June 2019, President Xi paid a state visit to Russia. During this visit, joint statements were signed on the development of the Russian-Chinese comprehensive partnership and strategic interaction for a new era,[14] and on strengthening global strategic stability.[15] Twenty-five intergovernmental, interagency, and corporate agreements were concluded. During the negotiations, an agreement on the establishment of two more formats of interregional cooperation were reached: 1) between the Central Federal District of Russia and northern China and 2) between the Russian Northwestern Federal District and the southeastern PRC coastal provinces.[16] At the end of the visit, Xi took part in the St. Petersburg International Economic Forum.

The trade turnover between Russia and China has been increasing. According to the Federal Customs Service of Russia, Russian-Chinese trade turnover in 2019 amounted to US$110.9 billion, an increase of 2.4 per cent compared to 2018. Exports grew to $56.8 billion, an increase of 1.3 per cent compared to 2018, and imports were $54.1 billion, an increase of 3.6 per cent compared to 2018.[17] Moscow accounts for roughly 2 per cent of Beijing's annual global trade.[18] For China, Russia's foreign trade turnover in 2019 amounted to 16.6 per cent versus 15.7 per cent in 2018, which represented first place in 2018 and 2019. Imports of Russian goods compared to all Chinese imports in 2019 represented 13.4 per cent against 12.4 per cent in 2018, while Chinese imports amounted to 22.2 per cent of all Russian imports in 2019 against 21.9 per cent in 2018. In both exports and imports, China registered first place in the Russian market for 2018 and 2019.[19] Most of the Russian imports are minerals, especially in energy. Arms comprise the bulk of manufactured goods that Russia sends to China, accounting for 12 per cent of the weapons exported from Russia.[20]

Russian-Chinese relations in the economic sphere currently are not balanced. Speaking at Columbia University's Harriman Institute in September 2018, a leading Russian expert in Sinology, Professor Alexander Lukin, said that from Moscow's point of view, convergence of geopolitical interests of the two states, namely, their desire to restrain American influence in the world, compensates for imbalance. Yet, while China is Russia's largest trading partner, from China's trade perspective, Russia is almost an economic afterthought. Lukin characterised the economic disparity as "unpleasant", and added that it was an "internal problem" for Russia.[21]

According to Lukin, a potential source of future tension in Russian-Chinese relations may be the Chinese $1-trillion Belt and Road Initiative (BRI). This Chinese integration initiative is based on five "communications": political coordination, infrastructure connectivity, free trade, financial flows, and strengthening mutual understanding between peoples.[22] One of the main routes to expand Chinese exports to Europe involves the active use of the Russian Trans-Siberian railway network. But, another option is to expand the railway network through China's Xinjiang Province and in the Central Asian states, thus establishing a route that bypasses Russia. Lukin believes that Russia will have few, if any items in its diplomatic toolkit to influence the Chinese decision on how to proceed.[23]

During the coronavirus pandemic, trade between Russia and China from January to June 2020 decreased by 5.6 per cent year on year, amounting to only $49.15 billion. According to the General Customs Administration of the PRC, exports to the Russian Federation fell by 6 per cent over the first six months of 2020 and amounted to about $20.94 billion dollars; imports of Russian goods and services to China decreased by 5.3 per cent to $28.21 billion.[24] However, 2020–2021 are declared the Years of Russian-Chinese scientific, technical and innovative cooperation, and it is planned to organise more than a thousand events, such as conferences, exhibitions, forums, competitions for joint research projects, and educational seminars. The opening teleconference ceremony took place on August 28, 2020.

China and Russia maintain a traditionally high level of cooperation in the military-technical and military spheres. China is one of Russia's key partners and importers of Russian weapons. There are regular joint manoeuvres and exchanges between the military of the Russian Federation and the PRC. The director of the Federal Service for Military-Technical Cooperation of Russia Dmitry Shugaev in January 2019 noted that the portfolio of orders amounted to more than $7 billion, more than 15 per cent of the total Russian military-technical export orders.[25] In 2015, Russia signed a contract with China to supply the S-400 Triumph anti-aircraft missile system (SAM). But in the fall of 2018, the US imposed sanctions on the Chinese Ministry of Defence over the purchase of 10 Su-35 aircraft and equipment for the S-400 Triumph air defence system. Russia and China also are cooperating in the development of software for a missile attack warning system (EWS).[26]

Since the beginning of the COVID-19 pandemic, Russia and China have been cooperating closely. In February 2020, Russian humanitarian aid including medical personal protective equipment (PPE) totalling over 23 tonnes was delivered to Wuhan. That month a group of experts from the Russian Ministry of Health and Rospotrebnadzor [Federal Service for Supervision of Consumer Protection and Welfare] was sent to Beijing to exchange experiences in the fight against the virus. Russian specialists from the Pasteur Research Institute of Epidemiology and Microbiology and the Russian Ministry of Health also joined the World Health Organization (WHO) mission which assessed the spread of the virus in China. In April the Moscow government invited a group of Chinese doctors to Russia to provide advice on the coronavirus infection.[27] In early April, Russian planes began the transport from Shanghai of large amounts of PPE purchased in China, including about 80 million medical masks and 700,000 medical protective suits. That same month the first batch of PRC-donated humanitarian cargoes weighing 25 tonnes arrived in Russia and in May there was a second batch of 103 tonnes.

The PRC is Russia's key partner in the world arena. Both countries adhere to similar positions on a wide range of international problems, such as multipolarity and polycentricity of the world, cautious attitude towards humanitarian interventions and ways to resolve situations in a number of problem countries and regions.[28] In addition to regular meetings of the heads of foreign affairs ministries during mutual visits and on the sidelines of international forums, a system of planned consultations at the level of deputy ministers and department directors operates between the Russian and Chinese foreign ministries. The Russian-Chinese political and diplomatic partnership has become one of the key factors in maintaining international security and stability, establishing a multipolar world order, democratising global governance mechanisms, and ensuring the rule of international law. The two countries are united largely by the existence of problems in relations with the US. Both states seek to develop relations with other countries in a polycentric world in which the nations of the East and West can cooperate on the basis of equality and mutual respect both bilaterally and within the framework of international organisations such as the United Nations (UN).

Russia supports China's BRI. In turn, China supports the advancement of integration processes within the Eurasian Economic Union (EAEU) and a Greater Eurasian Partnership. The two nations will intensify concerted efforts to combine the EAEU and the BRI. They believe that the BRI and the idea of the Greater Eurasian Partnership can develop in parallel and will contribute to the development of regional associations and integration processes for the benefit of the peoples of the Eurasian continent.[29] Beijing is Moscow's most important strategic partner, and thanks to this, it can more successfully join the integration processes in NEA and Asia as a whole.

Some experts believe that

> China holds the upper hand in the relationship, and this power asymmetry will continue to grow at the expense of Russia. But Russia and China have more to gain from cooperation than outright competition. Barring an unlikely course correction in Russia's relationship with the West, the partnership will strengthen.[30]

Through bilateral cooperation, both China and Russia strive to strengthen their positions in Asia and

> the greatest threat to the West of the Sino-Russian partnership emanates from their efforts to adjust the international system to their advantage. As both Russia and China pursue increasingly activist foreign policies, Western policy needs to come to terms with the fact that their partnership is here to stay.[31]

Russia-Japanese relations

Diplomatic relations between the USSR and Japan were established in January 1925.[32] In February 1945, at the Yalta Conference, the USSR, the United States and Great Britain reached a written agreement on the entry of the Soviet Union into the war with Japan under the condition that the South Sakhalin and the Kuril Islands would be returned to the USSR after World War II.[33] Diplomatic relations were interrupted on August 9, 1945, when the USSR declared war against Japan. On October 19, 1956, Moscow and Tokyo signed a declaration calling for the end to the state of war and restoration of diplomatic relations.[34] They agreed that to continue negotiations on the conclusion of a peace treaty, and after this is signed, to consider the possibility of transferring the island of Shikotan and the Habomai archipelago to Japan.[35] This document did not mention the Kuril Islands and Sakhalin Island.

In recent years, the problem of disputed territories in Russian-Japanese relations has become noticeably aggravated. After World War II, all the Kuril Islands were incorporated into the Soviet Union, but the ownership of the Iturup, Kunashir, Shikotan Islands, and the Habomai group of islands has been disputed by Japan. According to the Foreign Ministry, the problems of disputed territories "should be discussed within the framework of a calm and unbiased dialogue, including through historians of the two countries."[36] Dr. Brad Williams notes that

> in one of the strangest anomalies in international relations today, Japan and Russia have yet to sign a peace treaty and relations between the two countries have not been fully normalised, although more than six decades have passed since the end of the Second World War.[37]

Despite the absence of a peace treaty, in the early Twenty-first century Russian-Japanese relations have reached the highest level in history. These relations are developing actively in three areas: political, including issues of concluding a peace treaty; economic, where priority is given to trade and economic cooperation; and in the field of bilateral and multilateral international cooperation, as well as in other practical areas.

It is geo-strategically important for Russia to have strong, long-term, reliable, partnership relations with Japan. The Foreign Policy Concept of the Russian Federation (2016) states that "the Russian Federation will continue to build good-neighbourly relations and promote mutually beneficial cooperation with Japan, including with a view to ensuring stability and security in Asia-Pacific."[38] Such relations would make it possible to strengthen Russia's positions not only in the Asia-Pacific Region, but in the world as a whole.

At present, Japan's policy towards Russia is determined by a number of contradictory factors. On the one hand, Japan is interested in long-term mutually beneficial cooperation with its northern neighbour. It believes that realising the economic potential of the regions of the Far East and Eastern Siberia will strengthen economic, social, and humanitarian ties with the Asia-Pacific region and enable Russia to make a constructive contribution to strategic stability and sustainable mutually beneficial development of the region. On the other hand, Japan's foreign policy towards Russia is associated with its US military-political alliance and participation in the G7. Japan cannot take a position fundamentally different from the position of other Western countries that entered into confrontation with Russia after the imposition of 2014 sanctions.

Initially, Japan supported sanctions that significantly limited lending by Japanese banks to their Russian partners. Japanese sanctions are relatively milder than those of the US and European countries and do not do much damage to economic relations between Japan and Russia.[39] In 2016, it was reported that the State Agency for Financial Services, in private consultations on the eve of President Putin's visit to Japan, asked Japanese leading private banks to finance some Russian projects.[40] According to Japanese economics official Hiroshige Seko, Japanese financial institutions can lend to Russian regional banks that are not under sanctions.

The two countries at the highest levels pursue an active political dialogue focused mainly on the issue of concluding a peace treaty, the central problem in relations between the two countries. The special bilateral relationship is evidenced by the fact that Putin travelled to Japan five times and former Japanese Prime Minister Abe Shinzo visited Russia nine times. In 2018, at the plenary session of the IV Eastern Economic Forum, Abe addressed the Russian President with the words: "Vladimir, let us once again confirm our intentions here, in front of such a large audience as witnesses. Let's go ahead, asking ourselves such questions: 'If we don't do this now, then when?,' 'If we don't do this, then who besides us?'" Putin replied, "We want to reach the conclusion of a peace treaty with Japan....let's conclude a peace treaty—not now, but before the end of the year—without any preconditions."[41]

At a meeting with President Putin on November 14, 2018 in Singapore during the Russia-ASEAN summit, Prime Minister Abe announced his readiness to negotiate a peace treaty between Japan and Russia based on the "territorial clause" of the Joint Declaration of 1956.[42] This statement was interpreted by the Russians as meaning that the Japanese side was not demanding the return of all the islands of Kunashir, Iturup, Habomai, and Shikotan. In January 2019, negotiations on the conclusion of a peace treaty between Russia and Japan began but according to Russian experts, difficulties arose as to the content of the agreement. The Japanese side sought fixing agreement on the ownership of the islands and drawing an agreed upon borderline. The Russian side thought that the treaty would lay the foundations for the formation of a new Russian-Japanese relationship by including other important problems such as Japan's recognition of Russian possession of the Kuril Islands, guarantees of non-use of the Japanese-American military-political alliance against Russian interests, broad development of comprehensive bilateral cooperation and implementation of military confidence-building measures.[43] Negotiations also were influenced by popular movements in Japan and Russia that were against resolving the disputed islands issue on the basis of the "territorial" article of the 1956 Declaration. The adoption in 2020 of an amendment[44] to the Russian constitution prohibiting alienating Russian territory further complicated the process.

Nevertheless, trade and economic relations between Russia and Japan are developing steadily, although not at a high level. In 2019, trade between Russia and Japan amounted to $20.31 billion, decreasing by 4.5 per cent compared to 2018. Exports to Japan in 2019 were $11.35 billion, decreasing by 8.8 per cent compared to 2018, and imports from Japan in 2019 were

$8.96 billion, an increase of 1.6 per cent compared to 2018. Japan's share in Russia's foreign trade turnover in 2019 amounted to 3 per cent as opposed to 3.1 per cent in 2018,[45] and Japan ranked eighth as a Russian trade partner in 2019.[46] The volume of bilateral trade is affected by fluctuations in prices for mineral raw materials, in particular hydrocarbons. In terms of the number of FDI projects in Russia, Japan ranks fifth with a downward trend: 17 in 2017 and 10 in 2018.[47]

The main area of investment cooperation between the two countries remains the fuel and energy sector. Japan controls 30 per cent of the consortium Sodeco in the Sakhalin-1 project; in the Sakhalin-2 project, Mitsui and Mitsubishi own 12.5 per cent and 10 per cent, respectively. Twenty per cent of the oil produced at Sakhalin-1 and 30 per cent of the oil produced at Sakhalin-2 are exported to Japan. At the Sakhalin-2 project plant, 80 per cent of the liquefied natural gas production discovered since 2009 is sent to Japan.[48] Another important field of cooperation is the automotive industry. Japanese companies Toyota, Nissan, Mitsubishi, Yokohama rubber, Isuzu, Mazda, and Komatsu have opened factories or joint ventures in Russia.[49]

In 2007, at the G8 summit in Germany, Japan offered Russia its assistance in the development of the Far East region. This proposal involved the development of nuclear energy in order to establish a stable power supply in the Far East, the laying of optical internet cables through Russian territory to connect Europe and Asia, the development of infrastructure and cooperation in the field of tourism, ecology, and security.[50] Tokyo considers that the joint development of the Far Eastern territories of Russia will reduce the tension in the two countries over the disputed territories.[51] In May 2016, Abe proposed an Eight-Point Cooperation Plan to expand bilateral cooperation in medicine, urban planning, cooperation between small and medium-sized enterprises, energy, industrial structure diversification, industrial development in the Russian Far East, advanced technologies and humanitarian exchanges.[52] The parties also promised to facilitate the visa regime on a reciprocal basis from January 1, 2017.

In December 2016, Putin and Abe agreed to conduct joint economic activities in the Kuril Islands without discussing the signing of a peace treaty.[53] Also, they agreed to provide Japanese with access to the graves of their ancestors located on the Kuril Islands. The two sides also discussed the Sakhalin-Hokkaido gas pipeline project to be laid from Yuzhno-Sakhalinsk to a northern port on Hokkaido. According to Japanese calculations, a pipe with a capacity of 25 billion cubic metres of gas per year and costing about $6 billion can be launched in 2022. Thus Japan, as the world's largest importer of LNG, hopes to get gas 2.5 times cheaper.[54]

Russian experts consider that currently Russian-Japanese relations are at "a medium level of development."[55] Japan does not view Russia as its military adversary and does not regard Russia's military potential as a direct threat to its national security. Its current concept, enshrined in Japan's Basic Plan for National Defense, mainly is focused on military threats from China and the DPRK.[56] At the same time, because of the territorial claims of Japan, Tokyo negatively perceives the strengthening of Russia's military presence in the South Kuril Islands over the past several years, reinforcement of its military infrastructure there as well as the deployment of modern weapons, including the latest coastal defence Ball and Bastion missile systems.[57]

Russia-South Korea relations

The Republic of Korea (ROK or South Korea) is one of Russia's priority partners in NEA. Diplomatic relations between the Russian Federation and the ROK officially were established on September 30, 1990. The official visit of Russian President Putin to Seoul in November 2013, during which the Joint Statement of Russia and the ROK was adopted, was of great importance to advancing bilateral relations. The statement reflected the priority vectors in the near and medium term, which are aimed at maximising potential cooperation, increasing its effectiveness, and searching for new areas of practical interaction, primarily in innovative fields.[58] In Vladivostok on September 6, 2017, on the sidelines of the III Eastern Economic Forum, new impetus to the development of relations was given by talks and signed agreements between Putin and Korean President Moon Jae-in, who was invited as the main guest.

In June 2018, President Moon paid a state visit to the Russian Federation. The Kremlin hosted negotiations which resulted in the adoption of a Memorandum of Understanding between the Russian Ministry of Economic Development and ROK Ministry of Science and Information and Communication technologies on the creation of a Russian-South Korean innovation platform for the fourth industrial revolution; joint statement on a Free Trade Agreement; and a Memorandum of Understanding between the two foreign affairs ministries on the establishment of the Russian-Korean Forum of Interregional Cooperation.[59] There are interparliamentary contacts, and legal framework for bilateral cooperation has been created. Over 50 agreements have been concluded covering trade, investment, fishing, military-technical cooperation, peaceful use of atomic energy and culture. Since 2014, there has been an agreement on visa-free stay of citizens for 60 days for holders of all types of passports.

Russia is interested in strengthening cooperation with South Korea primarily in the economic sphere. Economic relations have existed since the late 1980s, which was prior to the establishment of official diplomatic relations. An important role in the development of bilateral economic cooperation is played by the Russian-Korean Joint Commission for Economic, Scientific, and Technical Cooperation. For many years South Korea has been one of the main strategic partners and investors in the Primorye, the most southerly of the Russian Far Eastern territory. Today, more than 50 enterprises with South Korean capital operate in the region in such sectors as trade, agriculture, manufacturing, transport and logistics, fishing, and hotel and restaurant business.[60] The priority area of bilateral economic cooperation is in development plans for the Siberian and Russian Far Eastern regions. According to President Putin, "the regions of the Far East account for more than 40% of trade with Korean partners, which have a truly unique potential for the implementation of joint projects in shipbuilding, fishing, gas production, sea transportation, agriculture, health care, tourism, and development of the Arctic."[61] The participation of ROK companies in projects around the free port of Vladivostok and infrastructure development of the Northern Sea Route, as well as the involvement of the ROK government within the Arctic Council, continue to be discussed. In November 2018, the first meeting of the Interregional Cooperation Forum was held in Pohang, ROK, a forum attended by government and business representatives from both countries.[62] The second Interregional Cooperation Forum held in 2019 was attended by representatives of seven provinces and cities of the ROK and eleven Russian jurisdictions.[63]

The New Northern Policy, proclaimed by South Korean President Moon Jae-in in Vladivostok in September 2017, involves cooperation among the countries of Eurasia in order to form a northern economic community in the interests of peace and common prosperity.[64] At that conference, President Moon announced an initiative to build "nine bridges" with Russia. The "nine bridges" of cooperation including gas, railways, Northern Sea Route, shipbuilding, job creation, and fisheries.[65] In June 2018, Russia and Korea signed a joint statement on establishing a free trade zone,[66] trade in services and mutual protection of investments.

Currently, Russian-South Korean bilateral trade reflects a modest revival.[67] South Korea has become the second largest economic partner of Russia in Asia in terms of trade. According to the Federal Customs Service of Russia, in 2019 trade turnover between the Russian Federation and the ROK amounted to $24.3 billion, a decrease of 1.94 per cent compared to 2018. Russia's exports to South Korea in 2019 stood at $16.3 billion, having decreased by 8.27 per cent from 2018. Russia's imports from South Korea in 2019 amounted to $8 billion, an increase of 14.17 per cent over 2018. In Russia's foreign trade balance, South Korea's share in 2019 was only 3.6 per cent. In terms of its share in Russian trade turnover in 2019, the ROK took eighth place, as it did in 2018.[68] Russia is in 10th or 11th place in South Korean trade relations.[69] Russia accounts for no more than 1–2 per cent of total ROK turnover. According to ROK Ambassador to Russia Lee Sok Bae, trade between Russia and South Korea in January–April 2020 had fallen by 11 per cent: "the overall decline in trade occurred because cars and oil, which are the main items of import and export between our two countries, have been influenced by the global environment and price fluctuations in international markets."[70]

Investment cooperation is less effective. For 30 years, direct investments from the ROK in the Russian economy amounted to only about $3 billion.[71]

The ROK ranks seventh among investing countries.[72] The most successful aspects of Russian-South Korean relations are found in such joint projects as the Hyundai motor car plant in St. Petersburg, which produces up to 200,000 cars a year; the Lotte Group confectionery factory in the Kaluga region; a business and hotel complex in Moscow; and the opening of large-scale production of consumer electronics by Samsung and LG.

Russia has made a significant contribution to the development of the South Korean space programme. On April 19, 2008, the first female ROK cosmonaut, Yi Soyeon, took off into space with two Russian cosmonauts aboard the Russian Soyuz TMA-11 spacecraft. A joint project developed by South Korea was the creation of a one-time two-stage space vehicle KSLV-1 that was launched successfully in January 2013.[73]

In recent years, the rapprochement of the positions of Moscow and Seoul on North Korean issues has become noticeable. Russia and South Korea share a lot of principles on the uniting of the Korean nation: the peninsula should be free of nuclear weapons, and all problems and disputes should be resolved exclusively through diplomacy, without the use of weapons. Under some previous presidents of South Korea, Moscow's position on how to interact with the DPRK at times seriously differed from Seoul's, but now they support trilateral cooperation with the participation of both Koreas and Russia. Plans for the future include further development of ROK-DPRK-Russia cooperation to construct a unified railway and to lay a gas pipeline and power lines.

No doubt, the US is South Korea's main partner and ally. American troops are stationed in South Korea, which means that Seoul generally follows Washington's policy, which cannot but affect relations with Russia. Over the past five years, the US has limited significantly the scope and scale of Russian-South Korean cooperation.[74] Despite this, Russia and South Korea are interested in further improving bilateral relations and in developing interaction on various aspects of regional security.

Russia and Mongolia—strategic partnership in NEA

Relations between Russia and Mongolia have had a long history distinguished by good-neighbourliness and mutual interest in expanding and improving ties. On November 5, 1921, an Agreement on the establishment of friendly relations between Russia and Mongolia declared mutual recognition and determined the main principles and directions of interaction.[75] In the Twentieth century, socialist-era cooperation between the two countries took place in the fields of politics, economy and trade, culture, science, education, medicine, health care, and the military sphere. However, these relations also had their downside—Mongolia fell into a strong ideological, political, and economic dependence on the Soviet Union.

In the early 1990s with the collapse of the USSR, the level of Russian-Mongolian relations significantly decreased, and the mechanisms of bilateral cooperation malfunctioned. This primarily affected the economic sphere, so by the beginning of the Twenty-first century, the economic influence that the Soviet Union held in Mongolia had been lost: "Russia practically lost access to the management of the economic agenda, which ended up in the hands of Chinese, Japanese and American business."[76] At present, Mongolia still occupies an important place in the eastern direction of Russian foreign policy. This situation particularly is influenced by a number of historical, political, geographical, and civilisational factors.

Relations are regulated by several fundamental interstate documents. The 1993 Treaty on Friendly Relations and Cooperation between the Russian Federation and Mongolia reflected the fundamental change from allied relations to a good-neighbourly partnership not burdened with an ideological component and characterised by greater pragmatism.[77] Other significant documents for the development of bilateral relations were the Ulaanbaatar Declaration (2000); Moscow Declaration (2006), which confirmed the strategic partnership for Russian-Mongolian relations; and Declaration on the development of strategic partnership between Russian Federation and Mongolia (2009). The 1993 treaty was replaced by the Treaty on Friendly Relations and Comprehensive Strategic Partnership between the Russian Federation and Mongolia that was signed by President Putin and Mongolian President Khaltmaa Battulga on September 3, 2019.[78] According to Putin, this document consolidated a new level of Russian-Mongolian interaction for the further expansion of strategic partnership.[79] The parties agreed to develop cooperation in the field of politics, defence, security, economy, trade, finance and investment, infrastructure, transport and communications, energy, information technology, humanitarian relations, culture, art, education, science and technology, ecology, health care and, sanitary epidemiological well-being.[80]

In recent years Russian-Mongolian trade and economic ties have grown slightly. Trade between Russia and Mongolia for the first nine months of 2019 amounted to $1.23 billion, an increase of 13.1 per cent compared to the same period in 2018. Russia's exports to Mongolia for same first nine months of 2019 amounted to $1.2 billion, an increase of 14 per cent compared to the same period in 2018. Russia's imports from Mongolia for this period in 2019 amounted to $24.7 million, a decrease of 19.48 per cent compared to 2018. At the same time, the share of Mongolia in the foreign trade turnover of Russia for the first nine months of 2019 increased 0.25 per cent compared to a 0.22 per cent increase in the same period of 2018. Mongolia took 55th place in Russia's trade turnover for the first nine months of 2019, while for 2018 it was 56th place.[81]

Several articles of the Comprehensive Strategic Partnership Treaty of 2019 relate to topical issues of national and international security. The parties pledge to cooperate on a bilateral and multilateral basis on arms control, disarmament, non-proliferation and to develop cooperation with the United Nations (UN) and other international organisations. Furthermore, they promise to contribute to the strengthening of stable, effective security architecture in the Eurasian space and in the Asia-Pacific region, and to promote ties in the economic, cultural, humanitarian, inter-civilisational, intercultural and interfaith dialogues among states of the region.[82]

To ensure NEA regional security for Mongolia and develop bilateral relations with its neighbours in Northeast Asia, Mongolia's foreign policy is aimed at minimising tension in the region. In 2013, former President of Mongolia Tsakhia Elbegdorj initiated an international conference on security in NEA called the Ulaanbaatar Dialogue (UBD) in order to build confidence in the region. The agenda of the UBD sessions cover a wide range of issues, including modern threats to security, strengthening confidence-building measures and developing economic and energy cooperation. The UBD is a good platform for deepening understanding of the positions of different states and organisations, since experts from Russia, China, Mongolia, Japan, North Korea, the ROK, US, European Union, and the UN participate.

In recent years an important component of Russian-Mongolian relations has become their interaction with the PRC in trilateral format in order to solve economic development problems. The mechanism of trilateral meetings of the leaders of Russia, Mongolia, and China was launched on September 11, 2014 in Dushanbe on the sidelines of the SCO summit. The roadmap for cooperation among the three countries was adopted on July 9, 2015 at the Ufa summit. The programme for creating a Russia-Mongolia-China Economic Corridor was signed at the Tashkent summit in June 2016. Its main goal is to form a cross-border infrastructure network of railways, highways, border points and production capacities to increase investment and trade.[83] In September 2018, a memorandum of understanding regarding the mechanism for jointly promoting the Economic Corridor project was concluded.[84] Within its framework Russia will carry out the modernisation of the Ulaanbaatar Railway (UBTZ), which will provide necessary increase in throughput both for the transportation of goods, primarily minerals from Mongolian fields in the direction of Russian Far Eastern ports, and for the growth of transit traffic between Russia and China. UBTZ modernisation will ensure the efficient transit of Russian goods within the framework of the Northern Logistics System and will unite the transport systems of Russia, Mongolia, and China.

In June 2019, at the fifth trilateral meeting of the leaders of the three nations, Mongolian President Battulga pointed out that from 2016 to 2018 Mongolia had achieved significant success in transit traffic by increasing the number of trains travelling from China to Russia and onward to European countries through Mongolia by more than 500 per cent.[85] However, in the three years since the adoption of the Economic Corridor, implementation of specific projects had not begun. Nonetheless, Battulga proposed the creation of a unified energy network in Northeast Asia.[86] In response, President

Putin said that Russia was interested in joint projects with its Chinese and Mongolian partners: "For our part, we propose to ensure uninterrupted supplies of Russian electricity to the energy-deficient regions of Mongolia and China."[87]

The examples of trilateral cooperation among Russia, China, and Mongolia testify to their interest in establishing closer NEA economic cooperation. The development of economic interaction among the countries of the region can become the basis for strengthening stability and mutual understanding. At the same time, such multi-level cooperation within the region and the entire Eurasian space can become a guarantee of security for all countries in the Economic Corridor zone.

Conflict potential on the Korean Peninsula

Northeast Asia is characterised by the constant potential of considerable conflict. The strengthening of China's position is being opposed actively by the US, which seeks to involve its allies, Japan and South Korea. Under these conditions, unpredictable consequences for regional and global security are possible, for example, concerning the DPRK's nuclear missile programme. Territorial disputes exist between Japan and China or South Korea and Japan, and there is still one unresolved territorial problem for Russia—that of Japan. However, the situation on the Korean Peninsula appears to be the most acute.

The Korean peninsula nuclear problem always has been a major issue for Russia because Russia is a direct neighbour of the DPRK, has a common border with it, and in the event of any armed conflict, the territory of the Russian Far East and the population living there will be under threat. From the point of view of Russian interests, it is important to prevent an armed conflict on the Korean Peninsula. Russia is not just a non-involved "actor", but a "stakeholder", that is, a party whose well-being depends directly on the outcome.[88] Russia is interested in maintaining the political and diplomatic process in the region and is convinced that progress in solving the entire range of problems existing there can be achieved only on the basis of the consistent movement of the parties towards each other and the joint efforts of all the states involved in any regional settlement.[89]

For South Korea and the DPRK, 2018 became an important starting point in bilateral relations. South Korean President Moon Jae-in had three meetings with DPRK leader Kim Jong-un which were spurred by summitry between the US and the DPRK. The first summit of the US and the DPRK was held in Singapore on June 12, 2018 in which the leaders of the two countries agreed on a model for dispute settlement: Washington would provide Pyongyang with security guarantees and Pyongyang would move towards complete denuclearisation. It should be admitted that it was thanks to United States President Donald Trump's consent (with the active support of significant actors—primarily South Korea, China, and Russia) to a phased solution that a favourable atmosphere of detente and reduction of the military threat was created.[90] The direct dialogue that began between the leaders of the US and the DPRK made it possible to reduce the level of tension on the Korean peninsula, but to date it has not actually solved the problem that gave rise to the acute Korean missile crisis of 2017.

Russia highly appreciates the movement on both sides to attempt to settle the Korean problem, since this corresponds to its interests in the region. Yet, Russia's approach to this problem clearly contradicts those of the US, which opposes the DPRK's preservation of its residual nuclear potential while pledging not to develop it and guaranteeing non-proliferation. Russian analysts believe it is not profitable for the US' strategic goals to reduce confrontation on the Korean Peninsula and move to a state of stability from the current "controlled chaos".[91]

Russia has proposed its own proposals for resolving the Korean peninsula crisis. In 2017, it, together with the PRC, adopted a roadmap for resolving the crisis. This document contains proposals on the basis of "double freeze", that is, freezing the nuclear missile activities of the DPRK in exchange for freezing military exercises; moving towards bilateral (North and South Korea, North Korea, and the United States) and multilateral negotiations; defining general principles of relations between the parties; and, subsequently, resuming the Six Party (two Koreas, the US, China, Russia, and Japan) talks with the ultimate goal of creating a collective architecture of peace and security in Northeast Asia.[92]

On the issue of the denuclearisation of the Korean peninsula and stabilisation of relations in the region, Russia conducts a dialogue on a regular basis with the US and with the DPRK. In 2019, the Russian side discussed with South Korea a number of steps proposed by Russia and China for a joint action plan for a comprehensive settlement, based upon the 2017 road map. A new joint initiative is the Korean Peninsula Comprehensive Settlement Action Plan.[93] It contains a set of coordinated steps towards denuclearisation and security guarantees for the DPRK. On November 8, 2019, at the Moscow Nonproliferation Conference, Russian Foreign Minister Lavrov said that the Action Plan, designed to normalise the peninsula, is based on the principles of reciprocity and proportionality and sets out "the steps that the United States could take without damage to its reputation, and the steps that the leaders of North Korea could take on the same basis."[94]

In considering these initiatives, South Korean Minister of Unification Kim Yong-chol stressed the importance of diplomatic efforts to resolve the DPRK problem and the need for an "interim agreement" between Washington and Pyongyang in order to move towards a mutually acceptable compromise.[95] An official of the same ministry, who asked not to be named, said in an interview to a Russian journalist that the proposal of the Russian Federation and the PRC is a good option, which many South Korean entities are ready to support:

> This gives us a chance, he said, to revive cooperation with the DPRK and, in general, move away from the danger of sliding into the situation that was on the peninsula in 2016–2017. But, as you know perfectly well, we have our obligations to the United States, and therefore we have to take this into account and hope that the American-North Korean dialogue will resume and, as a result, will help tointensify inter-Korean contacts.[96]

Russia is of the opinion that maintaining and improving the political and diplomatic process in the region plays an important role in normalising the Korean peninsula and in NEA as a whole. North Korea has been under UN sanctions since 2006, when it first tested nuclear weapons. Russia advocates the use of negotiation to resolve the problem of the DPRK's nuclear missile programme and believes that the ultimate goal of denuclearisation of the entire Korean peninsula includes both the termination of the DPRK's nuclear programme in exchange for security guarantees (primarily from the US) and the rejection of the deployment of strategic weapons at American military bases in the ROK.[97] Vice-President of the Russian Council on International Affairs Ambassador Gleb Ivashentsov considers it reasonable to return to the Six Party format of negotiations to resolve the nuclear problem on the Korean peninsula on the basis of a phased approach by applying the principle of "action in exchange for action." It would be

> …expedient at the initial stage to propose to separate the North Korean nuclear programme from the missile programme. The DPRK's nuclear status is included in the country's constitution, and for Pyongyang this topic is currently not subject to discussion. At the same time, the freezing of the missile development programme, as well as guarantees of the non-proliferation of missile and nuclear technologies, may well be a subject of discussion.[98]

Russia has condemned the actions of the DPRK related to the testing of nuclear weapons and ballistic missiles and considers that they harm the security situation in East Asia. In 2017, Russia and China with other members of the UN Security Council voted in support of the DPRK sanctions resolution.[99] The Russian Foreign Ministry expressed deep concern over the North Korean hydrogen bomb test of a "thermonuclear explosive device for an intercontinental ballistic missile" announced by North Korea on September 3, 2017: "this latest demonstrative disregard by Pyongyang of the requirements of the relevant UN Security Council resolutions and the norms of international law deserves the most resolute condemnation."[100] Speaking at a plenary session of the Valdai Discussion Club in Sochi on October 19, 2017, President Putin condemned the DPRK nuclear tests, but explained that "this problem must certainly be resolved through dialogue, and not drive North Korea into a corner, not threaten to use force, not stoop to outright rudeness or abuse."[101]

Moscow believes that a gradual revision of the UN Security Council sanctions against the DPRK is necessary, as well as the dismantling of some of the nuclear missile program of North Korea.[102] In this regard, on December 16, 2019, at the UN, Russia, and China put forward a joint draft resolution, which sought some relaxation of international sanctions against Pyongyang and the resumption of the negotiation process.

Conclusion

In its regional policy, Moscow proceeds from the need to build multilateral mechanisms for NEA regional integration. Russia continues to advocate a course towards strengthening good-neighbourly relations with all interested countries in the region and respects the efforts of the NEA countries to form a multilateral structure that could ensure security in the region. Formation of various regional partnerships, primarily in the economic space of NEA, will lead to interaction mechanisms that gradually will strengthen mutual trust. Then, the countries can move on to discussions on broader regional issues of peace, development, and security and ultimately create conditions towards a comprehensive NEA security system. The basis for the NEA security architecture can be laid by the joint implementation of mutually beneficial large-scale, long-term economic projects, including the EEU and the Chinese BRI. Other proposals include President Xi's "Economic Ring of North-East Asia," which would be financially supported by the Asian Infrastructure Investment Bank and the Silk Road Fund,[103] and Russia, China, Mongolia, Japan and ROK's "Asian Energy Super Ring" that would ensure energy security in NEA.[104]

Trilateral summits of the PRC, Japan and ROK, held annually since 2008, can play a significant role in the trust-building process and regional economic cooperation. In September 2011 in Seoul, the three countries established the Trilateral Cooperation Secretariat (TCS) to promote peace and common prosperity.[105] The TCS Consultative board has established a constant dialogue on trilateral cooperation in the fields of politics, education, culture, and economy. However, in 2020, South Korea did not host as planned because of differences between Tokyo and Seoul over compensation for wartime labour.[106]

NEA is a strategically important component of Russia's foreign policy. The position of Russia as a global and regional power and the development of the Russian Far East, which was proclaimed as a strategic priority of the Twenty-first century, require strengthening of political, economic, and humanitarian cooperation with the countries of the region. Russia is interested in preserving its status as a great power by increasing its influence in Asia-Pacific affairs. Considering the high rate of development of the Asia-Pacific region both in the economic and military fields, integration into the region holds great promise for Russia.

Russia's NEA policy in NEA aims to protect the national interests and security of the country on its eastern borders, use the economic and political potential of the various states of the region in order to modernise and develop Russia, and ensure a decent life for its population on the Pacific coast. To achieve these goals, it is necessary to build a new non-aligned regional system of international interaction based on the principles of openness and equal, indivisible security. This political structure could include all the states geographically belonging to NEA, that is, Russia, China, Japan, ROK, Mongolia, and DPRK. Russia is interested in cooperation with the US as a dialogue partner on NEA security issues such as nuclear non-proliferation, arms control, peaceful atomic development, and Korean peninsula settlement.

Notes

1 "Foreign Policy Concept of the Russian Federation. Approved by President of the Russian Federation Vladimir Putin on November 30, 2016," at https://www.mid.ru/en/foreign_policy/official_documents/-/asset_publisher/CptICkB6BZ29/content/id/-2542248 (accessed October 21, 2020).
2 M. Isayev, "Problemy ekonomicheskogo razvitiya Dal'nego Vostoka" ["Problems of the Economic Development of the Far East"] (in Russian), *Molodoy uchenyy* [*Young Scientist*], 2 (136), 2017, p. 437, at https://moluch.ru/archive/136/38114/ (accessed October 21, 2020).
3 "Rosstat podvel pervyye itogi sotsial'no-ekonomicheskogo polozheniya Dal'nevostochnogo federal'nogo okruga za 2019 god/Territorial'nyy organ Federal'noy sluzhby gosudarstvennoy statistiki po Primorskomu krayu" ["Rosstat has summed up the first results of the socio-economic condition of the Far Eastern Federal District for 2019/Territorial body of the Federal State Statistics Service for the Primorsky Territory"] (in Russian), February 10, 2020, at https://primstat.gks.ru/folder/49006/document/75891 (accessed October 21, 2020).
4 Ibid.
5 "About the Eastern economic forum–Address of the Chair," April 7, 2017, at https://forumvostok.ru/en/about-the-forum/ (accessed November 12, 2020).
6 "Mikhail Mishustin utverdil natsional'nuyu programmu razvitiya Dal'nego Vostoka" ["Mikhail Mishustin approved the national programme for the development of the Far East"] (in Russian), *Vostochnyy ekonomicheskiy forum/Новости [The Eastern economic forum/News]*, September 28, 2020, at https://forumvostok.ru/news/mihail-mishustin-utverdil-natsionalnuju-programmu-razvitija-dalnego-vostoka/ (accessed November 12, 2020).
7 In 2020, the Eastern Economic Forum was cancelled due to the coronavirus pandemic.
8 "O Vostochnom ekonomicheskom forume" ["About the Eastern Economic Forum"] (in Russian), at https://forumvostok.ru/about-the-forum/ (accessed November 10, 2020).
9 "Outcomes of the 5th Eastern Economic Forum 2019," at https://forumvostok.ru/en/outcomes-of-the-eef-2019/ (accessed November 10, 2020).
10 "Dogovor o dobrososedstve, druzhbe i sotrudnichestve mezhdu Rossiyskoy Federatsiyey i Kitayskoy Narodnoy Respublikoy" ["Treaty on Good Neighborliness, Friendship and Cooperation between the Russian Federation and the People's Republic of China"] (in Russian), July 18, 2001, at https://www.mid.ru/web/guest/maps/cn/-/asset_publisher/WhKWb5DVBqKA/content/id/576870 (accessed November 14, 2020).
11 "Dopolnitel'noye soglasheniye mezhdu Rossiyskoy Federatsiyey i Kitayskoy Narodnoy Respublikoy o rossiysko-kitayskoy gosudarstvennoy granitse na yeye

Vostochnoy chasti"] ["Additional agreement between the Russian Federation and the People's Republic of China on the Russian-Chinese state border on its eastern part"] (in Russian), May 31, 2005, *Elektronnyy fond pravovoy i normativno-tekhnicheskoy dokumentatsii [Electronic Fund of legal and regulatory and technical documentation]*, at http://docs.cntd.ru/document/901945334 (accessed November 14, 2020).
12 V. Shishlin, "Rossiya i Kitay podelili granitsu" ["Russia and China have divided the border"], *Interfax* (in Russian), July 21, 2008, at https://www.interfax.ru/russia/22633 (accessed November 15, 2020).
13 Ye. Studneva, "Pochemu Vladimir Putin i Si Tszin'pin vse chashche 'sveryayut chasy'?" ["Why are Vladimir Putin and Xi Jinping increasingly 'synchronizing watches'?"] (in Russian), *Mezhdunarodnaya zhizn' [International life]*, November 24, 2017, at https://interaffairs.ru/news/show/18837 (accessed October 29, 2020).
14 "Sovmestnoye zayavleniye Rossiyskoy Federatsii i Kitayskoy Narodnoy Respubliki o razvitii otnosheniy vseob'yemlyushchego partnerstva i strategicheskogo vzaimodeystviya, vstupayushchikh v novuyu epokhu" ["Joint statement of the Russian Federation and the People's Republic of China on the development of comprehensive partnership and strategic interaction relations entering a new era"] (in Russian), June 5, 2019, at http://kremlin.ru/supplement/5413 (accessed November 14, 2020).
15 "Sovmestnoye zayavleniye Rossiyskoy Federatsii i Kitayskoy Narodnoy Respubliki ob ukreplenii global'noy strategicheskoy stabil'nosti v sovremennuyu epokhu" ["Joint statement of the Russian Federation and the People's Republic of China on strengthening global strategic stability in the modern era"] (in Russian), June 5, 2019, at http://kremlin.ru/supplement/5412 (accessed November 14, 2020).
16 "Zayavleniya Vladimira Putina i Si TSzin'pina po itogam peregovorov v Moskve. Glavnoye" ["Statements by Vladimir Putin and Xi Jinping following the talks in Moscow. The main thing"], *TASS* (in Russian), June 5, 2019, at https://tass.ru/politika/6512313 (accessed October 17, 2020).
17 All data are provided by: "Otchot o vneshney torgovle mezhdu Rossiyey i Kitayem v 2019 godu: tovarooborot, eksport, import, struktura, tovary, dinamika" ["Report on foreign trade between Russia and China in 2019: trade turnover, exports, imports, structure, goods, dynamics"], *Obzory vneshney torgovli Rossii/Torgovlya mezhdu Rossiyey i Kitayem v 2019 g. [Russian Foreign Trade Reviews/Trade between Russia and China in 2019]* (in Russian), February 13, 2020, at https://russian-trade.com/reports-and-reviews/2020-02/torgovlya-mezhdu-rossiey-i-kitaem-v-2019-g/ (accessed November 16, 2020).
18 "Moscow not worried about trade disparity with China – Russian scholar," *Eurasianet*, October 16, 2018, at https://eurasianet.org/moscow-not-worried-about-trade-disparity-with-china-russian-scholar (accessed November 16, 2020).
19 Ibid.
20 A. Nikol'skiy, "Kitay okazalsya odnim iz glavnykh importerov rossiyskogo oruzhiya" ["China has turned out to be one of the main importers of Russian weapons"] (in Russian), *Vedomosti [Journal]*, July 12, 2018, at https://www.vedomosti.ru/politics/articles/2018/07/12/775357-kitai-okazalsya-importerov-oruzhiya (accessed November 11, 2020).
21 "Moscow not worried about trade disparity with China – Russian scholar."
22 Sun Zhuangzhi, "Sotrudnichestvo po sopryazheniyu mezhdu Kitayem i stranami Yevrazii v kontekste postroyeniya Initsiativy poyasa i puti" ["Cooperation between China and Eurasian Countries in the context of building the Belt and Road Initiative"], *Rossiyskiy Sovet po mezhdunarodnym delam [Russian Council on International Affairs]* (in Russian), September 18, 2020, at https://russiancouncil.ru/analytics-and-comments/analytics/sotrudnichestvo-po-sopryazheniyu-mezhdu-

kitaem-i-stranami-evrazii-v-kontekste-postroeniya-initsiativ/ (accessed November 24, 2020).
23 "Moscow not worried about trade disparity with China – Russian scholar."
24 "Tovarooborot Rossii i Kitaya za polgoda sokratilsya do $49,15 mlrd" ["Trade turnover between Russia and China decreased to $49.15 billion in six months"], *TASS* (in Russian), July 14, 2020, at https://tass.ru/ekonomika/8957449 (accessed November 15, 2020).
25 "Moskva zayavila ob otsutstvii planov sozdaniya voyennogo soyuza s Kitayem" ["Moscow announced no plans to create a military alliance with China"], *Interfax* (in Russian), December 19, 2019, at https://www.interfax.ru/world/688638 (accessed November 2, 2020).
26 Ibid.
27 "Voprosy dvustoronnikh otnosheniy Rossii s inostrannymi gosudarstvami i regional'nymi ob'yedineniyami/O rossiysko-kitayskikh otnosheniyakh strategicheskogo partnerstva" ["Issues of Russian Bilateral Relations with Foreign States and Regional Associations/On Russian-Chinese Strategic Partnership Relations"] (in Russian), at https://www.mid.ru/strategiceskoe-partnerstvo-s-kitaem/asset_publisher/uFvfWVmCb4Rl/content/id/3487407 (accessed November 2, 2020).
28 O. Timofeev, "Rossiysko-kitayskiye otnosheniya na sovremennom etape i perspektivy ikh razvitiya" ["Russian-Chinese relations at the present stage and prospects for their development"], *Perspektivy* [*Prospects*] (in Russian), December 15, 2014, at http://www.perspektivy.info/rus/ekob/rossijsko-kitajskije_otnoshenija_na_sovremennom_etape_i_perspektivy_ih_razvitija_2014-12-15.htm (accessed November 3, 2020).
29 "Kitay vystupil za formirovaniye bol'shogo Yevraziyskogo partnerstva" ["China has declared for the formation of a large Eurasian partnership"], *Regnum* (in Russian), June 5, 2019, at https://regnum.ru/news/polit/2642042.html (accessed October 29, 2020).
30 P. Stronski and N. Ng, "China in Central Asia, the Russian Far East, and the Arctic," Carnegie Endowment for International Peace, February 28, 2018, at https://carnegieendowment.org/2018/02/28/cooperation-and-competition-russia-and-china-in-central-asia-russian-far-east-and-arctic-pub-75673 (accessed October 28, 2020).
31 Ibid.
32 "Konventsiya ob osnovnykh printsipakh vzaimootnosheniy mezhdu SSSR i Yaponiyey"["The Convention embodying basic rules of the relations between the Union of Soviet Socialist Republics and Japan"] (in Russian), January 20, 1925, at https://www.prlib.ru/item/337144 (accessed November 3, 2020).
33 "Yaltinskoye soglasheniye trekh velikikh derzhav po voprosam Dal'nego Vostoka, 11 fevralya 1945 g."["The Yalta Agreement of the Three Great Powers on the Far East, February 11, 1945"] (in Russian), *Vneshnyaya politika Sovetskogo Soyuza v period Otechestvennoy voyny. Dokumenty i materialy* [*Foreign Policy of the Soviet Union during the Patriotic War. Documents and materials*], Volume 3, Gospolitizdat, Moscow, 1947, pp. 111–112.
34 "Joint Declaration by the Union of Soviet Socialist Republics and Japan (October 19, 1956)," *The World and Japan Database* (Project Leader: A. Tanaka)/Database of Japanese Politics and International Relations/National Graduate Institute for Policy Studies (GRIPS); Institute for Advanced Studies on Asia (IASA), The University of Tokyo, at https://worldjpn.grips.ac.jp/documents/texts/docs/19561019.D1E.html (accessed November 4, 2020).
35 Ibid.

36 S. Lavrov, "Suverenitet Rossii nad Kurilami obsuzhdeniyam ne podlezhit" ["Russia's sovereignty over the Kuriles is not negotiable"], *Rossiyskaya gazeta [Russian Newspaper]* (in Russian), January 18, 2012, at https://rg.ru/2012/01/18/suv-site-anons.html (accessed November 3, 2020).
37 Brad Williams, *Resolving the Russo-Japanese territorial dispute: Hokkaido-Sakhalin relations*, Routledge, London and New York, 2007, p. 20.
38 "Foreign Policy Concept of the Russian Federation."
39 D. Streltsov, "Rossiysko-yaponskiye otnosheniya v kontekste novykh i traditsionnykh vyzovov bezopasnosti" ["Russian-Japanese relations in the context of new and traditional security challenges"], *Perspektivy razvitiya rossiysko-yaponskikh otnosheniy na novom etape: rabochaya tetrad' [Prospects for the development of Russian-Japanese relations at a new stage: workbook]* (in Russian), Number 50/2019, Moscow: NP RSMD, 2019, p. 12.
40 A. Moskvichev, "Yaponiya de-fakto vykhodit iz rezhima antirossiyskikh sanktsiy" ["Japan is de facto leaving the anti-Russian sanctions regime"], *Vzglyad [Outlook]* (in Russian), November 5, 2016, at https://vz.ru/economy/2016/11/5/842033.html (accessed November 3, 2020).
41 A. Beluza, "Putin predlozhil zaklyuchit' mirnyy dogovor s Yaponiyey do kontsa goda bez usloviy" ["Putin proposed to conclude a peace treaty with Japan before the end of the year without conditions"], *Rossiyskaya gazeta [Russian Newspaper]* (in Russian), September 12, 2018, at https://rg.ru/2018/09/12/putin-predlozhil-zakliuchit-mirnyj-dogovor-s-iaponiej-do-konca-goda-bez-uslovij.html (accessed November 4, 2020).
42 Junnosuke Kobara, "Abe and Putin designate negotiators for peace treaty and islands," *Nikkei Asia*, December 2, 2018, at https://asia.nikkei.com/Politics/International-relations/Abe-and-Putin-designate-negotiators-for-peace-treaty-and-islands (accessed November 4, 2020).
43 A. Panov, "Predisloviye" ["Preface"], *Perspektivy razvitiya rossiysko-yaponskikh otnosheniy na novom etape: rabochaya tetrad' [Prospects for the development of Russian-Japanese relations at a new stage: workbook]* (in Russian), Number 50/2019, Moscow: NP RSMD, 2019, p. 5.
44 This states: "the Russian Federation ensures the protection of its sovereignty and territorial integrity. Actions (with the exception of delimitation, demarcation, re-demarcation of the state border of the Russian Federation with neighbouring states) aimed at alienating part of the territory of the Russian Federation, as well as calls for such actions, are not allowed." See "Novyy tekst Konstitutsii RF s popravkami 2020" ["New text of the Constitution of the Russian Federation with the 2020 amendments"] (in Russian), at http://duma.gov.ru/news/48953/ (accessed November 4, 2020).
45 All data provided by: "Otchot o vneshney torgovle mezhdu Rossiyey i Yaponiyei v 2019 godu: tovarooborot, eksport, import, struktura, tovary, dinamika" ["Report on foreign trade between Russia and Japan in 2019: trade turnover, exports, imports, structure, goods, dynamics"], *Obzory vneshney torgovli Rossii/Torgovlya mezhdu Rossiyey i Yaponiyei v 2019 g. [Russian Foreign Trade Reviews/Trade between Russia and Japan in 2019]* (in Russian), February 13, 2020, at https://russian-trade.com/reports-and-reviews/2020-02/torgovlya-mezhdu-rossiey-i-yaponiey-v-2019-g/#:~:text=В%202019%20году%20товарооборот%20России,11%20353%20033%20488%20долл (accessed November 16, 2020).
46 "Vneshnyaya torgovlya RF. Dannyye FTS Rossii za 2019 god" ["Foreign trade of the Russian Federation. Data of the FCS of Russia for 2019"] (in Russian), February 12, 2020, at https://gipp.ru/news/poligrafiya-rynok-bumagi/vneshnyaya-torgovlya-rf-dannye-fts-rossii-za-2019-god/ (accessed November 16, 2020).
47 "Ministerstvo ekonomicheskogo razvitiya Rossiyskoy Federatsii/Itogi vneshneekonomicheskoy deyatel'nosti Rossiyskoy Federatsii v 2019 godu" ["Ministry

of Economic Development of the Russian Federation/Results of foreign economic activity of the Russian Federation in 2019"] (in Russian), p. 58, at https://www.economy.gov.ru/material/file/66eec1250c653fc9abd0419604f44bbd/VED.pdf (accessed November 16, 2020).

48 "The Next Phase in Japan-Russia Oil & Gas Cooperation," November 2013, Ministry of Economy, Trade and Industry of Japan, p. 6, at https://www.erina.or.jp/wp-content/uploads/2014/10/K-MINAMI.pdf (accessed November 5, 2020).

49 V. Nelidov, "Dvustoronniye otnosheniya Rossii i Yaponii" ["Bilateral relations between Russia and Japan"], *Perspektivy razvitiya rossiysko-yaponskikh otnosheniy na novom etape: rabochaya tetrad'* [*Prospects for the development of Russian-Japanese relations at a new stage: workbook*] (in Russian), Number 50/2019, Moscow: NP RSMD, 2019, p. 34.

50 "Initsiativa po ukrepleniyu yapono-rossiyskogo sotrudnichestva v regionakh Dal'nego Vostoka i Vostochnoy Sibiri" ["Initiative to Strengthen Japanese-Russian Cooperation in the Far East and Eastern Siberia"], April 19, 2017 (in Russian), at https://www.ru.emb-japan.go.jp/itpr_ru/heiligendamm.html (accessed November 5, 2020).

51 "Yaponiya pomozhet Rossii razvivat' Dal'niy Vostok" ["Japan will help Russia to develop the Far East"], *Lenta.ru* (in Russian), July 2, 2007, at https://lenta.ru/news/2007/07/02/japrussia/ (accessed November 1, 2020).

52 "Plan sotrudnichestva iz 8 punktov (Plan sotrudnichestva dlya innovatsionnoy reformy v promyshlennosti i ekonomike dlya Rossii kak vedushchey strany s blagopriyatnymi usloviyami zhizni, Posol'stvo Yaponii v Rossii)" ["8-Point Cooperation Plan (Cooperation Plan for Innovative Reform in Industry and Economy for Russia as a Leading Country with Favorable Living Conditions")] (in Russian), Embassy of Japan in Russia], May 6, 2016, at https://www.ru.emb-japan.go.jp/economy/ru/index.html; and "Japan-Russia Summit Meeting," Ministry of Foreign Affairs of Japan, May 7, 2016 (accessed November 5, 2020).

53 At a joint press conference, Abe stated: "I have agreed with the Russian president to create a special regime for establishing joint economic activities on these islands. This joint economic activity will not be carried out to the detriment of the positions of both sides on the issue of the peace treaty. This government will aim to create conditions for a future solution to this problem." Putin proposed to introduce a free border movement regime for residents of Sakhalin Oblast and Hokkaido. "Putin i Abe dogovorilis' o sotrudnichestve na Kurilakh" ["Putin and Abe have agreed on cooperation in the Kuril Islands"], *BBC News/Russkaya sluzhba* [BBC News/Russian Service] (in Russian), December 16, 2016, at https://www.bbc.com/russian/news-38339106 (accessed November 1, 2020).

54 I. Lobovskiy and L. Ruban, "Ekonomicheskoye razvitiye Yaponii (energeticheskiy aspekt)" ["Economic development of Japan (energy aspect)"], *ATR glazami ekspertov (mezhdunarodnaya ekspertiza 2005–2019 gg.)* [*APR through the eyes of experts (international expertise 2005–2019)*] (in Russian), Academia, Moscow, 2019, p. 228.

55 A.N. Panov et al., *Sovremennyye rossiysko-yaponskiye otnosheniya i perspektivy ikh razvitiya,* [*Modern Russian-Japanese relations and prospects for their development/A.N. Panov*] (in Russian), M.: Spetskniga, p. 8.

56 Streltsov, "Rossiysko-yaponskiye otnosheniya," p. 13.

57 N. Grishchenko, "Na Kurilakh razvernuty raketnyye kompleksy 'Bal' i 'Bastion'" ["Ball and Bastion missile systems have been deployed in the Kuriles"], *Rossiyskaya* gazeta (*Russian Newspaper*) (in Russian), November 22, 2016, at https://rg.ru/2016/11/22/reg-dfo/na-kurilah-razvernuty-raketnye-kompleksy-bal-i-bastion.html (accessed November 3, 2020).

58 "Sovmestnoye zayavleniye Rossii i Respubliki Koreya 13 noyabrya 2013 g." ["Joint Statement by Russia and the Republic of Korea, November 13, 2013"] (in Russian), at http://kremlin.ru/supplement/1564 (accessed November 3, 2020).
59 The list of signed documents on the website: http://kremlin.ru/supplement/5320.
60 Ibid.
61 R. Ko, "Rossiysko-koreyskiy forum startoval v Primor'ye v dni VEF–2019" ["The Russian-Korean Forum opened in Primorye during the EEF–2019"], *Ofitsial'nyy sayt Pravitel'stva Primorskogo kraya* [*Official website of the Government of Primorsky Krai*] (in Russian), September 6, 2019, at https://www.primorsky.ru/news/164933/ (accessed November 3, 2020).
62 A. Latysheva, "V Koreye otkrylsya pervyy Rossiysko-Koreyskiy forum mezhregional'nogo sotrudnichestva" ["The first Russian-Korean forum of interregional cooperation opened in Korea"], *Press-sluzhba Ministerstva Rossiyskoy Federatsii po razvitiyu Dal'nego Vostoka i Arktiki* [*Press Service of the Ministry of the Russian Federation for the Development of the Far East and the Arctic*] (in Russian), November 7, 2018, at https://minvr.gov.ru/press-center/news/19677/ (accessed November 3, 2020).
63 Ko, "Rossiysko-koreyskiy forum."
64 Choi He-suk, "New Northern Policy committee seeks progress," *The Korea Herald*, March 27, 2019.
65 "S. Korea, Russia Sign Action Plans on 9 Bridges of Cooperation," *KBS World Radio*, February 13, 2019, at http://world.kbs.co.kr/service/news_view.htm?lang=e&Seq_Code=142964; V. Voloshchak, "A Closer Look at South Korea's Plan for Cooperation with Russia," *The Diplomat*, January 9, 2019, at https://thediplomat.com/2019/01/a-closer-look-at-south-koreas-plan-for-cooperation-with-russia/; "9-BRIDGE Strategy/The Presidential Committee on Northern Economic Cooperation," at https://www.bukbang.go.kr/bukbang_en/vision_policy/9-bridge/ (accessed November 10, 2020).
66 "Russia, South Korea to formally start free trade zone talks, says Lavrov," *TASS*, June 17, 2019, at https://tass.com/economy/1064214 (accessed November 15, 2020).
67 L. Zakharova, "Economic Relations between Russia and South Korea in the New Northern Policy," *Korea Economic Institute of America/Academic Paper Series*, December 10, 2019, p. 6, at http://www.keia.org/sites/default/files/publications/kei_aps_zakharova_191206.pdf (accessed November 11, 2020).
68 All data provided by: "Otchot o vneshney torgovle mezhdu Rossiyey i Respublikoy Koreya (Yuzhnoy Koreyey) v 2019 godu: tovarooborot, eksport, import, struktura, tovary, dinamika" ["Report on foreign trade between Russia and the Republic of Korea (South Korea) in 2019: trade turnover, exports, imports, structure, goods, dynamics"], *Obzory vneshney torgovli Rossii/Torgovlya mezhdu Rossiyey i Respublikoy Koreya (Yuzhnoy Koreyey) v 2019 g.* [*Russian Foreign Trade Reviews/Trade between Russia and the Republic of Korea (South Korea) in 2019*] (in Russian), February 13, 2020, at http://www.russian-trade.com/reports-and-reviews/2020-02/torgovlya-mezhdu-rossiey-i-respublikoy-koreya-yuzhnoy-koreey-v-2019-g/#:~:text= В%202019%2 (accessed November 16, 2020).
69 O. Kiryanov, "Chego dostigli Rossiya i Yuzhnaya Koreya za 30 let diplomaticheskikh otnosheniy" ["What Russia and South Korea have achieved in 30 years of diplomatic relations"], *Rossiyskaya gazeta* [*Russian Newspaper*] (in Russian), September 30, 2020, at https://rg.ru/2020/09/30/chego-dostigli-rossiia-i-iuzhnaia-koreia-za-30-let-diplomaticheskih-otnoshenij.html (accessed November 16, 2020).
70 "Posol otsenil tovarooborot mezhdu Rossiyey i Yuzhnoy Koreyey" ["The Ambassador assessed the trade turnover between Russia and South Korea"],

RIA Novosti (in Russian),June 5, 2020, at https://ria.ru/20200605/1572536075.html (accessed November 16, 2020).
71 A. Zhebin, "Tridtsat' let, kotoryye sblizili Rossiyu i Yuzhnuyu Koreyu" ["Thirty years that have brought Russia and South Korea closer"], *Nezavisimaya gazeta* [*Independent newspaper*] (in Russian), October 14, 2020, at https://www.ng.ru/dipkurer/2020-10-04/9_7980_korea.html (accessed November 10, 2020).
72 "Ministerstvo ekonomicheskogo razvitiya Rossiyskoy Federatsii/Itogi vneshneekonomicheskoy deyatel'nosti Rossiyskoy Federatsii v 2019 godu" ["Ministry of Economic Development of the Russian Federation/Results of foreign economic activity of the Russian Federation in 2019"] (in Russian), p. 58, at https://www.economy.gov.ru/material/file/66eec1250c653fc9abd0419604f44bbd/VED.pdf (accessed November 10, 2020).
73 O. Kiryanov, "Chego dostigli Rossiya i Yuzhnaya Koreya za 30 let diplomaticheskikh otnosheniy" ["What Russia and South Korea have achieved in 30 years of diplomatic relations"], *Rossiyskaya gazeta* [*Russian Newspaper*] (in Russian), September 30, 2020, at https://rg.ru/2020/09/30/chego-dostigli-rossiia-i-iuzhnaia-koreia-za-30-let-diplomaticheskih-otnoshenij.html (accessed November 16, 2020).
74 Zhebin, "Tridtsat' let."
75 *Sovetsko-mongol'skiye otnosheniya. 1921–1974. Dokumenty i materialy* [*Soviet-Mongolian relations. 1921–1974. Documents and materials*] (in Russian), Volume 1, Moscow, "International relations" Publishing house, 1975, pp. 58–61.
76 V. Rodionov, "Evolyutsiya podkhodov rukovodstva Rossii i Mongolii k dvustoronnim otnosheniyam" ["Evolution of the approaches of the leadership of Russia and Mongolia to bilateral relations"], *Vestnik Volgogradskogo gosudarstvennogo universiteta, Seriya 4. Istoriya. Regionovedenie. Mezhdunarodnye otnosheniya* [*Bulletin of Volgograd State University, Series 4. History. Area Studies. International Relations*] (in Russian), 2 (18), 2010, p. 138.
77 "Dogovor o druzhestvennykh otnosheniyakh i sotrudnichestve mezhdu Rossiyskoy Federatsiyey i Mongoliyey" ["Treaty on Friendly Relations and Cooperation between the Russian Federation and Mongolia"], January 20, 1993, *Elektronnyy fond pravovoy i normativno-tekhnicheskoy dokumentatsii* [*Electronic Fund of legal and regulatory and technical documentation*] (in Russian), at http://docs.cntd.ru/document/8314343 (accessed November 18, 2020).
78 "Dogovor o druzhestvennykh otnosheniyakh i vseob'yemlyushchem strategicheskom partnerstve mezhdu Rossiyskoy Federatsiyey i Mongoliyey" ["Treaty on Friendly Relations and Comprehensive Strategic Partnership between the Russian Federation and Mongolia"] September 3, 2019, *Elektronnyy fond pravovoy i normativno-tekhnicheskoy dokumentatsii* [*Electronic Fund of legal and regulatory and technical documentation*] (in Russian), at http://docs.cntd.ru/document/565307846 (accessed November 18, 2020).
79 V. Putin, "Zayavleniye dlya pressy po itogam rossiysko-mongol'skikh peregovorov" ["Statement to the press following Russian-Mongolian talks"], September 3, 2019, at http://kremlin.ru/events/president/transcripts/61435 (accessed November 19, 2020).
80 "Dogovor o druzhestvennykh otnosheniyakh i vseob'yemlyushchem strategicheskom partnerstve mezhdu Rossiyskoy Federatsiyey i Mongoliyey."
81 All data provided by: "Otchot o vneshney torgovle Rossii s Mongoliyey za 9 mesyatsev 2019 goda: tovarooborot, eksport, import, struktura, tovary, dinamika" ["Report on Russia's foreign trade with Mongolia for 9 months of 2019: trade turnover, exports, imports, structure, goods, dynamics"], *Obzory vneshney torgovli Rossii*/*Vneshnyaya torgovlya Rossii s Mongoliyey za 9 mesyatsev 2019*

goda [*Russian Foreign Trade Reviews/Foreign trade of Russia with Mongolia for 9 months of 2019*] (in Russian), November 14, 2019, at https://russian-trade.com/reports-and-reviews/2019-11/vneshnyaya-torgovlya-rossii-s-mongoliey-za-9-mesyatsev-2019-g/ (accessed November 19, 2020).

82 "Dogovor o druzhestvennykh otnosheniyakh i vseob'yemlyushchem strategicheskom partnerstve mezhdu Rossiyskoy Federatsiyey i Mongoliyey."

83 "Kitay–Mongoliya–Rossiya utverdili programmu sozdaniya ekonomicheskogo koridora" ["China–Mongolia–Russia have approved the Programme for the creation of the Economic Corridor"], *Ministerstvo ekonomicheskogo razvitiya Rossiyskoy Federatsii [Ministry of Economic Development of the Russian Federation]* (in Russian), June 24, 2016, at http://old.economy.gov.ru/minec/press/news/201606240 (accessed November 26, 2020).

84 "Initsiativa sovmestnogo stroitel'stva "Odnogo poyasa, odnogo puti": progress, vklad i perspektivy" ["Belt and Road Collaborative Initiative: progress, contributions and prospects"], *Greater Eurasia* (in Russian), April 25, 2019, at http://www.gea.site/2019/04/1735/ (accessed November 24, 2020).

85 "Vstrecha s Predsedatelem KNR Si Tszin'pinom i Prezidentom Mongolii Khaltmagiyn Battulgoy" ["Meeting with President of the People's Republic of China Xi Jinping and President of Mongolia Khaltmagiin Battulga"] (in Russian), June 14, 2019, at http://kremlin.ru/events/president/news/60753 (accessed November 25, 2020).

86 For Mongolia, such a mechanism is of particular interest due to the fact that it has a great energy potential, possessing coal reserves and renewable energy sources.

87 Xi Jinping also supported this Mongolian proposal to develop an electricity supply network in Northeast Asia.

88 A. Lukin and G. Toloraya, "Can Russia Play a Role in Resolving the Korean Crisis?" *Nuclear Weapons and Russian-North Korean Relations*, FPRI, Philadelphia, 2017, p. 64.

89 "Kommentariy Departamenta informatsii i pechati MID Rossii v svyazi s vizitom v Rossiyskuyu Federatsiyu Ministra inostrannykh del Respubliki Koreya Kan Gon Khva, 15 iyunya 2019" ["Commentary by the Information and Press Department of the Russian Foreign Ministry on the visit to the Russian Federation of the Minister of Foreign Affairs of the Republic of Korea Kang Kyung Hwa, 15 June 2019"] (in Russian), at https://www.mid.ru/ru/foreign_policy/news//asset_publisher/cKNonkJE02Bw/content/id/3685318 (accessed November 12, 2020).

90 G. Toloraya, "Prodlitsya li 'mirnaya pauza' na Koreyskom poluostrove do 2024 goda?" ["Will the 'peace pause' on the Korean Peninsula last until 2024?"], *Global'nyy prognoz RSMD, 2019–2024 [RIAC globalforecast for 2019–2024]* (in Russian), Moscow: NP RSMD, 2019, p. 202, at https://russiancouncil.ru/upload/iblock/992/riac_forecast_2019_2024.pdf (accessed November 16, 2020).

91 Ibid., p. 203.

92 "Sovmestnoye zayavleniye Ministerstva inostrannykh del Rossiyskoy Federatsii i Ministerstva inostrannykh del Kitayskoy Narodnoy Respubliki po problemam Koreyskogo poluostrova, 4 iyulya 2017 g" ["Joint Statement by the Ministry of Foreign Affairs of the Russian Federation and the Ministry of Foreign Affairs of the People's Republic of China on the Korean Peninsula, July 4, 2017"] (in Russian), at https://www.mid.ru/ru/maps/kp/-/asset_publisher/VJy7Ig5QaAII/content/id/2807662 (accessed November 12, 2020).

93 "Rossiya i Kitay podgotovili novuyu initsiativu po Koreyskomu poluostrovu" ["Russia and China have prepared a new initiative on the Korean Peninsula"], *RT na Russkom [RT in Russian]* (in Russian), June 15, 2019, at https://

russian.rt.com/world/news/641344-mid-rossiya-koreya (accessed November 12, 2020).
94 Lavrov stated that "The settlement of the nuclear problem of the Korean Peninsula is possible exclusively by diplomatic methods based on a dialogue between all interested countries. A full-fledged launch of the process of denuclearisation of the Korean Peninsula will become real only if political negotiations are promoted on the basis of reciprocal steps of the directly involved parties. Specific proposals on how to effectively move towards this goal were formulated by Russia and China, first in the roadmap, and now in the Action Plan, which we are completing to coordinate with the six members." See Vystupleniye Ministra inostrannykh del Rossiyskoy Federatsii S.V. Lavrovana Moskovskoy konferentsii po nerasprostraneniyu po teme "Vneshnepoliticheskiye prioritety Rossiyskoy Federatsii v sfere kontrolya nad vooruzheniyami i nerasprostraneniya v kontekste izmeneniy v global'noy arkhitekture bezopasnosti," Moskva, 8 noyabrya 2019 goda" ["Speech by the Minister of Foreign Affairs of the Russian Federation S.V. Lavrov at the Moscow Conference on Nonproliferation on the topic "Foreign Policy Priorities of the Russian Federation in the Sphere of Arms Control and Nonproliferation in the Context of Changes in the Global Security Architecture," Moscow, November 8, 2019"] (in Russian), at https://www.mid.ru/foreign_policy/news//asset_publisher/cKNonkJE02Bw/content/id/3891674 (accessed November 12, 2020).
95 O. Kiryanov, "Yuzhnaya Koreya zainteresovalas' rossiysko-kitayskim predlozheniyem po KNDR" ["South Korea is interested in the Russian-Chinese proposal for the DPRK"], *Rossiyskaya gazeta* [*Russian Newspaper*] (in Russian), December 27, 2019, at https://rg.ru/2019/12/27/iuzhnaia-koreia-zainteresovalas-rossijsko-kitajskim-predlozheniem-po-kndr.html (accessed November 16, 2020).
96 Ibid.
97 A. Kireeva, "Pozitsii Rossii i Yaponii po klyuchevym problemam regional'noy bezopasnosti i vzaimodeystviya" ["Positions of Russia and Japan on Key Problems of Regional Security and Interaction"], *Perspektivy razvitiya rossiysko-yaponskikh otnosheniy na novom etape: rabochaya tetrad'* [*Prospects for the development of Russian-Japanese relations at a new stage: workbook*] (in Russian), Number 50/2019, Moscow: NP RSMD, 2019, p. 25.
98 G. Ivashentsov, "O bezopasnosti v Severo-Vostochnoy Azii" ["On security in Northeast Asia"], *Global'nyy prognoz RSMD, 2019–2024* [*RIAC globalforecast for 2019–2024*] (in Russian), Moscow: NP RSMD, 2019, p. 185, at https://russiancouncil.ru/upload/iblock/992/riac_forecast_2019_2024.pdf (accessed November 16, 2020).
99 In 2016–2017 the DPRK conducted a series of tests of intercontinental ballistic missile tests, which brought the situation in NEA to the brink of a large-scale conflict.
100 "MID Rossii osudil yadernoye ispytaniye v Severnoy Koreye" ["Russian Foreign Ministry condemned nuclear test in North Korea"] (in Russian), *Interfax*, September 3, 2017, at https://www.interfax.ru/world/577534 (accessed November 16, 2020).
101 "Putin: Rossiya osuzhdayet yadernyye ispytaniya KNDR, no prizyvayet k dialogu" ["Putin: Russia condemns North Korean nuclear tests, but calls for dialogue"], *Vesti.ru* (in Russian), October 19, at https://www.vesti.ru/article/1544604 (accessed November 12, 2020).
102 Kireeva, "Pozitsii Rossii i Yaponii," p. 26.
103 "Sotrudnichestvo v Severo-vostochnoy Azii sozdayet novyye vozmozhnosti dlya razvitiya" ["Cooperation in Northeast Asia creates new opportunities for development"], *russia.people.cn* (in Russian), September 13, 2018, at http://

russian.people.com.cn/n3/2018/0913/c95181-9500161.html (accessed November 10, 2020).
104 "Asian Energy Super Ring Opens Up New Horizons for Economic Grows," *Sputnik International*, September 4, 2016, at https://sputniknews.com/russia/201609041044945899-asia-energy-cooperation/ (accessed November 16, 2020).
105 "What is TCS?" at https://www.tcs-asia.org/en/about/overview.php (accessed November 11, 2020).
106 "SMI: trekhstoronniy sammit Kitaya, Yaponii i Yuzhnoy Korei v 2020 godu ne sostoitsya" ["Media: Trilateral Summit of China, Japan and South Korea in 2020 will not be held"], *TASS* (in Russian), October 13, 2020, at https://tass.ru/mezhdunarodnaya-panorama/9700237.

4 Why Northeast Asian regional economic integration is important for Mongolia

Nanjin Dorjsuren

Geographically, the Northeast Asian (NEA) countries are China, Japan, Mongolia, DPRK (North Korea), ROK (South Korea), and Russia. But from a geopolitical approach, many scholars include the United States as one of the major players in NEA geopolitics. However, from the economic potential aspect, for instance, the World Bank refers to the major Northeast Asian economies as China, Japan, and South Korea.

Regardless of the economic potential, in terms of security, many scholars have argued that the power structure in NEA is one whereby "two states have a majority of economic, military, and cultural influence."[1] Recently, China has become "central to managing, if not resolving, many of the traditional and non-traditional security issues facing the international community."[2] Some Chinese scholars cite China's regional "activism" as contributing to "the coming of a new kind of geopolitics in Asia."[3] From this perspective, China's interests and strategies have more and more direct implications and impacts on stability and security in Asia and its regional neighbours. The implications of the trade war between the US and China especially is having a greater negative impact on the Asian economy. However, in terms of security, the so-called "radical changes" in the security environment in the region not only provide opportunities for increased negotiations among countries but also to strengthen their military capacities. Another issue is how the NEA countries are trying to manage their responses to health crises such as SARS in 2003, tuberculosis and COVID-19 in 2020.

These policy trends for Mongolia beg the following questions: How can countries in the region cooperate more "effectively" to enhance mutual trust and benefit? What are the core ideas behind the fundamental principles of Mongolian foreign policy towards NEA? What kind of strategic advantages and disadvantages does Mongolia have in the region regarding forwarding collaboration and exploration of economic integration in NEA?

To answer these questions this chapter focuses on three main areas: Firstly, this analysis attempts to summarise the strategic motivations behind the main principles of Mongolian foreign policy towards NEA. This is stimulated by the fact that in recent years, many foreign scholars and strategists, who are involved in research on NEA security issues, would like to

DOI: 10.4324/9781003148630-4

understand and learn more about Mongolian strategic directions and contributions towards regional community building in the coming decades. Secondly, this research explains what kind of challenges NEA integration mechanisms are facing and its perspectives. This chapter especially will focus on the China-Mongolia-Russia Economic Corridor and its implications for NEA economic integration. Finally, this study explores the strategic advantages and disadvantages Mongolia has in its region in regard to regional security. As of now, the big powers in the region have not paid enough attention to the greater NEA security situation. From a macro perspective, big power policies likely will increase future tensions. Situated in the middle of these great powers, Mongolia finds that its geostrategic role in promoting economic integration and reconciliation in the region has become more important. By understanding Mongolia's advantages, such analysis can reveal the common ground of cooperation and sharing of ideas. At the same time, by exposing Mongolia's disadvantages, the difference of perceptions and challenges for Mongolia to promote its role in the region are placed into context.

Brief introduction of Mongolian foreign policy towards NEA

Since the 1990s, East Asia has played a major role in Mongolian foreign policy, and, in terms of economic policy and people-to-people exchanges, Mongolia has been aiming to align with this region. It must be noted that the main reason for the willingness to cooperate among NEA nations is economic interdependence, while politically and security-wise, defence dialogue is becoming a significant matter.

Mongolia advocates for a NEA-oriented foreign policy concept in order to overcome its social and economic difficulties and benefit from the success of Asia-Pacific economies through integration. For instance, in 2011 Mongolian former President Tsakhia Elbegdorj proclaimed that Mongolia was supportive of the Japanese concept of establishing an East Asian Community. This embrace of connectivity was specified in the National Security Concept of Mongolia 2011, which states that the nation's foreign trade and integration policy will, "Make decisions on joining regional or international integration arrangements and concluding free trade agreements based upon Mongolia's economic security and economic development objectives as determined by research and studies."[4]

Unlike many countries in the region, Mongolia has good relations with all countries in the region, including both North Korea and South Korea. Thus, Ulaanbaatar has become a good third country location in which countries can meet for dialogue. For instance, in the past, Japan and the DPRK held bilateral meetings in Mongolia within the framework of the Six Party Talks. Mongolia also facilitated a North Korea-US track 2 level meeting in 2015 to help these two states search for mutual understanding. As we have seen with the US and North Korea especially while formal relations were at their worst over the past few years, track 2 meetings carry importance as a channel of communication between the two sides and in minimising misinterpretations of each other's actions.

In 2019, the two-day event of NEA young leaders, organised by the United Nations' Department of Political and Peacebuilding Affairs in partnership with the Ministry of Foreign Affairs of Mongolia, took place in Ulaanbaatar at the same time as the Sixth Ulaanbaatar Dialogue on Northeast Asian Security (UBD) international conference. The UBD conference was held in two plenary sessions devoted to "The Northeast Environment: Opportunities and Challenges" and "Cooperation and Competition Dynamics," and there were three parallel sessions on promoting energy cooperation in the region. During the UBD, the former Foreign Minister Damdin Tsogtbaatar noted:

> The Ulaanbaatar Dialogue's main purpose lies in having the regional countries meet, thus reach mutual understanding. Mongolia is well versed in the features, decision-making mechanisms and diplomacy of both systems as it once had a communist system and now is a democratic country with a market economy. That being so, we will endeavor to become the regional countries' bridge of peace. We have been and will work for this.[5]

Nevertheless, it appears that the current regional security framework in the region must confront the following two major issues: First, the lack of defining key terms, for example: "peace", "trust", and "stability". This can be explained by the lack of consensus on major issues such as North Korean nuclear weapons, which then are treated as subjects of failed negotiations. The 2018 summit between US President Donald Trump and North Korean leader Kim Jong-un in Singapore created hope for the resolution of the DPRK nuclear issue. But the second summit, which was held in Vietnam, broke down, and both sides chose not to issue a joint summit statement. Kim Jong-un has stated that he is open to meeting with the US President "one more time," but only if the US changes its attitude. President Trump responded that a third summit "would be good," and Secretary of State Mike Pompeo said he is "confident" of holding a third summit.

Yet, the term "peaceful coexistence" still is not well defined by the two Koreas. The difference in thinking and its implications for unification are important issues too. South Korea's President Moon Jae-in has met North Korean leader Kim Jong-un four times already and seeks a "peaceful coexistence" for both Koreas with economic cooperation, including re-opening inter-Korean projects. However, reality should compel all parties to rethink their negotiation strategies from two perspectives. First, bringing back the denuclearisation issue to the negotiation table is a long process, and still there is no basic agreement among the region's nations that would produce a "positive" result. This "flexible" security environment provides opportunities for some regional countries to say that they do not make any promises to anyone. Second, a realistic perspective leads to the conclusion that nations in the region should not base their security measures on bilateral frameworks any longer. The task for leaders, beyond seeking talks, is to agree on a new relationship by accepting each other's interest and then building mutual trust.

Right now, there are a few security frameworks in the Asia-Pacific that are promoted by the Association of Southeast Asian Nations (ASEAN). Examples are the East Asian Summit, ASEAN Regional Forum (ARF), and ASEAN Defence Ministry Meeting. Nevertheless, there still is no security cooperative framework that covers the NEA region and the whole of Eurasia. The Six Party Talks played an important role in dealing with the North Korean nuclear issue. But, they still have not resumed, and the parties have not met since 2008. However, it is true that the Six Party Talks are a "test of whether these countries can collectively deal with regional security concerns."[6] There are some discussions on "developing the Six-Party Talks to be a regional mechanism managing broader security issues…[and] build a regional security mechanism based on the Six-Party Talks."[7] Furthermore, the term "Indo-Pacific" has been promoted in recent years by the US, Japan, Australia, and India, which is a sign of envisioning the region collectively.

In 2018, professors from the Institute of Social Scientists of the DPRK visited the Mongolian Institute of Northeast Asian Security and Strategy—MINASS (a private non-profit organisation) to lecture on the DPRK's self-reliance policy. This channel aims to extend non-governmental exchanges between the two countries. Generally, civil society can play more of a role in the region, and construction of networks among experts, business and NGOs is becoming more important.

Northeast Asian integration mechanisms: challenges and perspectives

In recent years, countries have entered into Free Trade Agreements (FTA) and Economic Partnership Agreements (EPA) to deepen trade, investment and economic relations through the development of partnerships. For example, cooperation between China, Japan, and Korea has expanded, and the initiatives to make a free trade agreement and establish the Northeast Asian Development Bank were taken after they proclaimed the "Joint Declaration on the Promotion of Tripartite Cooperation" in 2003.

China is aiming to meet its growing domestic needs, and in the future it desires to increase its role in the region in order to become the leader. For Japan, Northeast Asia is the closest source for the domestic energy and raw materials it needs. This is the same situation for South Korea. Thus, the issue of energy supplies for these countries will continue to be important. Below are some of the mechanisms that currently exist in the region that hold promise for promoting Northeast Asian economic integration.

China-Mongolia-Russia Economic Corridor

The Mongolian Government announced its new national development strategy called Steppe Road Programme in 2014, which later was renamed the Development Road Programme. It was a very timely decision because it came at the time when Mongolia's two big neighbours had just revealed their regional development strategies. Announced in 2013, China's Belt and Road initiative (BRI) aims to strengthen Beijing's economic leadership through a vast programme of infrastructure building throughout China's neighbouring regions. Under the New Eastern policy, which was announced in 2012, Russia has been seeking to develop the Far East through cooperation among countries in the Asia-Pacific region. Mongolia's border neighbour countries Russia and China have set a goal to increase bilateral trade turnover to US$200 billion by 2020. Mongolia is well positioned between China and Russia to benefit from their plans to expand transportation cooperation throughout the Eurasian region.

As a landlocked Northeast Asian nation, Mongolia is seeking to have more access to the sea and become an international transportation hub while at the same time diversify its mineral exports and foreign investors. In other words, Mongolia is seeking to improve its own industrialisation within the BRI and not just act as a raw material supplier to Chinese industrialisation. Mongolia's geographic positioning between two fast-growing giant economies is a huge opportunity to overcome barriers arising from its landlocked status. In order to fully utilise its chance to serve as a transport hub connecting the two neighbours and Eurasian coasts, Mongolia is working towards robust implementation of the China-Mongolia-Russia Economic Corridor programme. To further this purpose, Mongolia introduced its "Development Road" programme and aims to become a transit corridor to facilitate trade between the two neighbours via rail, road, and pipe channels. Such a corridor will integrate the initiatives of the Eurasian Economic Union proposed by the Russian Federation and the BRI of China.

In September 2014 at the first trilateral meeting held among the leaders of China, Mongolia, and Russia in Dushanbe, Tajikistan, the three parties discussed a variety of joint economic projects, and Mongolian President Elbegdorj expressed his willingness to participate in China and Russia's infrastructure projects. So far, there have been five trilateral summits. In June 2016, the three governments reached agreement on the China-Mongolia-Russia Economic Corridor (CMREC) project, as part of China's BRI. The CMREC is one of the six main corridors of BRI and known as the "shortest" path between Europe and Asia. As for energy connectivity projects under the CMREC rubric, in December 2019, during the state visit to Russia of Mongolian Prime Minister Ukhnaa Khürelsükh, Mongolia and Russia signed a memorandum of understanding (MOU) on Mongolia's participation in the "Power of Siberia 2" project. In August 2020, the Russian company Gazprom signed an MOU with the Mongolian government to create a special company, which will develop a study for the construction of a natural gas pipeline.

It has been four years since CMREC was officially announced. Despite the fact that there have been some concrete achievements on implementing CMREC, as mentioned above, critics say that overall progress has been slow, and it has been no more than a dialogue with few tangible results. Obviously, synergising development strategies requires synergising everything from rail gauge incompatibility to the legal environment. Furthermore, implementation will take time, since any decision requires trilateral consensus. Financing, rail gauge incompatibility, customs procedures, legislation differences, and environmental and broader conceptual issues continue to be roadblocks for CMREC.

Greater Tumen Initiative

Recently, the construction of cross-border zones has given Mongolia the opportunity to promote economic interdependence via projects of cooperation in transportation, energy, tourism, investment, and environment under the framework of the Greater Tumen Initiative (GTI).[8] Mongolia has been a member of this organisation since 2006. In March 2019, in Ulaanbaatar at the Consultative Commission Meeting of the GTI, the Rajin-Khasan (the cities of Rajin in the DPRK and Khasan in Russia) Project was approved to be included in the list of GTI priority projects. In 2012, the Development Bank of Mongolia signed an MOU with the EXIM Banks of China and South Korea on the establishment of the NEA Exim Banks Association. In April 2018, the MINASS research institution, in cooperation with the Economic Research Institute of Northeast Asia (ERINA), International Think Tank for Landlocked Developing Countries (LLDC), and the GTI Secretariat organised an international conference on GTI's perspective and the role of Mongolia.

Northeast Asian Super Grid

Given the rising demand in NEA for energy, including coal, oil, gas, and nuclear energy, the energy security environment is rapidly changing. Therefore, countries in the region have been considering forming an energy cooperation network. Renewable energy and international grid initiatives especially are growing. Mongolian policymakers and scholars are proposing a role for Mongolia in the development of a Northeast Asian Super Grid (ASG). This is a project to establish an electrical power transmission network to connect China, South Korea, Mongolia, Russia and Japan. In September 2018 in Vladivostok, Mongolian President Khaltmaa Battulgaad advocated for the prompt commencement of the ASG. Also, he noted the importance of joint implementation of ASG in his speech in April 2019, at the leaders' roundtable of the second Belt and Road Forum for International

Cooperation in Beijing.[9] To date, in Northeast Asia, the Energy Charter Treaty only has been ratified by Japan and Mongolia. However, it has been suggested by some sources that when international grid connections are built, Japan could encourage potentially affected countries to join the treaty.

Strategic advantages compared to disadvantages of Mongolia in the region

Some researchers argue that countries in the same region should try to develop "deeper" economic integration by using their own advantages in the international field. In other words, opportunities for regional cooperation are determined by the necessity for regional economic integration to take place based on the natural resources of Russia and Mongolia, labour forces of DPRK and China, and technology, enormous money market and natural resources of Japan.

Looking at certain economic statistics of NEA countries, taking NEA as a whole, and calculating the percentage of each country's share, Mongolia's situation becomes clearer. Difficulties in economic cooperation arise because of trade gaps between developed and underdeveloped countries. For example, Japan has signed an Economic Partnership Agreement with Chile which exempts semi-finished copper and molybdenum products from customs duties, and in return Chile exempts Japanese cars from customs duties. This example tells us that, it is important to seek cooperation in different strategically beneficial sectors and not be limited just to the mining sector.

Despite some positive steps, tension between North Korea and South Korea still remains. Mongolia has declared its territory a nuclear-weapon-free state, and its nuclear-weapons-free status contributes to the strengthening of the Treaty on the Non-Proliferation of Nuclear Weapons. This action also is important in regards to resolving the nuclear issue on the Korean Peninsula. Although there is no sign of the return of the Six Party Talks, Mongolia is able to take advantage of its diplomatic relations with all of the six countries to hold meetings of Six Party working groups and interested research institutes in Mongolia in the future.

Mongolia's relationship with the DPRK

In 2018, North Korean leader Kim Jong-un declared victory on attaining nuclear development and shifted his focus from the nuclear issue to concentration on the economy. He declared a "new strategic line," while US President Donald Trump said that "...North Korea had a bright economic future if the two countries made a deal."[10] However, in the future even after the US removes North Korean-related sanctions, the result should be more than just economic growth. While the role of the great powers in strengthening peace and security in NEA is indeed important, the involvement of developing countries also is important. Therefore, attention must be paid to which nations North Korea trusts.

One of the primary ways Mongolia has sought to engage the DPRK is by presenting itself as an example of a country that was able to make economic reforms peacefully, while balancing its powerful neighbours. Much like Mongolia, the DPRK possesses substantial mineral deposits. Mongolia's economic transition to a market economy has been something that has long been of interest to the leadership in Pyongyang, if it were to choose to engage in economic reforms. Mongolia has offered its example as one path for North Korea to consider when developing its economy and also simultaneously retaining its sovereignty.

Mongolia was the second country to recognise the DPRK. Over the last decade thousands of North Koreans have worked in medical and acupuncture clinics, cashmere factories, road construction, and North Korean restaurants in Ulaanbaatar. These workers left the country in 2018 due to the pressure of international sanctions. The one key advantage the DPRK possesses for the landlocked country of Mongolia is North Korea's access to the sea. The Mongolian side tested rail shipping of 25,000 tonnes of coal to the DPRK's Rajin port in 2015–2016 and are ready to use this new route to Japanese and South Korean customers, as soon as the international climate permits.

Since 1990, when Mongolia became a democratic nation and officially recognised the Republic of Korea, the DPRK and Mongolia still have proceeded to sign a series of agreements related to science and technology, agriculture, trade, infrastructure, among other fields. Mongolia also in recent years has provided aid to the DPRK. In December of 2014, a North Korean plane was rumoured to have landed to pick up a large number of cows from a province in eastern Mongolia. This rumour was later confirmed by the Mongolian government as part of an aid agreement with the DPRK.

Conclusion

In conclusion, participating in regional economic integration is one of the main priorities of Mongolian foreign policy, and it could open up many opportunities for its economic development. However, for a country like Mongolia, which has a small economy and sparse population, the disadvantages of integration may likely be even greater. On the other hand, the strategic interests of the other countries in NEA, especially the impact of the policies of the future leading powers in the regional cooperation, need to be considered.

Furthermore, most countries in the region are dependent on energy imports, and the system of regional cooperation in this sector has not yet been formed. To date it is based only on bilateral negotiations and cooperation. Energy needs are high in countries such as China, which is experiencing rapid economic growth, South Korea, and Japan, which is a leader in economic development. Regional energy consumption is expected to continue to increase, and this is the main reason for the deepening of relations and cooperation among the countries in NEA.

Finally, a point to emphasise is that the NEA region is not the European Union. A key prerequisite for economic integration is political trust, and this has not yet been established in the region. This region's security is maintained with outside intervention, the policy of a great power with nuclear weapons and a large army, and the fear of small countries trying not to be influenced by these superpowers. In addition to the Korean Peninsula issue, there are territorial disputes, potential humanitarian crises, unpredictable political regimes, differences in ideologies, wartime historical grievances, and even an unresolved war. These are the reasons why issues on the political side are so complicated in this region. Nonetheless, Mongolian policymakers believe that their country should be committed to forwarding collaboration and exploration of economic integration in NEA.

Notes

1 Avery Goldstein, *Rising to the Challenge; China's Grand Strategy and International Security*, Stanford University Press, Stanford, California, 2005, p. 20.
2 Robert G. Sutter, *China's Role in Asia: Promise and Perils*, Rowman & Littlefield, Oxford, UK, 2005, p. 46.
3 Yang Jiechi, "Gaige Kaifang Yilai de Zhongguo Waijiao" ["China's Diplomacy Since Reform and Opening"], *Qiushi* (online), CPC Central Committee Bi Monthly, 18, September 16, 2008, p. 91.
4 "National Security Concept of Mongolia," 2011, Section 3.2.5.4, Mongolia National Security Council, at http://www.nsc.gov.mn/sites/default/files/images/National%20Security%20Concept%20of%20Mongolia%20EN.pdf (accessed October 29, 2020).
5 "Ulaanbaatar Dialogue taking place," www.montsame.mn, June 5, 2019.
6 James Goodby and Donald Gross, "From Six Party Talks to a Regional Security Mechanism," March 25, 2005, at http://www.glocom.org/debates/20050325_goodby_from/index.html (accessed October 15, 2020).
7 Chun Si Wu, "The Six-Party Talks: A Good Platform for Broader Security Cooperation in Northeast Asia," *Korean Journal of Security Affairs*, 2007, p. 45.
8 The Greater Tumen Initiative (GTI) (originally known as the Tumen River Area Development Programme) is an intergovernmental cooperation mechanism among four countries: China, Mongolia, Republic of Korea and Russian Federation, supported by the United Nations Development Programme (UNDP). See http://www.tumenprogramme.org/?info-505-1.html (accessed October 15, 2020).
9 "Asia International Grid Connection Study Group, Third Report," Renewable Energy Institute, *REI Publication,* July 2019, p. 47.
10 Reuters, "North Korea has no economic future if it has nuclear weapons: Trump," March 19, 2019 tweet. North Korea Has No Economic Future If It Has Nuclear Weapons: Trump (businessinsider.com) accessed May 19, 2021.

5 Japan's foreign policy security mechanisms in the Asia-Pacific and Northeast Asia

*Fujimaki Hiroyuki and
Tsedendamba Batbayar*

Introduction

Existing security mechanisms in the Asia-Pacific sphere have been challenged in three aspects: the United States' stronger commitment in the region; growing Chinese power; and the increasingly stronger role in the area of regional groupings, such as Association of Southeast Asian Nations (ASEAN), Asia Pacific Economic Forum (APEC), ASEAN plus three, and ASEAN Regional Forum (ARF).

Presidents of the United States consistently have supported the liberal international order after World War II. A fundamental regional order in Northeast Asia has been structured through a "hub and spoke" system[1] that has been provided by the US since the end of World War II. The "hub and spoke" system is based on bilateral alliances, such as Japan-US and South Korea-US. The system provides regional security not only among spoke states but also for the whole of Asia-Pacific region. The George W. Bush administration (2001–2009) dedicated enormous resources to resolving the North Korean, China-Taiwan, and Islamic fundamentalism in Southeast Asia issues. His successor, President Barack Obama's dedication to the region was no different, as he declared himself the "President of the United States as a Pacific nation,"[2] but President Donald Trump now has become the first of this era to prioritise American national interests over international cooperation. Japan is in the most vulnerable position in Northeast Asia and the Asia-Pacific region because of this Trump administration policy since it demands Japan's security independence. However, Japan under Prime Minister Abe Shinzo has shown a willingness to respond positively.

Since the latter half of the 1990s, a concept regarding the establishment of a formal East Asian community has been debated in Japan, especially between scholars of Asia and Europe. Every successive Japanese prime minister has had his own attitude towards regionalism in the Asia-Pacific. The biggest question has been whether a European Union (EU)-type regionalism will arise in East Asia or not. The majority of people that discuss the issue claim that this type of regionalism in East Asia has very little opportunity to be realised, even in the future.[3] Although these pessimistic opinions are

DOI: 10.4324/9781003148630-5

shared by the majority of academics in Japan, some point out that there are similar formations, because there are so many bilateral and multilateral political, economic, and cultural transactions in East Asia. This chapter argues that the need for formalised regionalism in the Asia-Pacific area has risen greatly due to the financial crises of 1997 and 2008. These two major crises proved that states are dependent on the free international market. This market is so untamed that sometimes nations are not able to survive without collective assistance.

In reviewing the historical factors that have led to the current situation, it seems clear that the power vacuums in Europe and the Middle East created a stronger US commitment in the Asia-Pacific region and a stronger-than-ever Japan-US alliance. The rise of China changed the security system in the area in many ways. Previously, neo-realists[4] viewed the "hub and spoke" system as an unbreakable fixture as long as US power remained in the Asia-Pacific, but the system was shaken by the rise of China, even though US power is still unmatched militarily, as well as economically and in terms of soft power.

The US' commitment in the Asia-Pacific is reinforced continuously, and regionalism in the area progresses simultaneously. This chapter will 1) describe how Japan's major successive administrations have reacted to ASEAN; 2) detail how regional conflicts always have occurred when power vacuums have existed in the area; and finally, 3) criticise the current "Proactive Contribution to Peace" policy that the Abe administration introduced as a regional architecture for Northeast Asia and the Asia-Pacific.

Japanese foreign policy in Post-World War II and Asia

Following World War II, Prime Minister Yoshida Shigeru (in office October 15, 1948–December 10, 1954), enacted a new foreign policy system dubbed the "Yoshida Doctrine". The main feature of the Yoshida Doctrine was "Unilateral Pacifism", based on light armament and economic diplomacy. Yoshida aimed to have Japan rely on the US' military power while Japan concentrated on post-war reconstruction. Japan set a national policy focused on trade and innovation in science and technology without having to budget much on military but still maintain national security. As a result, Japan achieved economic recovery after its defeat in World War II and became the world's No. 2 economic power in the 1980s. Generally, the Yoshida Doctrine was broadly seen in Japan as 1) Japan relying on the Japan-US alliance for its national security; 2) Japan keeping its defence costs low; and 3) Japan using its resulting surplus to activate its economy.

Japan expanded its tilt towards Asia, especially Southeast Asia, under Prime Minister Fukuda Takeo (in office December 24, 1976–December 7, 1978). The Fukuda Doctrine was declared in Manila, Philippines in August 1977, during Prime Minister Fukuda's tour of the ASEAN member-states. The Doctrine emphasised Japan's non-military role and pledged political, economic, and cultural cooperation. At that time, Japan's foreign policy already was stressing cultural exchanges as regional projects, especially in Southeast Asia. The foreign policy consisted of three pillars.

First, Japan, a nation committed to peace, rejected its potential role as a military power, and, on that basis, was resolved to contribute to the peace and prosperity of Southeast Asia and of the world community. Second, Japan, as a true friend of the countries of Southeast Asia, promised to do its best to consolidate a relationship of mutual confidence and trust based on "heart-to-heart" understanding with those countries, in wide-ranging fields covering not only political and economic areas but also social and cultural areas. Third, Japan would be an equal partner of ASEAN and its member countries. It would cooperate positively in their own efforts to strengthen solidarity and resilience together with other like-minded nations outside the region while aiming to foster relationships based on mutual understanding with the nations of the region and thus contribute to the building of peace and prosperity throughout Southeast Asia.[5]

In January 1997, despite a mounting Japanese hostage crisis in Peru, Prime Minister Hashimoto Ryutaro (in office January 11, 1996–July 30, 1998) visited the region (Brunei, Malaysia, Indonesia, Vietnam, and Singapore) and proposed the formation of a top-level forum between Japan and ASEAN. Furthermore, in Singapore, Hashimoto delivered the policy speech, "Reforms for the New Era of Japan and ASEAN for a Broader and Deeper Partnership," which described 1) ASEAN as an equal partner and proposed closer policy dialogues at the top levels; 2) greater exchanges between the private sectors, cultural exchange and cooperation; and 3) joint efforts at regional and international forums (including APEC, ASEM, and WTO) and on international concerns and issues such as the natural environment, food and energy resources, terrorism and narcotics.[6]

As per the doctrine newly proposed at the ASEAN summit in Singapore in 2002, the East Asian Community envisioned by Prime Minister Koizumi Junichiro (in office April 26, 2001–September 26, 2006) consisted not only of ASEAN and Northeast Asia but also included Australia and New Zealand. Koizumi's administration was distinct for its stronger than ever ties with the US. Another difference from previous administrations was Japan's security role. The problem of piracy alone made it clear that Japan could not expect to take part in the creation of an Asian community without contributing to East Asia's security. Prime Minister Koizumi received strong approval from ASEAN countries by indicating clearly that Japan would fulfil its responsibility, while positively acknowledging the US' involvement in Asia. To show the importance of economic ties with ASEAN member-states, Koizumi signed a free trade agreement (FTA) with Singapore—the first time Japan had concluded such an arrangement on a bilateral basis.

To what extent does the US see the Shanghai Cooperation Organisation (SCO) as influencing Japan's Central Asian policy, especially the "Arc of Freedom and Prosperity" policy that is synchronised with the US' policy in Central Asia? In 2007, Minister of Foreign Affairs (MOFA) Aso Taro

(September 26, 2006–September 26, 2007) in Abe Shinzo's first administration unveiled the "Arc of Freedom and Prosperity" policy.[7] The policy covers Northeast Asia and the Asia-Pacific, Central Asia, the Caucasus, Turkey, and East and Central Europe. According to the MOFA, "value-oriented diplomacy" involves placing emphasis on "universal values", such as democracy, freedom, human rights, the rule of law, and the market economy, as these values would advance diplomatic endeavours.[8] This diplomacy successfully targeted budding democracies that line the outer rim of the Eurasian continent, forming an arc. Thus, as the name implies, Aso wanted to design an "Arc of Freedom and Prosperity."

It should be noted that the concept was the first of Japan's foreign policies to address Central Asia in the post-Cold War era, because, previously, Japan did not possess its own foreign policy towards Central Asia. Japan's foreign policy towards the region always was subordinate to Russian and Chinese policies, but this Arc policy illustrated how Japan could enhance its own presence and national interest in the region.

The "Arc of Freedom and Prosperity" policy also needs to be criticised because this policy started Japan's pursuit of its own national interest, while it was created to be a part of US foreign policy towards Russia, China, and Central Asia. The US' foreign policy in the region is based on a containment policy against Russia and China, and the Japan-US alliance created the "Arc of Freedom and Prosperity" policy. Iwashita Hiroaki of the Slavic Research Center has pointed out that the policy argued in support of geopolitics in Eurasia, but it tried to remove Russia and China from the policy debate.[9] According to this policy, Japan's foreign policy in the region was meant to contain Russia and China to the detriment of Japan's national interests but did allow for opportunities for cooperation with Central Asia.

From outside power to regional power

Traditionally, Japan's security architecture in the region had focused on Northeast Asia and ASEAN, but the situation has changed. Previously, Japan saw itself as removed from Southeast Asia, and Japan's foreign policy towards Asia was shaped by this perception. However, after the Cold War, Japan identified itself as an East Asian or Asia-Pacific state. Debate began on redefining old boundaries to conceptualise one broad region including Japan and Southeast Asia, with importance placed upon the Japan-US alliance and an eye on the rise of China. Japan believed that China, due to its growth, would naturally be a new regional member of the East Asian Community debate, just like Australia, New Zealand, and India (Table 5.1).

When power vacuums happen in the Asia-Pacific region

International relations' espousing Realist theory argues that a balance of power always has been the principle of international relations, and there is

Table 5.1 Japan's regional policy towards the Asia-Pacific region

Period	Ideal circumstances	Major policy	Target
Cold War	Peaceful SE Asia	Economic Development	ASEAN
1990s	Asia-Pacific cooperation	Security/Economic Cooperation	Indochina
2000s	Creating a Regional Community	Economic Cooperation	Indochina/Mekong river project
2010s	Peaceful Maritime Order	Security and TPP, Balance and Engagement with China	ASEAN, China, Indo-Pacific region

Source: Refer to Susumu Yamakage, "Japan's regional conception and growth of China," Mie Ooba., eds, "Higashi Ajia no Katachi," *Chikura Shobo*, 2016.

no peace without a balance of power. In history, when one state's power increases dramatically, or one state's power decreases dramatically, the international or regional order always has become unstable, and sometimes a war has occurred.[10] In the Asia-Pacific region, a "power vacuum" has been created twice in recent history in the Twentieth and early Twenty-first centuries. The first time, the collapse of the Empire of Japan resulted in a power vacuum, and the second time was caused by a reduction of the influence of the US in the area.

First power vacuum in Asia-Pacific: collapse of the Empire of Japan in 1945

The area occupied by the Empire of Japan before and during World War II was enormous and included a part of mainland China, the Korean Peninsula, Taiwan, and a huge part of Southeast Asia. After the war, this resulted in a large contested area and, to prevent communist influence from overtaking the area, the opponents of communism believed that someone else had to exert control. The US attempted to become the "cap" of the "bottle" in the region to contain any ambitions of rearmament of the Japanese empire in the bottle. Thus, the US vied with the Soviet Union to fill the huge area that Japan's empire formerly had occupied as a new friend of damaged Asia-Pacific states after World War II, declaring that the US' role would prevent the rise of Japan again in the region. As part of the process where the US sought to provide a new security policy in the Asia-Pacific, a series of wars occurred, namely the Chinese Civil War, Korean War, and Vietnam War.

Second power vacuum in Asia-Pacific: retreat of American military power

After the end of the Cold War in the early 1990s, the Clinton administration announced a new US security policy called the "National Strategy of

Engagement and Enlargement" policy. The US leadership at this point felt it had to take preventive actions, through such means as support for democracy, economic assistance, overseas military presence, military-to-military contacts, and involvement in multilateral negotiations in the Middle East and elsewhere, to avoid crises.[11]

This policy featured engagement and enlargement in East Asia, the Middle East, and Europe. The US planned to dispatch 100,000 servicemen in the Asia-Pacific, as per a promise made between Prime Minister Hashimoto Ryutaro and President William (Bill) Clinton.[12] Maintaining US military power in the world was not only for security reasons in terms of the global stability alliance but also to help spread liberal democracy to create a safer world for global business. The Clinton administration defined East Asia as a New Pacific Community, which was deemed a region of growing importance for US security and prosperity, and where the need for continued US engagement had never been more evident. In the post-Cold War era of the mid-1990s, it was viewed that security must be paired with open markets and democracy in any approach to the region. So, the New Pacific Community linked security requirements with economic realities and their concerns for democracy and human rights.[13]

In January 2012, the US Department of Defense announced its Defense Strategic Guidelines.[14] Under these, the US in the last decade has undertaken extended operations in Iraq and Afghanistan to bring stability to those countries. As the US measuredly has drawn down from these two operations, it has taken steps to protect its own economic vitality and protect its national interests in a world of accelerating change. Thus, the US faced an inflection point.[15] It was challenged with being able to intervene to prevent North Korean attacks when conflicts simultaneously might occur in the Middle East. However, in this new defence policy, the United States focused on one strategic region, the Asia-Pacific, because this is a region that possessed potential regional conflict zones and also is home to the United States' potential competitor, China.

The Barack Obama administration in 2012 announced a policy to reduce the defence budget total by US$450 billion over 10 years and rethink US Army global deployment. Because of these fiscal cuts, the US military was forced to abandon its capability to fight a two-front war, which it had maintained for many years. The main objective of the new policy was to reduce military spending, which put financial pressure on dealing with two large-scale regional conflicts at the same time and to engage in a long-term military operation. Moreover, the policy stressed that China was a potential threat that impacted the American economy and security in the long term.

This US rebalance policy created two power vacuums, namely in Europe and the Middle East. This meant that, although it would be in the interest of the US to rebuild this security commitment if possible, in reality it could not. As a result, instead, the US must forge a stronger-than-ever alliance with Japan in the Asia-Pacific; an alliance that Japan also needs due to China and North Korea.

Regionalism debate in Eurasia and the Asia-Pacific's "Proactive Contribution to Peace" policy of the Abe administration

Regionalism in Asia-Pacific

During the Cold War, the Japan-US alliance was a major pillar of foreign policy. Since the end of World War II, the Japanese government has tried to maintain a multilateral diplomacy with Asia-Pacific states, despite the economic centre having shifted from Tokyo to other areas of Asia, such as Singapore and Hong Kong. Japan explored how to achieve economic prosperity with Asian states through regionalism. During this process, Japan had to be very careful not to be criticised due to past mistakes.

Since the end of the 1980s, for almost 30 years, some important progress has been made in forming regional institutions in the Asia-Pacific. In 1989, APEC was formed as the first regional cooperation group. In 1994, the first political security dialogue forum, ARF, was formed, followed by ASEAN plus 3 in 1997, East Asian Summit (EAS) in 1997, and ASEAN Defense Minister's Meeting-Plus (ADMM+) in 2010. These regional frameworks included ASEAN, Japan, China, the United States, South Korea and, sometimes, Mongolia.

The regional security and economy in Asia-Pacific contains "regionalism" and "regionalisation". "Regionalism" is thought of as the political will to pursue the implementation of peace and prosperity in certain areas and states. In many cases, this type of international cooperation sets as its goal to create international organisations which are formally legally binding. Only ASEAN, since 1967, has been successful in the area. In contrast, "regionalisation" refers to an increment of transactions between non-state actors, and it creates economic and social cohesion in certain areas. The Asia-Pacific has witnessed great progress in "regionalisation", but not as much in "regionalism". This view is applicable especially as economic transactions between companies and security systems still depend on the "hub and spoke" system. However, in the Asia-Pacific the issue of building institutions which would be superior to bilateral relations as a means of securing regional stability, as opposed to regional cooperation, has become a major topic of debate.

Although ASEAN was formed by small states, it has started taking an important role in regional security. Approaching regionalism in the Asia-Pacific requires the existence of regional institutions, such as ASEAN, since individual member-states of ASEAN on their own are not capable of making strong impacts on international relations. The collection of small powers, however, was shown to be capable of stronger impacts, if common interests can be found. APEC, ASEAN plus three, East Asian Summit (EAS), ARF, and ADMM+ all set their meetings along the sidelines with ASEAN meetings and, EAS, in particular, requires a dialogue membership of ASEAN and the Treaty of Amity and Cooperation in Southeast Asia (TAC). These forums are at the centre of ASEAN and regionalism in the Asia-Pacific.

China and regional security architecture

How could ASEAN, a regional institution comprised of small states, create such presence in the Asia-Pacific? One major reason is that there was no powerful single state actor dominating that region. Neither Japan nor China would allow the other to take the initiative.[16] The structure in which Japan and China do not yield to each other as the pre-eminent regional power that influences ASEAN has become particularly strong since the Tiananmen Square Incident in 1989. In fact, after this incident, Japan joined Western countries in placing economic sanctions on China and, subsequently, Japan-Chinese relations deteriorated. The US had commitments there but it did not know how to deal with Southeast Asian states historically. Also, no single ASEAN member-state wished to play a leading role. These reasons allowed ASEAN as an organisation to become a major player.

The situation, however, now is different. Around 2010, the rise of China ushered in many changes, with two especially standing out. First, China took a firm attitude towards territorial disputes with Japan and the Philippines. Vietnam, Malaysia, and Indonesia also claim China is in violation of their respective territorial water claims. The Senkaku Islands are one major example of an island-based dispute becoming a symbol of the deterioration of relationships. Second, China started taking an aggressive position in organising a regional security architecture. The rise of China introduced new realities to Asian states, and the Chinese viewpoint does not require a centralised ASEAN. Examples of Chinese-led initiatives include the "New Asian Security Concept," "One Belt and One Road Initiative" (BRI), and Asia Infrastructure Investment Bank (AIIB).[17] Beijing has a plan, which was announced a decade previous, that would establish a new regional security architecture not based on any formal alliance system but rather on weaving together a tighter web of existing organisations and entities and bending them towards Beijing's desired strategic ends. Beijing's proposal warrants serious consideration and thus should not be rejected by Japan, the US, or other Asian neighbours. Still, China needs to adjust its message to assuage the concerns of both Washington and regional neighbours who see benefit in a continued active US role in Asian security. These countries clearly hope to not be forced to choose between US security assistance and China-funded economic development.

The rise of China has had an effect upon regional integration and also provided positives and negatives for regional states. The merits of the Chinese strategy in security and economic areas can be enjoyed by Eurasian states, such as Russia, Mongolia, the Central Asian republics, Turkey, Pakistan, and states with authoritarian regimes. These nations need to strengthen their political establishments via economic development, and some of them have realised that economic development does not necessarily require democratisation. The US and its allies have believed that democratisation follows economic development, as was the case during and after the Cold War in South Korea, Taiwan, and Eastern Europe, but Chinese economic growth did not require democratisation nor was it followed by democratisation. Thus, the Chinese model came to be seen as an alternative new Asian miracle by many newly independent Eurasian states.

Northeast Asia and Mongolia

A "Strategic Partnership" was established between Mongolia and Japan in 2010, and in June 2016 an "Economic Partnership Agreement" was signed, which boosted the bilateral relationship to a higher level. The Japanese Ministry of Foreign Affairs document, "White Paper on Developmental Cooperation 2018," mentions Japanese policy towards Mongolia as "the country situated between the Russian Federation and the PRC and friendly towards Japan, therefore, Mongolia's sustainable growth is beneficial for regional stability and bilateral relationship."[18] Mongolia is regarded as a reliable partner who strongly supports Japan at various international organisations. Officially, these factors were prime motives why Japan agreed to develop a "strategic partnership" with Mongolia.

Japanese development assistance was the main form of bilateral cooperation until 2010. Development assistance included both grant aid and Japanese yen-denominated soft loans. Grant aid started in 1977 with the construction of the cashmere processing "Gobi" factory and continued after 1990 with more coordinated and focused efforts. Grant assistance also included a "Grassroots aid" special programme which primarily targets the construction and renovation of rural schools and rural hospitals.[19] Yen-denominated soft loans were directed towards such infrastructure projects as the construction of a new international airport in Ulaanbaatar and renovation works on coal-powered thermal power stations.[20] The Japanese government has decided to gradually lessen grant aid while increasing long-term yen-denominated soft loans. Ota Akihiro, Japanese Minister for Infrastructure, Transportation and Tourism, during his visit to Mongolia in 2014, expressed Japanese interest to have a share in the Tavan Tolgoi coking coal company and to undertake complete management of the new Ulaanbaatar region capital international airport.[21]

According to the viewpoint of most Japanese experts, Mongolia, as "the island of democracy" in Eurasia, is highly regarded as a strategic partner with shared values. Besides, Mongolia possesses an important geographic position indispensable for strengthening relations with both Russia and China and for maintaining the balance of power in Eurasia. Japan also has a particular interest in "tapping into Mongolia's close ties with North Korea" and making progress on the issue of North Korea's abductions of Japanese nationals during the 1970s and 1980s.[22]

The mid-term programme of Mongolian-Japanese strategic partnership for 2013–2017 was established during Mongolian Prime Minister Norov Altankhuyag's official visit to Japan in September 2013. Encouraged by the accomplishments of the first mid-term programme of strategic partnership, the two governments signed a second agreement to implement the "Mid-term Programme of Mongolian-Japanese Strategic Partnership for 2017–2021" in March 2017. These two mid-term programmes were designed to promote not only political, security and economic cooperation but also humanitarian and people-to-people contacts, which are the foundation of the bilateral strategic partnership.[23]

In the sphere of political and security relations, mid-term programmes have strengthened bilateral relations and partnership for regional stability and prosperity. Japanese Prime Minister Abe Shinzo over his term of office developed a strong relationship with Mongolian President Tsakhia Elbegdorj and visited Mongolia in 2013, 2015, and 2016. Overall bilateral summit meetings between Abe and his counterpart took place nine times during 2013–2017, which demonstrated that Mongolia's role as an indispensable strategic partner in East Asia has been vital for Japan. Newly elected Prime Minister of Mongolia Ukhnaa Khürelsükh was invited to Japan in December 2018 to reconfirm the strategic partnership between the two countries. Thereupon, Foreign Minister of Japan Kono Taro made an official visit to Mongolia in June 2019, which was significant because a similar visit happened nine years ago. Strategic consultative meetings between two foreign ministries have been organised regularly since 2014.[24]

The first-ever meeting involving foreign and defence officials of the two countries was held in 2013 in Tokyo, and the two countries decided to continue such dialogues in the future. The two defence ministries have concluded memorandum of cooperation in the sphere of defence, which have promoted bilateral visits by defence officials and consultative meetings. The Self-Defence Force of Japan since 2009 has been sending a participating team to international military field exercises called "Khaan Quest", which are organised by Mongolia.

The mid-term action plan between Japan and Mongolia mentioned that the "two Governments will continuously work to organize trilateral meetings among Mongolia, the United States, and Japan at the initiative of Mongolia."[25] The inaugural trilateral meeting at the foreign ministry level among Mongolia, the US, and Japan was held in September 2015 in New York City to discuss "some topics of deepening regional security cooperation and expanding economic relations."[26] The second trilateral meeting was held in August 2017 to discuss regional security and economic cooperation issues. In January 2020, the third trilateral meeting was conducted in Washington, D.C. to discuss "strengthening of strategic partnership between three countries and issues related to regional stability and the Korean Peninsula."[27]

The Japanese side explained its efforts to promote a "Free and Open Indo-Pacific" and to work closely with Mongolia through bilateral and trilateral mechanisms during the official visit to Tokyo by Prime Minister Khürelsükh in December 2018. The Mongolian side also expressed its interest in participating in integration processes throughout the Asia-Pacific and voiced its understanding that the idea of "free and open Indo-Pacific" by Japan was an initiative to promote open development and cooperation in the region. Both Mongolia and Japan are eager to strengthen regional cooperation, especially to make the Korean Peninsula free of nuclear weapons and to make Northeast Asia stable and prosperous. In that context, Japan has been strongly supporting Mongolian initiatives including the "Ulaanbaatar Dialogue for Northeast Asia Security."

The mid-term action plan of strategic partnership is designed to revitalise the Mongolian economy and to intensify bilateral trade and economic cooperation. An "Economic Partnership Agreement" between Japan and Mongolia was established in June 2016.[28] During the last four years, consultative meetings between the two countries, involving both public and private entities, have been held regularly, which have contributed to greater interaction between the two business communities. Both sides are doing their utmost efforts to build a foreign direct investment (FDI) friendly environment to promote the participation of private sectors of both countries in the implementation of major bilateral infrastructure projects. Importantly, the Development Bank of Mongolia raised 30 billion yen (US$300 million) "samurai bonds" in the Japanese stock market with the help of the Japan Bank for International Cooperation. This Japanese bank pledged to support such fundraising activities by the Mongolian bank up until 2023. Money raised by these "samurai bonds" has been spent to support major infrastructure projects such as the Darkhan oil refining facility and the fifth thermal station in Ulaanbaatar.[29]

Japan also strongly has supported the Mongolian government's "economic stabilisation programme" with the help of the International Monetary Fund (IMF) and pledged to support Mongolia' efforts to overcome economic and financial difficulties and to secure economic stability and mid- and long-term economic growth. Japan has been providing yen-denominated soft loans equivalent to $850 million within the implementation of a three-year IMF-led programme in Mongolia. Japan is encouraging Mongolia's efforts to become a transit corridor in the region and especially to benefit from exploding Sino-Russian trade. Ultimately, this plan can help Japan to play a more active role in the Mongolian market by making connectivity between Japan and Mongolia more convenient through improved transit routes among Russia, Mongolia, and China.

The "Proactive Contribution to Peace" policy and the "Free and Open Indo-Pacific" in the second Abe administration

On December 26, 2012, at the outset of his second administration, Abe invited Aso Taro to serve as Vice-Prime Minister. This led to a revival of the

"Arc of Freedom and Prosperity" policy which was introduced after Aso's "value-oriented diplomacy". The reason why Aso's policy was criticised is because this policy itself criticised the value of China and Russia, and it would thus encourage suspicion and fear regarding the true meaning of Japanese foreign policy.

However, due to the change of the power balance in East Asia, the "value policy" is being revaluated domestically and regionally.[30] First, the conflict between Japan and China over the Senkaku Islands symbolises China's seriousness and military capability and shows a power shift between the two countries is underway. Second, the policy is able to avoid a powerful head-on collision between Japan and China because, while Japan criticised Chinese policy, it did not challenge it in terms of military power. Third, the policy is able to pull India and the ASEAN states into the discussion, because the value of those states is extremely high and they would be able to share their values with Japan.

The "Abe Doctrine" was declared in Myanmar from January 16–18, 2013, by Vice-Prime Minister Aso during Abe's first foreign trip.[31] The points below from the Abe Doctrine towards ASEAN show the value of law, democracy, and economic networks.

1. We will work together with ASEAN countries to establish and expand universal values such as freedom, democracy, and basic human rights.
2. The free and open ocean, which is governed by "law" rather than "power", is a "public good", and we will do our best to protect it with the ASEAN countries. We welcome the United States' emphasis on Asia.
3. Through various economic partnership networks, we will further promote the flow of trade and investment such as goods, money, people, services, and lead to the revival of the Japanese economy and prosper together with ASEAN countries.
4. We will protect and nurture the diverse cultures and traditions of Asia.
5. We will promote a mutual understanding through more active exchanges among the younger generation, who will bear the future.[32]

The Indo-Pacific and the US, China, India, Australia, and Japan

Abe introduced a series of new security policies to make "proactive contributions to peace" in Japan's own defence through the Japan-US alliance and for the security of the Asia-Pacific region. In December of 2013, the Abe administration revised the National Defense Program Guidelines (NDPG) for fiscal 2014 and beyond, founded the National Security Council (NSC), and issued Japan's first National Security Strategy (NSS).[33]

Prime Minister Abe advocated the "Free and Open Indo-Pacific Strategy" at the Sixth Tokyo International Conference on African Development (TICAD VI) held in August 2016. The importance of achieving a free and open maritime order based on the rule of law in the Indo-Pacific region, stretching from the Asia-Pacific through the Indian Ocean to the Middle East and Africa, has been widely agreed upon across the international community. With the further emergence of various threats, including the severe security environment in the Indo-Pacific region, piracy, terrorism, proliferation of weapons of mass destruction, natural disasters, and illegal fishing, there is a growing need for the countries of the region to cooperate towards a "Free and Open Indo-Pacific." Japan is promoting the "Free and Open Indo-Pacific Strategy" in order to develop the region as part of "international public goods" that bring stability and prosperity for any country. This vision involves maintaining and strengthening a free and open maritime order based on the rule of law across the region through the elimination of those various threats, as well as through enhancing connectivity by developing quality infrastructure in accordance with international standards. This policy is based on the three pillars below.[34]

1. The promotion and solidifying of the rule of law, freedom of navigation, free trade, etc.
2. The pursuit of economic prosperity through enhancing connectivities, including through quality infrastructure development in accordance with international standards.
3. Commitment for peace and stability that includes assistance for the capacity building of maritime law enforcement, and cooperation in such fields as disaster risk reduction and non-proliferation.

In November 2017 in Vietnam, US President Donald Trump announced a vision for a free and open Indo-Pacific. Under his Indo-Pacific strategy, the US has increased its tempo and level of cooperation with allies and partners in the region.[35] At the Shangri-La Dialogue in 2017, US Secretary of Defense Jim Mattis also announced the Trump administration's first Asian policy, although the US' commitment to the region is a structural, not situational, issue, which bedevils every administration.[36] In the conference, Mattis censured China. Later in 2019, US Vice President Mike Pence clarified that Western initiatives towards China had failed in the democratisation of China after its economic development.[37] Then in 2020, US Secretary of State Mike Pompeo denounced China's actions in the waters of the Spratly Islands as illegal and said that the US could not tolerate the construction of a maritime empire by China. He further added that the Chinese government had changed the status quo against the backdrop of military power.[38] To prove the point, the Ministry of Defense of Japan announced that the number of emergency starts (scrambles) of the Air Self-Defence Force was 947 times in 2019, the third highest in the history.[39]

Japan's "Free and Open Indo-Pacific Strategy" called on the US' Indo-Pacific strategy and also on the recently created Quad (Quadrilateral Security Dialogue) system. The Quad system is a security cooperation initiative of four countries, namely India, Japan, the US, and Australia, which are democratic countries in the greater region. It had been advocated by Prime Minister Abe as far back as 2007, and although defence ministry-level talks among the four countries were held in May of that year, the concept was virtually shelved due to the withdrawal of the Australian side and the resignation of Prime Minister Abe. The idea resurfaced as India became more concerned about China's deeper relations with South Asian countries and its expansion into the Indian Ocean, and as security relations among Japan, the US, Australia, and Japan, and especially the US and India, were strengthened.

The Abe administration and the "One Belt, One Road Initiative"

The Japanese government initially did not show a positive attitude towards the "One Belt, One Road Initiative" or BRI, but it modified its stance as conditions changed. In May 2017, Prime Minister Abe dispatched a government delegation to the first "One Belt, One Road" International Cooperation Summit Forum held in Beijing, and the next month he expressed his support in Tokyo. However, he placed conditions on Japan's participation: 1) There should be open access to the BRI's infrastructure, transparent and fair procurement methods, economic efficiency of any project, debt repayment and financial soundness. 2) By incorporating such common values in the regional community, the BRI should be integrated into the free and fair economic zone of the Asia-Pacific.[40]

The Abe administration recognised that developing joint business between Japan and China is beneficial not only for the development of both countries but also for the region. From the end of 2017, cooperation between the "Free and Open Indo-Pacific" concept and the BRI began to be discussed. Chinese Prime Minister Li Keqiang visited Japan in May 2018 and promoted exchanges between private companies in Japan and China, aiming at private economic cooperation projects.[41] The "First Japan-China Forum on Third Country Business Cooperation" was established during that visit, and members included managers of a wide range of companies and related ministers to further promote exchanges between private companies in Japan and China.

However, there are aspects in Japan's "Free and Open Indo-Pacific" policies which conflict with geopolitics coordination between the governments in the private sector. It is considered that Japan has a strategy of promoting the BRI to operate in line with international standards through third-country cooperation with China.

Conclusion

A broad region including Japan, Northeast Asia, and Southeast Asia has started debating bonding as one region. This has revealed many considerations, including the importance of the Japan-US alliance, the effects of the rise of China, and, most importantly, how Japan should react to the security architecture in the region. Regarding all of the above, three models have been advocated. First, the traditional power model is the one which Japan now employs to respond to the growing Chinese threat. An increasing number of domestic right-wing groups and individuals since 2010 have been supporting the Abe administration's defence policies in tandem with growing Chinese influence over the Asia-Pacific. As a result, the Japan-US alliance would take on a more important role in the Northeast region and throughout the Indo-Pacific as a major power pole. This powerful regional security model prevents Asia from realising its long-held desire of integrating the greater Asia-Pacific. Second, liberalists within Japan believe that free and open regional cooperation guarantees movement of people, goods, money, and services. Thus, Japanese foreign policy towards the Indo-Pacific should maintain a value-oriented position, because a power model would lead to military competition between the Japan-US alliance and SCO. Competition between Japan and China must not be restricted to one option or the other: Japan should pursue an economic and value diplomacy model with the Japan-US alliance and with China pursue the BRI in balance with neighbouring countries, such as Mongolia with which it has a strategic partnership. Third, the balance of power could be created by regional powers such as Japan, the US, China, India, Russia, and potentially the United Kingdom. This model is based on the theory that to share the fruit of economic gains and value diplomacy, states in the region must recognise the importance of the nature of nation states throughout history.

Despite the fact that the debate over the future of regional integration has not been resolved, overall, there are some positive aspects of Japan's Indo-Pacific policy. While Abe recently has been succeeded by the new Prime Minister Suga Yoshihide, Abe's legacy continues to leave both positive perspectives and difficult issues. Japan's one main pillar, the "Free and Open Indo-Pacific," created a stronger Japan-United States alliance and possibly may see the realisation of a fully functioning Quad relationship in the future. Nonetheless, on the "value" side, Japan sometimes displays contradictory diplomatic attitudes. Japan faces growing negative views of western countries, which should share the same values with Japan, towards China. For example, western countries have seen the Hong Kong demonstrations as an act of democratisation and thus cannot forgive China's power grabbing stance, or its open ocean policies in the South China Sea. Because of Hong Kong and problems emanating from the COVID-19 pandemic, US-Chinese trade relations have caused division in the high-tech field. As a result, the number of American-made parts used in Huawei's latest smartphones has plummeted, and, instead, the number of Japanese and Korean-made parts has increased.[42] Still, although initially postponed by COVID-19, the plans for a state visit by Chinese President Xi Jinping to Japan have been adjusted by Tokyo. [43]

If the competition between the US and China intensifies, the impact on Japan will be inevitable. The Japanese government is enthusiastic about how to keep the "Leaving United States" in the Asian region. According to Professor Murata Koji of Doshisha University, the US is taking a very strict attitude towards China, while Japan is more reluctant. However, on the contrary, Japan feels that North Korea is a threat, but the US may be willing to compromise.[44] Furthermore, there is the question of what the Japan-US alliance will look like in the future, as the two nations hold very different positions regarding the burden of expenses of the US military stationed in Japan. This links to another question, namely, how should Japan protect its own security, and what role should it play in the international community, especially in Northeast Asia?

Japanese Prime Minister Suga and Chinese President Xi need to discuss repeatedly the future of Asia and Japan-Chinese relations in order to create mutual understanding and trust. The potential is there because Japan is able to play a major role by leading the Asian Development Bank (ADB) and participating in Chinese-led AIIB. All of this would promote economic order in Asia and encourage China to act in accordance with multilateral frameworks and international rules.

Notes

1 "Hub and Spoke" also known as the San Francisco system was created by the US to maintain its alliance with East Asian states after World War II. The concept is well explained in Victor Cha, "Powerplay: The Origins of the U.S. Alliance System in East Asia," *International Security*, 34 (3), Winter, 2009/2010, pp. 158–196.
2 "Remarks by President Barack Obama at Suntory Hall, Tokyo, Japan," November 14, 2009, at http://www.whitehouse.gov/the-press-office/remarks-president-barack-obama-suntory-hall (accessed October 26, 2020).
3 For regionalism in East Asia, see T.J. Pempel, "Introduction: Emerging Webs of Regional Connectedness," *Remapping East ASIA – The Construction of a Region*, T. J. Pempel (ed.), Cornell University Press, 2004, pp. 3–6, and Akiko Fukushima, "Japan's Perspective on Asian Regionalism," *Asia's New Multilateralism*, Michael J. Green and Bates Gill, eds, Colombia University Press, pp. 103–106.
4 Neorealism or structural realism is a theory of international relations that says power is the most important factor in international relations. It was first outlined by Kenneth Waltz. See his *Theory of International Politics*, McGraw Hill, New York, 1979.
5 "Fukuda Doctrine," *ASJA International*, at https://asja.gr.jp/en/asja/fukuda.html (accessed June 6, 2020).
6 Ryutaro Hashimoto, *Reforms for the New Era of Japan and ASEAN: for a broader and deeper Partnership*, ISEAS Publishing, Singapore, 1997, p. 23.
7 Taro Aso, "Arc of Freedom and Prosperity: Japan's Expanding Diplomatic Horizons," Japanese Institute of International Affairs Seminar, November 30, 2006, at http:www.mofa.go.jp/announce/fm/aso/speech0611.html (accessed April 20, 2020).

Japan's foreign policy security mechanisms 101

8 "Value Oriented Diplomacy and Strive to From the 'Arc of Freedom and Prosperity'," Ministry of Foreign Affairs, July 2007, at https://www.mofa.go.jp/policy/pillar/index.html (accessed on October 26, 2020).
9 Hiroaki Iwashita, "Japan's Eurasia Diplomacy," *JIIA: The Japan Institute of International Affairs*, 2007, at http://www2.jiia.or.jp/pdf/report/h18_eurasia.pdf (accessed on July 5, 2020).
10 Yuichi Hosoya, *Japan's Security and Changing Global Power Balance*, Kouken, September 2015, p. 62.
11 The White House, "Security Strategy of Engagement and Enlargement," July 1994, pp. 5–6, at https://history.defense.gov/Portals/70/Documents/nss/nss1994.pdf?ver=2014-06-25-121219-500 (accessed on June 10, 2020).
12 Ibid., p. 23.
13 Ibid.
14 Department of Defense, "Sustaining U.S. Global Leadership: Priorities for 21st Century Defense," January 2012, at https://archive.defense.gov/news/Defense_Strategic_Guidance.pdf (accessed June 10, 2020).
15 Ibid., p. 1.
16 Mie Ooba, "Memo for East Asian regional integration-post ASEAN community," Council on East Asian Community, at http://www.ceac.jp/j/pdf/study1/73.pdf (accessed June 30, 2020).
17 President Xi Jinping published what he called the "New Asian Security Concept" during the fourth Summit of the Conference on Interaction and Confidence Building Measures in Asia (CICA) in May 2014. See David C. McCaughrin, "What Does China's New Asian Security Concept' Mean for The US?," *The Diplomat*, January 21, 2017, at https://thediplomat.com/2017/01/what-does-chinas-new-asian-security-concept-mean-for-the-us/ (accessed July 15, 2020).
18 Japanese Ministry of Foreign Affairs, "White Paper on Development Cooperation 2018," at https://mofa.go.jp/policy/oda/page_000017.html (accessed on October 30, 2020).
19 Batbayar Tsedendamba, *The Dynamic Decade: Mongolian Sovereignty and Foreign Policy Between East and West, 1990–2000*, Admon Print, Ulaanbaatar, 2019, pp. 194, 207–209.
20 Mongolian Ministry of Foreign Affairs, *The Blue Book of Mongolia's Foreign Policy 2016*, BCI Printing, Ulaanbaatar, 2017, pp. 21–22.
21 "Transport Minister to visit Mongolia, South Korea," at https://mongolia-economy.blogspot.com/2014/04/transport-minister-to-visit-mongolia-s.html (accessed on October 30, 2020).
22 Sharad K. Soni, "The Geopolitical Dilemma of Small States in External Relations: Mongolia's Tryst with "Immediate" and "Third" Neighbours," *The Mongolian Journal of International Affairs*, 20, 2018, pp. 40–41.
23 "Japan-Mongolia Foreign Minister's Meeting and Signing ceremony for the Japan-Mongolia Mid-term Action Plan," Japanese Ministry of Foreign Affairs, March 29, 2017, at https://mofa.go.jp/press/release/press4e_001533.html (accessed on October 27, 2020).
24 "Foreign Minister Kono visits Mongolia," *Japan Times*, June 16, 2019.
25 "Japan-Mongolia Foreign Minister's Meeting and Signing ceremony for the Japan-Mongolia Mid-term Action Plan."
26 Alicia Campi, "Mongolia and the Dilemmas of Deepening Eurasian Continentalism," *The Mongolian Journal of International Affairs*, 20, 2018, pp. 16–17.
27 "Joint Statement on the Japan-U.S.-Mongolia Trilateral Meeting," at https://mofa.go.jp/mofaj/files/000556605.pdf (accessed on October 30, 2020).
28 *The Blue Book of Mongolia's Foreign Policy 2016*, pp. 21–22.

29 Japan Bank for International Cooperation, "Guarantee for Privately Placed Samurai Bonds Issued by Development Bank of Mongolia," at https://jbic.go.jp/en/information/press/press-2013/1225-16316.html (accessed on October 30, 2020).
30 Japan Forum on International Relations, "Report of Japan's Values and Foreign Policy: Intangible Power in International Relations," March 2014, at https://jfir.or.jp/e/regular-research/201403.pdf (accessed on October 30, 2020).
31 Japanese Ministry of Foreign Affairs, "Prime Minister Abe's visit to Southeast Asia in 2016," January 18, 2013, at https://www.mofa.go.jp/mofaj/kaidan/s_abe2/vti_1301/gaiyo.html (accessed July 5, 2020).
32 Ibid.
33 Tsuneo Watanabe, "Japan's Rationale for the Free and Open Indo-Pacific Strategy [1]," *International Information Network Analysis,* October 30, 2019, at https://www.spf.org/iina/en/articles/watanabe_01.html (accessed July 5, 2020).
34 Japanese Ministry of Foreign Affairs, *Diplomatic Blue Book 2019 Japanese Diplomacy and International Situation 2018,* at https://www.mofa.go.jp/files/000527162.pdf (accessed July 16, 2020).
35 "A Free And Open Indo-Pacific-Advancing a Shared Vision," U.S. Department of State, November 4, 2019, at https://www.state.gov/wp-content/uploads/2019/11/Free-and-Open-Indo-Pacific-4Nov2019.pdf (accessed August 23, 2020).
36 Prashnth Parameswaran, "What Mattis' Shangri-La Dialogue Speech Revealed About Trump's Asia Policy," *The Diplomat,* June 6, 2017, at https://thediplomat.com/2017/06/what-mattis-shangri-la-dialogue-speech-revealed-about-trumps-asia-policy/ (accessed August 26, 2020).
37 "Remarks by Vice President Pence at the Frederic V. Malek Memorial Lecture," October 24, 2019, at https://www.whitehouse.gov/briefings-statements/remarks-vice-president-pence-frederic-v-malek-memorial-lecture/ (accessed August 26, 2020).
38 "Pompeo addresses Republican National Convention," *Asahi Shinbun,* August 26, 2020, at https://www.asahi.com/articles/ASN8V44JLN8VUHBI016.html (accessed September 5, 2020).
39 "Air Self-Defense Force scramble, 947 times in the first year of Reiwa, increase in aircraft to China," April 9, 2020, at https://www.sankeibiz.jp/macro/news/200409/mca2004091724025-n1.htm (accessed October 26, 2020).
40 "Belt and Road, 4 conditions for cooperation Prime Minister 'I do not totally agree'," *Nikkei,* March 25, 2019, at https://www.nikkei.com/article/DGXMZO42874300V20C19A3000000/ (accessed October 26, 2020).
41 Ministry of Foreign Affairs of Japan, "Premier of the State Council of China Li Keqiang Visits Japan," May 9, 2018, at https://www.mofa.go.jp/a_o/c_m1/cn/page3e_000857.html (accessed October 26, 2020).
42 "U.S. strengthens Huawei sanctions-China retaliate U.S. companies," *Nihon Keizai Shinbun,* May 15, 2020, at https://www.nikkei.com/article/DGXMZO591-83930V10C20A5MM8000/ (accessed August 23, 2020).
43 Toshihiro Minohara, "Recognize the significance of the Japan-US alliance," *Sankei Shinbun,* July 25, 2020.
44 "US seeking in return for the alliance," *Asahi Shinbun,* January 13, 2020.

6 India, Mongolia, and Northeast Asia: between geography and the geopolitical realities

Mahima N. Duggal and Jagannath P. Panda

India's foreign policy is becoming increasingly proactive as the middle power maps a route to realise its major power aspirations. New Delhi's standoff with Beijing at their disputed border along the Line of Actual Control (LAC) and their deadly skirmish in June 2020, which left 20 Indian soldiers (and an undisclosed number of Chinese soldiers) dead, has greatly impacted democratic India's foreign policy calculus. Instead of following a strategically cautious path of managing bilateral ties with two competitive and at odds with each other great powers, New Delhi is exercising diplomatic activism to build pointed alignments in the region. Under this calculus, India's interests in the Indo-Pacific region have quickly expanded and enhancing its strategic partnerships have become a veritable priority as a means of safeguarding the country's strategic autonomy, as well as actualising its major power inclinations.

In this context, this chapter seeks to investigate India's foreign policy in relation to Northeast Asia, particularly with regards to its relations with Mongolia. The paper examines India's evolving foreign policy arc in the aftermath of the end of the Cold War—an event that essentially mandated a fundamental reorientation of India's then international outlook, which broadly consisted of a non-alignment strategy driven by the need to remain autonomous of the influence of the United States and Russia, the two ideological poles in a bipolar world order. Furthermore, the chapter places Mongolia in India's outlook towards the Northeastern region by looking at a brief history of their bilateral ties and examining how they have progressed since Prime Minister Narendra Modi's landmark trip to Ulaanbaatar in 2015. Subsequently, the paper also asserts that the momentum in India-Mongolia relations is arguably driven more by Ulaanbaatar's Third Neighbourhood foreign policy, which places India in a prominent position in the state's outlook. Through this discussion, the chapter examines India-Mongolia ties in the context of their shared concern of China's rise and demonstrates the shared interest of both states in managing Beijing, which has, in the past year, shown its worst face and proved that its rise in the coming times will not be without aggression and expansionism.

In light of these factors, this paper contextualises the progress and momentum in India-Mongolia ties and argues that despite the recent upswing

DOI: 10.4324/9781003148630-6

in ties promoted primarily by Modi's 2015 visit, the true potential of India-Mongolia ties still remains unrealised. Although India's historical ties to Mongolia can be traced back to ancient times, with cultural heritage including the Buddhist legacy becoming the bonding factor between the two sides, Mongolia barely has featured in India's strategic imagination. Despite some momentum in India-Mongolia bilateral ties in the past five-odd years, cooperation in the field of economy, security and political partnership is still a low-key affair with no upward movement in bilateral ties. Moving forward, the chapter contends that both countries must urgently look towards not only adding momentum to their already ongoing joint projects but also seek to transcend their Strategic Partnership to a comprehensive one as well. Lastly, the chapter looks at potential areas of cooperation in both regional and global dimensions. As part of this consideration, it explores the extent of cooperation that New Delhi and Ulaanbaatar can employ in relation to North Korea and establishing peace and stability in the Korean Peninsula and postulates that joint efforts in this regard can be instrumental in furthering their goals. Essentially, the chapter argues that as the Indo-Pacific concept gains greater import, Mongolia and India's shared democratic values, commitment to a free and inclusive region, and a pluralistic multi-nodal world order creates room for exploring a global, comprehensive strategic partnership.

A transitional foreign policy post Cold War

Changes with a subtle transition have been a constant doctrine in India's post-Cold War foreign policy. From a principle of "non-alignment" to "multi-alignment" to a concept of "pointed alignment" with a prime focus on neighbourhood and extended neighbourhood have been the highlights of Indian foreign policy transition.[1] This included, for instance, a recalibration of India's economic policy, which meant a departure from socialist economic ideals and an import substitution policy. Such economic liberalisation reforms were accompanied by New Delhi's search for a more proactive participation in world politics, in an attempt to carve out India's new role in a staunchly *Pax Americana* international order.[2]

However, this search for a contemporary, well-defined, and well-articulated foreign policy grand strategy was hindered by a number of domestic factors, not the least of which was the persistence of coalition governments at the central government level. This hindered the formulation, as well as the implementation, of coherent international strategies and weakened the effectiveness of institutions responsible for it.[3] Faced with unprecedented challenges amidst the dawning of a new era of globalisation, India's foreign policy remained largely reactive and cautious, with the country's principal interests being limited to its immediate neighbourhood[4] and ties with great powers. India focused on domestic growth and development, including building capacity for the conventional security of its people and territory, pursuing greater economic growth, ensuring energy security to support rapid economic expansion, cementing its nuclear power status while at the same time promoting non-proliferation objectives, and to some extent seeking ways to be recognised as a leading power in the developing world.[5]

In light of such, albeit unspoken, aspirations, India launched a number of foreign policy initiatives to better connect with its neighbourhood. India's neighbourhood policy was articulated first by Prime Minister Inder Kumar Gujral (the Gujral doctrine) and focused on enhancing cooperation amongst the South Asian states in dealing with shared security issues (particularly terrorism, human trafficking, outbreak of infectious diseases), enhancing regional trade, and amplifying people-to-people contacts.[6] This neighbourhood policy, further developed under Atal Bihari Vajpayee, resulted in India opening its borders wider. Although New Delhi's vigorous pursuance of nuclear capabilities caused concerns over India's hegemonic ambitions, its explicit commitment to a nuclear-weapons-free international society and continued engagement with the region served to alleviate such apprehensions.

At the same time, India also expanded its interests eastwards, with the foundation of the Look East Policy (LEP) in 1992 under Prime Minister Narasimha Rao and former Prime Minister Manmohan Singh (then, Finance Minister). The aim was to develop deeper diplomatic ties, enhance bilateral trade and fashion security partnerships.[7] The policy saw little follow-up in the following years with changes in national government administrations but returned into focus at the beginning of the Twenty-first century and has progressively gained momentum since then, with an expanded agenda which encompassed an area stretching from Australia to East Asia.[8] Although the LEP undoubtedly marked a change in India's global perspectives, it was focused largely on Southeast Asia and later the Association of Southeast Asian Nations (ASEAN)—a region with which India had considerable cultural, social and civilisational connections. With a large diaspora of non-residential Indians living in the Southeast Asian area and deep historical links between the two, this region is a natural partner for India.

Under Prime Minister Narendra Modi, India's foreign policy strategy and ambitions have become much more nuanced. Perhaps for the first time, India publicly and explicitly enunciated the ambitions that guide its foreign policy and made it abundantly clear that it was looking to play a greater and more "proactive" international role.[9] At the beginning of his first term, Modi instructed Indian missions abroad to emphasise the administration's intention to establish India as a regional and world leader, instead of being merely a balancing power.[10] Furthermore, India's Minister of External Affairs Subrahmanyam Jaishankar (foreign secretary at the time) articulated New Delhi's ambition to cement its position as a "leading power" at an International Institute for Strategic Studies-Fullerton Lecture in Singapore in 2015.[11] This change in foreign policy trajectory and the emergence of a driving strategy underpinning India's international outlook manifested in a number of ways. Most significantly, Modi embarked on a "Neighbourhood First" policy to increase integration in the South Asian sub-continent and forge "mutually beneficial, people-oriented, regional frameworks for stability and prosperity."[12] A key and distinct aspect of this has been India's pursuance of a development-focused approach by which Modi has attempted to increase Indian foreign aid and deliver benefits like improved connectivity, infrastructure, and bilateral government-private sector, and people-to-people engagement. Most importantly, in a move reminiscent of Prime Minister Jawaharlal Nehru, Modi added a personal touch to his foreign policy approaches, with multiple visits abroad, particularly in Asian countries, in a bid to accelerate diplomatic efforts and build better synergy.[13]

In this vein, much focus has been devoted to a rebranding of the LEP into an Act East Policy (AEP) to signify the region's "great sense of priority" in Indian politics, which was announced at the 2014 East Asia Summit in Myanmar.[14] Although ideologically guided by a vision of India's rise as a great Asian power, the move also was a structural response to China's growing influence in what India firmly viewed as its neighbourhood, as well as other factors like US increasing strategic interest in Asia, Japan's re-emergence as a key Asian actor, and rapid economic growth in Southeast Asia. Although the policy broadly incorporates Southeast Asia, Oceania, and Northeast Asia, AEP has remained largely ASEAN-centred even after its reboot under Modi.[15]

When it comes to Northeast Asia, there has been a limited focus. The initiatives that do exist have been driven by strategic interests of balancing China in light of India's concerns over China's rise and their complex history.[16] India's partnership with Japan, for instance, which has found significant synergy in recent years, has been underpinned by Modi's commitment to the idea of a free and open Indo-Pacific (FOIP) first advocated by the former Japanese Prime Minister Shinzo Abe.[17] Under the bilateral synergy of AEP and FOIP, the India-Japan partnership has flourished with Japan joining the Malabar exercises,[18] their landmark civil nuclear pact,[19] their ACSA[20] and their joint efforts via platforms like the Quadrilateral Security Dialogue (Quad 2.0),[21] and more recently, the Supply Chain Resilience Initiative (SCRI), which was instituted in the aftermath of the COVID-19 pandemic and made countries realise the risk they face in the over-dependence of their value chains on China.[22]

The strategic nature of New Delhi and Tokyo's relationship indicates that there exists a tacit acknowledgement that their ties are meant to better manage the rise of China and balance out Chinese adventurism. By comparison, smaller states like Mongolia and North Korea have been largely inconspicuous in India's Northeast Asian outlook, despite New Delhi sharing a maturing relationship with both Ulaanbaatar and Pyongyang. In other words, India's foreign policy transitioned from its intensive focus on its immediate neighbourhood to an extensive neighbourhood, which encompasses the entirety of the Asian continent (including Eurasia, Central

Asia and Northeast Asia) and the Indo-Pacific region. In this context, New Delhi's plans of engagement with Mongolia have figured only under India's "extended neighbourhood" framework in recent years and remain a rather novel development in India's diplomatic outlook.

While India's AEP is an assertive way to initiate deeper engagement with states to the country's east, in the sense that it makes explicit India's intention to become a proactive regional power, its focus has remained on the Southeast Asian region. India's Northeast Asian policy is, therefore, yet to take concrete shape or formulation. While Southeast Asian was overemphasised in New Delhi's policy outlooks, India never viewed, or even foresaw, the Northeast Asian region as one that was, or could be, exclusively and strategically significant to Indian interests. Its interests in Northeast Asia arguably have been driven by New Delhi's concerns of a growing China, which has led India's emerging outlook towards this region to focus acutely on ties with strategic allies like Japan, and, to some extent, South Korea. While Mongolia figures as a key country under India's extended neighbourhood policy, it has yet to emerge as a critical partner within the premise of India's evolving Northeast Asian policy prism. Nonetheless, it is far from neglected in Indian diplomacy; both countries have robust bilateral ties historically, and they have only gained momentum under Modi.

India-Mongolia: the emerging chapter

Geographical barriers, geopolitical realities and geo-economics of Northeast Asia are the constant factors influencing India-Mongolia ties. Mongolia is landlocked between Russia and China, meaning that are both countries are separated by a considerable geographical distance with China lying in between them, which considerably limits their connectivity options. At the same time, Mongolia's geographical position inevitably puts it at amidst not only the complex dynamics of the China-Russia relationship, particularly their competition in Central Asia,[23] but also as an actor in the conflict between the Democratic People's Republic of Korea (DPRK) and the Republic of Korea (ROK). Such geopolitical realities inevitably render Mongolia vulnerable to changing regional dynamics, constraining its foreign policy options and shaping its international strategies. In terms of geo-economics as well, India's lack of, or rather delay in, factoring the economic significance of Mongolia (and the Northeast Asian region as a whole) in its immediate foreign policy has hindered a true flourishing in India-Mongolia ties.

India and Mongolia's bilateral ties can be best characterised as enduring, positive, and strategic. The two civilisations share deep historical and cultural links, which have grown progressively stronger with missionaries travelling to the Mongolian region to share their Buddhist philosophies, languages and cultures.[24] These deep-rooted historical-cultural links have accorded Mongolia the status of a "Spiritual Neighbour" in the Indian outlook.[25] Building on such historical ties, Indian-Mongolian relations have continued to flourish to an extent in the modern age, since India's independence in 1947. Indian diplomatic missions to Mongolia consistently have emphasised their Buddhist connection and sought to deepen cultural, diplomatic and security ties by consolidating this religious legacy. Perhaps one key indicator of Indian-Mongolian ties is their close cooperation in the international arena. India established formal diplomatic ties with Ulaanbaatar in 1955 and subsequently became an ardent supporter of Mongolia's pursuit to be recognised as an independent state in the United Nations (UN).[26] Mongolia became a full-fledged member state of the UN in 1961, with Nehru championing the country's efforts for UN entrance as well as forging the foundation of their bilateral ties.

In turn, Mongolia has been a key partner in international forums for India. It co-sponsored India's landmark UN Resolution that recognised Bangladesh as an independent nation after its separation from Pakistan in 1972 and supported India's bid for a non-permanent seat on the UN Security Council (UNSC) in 2011. Mongolia has vigorously supported reformation of the UNSC and reiterated its backing for India's inclusion as a Permanent Member, in interest of a more diverse panel that fairly represents the developing world. More recently, Mongolia backed Indian candidates for positions on the International Tribunal for the Law of the Sea, the Executive Board of UNESCO, the Council of the International Maritime Organization, and the International Court of Justice. Such overtures have been reciprocated by India, with New Delhi voicing its own endorsement of Mongolia's candidature as a non-permanent UNSC member and an Executive Board member of the United Nations Children's Fund.[27]

This international dimension of Indian-Mongolian ties has been underpinned by their gradually growing bilateral synergy. Over the years, both India and Mongolia have signed a number of treaties and initiated cooperation in a diverse range of fields, often driven by high-level visits of dignitaries. Table 6.1 lists pacts between both countries starting in 1961 and spanning over fields such as defence, trade, education and training, technology, agriculture, natural resources, development and culture. New Delhi also has extended frequent lines of credit and aid to Mongolia for launching bilateral cultural exchange projects as well as for economic and humanitarian assistance.[28]

Gaining momentum under the Modi administration

Despite the presence of the aforementioned bilateral agreements between India and Mongolia, India's relationship with Mongolia prior to 2015 was, in fact, significantly limited in substance. Cooperation, for instance, consisted mostly of low- and medium-level diplomatic exchanges. This restrictive nature of Indian-Mongolian ties can be attributed to a number of reasons, not the least of which is their considerable geographical distance.

Table 6.1 List of bilateral agreements and treaties between the Republic of India and Mongolia

1961	India-Mongolia Agreement on Cultural Cooperation
	• To initiate a Cultural Exchange Programme between the two countries
1968	Trade Agreement between India-Mongolia
	• Agreement later was extended in 1971, 1974 and revised in 1978
1994	Treaty of Friendly Relations and Cooperation
1996	Agreement on Trade and Economic Cooperation
	• To provide MFN status to each otherAgreement in the field of Geology and Mineral Resources
	Agreement in the field of Agriculture
2001	Investment Promotion and Protection Agreement
	• To address modest bilateral trade
	Extradition Treaty
	Treaty on Legal Assistance and Legal Relations Concerning Civil and Commercial Matters
	• To coordinate legal processes and mutually offer citizens the same legal protections in each other's territories
2004	Agreement on Cooperation in Biotechnology
	Agreement on Cooperation in Animal Health and Dairy
	Agreement on Cooperation in Space Science, Technology, and Applications
2005	Agreement on Mutual Waiver of Visa Requirements Memorandum of Understanding on Establishment of an Agropark for Research and Demonstration
	For coordination between farmers of both countries to improve production efficiency through introduction of new technologies and better practices
2009	Agreement on Cooperation in Health and Medical Sciences
	Memorandum of Understanding on Cooperation for Peaceful Use of Radioactive Mineral and Nuclear Energy
	A civil nuclear agreement for the supply of uranium
2011	India extended a line of credit of US$20 million for establishment of Centre of Excellence for IT, Communication and Outsourcing
	• Later renamed the Atal Bihari Vajpayee Centre of Excellence on Information, Communication and Technology (ABVCE-ICT)
	Defence Cooperation Agreement
	Memorandum of Understanding on Cooperation between Planning commission of India and National Development and Innovation Committee (NDIC)
	Memorandum of Understanding on Media Exchanges
2013	India extends a grant for upgradation and modernisation of Rajiv Gandhi Polytechnic college of Production an Art in Mongolia
2015	Joint Statement for India-Mongolia Partnership
	Air Services Agreement (Revised)
	Memorandum of Understanding for cooperation between National Security Councils of India and Mongolia
	Memorandum of Understanding between Ministry of External Affairs (India) and the Ministry of Foreign Affairs (Mongolia)
	Memorandum of Understanding between Foreign Service Institute of the Ministry of External Affairs (India) and the Diplomatic Academy of the Ministry of Foreign Affairs (Mongolia)

(*Continued*)

110　*Mahima N. Duggal and Jagannath P. Panda*

Table 6.1 (Continued)

	Memorandum of Understanding on establishing a Joint Cyber Security Training Centre
	Memorandum of Understanding for Cooperation in Border Patrolling and Surveillance
	Memorandum of Understanding between Ministry of New and Renewable Energy (India) and the Ministry of Energy (Mongolia)
	Memorandum of Understanding on the establishment of a Joint Friendship Secondary School in Mongolia
	Cultural Exchange Programme (2015–2018)
	Agreement on cooperation in the field of Animal Health and Dairy
	Treaty on Transfer of Sentenced persons
	Memorandum of Understanding on cooperation in Traditional Systems of Medicine
2016	Memorandum of Understanding on Friendly Relations Cooperation
2019	Cultural Exchange Protocol (2019–2023) Memorandum of Understanding in the field of Disaster Management between National Disaster Management Authority (India) and National Emergency Management Agency (Mongolia) Memorandum of Understanding in Space between Department of Space (India) and Communications and Information Technology Authority (Mongolia)
	• To promote bilateral efforts in space exploration for peaceful reasonsComprehensive Work Plan between Ministry of Fisheries, Animal Husbandry and Dairying (India) and Ministry of Food, Agriculture and Light Industry (Mongolia)

Source: Ministry of External Affairs documents.[29]

With New Delhi's attention confined to its immediate neighbourhood (the South Asian sub-continent), and even its LEP centred on Southeast Asia to a great extent, their relationship was confined to and failed to transcend beyond bilateral characteristics, so as not to reach its political potential.

However, India and Mongolia's relationship gained significant momentum since Modi's visit to Mongolia in 2015, which marked the first-ever trip to Mongolia by an Indian Prime Minister since independence. Notably, the visit came as a part of Modi's East Asian tour that initiated the reinvigorated Act East policy, aimed at demonstrating India's efforts to extend its neighbourhood, and highlighted New Delhi's expanding interests beyond its borders.[30] The very inclusion of Mongolia (alongside China and South Korea) was suggestive of the position that the Northeast Asian state could expect to occupy in India's emerging outlook and foreign policy strategy. It highlighted Modi's perception of the vital role that Ulaanbaatar could play in the coming era—the Asian Century—and the necessity of deeper, strategic, and mutually beneficial ties between them.

This is perhaps best reflected by the fact that both countries formally elevated their ties to a Strategic Partnership, building on their historical and spiritual links, commitment to global peace and prosperity, and their shared democratic values. They also affirmed their resolve to promote an "open, balanced and inclusive security architecture in the Asia-Pacific" signifying their strategic synergy.[31] At the same time, the two countries consolidated their partnership within the political, security, defence, health, scientific and cultural sectors, while laying out concrete steps for collaboration. Their practical agreement for cooperation manifested in the inking of 13 bilateral agreements that amplified collaboration in areas of border security, air connectivity, agriculture, medical sciences, renewable energy and cyber security (see Table 6.1). In addition, in a commitment to lay the foundations for still stronger and more strategically driven relations, New Delhi and Ulaanbaatar instituted regular dialogue mechanisms between their respective foreign ministries and national security councils so as to forge better political and security synergy and underline the value they place on each other's international outlooks in face of shared challenges.[32]

Modi's success in deeply embedding Indian-Mongolian ties has been visible in the years since his landmark visit. In the past five years, India has increased scholarships and grants to Mongolian citizens from 150 to 200, especially under India's Technical and Economic Cooperation (ITEC) Programme.[33] India also has accelerated its efforts to enhance trade with the mineral-rich country, although they still remain far from their potential.[34] Notably, the Modi trip spurred several high-level diplomatic visits between the nations.[35] The import accorded to such high-level exchanges was exemplified in the statement issued by India's former External Affairs Minister, Sushma Swaraj, during a joint press briefing held during her visit to Mongolia, in which she called Mongolia a "factor of stability in East Asia" and its social and economic development as a first step in cementing regional peace.[36] The most recent of these exchanges was a state visit by the President of Mongolia Khaltmaa Battulga to New Delhi in September 2019,[37] wherein both states not only resolved to further consolidate their Strategic Partnership,[38] but also signed pacts bolstering coordination in disaster management and, interestingly, space exploration for civilian, peaceful reasons.[39]

Battulga's visit was significant in the sense that it marked a clear political acknowledgement by both sides of the weight equated to their strategic relationship, as well as a mutual agreement to further bilateral ties at the highest level. The strategic and comprehensive nature of the state visit was an overt nod by both countries to intensify noteworthiness, substance and momentum to Indian-Mongolian bilateral ties. Notably, the visit came against a backdrop of a drastically different geopolitical environment compared to Modi's prime ministerial visit in 2015. Instead of a strategic competitiveness that the US and China had previously shared, their ties had deteriorated swiftly and considerably in a bitter, drawn-out trade war between the two giant economies that invariably impacted the entire region as well as the global economy.[40] At the same time, as the Indo-Pacific region grew into a theatre of confrontation between the US and China's rising hostilities, the region saw the rise of a revisionist Chinese power, particularly in the context of soaring adventurism in the highly disputed South China Sea maritime region.[41]

India, too, increasingly was becoming aware of the threat of a rising China, as their rivalry developed into the Doklam plateau military stand-off in June 2017 in which New Delhi came to Bhutan's aid in resisting People's Liberation Army (PLA) activities along the disputed region at the India-Bhutan-China tri-junction.[42] Although there were attempts at rapprochement after the stand-off,[43] the incident was no doubt a key factor in India's shifting political calculations, as it sought to map its future foreign policy trajectory to best prepare for the rise of a revisionist China.[44] In this sense, Chinese activism encouraged Modi to look at Mongolia in a new light and re-evaluate its strategic import to New Delhi, thus pushing forward Indian-Mongolian ties. Battulga's 2019 presidential visit, therefore, was an explicit acknowledgement by both sides to deepen their ties in face of a rising Chinese power in Central and Northeast Asia, while at the same time re-invigorating limited, realistic and practical cooperation to expand their bilateral partnership with increased economic, cultural, technological and security interaction.

Consequently, it is important to note that India's attempts to initiate a new chapter in Indian-Mongolian ties is not merely a product of their religious affiliations but also a pragmatic and calculated move that came against the backdrop of a growing revisionist China. Even as India has sought to build power parity in its relations with Beijing,[45] Modi has been wary of the potential ramifications of the rising giant's economic and military might. New Delhi's Northeast Asian outlook, as well as its AEP, were devised to counterbalance and manage China, and Mongolia's inclusion under this umbrella is clearly an elucidation of this strategic interest.

In 2016, Mongolia suffered from an economic crisis when China imposed stringent trade sanctions on the country in retaliation for Ulaanbaatar hosting the Dalai Lama.[46] Notably, the Foreign Ministry spokesperson refused to confirm whether the new fees were applied in conjunction with the Dalai Lama's visit, although there was a clear connection. Not only had China warned of extensive consequences but also the sanctions eased once Mongolia apologised later in the month.[47] Under such circumstances, New Delhi reaffirmed its support to the landlocked nation by promising to work in tandem to implement effectively their previously announced US$1 billion credit line in order to overcome their difficulties.[48] The offer drew immediate and harsh criticism from Beijing, with the state-owned media outlet *Global Times* justifying the sanctions as punishment for defying China and harming its interests. It expressed hope that the crisis-hit state would "learn its lesson" and opined that it would be "politically harebrained" and "naive" to compromise its neutrality by accepting Indian aid.[49] A second article also censured New Delhi for "over-reaching" and "meddling" in Beijing's neighbourhood.[50]

Yet, at the same time, India until now has been exceedingly careful to not antagonise China and maintain cordial ties with the neighbour. In a telling sign of India's cautiousness, New Delhi did not explicitly side with Ulaanbaatar, despite the Mongolian ambassador's appeal for moral support.[51] Already in a downturn,[52] the Mongolian economy received a further hard blow from the sanctions. Having seen the jarring aftermath of Chinese economic retaliation in South Korea and Australia and acutely aware of what China's coercive, "wolf warrior" diplomacy could lead to, Mongolia ultimately conceded to Chinese pressure (although ambiguously) in an attempt to normalise the situation.[53]

Both countries also hold regular joint military (army) exercises—Nomadic Elephant in India and Khaan Quest in Mongolia—with the aim of bolstering their preparedness for UN peacekeeping operations.[54] Mongolia's Khaan Quest, which is co-led with the US, in particular, has become one of the leading peacekeeping exercises for all its participating states.[55] Although India's participation has been ongoing for several years now (Nomadic Elephant since 2010 and Khaan Quest since 2006), advancement of India-Mongolia security links has elevated Chinese concern over India intruding into what it sees as its backyard. Despite Beijing's apprehensions, India and Mongolia's security partnership above all is an extension of India's desire to play a greater role in and reinforce greater integration with the Northeast and Central Asia, rather than an attempt to monitor Chinese military expansion,[56] as well as an expression of their shared values. Notwithstanding concerns amongst both states in regards to drawing China's ire, India's expansive assistance packages coupled with high-level diplomatic exchanges and military cooperation have enabled both nations to deepen ties beyond their spiritual connection, although that remains an important avenue. For India, they extended India's soft diplomacy approach to what initially was a largely peripheral state.

India in Mongolia's "Third Neighbour" policy

As a landlocked state sandwiched between two great powers, Mongolia historically has been caught between the dominance of Russia and China. However, the end of the Cold War offered the nation an opportunity to reorient its external outlook and move away from its position as a Soviet proxy. Mongolian foreign policy's principal motivation became protecting its political independence and self-determination.[57] In the past decade, Mongolia's foreign policy has been redefined to adapt to the changing geo-strategic and geopolitical conditions by introducing a new approach of balance that is now recognised as the "third neighbour" approach.[58] Essentially driven by geographic concerns and a refusal to depend on either Russia or China,[59] Mongolia's third neighbour policy sought to expand its neighbourhood beyond these two states by developing deeper engagement with "virtual neighbour" and "like-minded" countries such as India, US,

South Korea, Turkey, Japan, Canada, and Australia—which also are geographically distant and do not present the same risks as Russia and China.[60] First referred to by US Secretary of State James Baker in 1990 during his Mongolian trip that marked the first democratic free elections in the country, the policy has since evolved and been formally instituted in Ulaanbaatar's international policy planning.[61]

India's inclusion in Mongolia's redefined vision stems not only from the two nations' deep spiritual and historic-cultural links but also their shared values of democracy.[62] Since India and Mongolia's independence in 1947 and 1990, respectively, both states have become vibrant (although admittedly flawed) democracies.[63] In fact, Mongolia has been consistently ranked a successful Central Asian democracy.[64] Mongolia's success in fighting the COVID-19 pandemic has been accompanied by adjustments to the electoral process[65] to ensure that the democratic system of the country remains resilient and can thrive despite limitations imposed by the virus, a sign of the country's abiding commitment to democratic and liberal values. The foundations for the synergy that both countries find in their foreign and security policies can be traced back to their robust propagation of non-alignment ideals. While India was one of the founding members of the Non-alignment Movement (NAM)[66] at the onset of the Cold War, Mongolia adopted it with equal voracity since joining the movement in 1992.[67] Although Mongolia has not declared itself "permanently neutral", its neutrality is reflected in the "substance, form and action" of its foreign policy as well as its signed international treaties and agreements—likely in an attempt to avoid being reduced to a buffer state.[68] In this context, Mongolia's adherence to NAM principles has become deeply embedded in Mongolian diplomacy.[69] Ulaanbaatar has made every effort to maximise international and multilateral engagements using NAM as a platform to seek enhanced relations with developing countries and facilitating South-South and North-South dialogues. It has, in other words, attempted to ensure its national security[70] by cooperating with countries within the NAM framework to further its national interests, safeguard its self-determination, strengthen its nuclear-free status, and reinforce its global posture. Thus, India has been a critical partner in this respect.

Much of the credit for the reinvigoration of Indian-Mongolian ties must be attributed to Mongolia's third neighbour policy. The elevation of India to a third neighbour in Mongolia's outlook, without doubt, put both countries on track to develop a comprehensive strategic partnership. Mongolia's multi-pillar framework of diplomacy has been critical in furthering bilateral ties with India. Here, the multi-pillar policy is one based on rationalist state behaviour, meaning that foreign policy decision making is guided primarily by self-interest.[71] In this context, the third neighbour policy exemplifies the "multipolarity, complexity and openness of Mongolia's foreign policy" and demonstrates Ulaanbaatar's adept diplomatic techniques in forging security relationships with states outside its immediate vicinity.[72] In the past decade,

Mongolia's foreign policy tacitly has identified China, and, to a lesser extent, Russia, as its chief security concern,[73] which has only made the security aspect of the country's third neighbour approach more important, particularly as a means of ensuring that the state is not made a pawn of great power competition. Relying on multiple states and international organisations allows Ulaanbaatar greater control, with additional stakeholders willing to support the country's development and thus secure its economic, ideological, and strategic security by balancing Russia and China. Therefore, the third neighbour policy is aimed not only at enhancing trade ties in the region and beyond but also at lessening the pressure that Mongolia's immediate neighbours can unduly exert on the country.

As a result, India's inclusion in Mongolia's third neighbour policy was, in fact, a key force driving their bilateral security relations forward. In 2009, notably at the same time that India gained a prominent position in Ulaanbaatar's regional and international outlook as a third neighbour, Mongolia signed a civil nuclear agreement for the peaceful use of radioactive minerals with India,[74] over China and Russia, both of whom have sizeable interests in Mongolia's mining industry.[75] India has sought to support Mongolia's mining sector through capacity building measures including advancement in areas like IT and telecommunications through training and educational support.[76]

Modi's 2015 state visit, which was instrumental in invigorating ties, also arguably came about as a result of Mongolia's deft third neighbourhood policy. Apart from marking the first Indian prime ministerial visit, the trip was historic in the grand welcome that Ulaanbaatar bestowed upon Modi. In a move symbolic of Mongolia's regard for New Delhi, Modi was granted the rare honour of addressing a specially convened session of the Mongolian parliament on a holiday.[77] The resulting declaration of elevating bilateral relations to a Strategic Partnership was essentially a reciprocation of Mongolia's decision to rank India as a key third neighbour. Mongolia's emergence as a key part of India's Northeast Asian policy enabled both states to pursue deeper political, economic, and security partnerships. Apart from their agreements in cooperation in cybersecurity, both states also stressed the need for coordinating their responses to terrorism and extremism, while also committing to safeguard the economic security of the region by preventing criminals from abusing their financial systems. This cooperation was further supported by high-level Ministry of Defence exchanges, cooperation between border security forces, and provision of training and assistance to Mongolian defence personnel.[78] India and Mongolia also have accelerated their cooperation in the field of energy security, with a US$1 billion Mongol refinery project supported by New Delhi, with considerations for Ulaanbaatar's inclusion in the New Delhi driven International Solar Alliance (ISA).[79]

It is important to note that India and Mongolia have a convergence of views on matters of global and regional security and a shared vision of a multipolar world order. In this spirit, both have several commitments to support one another in regional and international multilateral forums, so that they may effectively address both traditional and non-traditional security challenges. These concepts were reiterated in a Joint Statement following President Battulga's visit to India last September. Moreover, in a representation of their shared vision, Mongolia affirmed its support of India's Indo-Pacific vision that aims to establish a stable, prosperous, free, open and inclusive region guided by a rules-based system, and firmly founded in international law.[80] This shared Indo-Pacific vision, that India is leaning heavily on amidst its current geopolitical and security environment, can be a key aspect as both states take national security cooperation further.

The making of a strategic partnership?

Despite the injection of new energy into Indian-Mongolian ties, there remains considerable need and scope for furthering bilateral strategic relations, especially under the current, post-pandemic scenario. The pandemic has, to put it simply, sent the region's and the world's economic and security environment into a flux. It has caused countries to recalibrate their domestic and international outlooks as they not only attempt to deal with the ramifications of COVID-19 but also maximise the situation and rebuild resilient economies and global value chains. At the same time, they also are attempting to deal with the changing security dynamics.

The first half of the Twenty-first century possibly has shown the world what China's rise could look like if Beijing does not temper its international outlook and ambitions. Many states, including India, Australia, and Japan have felt the ill-effects of Beijing's adventurism, leading to a recalculation of their economic, foreign, and security policies, even as they remain considerably dependent on the Chinese economy.[81] In this context, India and Mongolia must also seek to revitalise their bilateral ties if they are to take advantage of the regional flux and further their shared ambitions.

Deeper economic integration

Although both India and Mongolia have sought to deepen trade ties through multiple agreements and memorandums, their bilateral trade has not grown as expected and is not particularly impressive. At the beginning of the decade, Mongolia was lauded as the world's fastest-growing economy, with more than 17 per cent GDP growth, in 2011, and its rich mineral reserves, worth roughly US$1 trillion gave the land-locked nation the title of "Mine-golia".[82] With vast natural resources, Mongolia joined a list of other Eurasian nations, such as Kazakhstan, Kyrgyzstan, and Uzbekistan, that are selling these to a rapidly growing China with its almost insatiable energy demands.[83] Mongolia's abundant reserves of minerals such as coal, uranium, gold, and copper—exactly what China has an insatiable appetite for—meant that the country was perfectly positioned to supply to a growing China and, therefore, boost its own economy. As China's coal needs grow exponentially, its key target to meet these ever-increasing demands for fuel has been Mongolia's Tavan Tolgoi—one of the world's largest undeveloped coal reserves.[84] Consequently, many analysts predicted that the GDP in real terms would more than double or possibly even triple with an average growth of 12 per cent year-on-year.[85]

However, this mineral boom quickly died down with falling commodity prices sharply driving down economic growth, which reached an all-time low of 1.17 per cent in 2016. The decline was prompted by numerous factors. Mongolia's economy was unsustainably dependent on Beijing; China formed over 88 per cent of Mongolia's total export market—a number, which stands at 82.5 per cent as of 2018.[86] As the Chinese economy slowed, mineral prices fell substantially, and, as a result, the Mongolian economy plunged.[87] At the same time, the economy was impacted by the "Dutch disease",[88] meaning that the overwhelming focus on mining led to a neglect of existing sectors like agriculture. The Mongolian government also undertook an ill-advised spending spree in order to build infrastructure. Much of the funds were spent badly, leading to government massive debt to the tune of almost 80 per cent of GDP.[89] These problems were compounded further by China's trade sanctions following the Dalai Lama's 2016 visit to Ulaanbaatar. Although there has been gradual return to economic growth since then, the COVID-19 pandemic seems to have set it back once again.[90]

Under such circumstances, there has been limited momentum in Indian-Mongolian trade ties. Currently, India accounts for only 0.02 per cent of Mongolian exports and 1.51 per cent of its imports, significantly less than China and countries in Northeast and Southeast Asia, including Japan, South Korea, Singapore and Vietnam, not to mention other global partners like the US, United Kingdom, Italy and Russia.[91] Although trade has grown over the last two decades, it remains impeded by a lack of connectivity. As India looks to strategically enhance its outreach in the greater Asian region, amplifying trade links with Mongolia must be a key priority for India's Northeast Asian policy. In fact, India's focus on economic growth through enhancing manufacturing and production under Modi's domestic initiatives, such as "Make in India" and "Atmanirbhar Barat" ("Self-reliant India"), its own energy needs likely will increase considerably.[92] This offers immense potential for scaling economic interactions through both bilateral trade as well as foreign direct investments (FDIs) between the countries. There is, hence, immense untapped potential to expand the scope of Indian-Mongolian trade ties in the energy sector.

However, both countries must accelerate their initiatives in building infrastructure for direct air connectivity in order to tap into this potential. With Mongolia completely encircled by Russia and China, all its external communication and trade is dependent on these two countries, which means that India's land-based links must necessarily pass through China. If Indian-Chinese ties deteriorate, as they are likely to under the current circumstances, India's trade connectivity with Mongolia will be at risk. At the same time, New Delhi and Ulaanbaatar also will need to improve their ease of doing business and prioritise creating a business-friendly environment that reduces restrictions and attracts FDI, if they are to speed up their economic integration. India's US$1 billion grant announced in 2015 during Modi's visit was a critical step in this direction. This line of credit is being used to finance infrastructure and provide technical support for an oil refinery set to be completed by 2022 that will be capable of producing 1.5 million tonnes of crude oil per year.[93]

For Mongolia, the fundamental aim moving forward will be to diversify its exports and its trade competitiveness. Ulaanbaatar will need to prioritise strengthening its value supply chains and enhancing the efficiency of its economic corridor.[94] This will translate into a two-fold focus: Firstly, to bolster industries other than mining, such as renewable energy, agriculture, and tourism to name a few, so as to reduce over-dependence on mineral wealth. The aim will be to maximise its mineral endowments for a more variegated and inclusive growth that ultimately will enable sustained productivity growth. This will, as Andrei Mikhanev, World Bank Country Manager for Mongolia, stated, require a "fundamental shift in approach the puts investing in minds on an equal footing with mines."[95] Secondly, Mongolia also must make every effort to diversify its economy to reduce overdependence on its immediate powerhouse neighbours, if it is to grow sustainably. The Mongolian economy already has felt the impact of over-reliance on China in the past decade with economic busts corresponding to falling demand in China or geopolitical tensions with Beijing. As a result, the focus of the country should be to promote trade relations with its "third neighbours", and India can emerge as a key partner in this arena.

India and Mongolia must, in this context, expand their relationship beyond their mineral trade into sectors that include information and communication technology, renewable energy, and mining sectors where, despite some progress, significant unfulfilled potential exists for cooperation. In particular, solar energy remains a field in which India can offer immense support, both financial and expertise, to Mongolia. New Delhi also could emerge as a key partner by investing in infrastructure and connectivity development alongside projects such as building of Information Technology (IT) parks and special economic zones (SEZs).[96] With the pandemic highlighting the shortcomings in Mongolia's health infrastructure, this could be another area for coordination between both countries.

In other words, moving forward, India and Mongolia must focus on building a comprehensive trade partnership that is diverse and inclusive, and seek to situate their trade ties as a developmental partnership, within the scopes of India's AEP and Mongolia's third neighbour policies. While India may have little hope of matching China's economic clout in Mongolia any time soon, it must, nonetheless, continue to enhance trade and establish itself as a responsible economic partner for Mongolia's vast natural resources. Both countries must build on their spiritual and democratic links in order to realise the significant potentials in their complementary economies.

The China factor

Both India and Mongolia also face a shared strategic concern in China, even as both are considerably dependent on the Chinese economy. As India faces a rapidly bellicose China, particularly in the post-Galwan era,[97] the Indo-Pacific ideal is gaining momentum in its political-security nexus at both the international and domestic levels. As a part of this initiative, India increasingly has been active in establishing deeper ties with strategically critical states. This has included the signing of defence logistics pacts with Australia and Japan,[98] as well as the launching of new forums such as the India-France-Australia dialogue.[99] Although not always created with the idea of containing China, many of the Indo-Pacific groupings, including the Australia-Japan-India (AJI) and Japan-America-India (JAI) trilateral groupings,[100] and the Quadrilateral Security Dialogue (Quad 2.0) are quickly gaining this characteristic since managing China's rise has become one of the key priorities for most states in the region.

Mongolia, too, sees China as a major security concern, both in terms of its economic and political clout. As Reeves has argued, "Mongolia's economic dependence on China coupled with weak political security have allowed China to develop structural power over Mongolia's domestic institutions."[101] This power presents a threat to Mongolian cultural and environmental security. Even as economic relations have intensified, Ulaanbaatar has remained wary of Chinese influence. This is evidenced by the recent tensions between both countries over China's heavy-handed new language policy replacing Mongolian with Mandarin in its Inner Mongolian Autonomous province, in a further attempt to assimilate the country's national minorities. The move caused not only widespread protests[102] in the province but also raised concern amongst Mongols across the border.

Mongolians from both areas saw the policy as Beijing's attempt to suppress their culture and subvert their inalienable right to learn their language. When Chinese Foreign Minister Wang Yi visited Ulaanbaatar on September 15–16, 2020,[103] the city saw the breakout of a rare protest, not often witnessed in the last 30 years.[104] Hundreds of people gathered shouting slogans such as "Wang Yi go away" and "Let's protect our native language",[105] demanding their government take action. Mongolia's former president Tsakhia Elbegdorj added his voice in a tweet about the protests by calling the situation "cultural genocide" and stating that "No matter where you live, as long as you are a Mongolian, you should join this movement. Without the Mongolian language, there is no Mongolian nation we can speak of."[106]

However, even though there clearly is widespread fear and suspicion of China, Mongolia realises that any official statement on the issue could invite violent backlash in the form of trade interruptions from Beijing. China has time and again employed its own particular brand of "wolf warrior" diplomacy and coercive tactics with its trade partners to inflict swift retaliation for any perceived slights (cases in point being Australia and South Korea). Therefore, while Mongolia obviously can ill afford to alienate the economic giant, it is no doubt gravely concerned about how Beijing may use undue influence if it grows more belligerent, thus giving New Delhi and Ulaanbaatar a key reason to accelerate ties and diversify from the PRC now.

From this perspective, Mongolia too can become a state of particular interest to India's vision in the near future. Mongolia's role in the region is gradually becoming more important, as it moves away from its perception as a buffer state to that of a bridge between great Northeast Asian powers and a perfect site for peaceful negotiations, much like Helsinki in Europe.[107] With both nations shaping a joint vision for the Indo-Pacific, their ties can translate into a strategic global partnership, with room for cooperation through various emerging multilateral platforms in the Indo-Pacific. More importantly, three of Mongolia's strategic third neighbours include Japan, the US, and, to some extent, Australia—India's Quad partners. This allows both New Delhi and Ulaanbaatar to explore opportunities for Mongolia's inclusion, alongside South Korea, in an expanded Quad framework—the Quad Plus. As they seek to enhance cooperation, India and Mongolia also can consider forming trilateral groupings with other partners in the Northeast Asian region, especially Japan, in order to add a new dimension to their ties. The emergence of such platforms could provide both countries additional avenues to deepen their security partnership and open opportunities for enhancing military cooperation. For instance, India and Mongolia can develop further synergy by New Delhi stepping up its capacity building programmes in the country. With platforms like the Ulaanbaatar Dialogue on Northeast Asia Security (UBD), the country's most prominent initiative,[108] Mongolia has begun to establish itself as a bridge in Northeast Asia. Therefore, if India wants to realise its foreign policy ambitions, driving its partnership with the geo-strategically located state of Mongolia could be critical and complementary to its objectives in the region.

The North Korea matrix

One key aspect of further cooperation between India and Mongolia can come from their respective bilateral ties with the reclusive North Korean state. In India's Mongolian policy, India maintains a fine balance of the third neighbour without running into Russia and China. Similarly, with North Korea, India avoids confrontations in its ties with South Korea and US-China rivalry. Advocating peace has been at the centre of India's Northeast Asia policy. Since the 1950s, New Delhi has been a staunch supporter of denuclearisation as a means to peace and stability on the Korean peninsula. Embedded in its tradition of non-alignment, India has been one of the few countries outside of China to establish diplomatic ties with the hermit nation and maintain an embassy in Pyongyang.[109] Unlike the Western states, most of whom share a contentious, or negligible, relationship with the DPRK, India has endeavoured to engage in "dialogue diplomacy" with the country instead of isolating it.[110] In this spirit, despite UN sanctions limiting the extend of ties India could feasibly pursue with Pyongyang, as well as India's own concerns regarding the DPRK's nuclear missile programme, New Delhi has maintained strong bilateral ties through areas such as humanitarian (largely food and medical) aid, technical assistance and training, and trade ties.[111] In fact, until the UN's economic sanctions halted all but essential food and medicinal trade in 2017, India was North Korea's second-largest trading partner.[112]

India's ties with the reclusive nation are underpinned by growing Indian ambitions to broaden its influence in the Indo-Pacific and to be a more proactive player in regional security matters. Keeping this in mind, New Delhi has pursued a growing engagement with the DPRK despite US criticism and under conditions wherein a shift away from Pyongyang, in fact, could be more conducive to enhancing its partnerships with the Quad nations. This suggests that New Delhi is interested in playing the long game. It is, for all intents and purposes, seeking to position itself as a vital channel of communication with the DPRK, so as to carve a role for itself in peace and denuclearisation negotiations.

However, this will be exceedingly complicated considering the deep-rooted involvement of major powers, such as China and the US, on the Korean Peninsula. In fact, in the past, critical players in the region (US, China, Japan, Russia, and South Korea) have not been entirely forthcoming about inviting Indian participation in the peace process for the Korean Peninsula. At the same time, India traditionally has not been included in South Korean Prime Minister Moon Jae-in's main peace-building strategy in the region, the Northeast Asia Plus Community of Responsibility-sharing (NEAPC).[113] The NEAPC was outlined first by Moon in his election manifesto but it remained limited to the US, China, Japan, and Russia. Although seeking multilateral support in face of the DPRK's threat and bolstering international diplomatic and security cooperation to propagate peace processes on the peninsula have long been the ROK's primary approaches in its North Korea policy,[114] India has not figured as a prominent player in the same.

That is not to say that India does not hold a prominent place in the ROK's international outlook. In addition to ASEAN,[115] New Delhi is a prominent focus of Seoul's New Southern Policy (NSP) that falls under the NEAPC framework that emerged as a part of the Moon administration's agenda after his election.[116] Nevertheless, India-ROK ties have yet to reach their full potential under the NSP, in terms of both peace cooperation on the Korean Peninsula and traditional political-security coordination. The involvement of major regional players, who are seemingly reluctant to grant India a seat at the table, presents a structural barrier to New Delhi's active contribution, particularly seeing as both the ROK and India are global middle powers. This considerably limits India's strategic choices, despite the potential it holds in facilitating peace and perhaps even making North Korea a "normal state."[117] In order to build a substantive presence in Northeast Asia and the Indo-Pacific and achieve its major power aspirations, New Delhi must positively harness its ties to both North and South Korea. By investing in deeper societal, cultural and economic engagement, India can strengthen and sustain peace-building initiatives and facilitate Korean rapprochement, perhaps even unification.[118]

North Korea also features prominently in Mongolia's regional foreign policy, with both countries sharing a long history and broad diplomatic ties, reinforced in recent years by their shared challenges of unsustainable dependence on China and geographical isolation from the broader region. Although the DPRK has not been explicitly mentioned under Mongolia's third neighbour policy, unlike South Korea, it is considered a partner state under foreign policy protocols calling for establishing ties with developing nations and former Soviet territories. In 2013, Mongolian President Elbegdorj visited Pyongyang, the first head of state to do so under a Kim Jong-un led DPRK although he did not actually meet Kim during the trip. The visit witnessed the signing of numerous bilateral agreements spanning agricultural, economic and societal cooperation.[119] Most prominently, the Mongolian President delivered a lecture entitled "It is the Human Desire to Live Free that is the Eternal Power" at Kim Il-Sung University. This speech not only demonstrated the closeness of Mongolia-DPRK ties but also did much to elevate Elbegdorj's international profile, and thereby place Mongolia as a potential arbitrator in international discussions over the Korean Peninsula.[120] Here, it is important to note that despite positive ties, Mongolia has criticised the DPRK's nuclear programme as a threat to regional stability.[121]

Described as a "unique relationship"[122] of "traditional allies,"[123] Mongolia's ties with the DPRK have long been considered a potential avenue for establishing peace and security mechanisms on the Korean peninsula. Mongolian politicians frequently have suggested that Ulaanbaatar could play the role of an intermediary to arbitrate normalisation of ties between the North and the South. The embeddedness of neutrality in Mongolian foreign policy presents it with a critical advantage here by allowing it to share a robust relationship with the US, Japan and South Korea under the third neighbour policy, a strong tie with its southern neighbour China that is rooted in its economic dependence, and a close connection to the largely isolated North Korea, which has only enhanced over time. Mongolia's history of facilitating talks between the US and the DPRK and Japan and the DPRK adds to its position as a potential broker in the future. The UBD, which has been successfully organised since 2013, is an example of the unique role that the country can play in promoting transnational dialogues and cooperation in areas such as economic integration, cross-border infrastructure development, and environmental issues.[124] North Korea's notable participation in the UBD three times clearly demonstrates that such a platform, particularly when held in a neutral state like Mongolia, can open doors.

Therefore, with both India and Mongolia looking to support the peace-making process and facilitating inter-Korean rapprochement, they can benefit by coordinating their policies. Ulaanbaatar and New Delhi could explore new dimensions to their ties by examining ways that they could collaborate and dovetail their respective Korean policies in order to play a more tangible and effective role in the future in the Korean peninsula and in Northeast Asia. With Korea essentially being a site for contest between not only the DPRK and ROK but also among great powers such as the US and China, New Delhi and Ulaanbaatar can identify themselves as neutral parties with no direct stake in the region and a genuine commitment to peace and stability. Not only could joint efforts between the two countries prove to be more effective and offer concrete and meaningful contributions to the regional security architecture, but they also might serve furtherance of their interests and aspirations in Northeast Asia and the whole Indo-Pacific region.

Conclusion

Despite the deep-rooted spiritual bonds that India and Mongolia have shared since antiquity, these ties have not yet translated into a robust partnership today. However, Modi's historic 2015 visit to Ulaanbaatar added momentum to their bilateral ties, even elevating them to the status of a Strategic Partnership and dispelling feelings of neglect amongst Mongolians that have persisted despite their own regard for India. Nevertheless, considering the true and expansive potential that their relationship holds, both sides moving forward must accord greater priority to the other. Much like in today's India, there exists a widespread discontent with Beijing and a profound wariness of what the rise of a revisionist China, and consequently a world made in the image of Chinese socialist thought, may mean for the territorial sovereignty and self-determinism of small power states. As a result, with current global power shifts and a region in flux with tensions heightened along flashpoints, New Delhi and Ulaanbaatar must explore avenues to enhance engagement in a comprehensive and strategic manner. In other words, as geopolitics in the region intensify, Mongolia no doubt will play a critical role, and if India is to realise its ambitions to establish itself as a major Asian power, it must accord Mongolia a greater status and priority in its diplomatic policy towards Northeast Asia and the world.

In this context, this chapter has highlighted key areas where both nations can pursue deeper ties. Economic engagement, in particular, remains an avenue which is far from being fully realised. As Mongolia seeks to diversify its trade, not only in terms of its partners but also its commodities, India can be a critical future partner. Urgent progress in establishing lines of direct air connectivity can help to overcome key obstacles to trade and to boost commerce between both countries. As a rising power with a focus on manufacturing, India is essentially in the same position as China was a decade or so ago; therefore, its energy needs are expected to rise exponentially. With Mongolia's considerable mineral reserves, India can become a key market in this arena, while helping reduce Mongolia's unsustainable reliance on China.

At the same time, with both countries focusing on renewable sources of energy to meet their demands and to create a sustainable, green economy to tackle climate change, there exists ample room for coordination moving forward in areas such as solar power. In addition, both countries must seriously explore ways to enhance their security partnership, considering their synergised international outlooks and shared challenges in managing China's rise while being considerably dependent on it. For this, New Delhi and Ulaanbaatar must consider adding a global dimension to their partnership. Both countries in the past already have successfully supported each other on multilateral platforms like the UN and NAM. Now, with changing global dynamics raising the criticality of the Indo-Pacific region, this can, and should, feature as a prominent element of their bilateral calculus in the future. In this vein, it is time for India and Mongolia to build on their "spiritual neighbour" ideals and mobilise the convergence in their strategic security outlooks, in terms of both traditional and non-traditional security, to advance their strategic partnership towards a comprehensive, global one.

Notes

1 For arguments surrounding India's shift to a "pointed alignment" strategy, see Jagannath Panda, "Modi's 'self-reliant India' has key foreign policy aspects," *Asia Times,* July 13, 2020, at https://asiatimes.com/2020/07/modis-self-reliant-india-has-key-foreign-policy-aspects/ (accessed September 29, 2020); Jagannath Panda, "A Moving Partnership of Consequential Democracies," *Japan Forward,* September 28, 2020, at https://japan-forward.com/asias-next-page-a-moving-partnership-of-consequential-democracies/ (accessed September 29, 2020); Marco Giannangeli, "UK could bolster India's military as Brexit Britain stands up to China's aggression," *Express,* July 12, 2020, at https://www.express.co.uk/news/politics/1308458/china-vs-india-china-news-UK-world-war-3 (accessed September 29, 2020).

2 For an account of the transformation in Indian foreign policy from regional to a global orientation, see Takenori Horimoto, "Explaining India's Foreign Policy: From Dream to Realization of Major Power," *International Relations of the Asia-Pacific,* 17 (3), 2017, pp. 463–496, at https://doi.org/10.1093/irap/lcx011. Also see Rani Vinti, "India's foreign policy and economic liberalization," *TRANS Asian Journal of Marketing & Management Research* 6 (7), 2017, pp. 10–17, at http://www.indianjournals.com/ijor.aspx?target=ijor:tajmmr&volume=6&issue=7&article=002 (accessed September 20, 2020); Chris Ogden, *Indian Foreign Policy: Ambition and Transition,* Polity Press, Cambridge, 2014, Chapters 3–4. For a more complete picture of India's foreign policy, see Harsh

V. Pant, *Indian Foreign Policy: An Overview*, Manchester University Press, Manchester, 2016.
3 Arijit Mazumdar, "India's Search for a Post-Cold War Foreign Policy: Domestic Constraints and Obstacles," *India Quarterly: A Journal of International Affairs* 67 (2), SAGE Journals, June 2011, pp. 165–182.
4 To better understand India's neighbourhood policies since 1947 and their continuity and change, see Prasanta Sahoo, "A History of India's Neighbourhood Policy," *World Affairs: The Journal of International Issues* 20 (3), JSTOR, Autumn 2016, pp. 66–81. For a broad outlook on Indian foreign policy, also see works like C. Raja Mohan, *Crossing the Rubicon: The Shaping of India's New Foreign Policy*, Palgrave Macmillan, New Delhi, 2004; Achal Malhotra, "India's Relationship with its Neighbours: Conflict and Cooperation," Ministry of External Affairs, Government of India, March 6, 2014, at https://mea.gov.in/conflit-cooperation.htm (accessed September 21, 2020).
5 Xenia Dormandy, "India's Foreign Policy," Harvard Kennedy School Belfer Center for Science and International Affairs, November 5, 2007, at https://www.belfercenter.org/publication/indias-foreign-policy (accessed September 21, 2020). Also see James Chiriyankandath, "Realigning India: Indian foreign policy after the Cold War," *The Commonwealth Journal of International Affairs* 93 (374), 2004, pp. 199–211, at https://doi.org/10.1080/00358530410001679567. For a historical context of India's rise and the potential role it could play in leading Asia, see Varun Sahni, "India and the Asian Security Architecture," *Current History* 105 (690), 2006, at https://doi.org/10.1525/curh.2006.105.690.1 63. For a background on India's rise as a nuclear power, its motivations and commitment to non-proliferation, see Tanvi Madan, *The Brookings Foreign Policy Studies Energy Security Series: India*, The Brookings Institution, Washington DC, November 2006, at https://www.brookings.edu/wp-content/uploads/2016/06/2006india.pdf (accessed September 21, 2020).
6 See Part II titled "The Gujral Doctrine" in Inder Kumar Gujral, *Continuity and Change: India's Foreign Policy*, Macmillan, New Delhi, 2003. Also see Padmaja Murthy, "The Gujral Doctrine and Beyond," *Strategic Analysis* 23 (4), July 1999.
7 Manmohan Singh, "Make 21st Century Truly an Asian Century: PM, Prime Minister's Office," Government of India, December 12, 2005, at http://pib.nic.in/newsite/erelease.aspx?relid714102 (accessed September 22, 2020); Manmohan Singh, "Opening Remarks By Prime Minister at 10th India-ASEAN Summit, Prime Minister's Office," Government of India, November 19, 2012, at http://pib.nic.in/newsite/erelease.aspx?relid789110 (accessed September 22, 2020); Thongkholal Haokip, "India's Look East Policy: Its Evolution and Approach," *South Asian Survey* 18 (2), September 2011, pp. 239–257, at https://doi.org/10.1177/0971523113513368.
8 Ministry of External Affairs, "Looking East," *Pioneer*, January 9, 2001, at https://mea.gov.in/articles-in-indian-media.htm?dtl/18431/Looking+East;
Harsh V. Pant, "India's 'Look East' policy gathers momentum," *Business Standard*, February 27, 2011, at https://mea.gov.in/articles-in-indian-media.htm?dtl/14379/Indias+Look+East+policy+gathers+momentum (accessed September 22, 2020).
9 S. Jaishankar elaborated his case for India's new, ambitious and proactive foreign policy in contradiction to voices arguing that despite a rebranding, Modi's foreign policy lacked substantive change. See Prashanth Parameswaran, "A New 'Proactive' Indian Foreign Policy under Modi?," *Diplomat*, July 21, 2015, at https://thediplomat.com/2015/07/is-india-advancing-a-new-proactive-

foreign-policy-under-modi/, (accessed September 23, 2020); Prashanth Parameswaran, "India Needs a More Ambitious Foreign Policy, Says Country's Top Diplomat," *Diplomat,* July 21, 2015, at https://thediplomat.com/2015/07/india-needs-a-more-ambitious-foreign-policy-says-countrys-top-diplomat/ (accessed September 23, 2020). Also see Raja Mohan, *Modi's World: Expanding India's Sphere of Influence,* HarperCollins, New Delhi, 2015.

10 Prime Minister's Office, "PM to Heads of Indian Missions," *PM India,* February 7, 2015, at https://www.pmindia.gov.in/en/news_updates/pm-greets-engineers-on-engineers-day/?comment=disable (accessed September 22, 2020).

11 Subrahmanyam Jaishankar, "India, the United States and China," International Institute for Strategic Studies, July 20, 2015, at https://www.iiss.org/en/events/events/archive/2015-f463/july-636f/fullerton-lecture-jaishankar-f64e (accessed September 22, 2020).

12 Sanjay Singh, "Question No. 3692 Neighbourhood First Policy: Rajya Sabha," Ministry of External Affairs, July 25, 2019, at https://mea.gov.in/rajya-sabha.htm?dtl/31673/QUESTION+NO3692+NEIGHBOURHOOD+FIRST+POLICY (accessed September 23, 2020). Also see Rani D. Mullen, "Indian Development Assistance: The Centralization and Mercantilization of Indian Foreign Policy," in Surupa Gupta, Rani D. Mullen, Rajesh Basrur, Ian Hall, Nicolas Blarel, Manjeet S. Pardesi, Sumit Ganguly (eds), "Indian Foreign Policy under Modi: A New Brand or Just Repackaging?," *International Studies Perspectives* 20 (1), February 2019, pp. 1–45, at https://doi.org/10.1093/isp/eky008.

13 Prime Minister's Office, "Details of Foreign/Domestic Visits," *PM India,* updated April 8, 2020, at https://www.pmindia.gov.in/en/details-of-foreigndomestic-visits/ (accessed September 23, 2020).

14 Press Trust of India, "'Look East' policy now turned into 'Act East' policy: Modi," *Hindu,* November 13, 2014, at https://www.thehindu.com/news/national/look-east-policy-now-turned-into-act-east-policy-modi/article6595186.ece (accessed September 23, 2020).

15 Manjeet S. Pardesi, "Modi, from 'Look East' to 'Act East': Semantic or Substantive Change?" in Surupa Gupta, et al,

16 For an outline of India's outreach to Northeast Asia in context of China, Japan and South Korea, see Wooyeal Paik and Rajiv Kumar, "India's Extended "Act East" Outreach to Northeast Asia: Its Economic and Security Interactions with China, Japan, and South Korea," *The Korean Journal of International Studies* 17 (1), April 2019, pp. 1–29, at http://dx.doi.org/10.14731/kjis.2019.4.17.1.1.

17 See Prime Minister's Office, "India-Japan Vision Statement," press release, Release ID: 1551159, Press Information Bureau, Government of India, October 29, 2018, at https://pib.gov.in/PressReleasePage.aspx?PRID=1551159 (accessed September 24, 2020); Ministry of Foreign Affairs of Japan, "Japan-India Joint Statement," Government of Japan, September 14, 2017, at http://www.mofa.go.jp/files/0002 89999.pdf (accessed September 24, 2020); Ministry of External Affairs, "Joint Statement on India and Japan Vision 2025: Special Strategic and Global Partnership Working Together for Peace and Prosperity of the Indo-Pacific Region and the World (December 12, 2015)," Government of India, December 12, 2015, at https://www.mea.gov.in/bilateral-documents.htm?dtl/26176/Joint_Statement_on_India_and_Japan_Vision_2025_Special_Strategic_and_Global_Partnership_Working_Together_for_Peace_and_Prosperity_of_the_IndoPacific_R (accessed September 24, 2020).

18 Ministry of External Affairs, "Joint Statement on India and Japan Vision 2025."

19 Ministry of External Affairs, "The entry into force of India-Japan Agreement for Cooperation in the Peaceful Uses of Nuclear Energy," Government of India,

July 20, 2017, at https://mea.gov.in/press-releases.htm?dtl/28678/The_entry_into_force_of_IndiaJapan_Agreement_for_Cooperation_in_the_Peaceful_Uses_of_Nuclear_Energy (accessed September 24, 2020).
20 Ministry of Foreign Affairs of Japan, "Agreement Between the Government of Japan and the Government of the Republic of India Concerning Reciprocal Provision of Supplies and Services Between the Self-Defense Forces of Japan and the Indian Armed Forces," Government of Japan, September 10, 2020, at https://www.mofa.go.jp/files/100091751.pdf (accessed September 24, 2020).
21 The Quad 2.0 is a security dialogue between the United States, Japan, Australia and India, which analysts have referred to as a "democratic security diamond." Although the idea for the grouping was first envisioned in a speech (entitled "Confluence of the Two Seas") by Japanese Prime Minister Shinzo Abe in 2007 at the Indian Parliament, the Dialogue was only revived in November 2017 amidst growing tensions between the US and China and a widespread wariness of Beijing's growing aggression. For an interesting take on the Quad's future with India's post-Galwan shift in foreign policy, see Jeff M. Smith, "Democracy's Squad: India's Change of Heart and the Future of the Quad," *War on the Rocks,* August 13, 2020, at https://warontherocks.com/2020/08/democracys-squad-indias-change-of-heart-and-the-future-of-the-quad/ (accessed September 24, 2020). Also see Patrick Gerard Buchan and Benjamin Rimland, *Defining the Diamond: The Past, Present, and Future of Quadrilateral Security Dialogue, CSIS Briefs,* March 2020, Centre for Strategic and International Studies, Washington DC, at https://csis-website-prod.s3.amazonaws.com/s3fspublic/publication/200312_BuchanRimland_QuadReport_v2%5B6%5D.pdf (accessed September 24, 2020).
22 This initiative was first proposed and pushed by Japan and is set to launch later in 2020. See Ministry of Economy, Trade and Industry, "Australia-India-Japan Economic Ministers' Joint Statement on Supply Chain Resilience," Government of Japan, September 1, 2020, at https://www.meti.go.jp/press/2020/09/20200901008/20200901008-1.pdf (accessed September 25, 2020).
23 For a detailed analysis of China-Russia dynamics, see Paul Stronski and Nicole Ng, *Cooperation and Competition: Russia and China in Central Asia, the Russian Far East, and the Arctic,* Carnegie Endowment for International Peace, Washington DC, 2018, at https://carnegieendowment.org/files/CP_331_Stronski_Ng_Final1.pdf (accessed September 25, 2020); Nadége Rolland, "A China-Russia Condominium over Eurasia," *Survival: Global Politics and Strategy* 61 (1), 2019, pp. 7–22, at https://doi.org/10.1080/00396338.2019.1568043; Alexander Korolev, "Systemic Balancing and Regional Hedging: China-Russia Relations," *The Chinese Journal of International Politics* 9 (4), 2016, pp. 375–397, at https://doi.org/10.1093/cjip/pow013.
24 Ministry of External Affairs, "Brief on India-Mongolia Bilateral Relations," Government of India, January 2020, at https://mea.gov.in/Portal/ForeignRelation/India_Mongolia__December_2018.pdf (accessed September 25, 2020).
25 Oidov Nyamdavaa, *Mongolia-India Relations,* Pentagon Press, New Delhi, 2003, pp. 14-21; Oidov Nyamdavaa, "Ancient Cultural, Ethnic And Religious Ties Between Mongolia And India," *World Affairs: The Journal of International Issues* 19 (4), 2015, pp. 150–59, at https://www.jstor.org/stable/48505253; Agata Bareja-Starzynska and Hanna Havnevik, "A Preliminary Study of Buddhism in Present-Day Mongolia," in *Mongols from Country to City: Boundaries, Pastoralism and City Life in the Mongol Lands,* Ole Brunn and Li Narangoa (eds), NIAS, Copenhagen, 2006, pp. 212–236.
26 Ministry of External Affairs, "Brief on India-Mongolia Bilateral Relations."
27 Ibid.

28 Ibid.
29 Table compiled by authors based on documents retrieved from the Ministry of External Affairs of the Government of India. See Ministry of External Affairs, "Documents: Treaty/Agreement," Government of India, at https://www.mea.gov.in/TreatyList.htm?1 (accessed September 26, 2020); Ministry of External Affairs, "Brief on India-Mongolia Bilateral Relations"; Ministry of External Affairs, "Joint Statement for India-Mongolia Strategic Partnership (May 17, 2015)," Government of India, May 17, 2015, at https://www.mea.gov.in/bilateral-documents.htm?dtl/25253 (accessed September 26, 2020); Ministry of External Affairs, "List of MOUs/Documents signed between India and Mongolia during the State Visit of President of Mongolia to India (September 19–23, 2019)," Government of India, September 20, 2019, at https://www.mea.gov.in/bilateral-documents.htm?dtl/-31842/List_of_MoUsDocuments_signed_between_India_and_Mongolia_during_the_State_Visit_of_President_of_Mongolia_to_India_September_1923_2019 (accessed September 26, 2020).
30 Ministry of External Affairs, "Joint Statement for India-Mongolia Strategic Partnership (May 17, 2015)."
31 Ibid.
32 Ibid. and Ministry of External Affairs, "Brief on India-Mongolia Bilateral Relations."
33 Ministry of External Affairs, "Brief on India-Mongolia Bilateral Relations."
34 Ministry of External Affairs, "Press Statement by External Affairs Minister during the Joint Media Briefing with Foreign Minister of Mongolia," Government of India, April 25, 2018, at https://fsi.mea.gov.in/outgoing-visit-detail.htm?29843/Press+Statement+by+External+Affairs+Minister+during+the+Joint+Media+Briefing+with+Foreign+Minister+of+Mongolia (accessed September 26, 2020). Also see Prabir De and Sreya Pan, "India-Mongolia Economic Relations: Current Status and Future Prospect," *The Northeast Asian Economic Review* 5 (2), October 2017, at https://www.erina.or.jp/en/wp-content/uploads/2018/05/naer52-3_tssc.pdf (accessed September 26, 2020). For limitations on their trade ties and areas for expanding their scope, see Imtiyaz Ahmad Shah and Neelofar Rashid, "Economic Analysis of Bilateral Trade: A Case Study of India-Mongolia," *International Journal of Economics* 7 (3), June 2019, pp. 1–6, at https://doi.org/10.34293/economics.v7i3.408.
35 For a list of these diplomatic visits to both India and Mongolia, see Ministry of External Affairs, "Brief on India-Mongolia Bilateral Relations."
36 Ministry of External Affairs, "Visit of External Affairs Minister to Mongolia (April 25–26, 2018)," Government of India, April 26, 2018, at https://www.mea.gov.in/press-releases.htm?dtl/29847/Visit_of_External_Affairs_Minister_to_Mongolia_2526_April_2018 (accessed September 26, 2020); Ministry of External Affairs, "Press Statement by External Affairs Minister during the Joint Media Briefing with Foreign Minister of Mongolia."
37 See Ministry of External Affairs, "State Visit of President of Mongolia to India (September 19–23, 2019)," Government of India, September 16, 2019, at https://www.mea.gov.in/press-releases.htm?dtl/31826/State_Visit_of_President_of_Mongolia_to_India_September_1923_2019 (accessed September 26, 2020); Ministry of External Affairs, "Visit of President of Mongolia to India (September 19–23, 2019)," Government of India, September 20, 2019, at https://mea.gov.in/press-releases.htm?dtl/31840/Visit_of_President_of_Mongolia_to_India_September_1923_2019 (accessed September 26, 2020); Prime Minister's Office, "PM meets the President of Mongolia, Mr. Khaltmaagiin Battulga, in New Delhi (September 20, 2019)," *PM India*, September 20, 2019, at https://

www.pmindia.gov.in/en/eventgallery/pm-meets-the-president-of-mongolia-mr-khaltmaagiin-battulga-in-new-delhi-september-20-2019/ (accessed September 26, 2020).
38 Ministry of External Affairs, "Joint Statement on Strengthening the Strategic Partnership between India and Mongolia," Government of India, September 20, 2019, at https://www.mea.gov.in/bilateral-documents.htm?dtl/31841/Joint_Statement_on_Strengthening_the_Strategic_Partnership_between_India_and_Mongolia (accessed September 26, 2020).
39 See Department of Space, "Cabinet approves agreement between India and Mongolia on Cooperation in the Exploration and Uses of Outer Space for Peaceful and Civilian Purposes," press release, Press Information Bureau, Government of India, January 8, 2020, at https://pib.gov.in/Pressreleaseshare.aspx?PRID=1598725 (accessed September 26, 2020); Ministry of External Affairs, "List of MOUs/Documents signed between India and Mongolia during the State Visit of President of Mongolia to India (September 19–23, 2019)."
40 For a brief overview of the US-Chinese trade war, see Dorcas Wong and Alexander Chipman Koty, "The US-China Trade War: A Timeline," *China Briefing,* August 25, 2020, at https://www.china-briefing.com/news/the-us-china-trade-war-a-timeline/ (accessed September 27, 2020). For a detailed analysis of the impact that the trade war had and will likely continue to have seen Eddy Bekkers and Sofia Schroeter, "An Economic Analysis of the US-China Trade Conflict," Working Paper, Economic Research and Statistics Division, World Trade Organization, February 2020, at https://www.wto.org/english/res_e/reser_e/ersd202004_e.pdf (accessed September 27, 2020); Marianne Schneider-Petsinger, Jue Wang, Yu Jie and James Crabtree, *US-China Strategic Competition: The Quest for Global Technological Leadership,* Royal Institute of International Affairs, Chatham House, London, 2019, at https://www.chathamhouse.org/sites/default/files/publications/research/CHHJ7480-US-China-Competition-RP-WEB.pdf (accessed September 27, 2020).
41 Dipanjan Roy Chaudhary, "China ups aggression in South China Sea through military exercises," *Economic Times,* July 9, 2019, at https://economictimes.indiatimes.com/news/defence/china-ups-aggression-in-south-china-sea-through-military-exercises/articleshow/70136317.cms?from=mdr (accessed September 26, 2020); Minnie Chan, "China is putting troops, weapons on South China Sea islands, and has every right to do so, PLA official says," *South China Morning Post,* June 2, 2018, at https://www.scmp.com/news/china/diplomacy-defence/article/2148979/china-putting-troops-weapons-south-china-sea-islands (accessed September 26, 2020). For an overview of the dispute and China's claims in the region, see Ronald O'Rourke, *U.S.-China Strategic Competition in South and East China Seas: Background and Issues for Congress,* CRS Report R42784, Congressional Research Service, Washington DC, 2020, at https://fas.org/sgp/crs/row/R42784.pdf (accessed September 26, 2020).
42 See Sumit Ganguly and Andrew Scobell, "The Himalayan Impasse: Sino-Indian Rivalry in the Wake of Doklam," *Washington Quarterly* 41 (3), 2018, pp. 177–190, at https://doi.org/10.1080/0163660X.2018.1519369.
43 See Chao Xie, "How Status-seeking States Can Cooperate: Explaining India-China Rapprochement After the Doklam Standoff," *India Quarterly* 75 (2), 2019, pp. 172-189, at https://doi.org/10.1177/0974928419841771.
44 For an analysis of how experts figured India would adjust its international outlook in reaction to the rise of China and pursue increased cooperation and coordination with strategic states in the Indo-Pacific, see T.V. Paul, "How India Will React to the Rise of China: The Soft-Balancing Strategy Reconsidered," *War on the Rocks,* September 17, 2018, at https://warontherocks.com/2018/09/

india-and-the-rise-of-china-soft-balancing-strategy-reconsidered/ (accessed September 26, 2020).
45 Jagannath Panda, "Narendra Modi's China policy: between pragmatism and power parity," *Journal of Asian Public Policy* 9 (2), 2016, pp. 185–197, at https://doi.org/10.1080/17516234.2016.1165334.
46 "China slaps new fees on Mongolian exporters amid Dalai Lama row," *Reuters*, December 1, 2016, at https://in.reuters.com/article/us-china-mongolia/china-slaps-new-fees-on-mongolian-exporters-amid-dalai-lama-row-idUSKBN13Q3I7 (accessed September 26, 2020); "China 'blocks' Mongolia border after Dalai Lama visit," *Al Jazeera*, December 10, 2016, at https://www.aljazeera.com/economy/2016/12/10/china-blocks-mongolia-border-after-dalai-lama-visit/?gb=true (accessed September 26, 2020).
47 See Geng Shuang, "Foreign Ministry Spokesperson Geng Shuang's Regular Press Conference on December 1, 2016," Ministry of Foreign Affairs, People's Republic of China, December 1, 2016, at https://www.fmprc.gov.cn/nanhai/eng/fyrbt_1/t1420605.htm (accessed September 26, 2020); Edward Wong, "Mongolia, With Deep Ties to Dalai Lama, Turn From Him Toward China," *New York Times*, December 30, 2016, at https://www.nytimes.com/2016/12/30/world/asia/china-mongolia-dalai-lama.html (accessed September 26, 2020).
48 Vikas Swarup, "Transcript of Weekly Media Briefing by Official Spokesperson (December 8, 2016)," Ministry of External Affairs, Government of India, December 9, 2016, at https://www.mea.gov.in/media-briefings.htm?dtl/27780/Transcript_of_Weekly_Media_Briefing_by_Official_Spokesperson_December_08_2016 (accessed September 26, 2020).
49 Wen Dao, "Mongolia should soul-search on hosting separatist figure," *Global Times*, December 8, 2016, at https://www.globaltimes.cn/content/1022715.shtml (accessed September 26, 2020).
50 Wen Dao, "New Delhi overreaches to meddle in China's core interests," *Global Times*, December 21, 2012, at https://www.globaltimes.cn/content/1025055.shtml (accessed September 26, 2020).
51 In an interview with an Indian newspaper, the *Times of India*, the Mongolian Ambassador to India, Gonchig Ganbold, stated that it was vital that "India raises its voice against the unilateral measures China [was] taking against [them]" especially when they were hurting the local people during a harsh winter. See Indrani Bagchi, "India to help Mongolia, staying away from its spat with China," *Times of India*, December 8, 2016, at https://timesofindia.indiatimes.com/india/India-to-help-Mongolia-staying-away-from-its-spat-with-China/articleshow/55879044.cms (accessed September 26, 2020).
52 Rob Scmitz, "Once Booming, Mongolia's Economy Veers From Riches To Rags," *National Public Radio*, December 5, 2016, at https://www.npr.org/sections/parallels/2016/12/05/504411983/once-booming-mongolias-economy-veers-from-riches-to-rags (accessed September 26, 2020).
53 It should be noted that in contrast to suggestions by the Chinese media and western political commentators, Mongolia did not issue an outright, official apology or ban future visits by the Dalai Lama. See Liu Caiyu and Yang Teo, "Mongolian government expresses regret over Dalai Lama's visit," *Global Times*, December 21, 2016, at https://www.globaltimes.cn/content/1024909.shtml (accessed September 26, 2020); Jichang Lulu, "The costs of normalisation: Norway and Mongolia respond to Chinese sanctions," *The Asian Dialogue*, February 22, 2017, at https://theasiadialogue.com/2017/02/22/the-costs-of-normalisation-norway-and-mongolia-respond-to-chinese-sanctions/ (accessed September 26, 2020).

54 Ministry of Defence, "Curtain raiser: Indo-Mongolian Joint Nomadic Elephant 2019," press release, Press Information Bureau, Government of India, October 3, 2019, at https://pib.gov.in/PressReleseDetailm.aspx?PRID=1587147 (accessed September 26, 2020); Ministry of External Affairs, "Brief on India-Mongolia Bilateral Relations."
55 United States Embassy in Mongolia, "Mongolia and U.S. Announce Their Participation in Khaan Quest 2019," press release, Public Affairs Section, June 11, 2019, at https://mn.usembassy.gov/2019-pr-khan-quest/ (accessed September 26, 2020).
56 Sharad K. Soni, "The 'Third Neighbour' Approach of Mongolia's Diplomacy of External Relations: Effects on Relations between India and Mongolia," *India Quarterly* 7 (1), 2015, pp. 37–52, at https://doi.org/10.1177/0974928414554975.
57 Vaishali Krishna, "Mongolian Foreign Policy Implications for Russia and China," *Mongolian Journal of International Affairs* 19, 2014, pp. 67–81, at https://doi.org/10.5564/mjia.v19i0.406. Also, see Ts. Batbayar and Sharad K. Soni, *Modern Mongolia: A Concise History,* Pentagon Press, New Delhi, 2007; Alicia J. Campi, "Moving Mongolian Nomadism into the 21st Century: Cultural and Ecological Preservation Coupled with Economic Vitality and National Security," *Mongolica* 9 (30), 1999; Sharad K. Soni, "Mongolia's Foreign Policy Priorities," *Himalayan and Central Asian Studies* 5 (1), January-March 2001, pp. 55–104, at https://search.proquest.com/docview/1325025318?pq-origsite=gscholar&fromopenview=true (accessed September 27, 2020); Sarah Telford, "To What Extent Does Post-1990 Mongolia Pursue an Independent Foreign Policy?," *Revista UNISCI*, 6, 2004, pp. 1–15, at https://www.redalyc.org/articulo.oa?id=76711307013 (accessed September 27, 2020).
58 Mongolia's "third neighbour" approach is essentially a foreign policy strategy that seeks to build closer bilateral relationships with countries other than Russia and China, which encircle Mongolia and have historically enjoyed influence over the country. With an aim of balancing Ulaanbaatar's bilateral equation with Moscow and Beijing, the third neighbor policy seeks to bolster Mongolia's cooperation with strategically identified nations, thereby boosting its development, in diverse areas. For a more comprehensive understanding of the third neighbourhood policy in Mongolia's foreign outlook, see Julian Dierkes, "Mongolia's 'third neighbour' policy and its impact on foreign investment," *East Asia Forum,* February 15, 2011, at https://www.eastasiaforum.org/2011/02/15/mongolias-third-neighbour-policy-and-its-impact-on-foreign-investment/ (accessed September 27, 2020); Sharad K. Soni, "Looking beyond geographic neighbours: Post-Soviet Mongolia's third Neighbour policy," in *Eurasia: Twenty years After,* Suchandana Chatterjee, Anita Sengupta and Shushmita Bhattacharya (eds), Shipra Publications, New Delhi, 2012, pp. 489; Allan Wachman, "Mongolia's geopolitical gambit: Preserving a precarious independence while resisting 'soft colonialism'," Working Paper, The East Asia Institute, 2009, at http://www.eai.or.kr/data/bbs/eng_report/2009052017262087.pdf (accessed September 27, 2020).
59 Alan Wachman, "Mongolia: Growth, Democracy, and Two Wary Neighbours," interview by Allen Wagner, National Bureau of Asian Research, May 3, 2012, at http://www.nbr.org/research/activity.aspx?id=245#.Uic9tzbI1K0 (accessed September 28, 2020).
60 Ministry of Foreign Affairs, "Diplomatic Relations—Third Neighbors," Government of Mongolia, at http://www.mfa.gov.mn/?page_id=16937&lang=en (accessed September 30, 2020); Jargalsaikhan Mendee, *Mongolia's Quest for Third Neighbours: Why the European Union?,* EUCAM Policy Brief, Centre for European Policy Studies, Brussels, 2012, at https://eucentralasia.eu/2012/07/mongolias-quest-for-third-neighbours-why-the-european-union/ (accessed September 30, 2020).

61 See Ministry of Foreign Affairs of Mongolia, "Concept of Mongolia's Foreign Policy," Government of Mongolia, February 21, 2011, at http://www.mfa.gov.mn/?page_id=26263&lang=en (accessed September 30, 2020). It should be noted that although the idea for the policy stemmed from Secretary of State James Baker's comments, the US only adopted the term officially in the late 1990s.

62 For an argument that the third neighbour policy draws on historic-cultural links as well as shared values, see Munkh-Ochir Dorjjugder, "Mongolia's "Third Neighbor" doctrine and North Korea," Brookings, January 28, 2011, at http://www.brookings.edu/papers/2011/0128_mongolia_dorjjugder.aspx, accessed September 30, 2020 (accessed September 30, 2020).

63 For an account of Mongolia's transition to a democracy, see Richard Pomfret, "Transition and Democracy in Mongolia," *Europe-Asia Studies* 52 (1), 2000, pp. 149–160, at https://doi.org/10.1080/09668130098316. For a discourse on the state of democracy in Mongolia, see Verena Fritz, "Mongolia: The Rise and Travails of a Deviant Democracy," *Democratization* 15 (4), 2008, pp. 766–788, at https://doi.org/10.1080/13510340802191060.

64 See country data for Mongolia in "Freedom in the World 2020: Countries and Territories," Freedom House, at https://freedomhouse.org/countries/freedom-world/scores (accessed October 2, 2020); "Corruption Perceptions Index," Transparency International, at https://www.transparency.org/en/cpi# (accessed October 2, 2020); "Mongolia," Bertelsmann Foundation Transformation Index, at https://www.bti-project.org/en/reports/country-dashboard-MNG.html (accessed October 2, 2020).

65 Mark Koenig, "Mongolia's Lessons on Democracy during a Pandemic," The Asia Foundation, June 24, 2020, at https://asiafoundation.org/2020/06/24/mongolias-lessons-on-democracy-during-a-pandemic/ (accessed October 2, 2020).

66 Ministry of External Affairs, "History and Evolution of Non-Aligned Movement," Government of India, August 22, 2012, at https://www.mea.gov.in/in-focus-article.htm?20349/History+and+Evolution+of+NonAligned+Movement (accessed October 2, 2020).

67 Non-Aligned Movement (NAM) Disarmament Database, James Martin Center for Nonproliferation Studies (CNS), at http://cns.miis.edu/nam/about.html (accessed December 2, 2020).

68 Tsakhia Elbegdorj, "Mongolia as a neutral state," World Economic Forum, January 18, 2016, at https://www.weforum.org/agenda/2016/01/mongolia-as-a-neutral-state/#:~:text=As%20far%20as%20Mongolia%20is,a%20%E2%80%9Cpermanently%20neutral%20state%E2%80%9D.&text=Neutrality%20enables%20a%20country%20to,quo%20of%20a%20neutral%20state (accessed December 6, 2020).

69 Permanent Mission of Mongolia to the United Nations, "Mongolia and the United Nations," United Nations, at https://www.un.int/mongolia/mongolia/mongolia-and-united-nations-0 (accessed September 28, 2020).

70 Mongolia's national security goals are incorporated and made explicit in its National Security Concept. See Government of Mongolia, "Annex to the Resolution No. 48 of the Parliament of Mongolia of 2010: National Security Concept of Mongolia," July 15, 2010, at https://www.legalinfo.mn/annex/details/8070?lawid=6163 (accessed September 28, 2020); Government of Mongolia, "National Security Concept of Mongolia," at http://www.nsc.gov.mn/sites/default/files/images/National%20Security%20Concept%20of%20Mongolia%20EN.-pdf (accessed September 28, 2020). For an overview of how Mongolia's national security doctrine developed since the beginnings of the 1990s, see Ariunsanaa Tunjin,

"Mongolia's National Security and Nuclear-Free Policy," *Korean Journal of Defense Analysis* 15 (1), 2003, pp. 101–130, at https://doi.org/10.1080/10163270309464035.
71 Soni, "The 'Third Neighbour' Approach of Mongolia's Diplomacy of External Relations: Effects on Relations between India and Mongolia."
72 A. Tuvshingtugs, "Mongolia's national security: Past, present and future perspectives," in *Mongolia in the 21st century: Society, culture and international relations*, in K. Warikoo and Sharad K. Soni (eds), Pentagon, London, 2010, p. 76. For a discussion on Mongolia's multi-pillared foreign policy, see Vaishali Krishna, "Mongolia's Foreign Policy: Profiling Fundamental Aspects," *International Journal of Applied Social Science* 4 (9 and 19), September and October 2017, pp. 402–414, at http://scientificresearchjournal.com/wp-content/plugins/download-attachments/includes/download.php?id=2569 (accessed December 6, 2020).
73 Jeffrey Reeves, "Mongolia's evolving security strategy: omni-enmeshment and balance of influence," *The Pacific Review* 25 (5), 2012, pp. 589–612, at https://doi.org/10.1080/09512748.2012.728241.
74 K. V. Prasad, "India, Mongolia ink pact for uranium supply," *Hindu*, September 14, 2009, at https://www.thehindu.com/news/national/India-Mongolia-ink-pact-for-uranium-supply/article16881429.ece (accessed October 5, 2020).
75 Brandon Joseph Miliate, "India's role in Mongolia's third neighbor policy," *Mongolia: Nomadic Culture and Globalization, Independent Study Project (ISP) Collection*, Paper 802, Fall 2009, p. 17, at http://digitalcollections.sit.edu/isp_collection/802 (accessed October 5, 2020).
76 These capacity-building efforts can be measured not only by India's multiple Line of Credits in the past decade but also by India's establishment of two training centres in Ulaanbaatar (the Atal Bihari Vajpayee Centre of Excellence in Information and Communication Technology and the Rajiv Gandhi Art and Production School), scholarships, and ITEC grants to Mongolian citizens, as well as other technical support. See Soni, "The 'Third Neighbour' Approach of Mongolia's Diplomacy of External Relations: Effects on Relations between India and Mongolia."
77 "Text of remarks by Prime Minister Narendra Modi in the Mongolian Parliament," *Hindu*, May 17, 2015, at https://www.thehindu.com/news/resources/text-of-remarks-by-prime-minister-modi-in-the-mongolian-parliament/article721 6240.ece (accessed October 5, 2020); Press Trust of India, "In a first, Narendra Modi addresses Mongolian Parliament; discovers 'special connection'," *Deccan Chronicle*, May 17, 2015, at https://www.deccanchronicle.com/150517/world-neighbours/article/first-narendra-modi-addresses-mongolian-parliament-discovers-?page=2 (accessed October 5, 2020); "PM Modi at the Ceremonial welcome in Mongolia," May 16, 2015, posted by Narendra Modi, video, 9:31, at https://www.youtube.com/watch?v=T_0OCORqjpY; "PM Modi's Historic and Path-Breaking Visit to Mongolia," Narendra Modi, May 18, 2015, at https://www.narendramodi.in/pm-modi-s-historic-and-path-breaking-visit-to-mongolia-12 6448 (accessed October 5, 2020).
78 Ministry of External Affairs, "Joint Statement on Strengthening the Strategic Partnership between India and Mongolia." For further details see Ministry of External Affairs, "Minutes of India-Mongolia Joint Committee on Cooperation," Government of India, April 25, 2018, at http://www.mea.gov.in/Uploads/PublicationDocs/29845_New_Doc_2018-04-25.pdf (accessed October 6, 2020).
79 Ministry of External Affairs, "Joint Statement on Strengthening the Strategic Partnership between India and Mongolia."

80 Ibid.
81 For Japan-China tensions in the East China Sea, see Jagannath Panda, "Why Chinese Adventurism Soars in East China Sea?," *Japan Forum for Strategic Studies,* August 3, 2020, at http://www.jfss.gr.jp/article/1263 (accessed October 6, 2020); Brahma Chellany, "China's expansionism enters dangerous phase," *Japan Times,* August 25, 2020, at https://www.japantimes.co.jp/opinion/2020/08/25/commentary/world-commentary/china-expansionism/ (accessed October 6, 2020); O'Rourke, *U.S. - China Strategic Competition in South and East China Seas: Background and Issues for Congress.* For Australia's declining relationship with China, see Anthony Galloway, "The China strategy: Australia prepared to play the long game," *The Sydney Morning Herald,* August 28, 2020, at https://www.smh.com.au/politics/federal/the-china-strategy-australia-prepared-to-play-the-long-game-20200828-p55qbe.html (accessed October 6, 2020); Felix K. Chang, "Social Distancing: Australia's Relations with China," Foreign Policy Research Institute, May 22, 2020, at https://www.fpri.org/article/2020/05/social-distancing-australias-relations-with-china/ (accessed October 6, 2020); International Institute for Strategic Studies, "The deterioration of Australia-China relations," *Strategic Comments* 26 (3), June 2020, at https://doi.org/10.1080/13567888.2020.1783863. For India-China tensions over their border dispute, see Jeff M. Smith, "The Galwan Killings Are the Nail in the Coffin for China and India's Relationship," *Foreign Policy,* June 26, 2020, at https://foreignpolicy.com/2020/06/26/galwan-border-china-india-war-conflict/ (accessed October 6, 2020); Toby Dalton and Tong Zhao, "At a Crossroads? China-India Nuclear Relations After the Border Clash," Working Paper, Carnegie Endowment for International Peace, August 2020, at https://carnegieendowment.org/files/Dalton%20Zhao%20-%20China-India%20Nuclear%20Relation.pdf (accessed October 6, 2020).
82 See Frank Langfitt, "Mineral-Rich Mongolia Rapidly Becoming 'Mine-golia'," National Public Radio, May 21, 2012, at https://www.npr.org/2012/05/21/152683549/mineral-rich-mongolia-rapidly-becoming-minegolia?singlePage=true (accessed October 7, 2020).
83 See Christina Ruth, "China's hunger for energy is insatiable," *Deutsche Welle,* July 27, 2012, at https://p.dw.com/p/15fT8 (accessed October 7, 2020); Spencer Swartz and Shai Oster, "China Tops U.S. in Energy Use: Asian Giant Emerges as No. 1 Consumer of Power, Reshaping Oil Markets, Diplomacy," *Wall Street Journal,* July 18, 2010, at https://www.wsj.com/articles/SB10001424052748703720504575376712353150310 (accessed October 7, 2020); "Could Mongolia Be the Next Dubai?," *The Atlantic,* November 9, 2011, at https://www.theatlantic.com/international/archive/2011/11/could-mongolia-be-the-next-dubai/248136/ (accessed October 7, 2020).
84 Also a source of large gold and uranium deposits. See Barry Baxter, "Insatiable Appetites," *World Coal Magazine,* May 27, 2010, at https://www.worldcoal.com/coal/27052010/insatiable_appetites/ (accessed October 7, 2020).
85 Jonathan Watts, "Gobi mega-mine puts Mongolia on brink of world's greatest resource boom," *Guardian,* November 7, 2011, at https://www.theguardian.com/environment/2011/nov/07/gobi-mega-mine-mongolia (accessed October 7, 2020); Langfitt, "Mineral-Rich Mongolia Rapidly Becoming 'Mine-golia'," National Public Radio, May 21, 2012, at https://www.npr.org/2012/05/21/152683549/mineral-rich-mongolia-rapidly-becoming-minegolia?singlePage=true (accessed October 7, 2020).
86 World Bank National Accounts Data (GDP growth (annual %) – Mongolia, at https://data.worldbank.org/indicator/NY.GDP.MKTP.KD.ZG?end=2019&locations=MN&start=2010 (accessed September 30, 2020); The Observatory of

Economic Complexity Database, Mongolia country profile, at https://oec.world/en/profile/country/mng/ (accessed September 30, 2020).
87 "How the World's Fastest-Growing Economy Went Bust," *Bloomberg*, February 13, 2017, at https://www.bloomberg.com/opinion/articles/2017-02-12/how-the-world-s-fastest-growing-economy-went-bust. Also see Alimaa Batai, Bujiimaa Enkhsaikhan, Siilen Tumurtogoo and Wing-Keung Wong, "China's Impact on Mongolian Economy," Working Paper, Asia University, 2017, at http://dx.doi.org/10.2139/ssrn.2999019.
88 "Dutch Disease" refers to the recession that hit the Netherlands' economy after the discovery of natural gas reserves in 1959 due to decline in the output of the country's traditional sector. This has frequently been compared to Mongolia's situation. Dagys, W.J.M. Heijman, Liesbeth Dries and Bake Agipar, "The mining sector boom in Mongolia: did it cause the Dutch disease?," *Post-Communist Economies* 32 (5), 2020, pp. 607–642, at https://doi.org/10.1080/14631377.2019.1689002; Wei Ge, and Henry W. Kinnucan, "The effects of Mongolia's booming mining industry on its agricultural sector: A test for Dutch disease," *Agricultural Economics* 48 (6), 2017, pp. 781-791, at https://doi.org/10.1111/agec.12374;Tserendorj Batsukh and Purevjav Avralt-Od, "Risk assessment of "Dutch Disease" in Mongolia," Discussion Paper Series No. 1, Ulaanbaatar, The Economic Research Institute, 2012, at https://www.eri.mn/download/vtzbrmbp (accessed October 7, 2020).
89 William Bikales, "Mongolia Faces a Debt Crisis," *Wall Street Journal*, August 4, 2016, at https://www.wsj.com/articles/mongolia-faces-a-debt-crisis-1470331031 (accessed October 7, 2020); Lkhagva Erdene, "Panama Papers helps break new reporting ground in Mongolia," International Consortium of Investigative Journalists, August 4, 2016, at https://www.icij.org/investigations/panama-papers/panama-papers-helps-break-new-reporting-ground-mongolia/ (accessed October 7, 2020); Rob Schmitz, "Once Booming, Mongolia's Economy Veers From Riches To Rags," National Public Radio, December 5, 2016, at https://www.npr.org/sections/parallels/2016/12/05/504411983/once-booming-mongolias-economy-veers-from-riches-to-rags (accessed October 7, 2020).
90 "Mongolia's Growth to Remain Solid in 2019 and 2020 - ADB," Asian Development Bank, April 3, 2019, at https://www.adb.org/news/mongolias-growth-remain-solid-2019-and-2020-adb; "The World Bank in Mongolia," The World Bank, at https://www.worldbank.org/en/country/mongolia/overview#1 (accessed September 30, 2020).
91 *The Observatory of Economic Complexity Database*. Also see *World Integrated Trade Solution*, World Bank, Mongolia trade balance, exports and imports by country 2018, at https://wits.worldbank.org/CountryProfile/en/Country/MNG/Year/2018/TradeFlow/EXPIMP/Partner/by-country (accessed September 30, 2020). For trade in absolute terms, see *UN Comtrade Database*, Mongolia-India import export 2015-2019, at https://comtrade.un.org/data (accessed September 30, 2020).
92 "Make in India" was introduced in 2014 by the Modi administration to increase export production in the country and carve out a role for India as a global manufacturing hub. However, the programme achieved limited success and was in a slump even before the pandemic. "Atmanirbhar Bharat" ("Self-reliant India") was introduced as a post-pandemic recovery package, which is expected to provide impetus to the Make in India programme and boost manufacturing amidst changing global supply chains. See Raghuram Rajan, "Make in India, Largely for India," *The Indian Journal of Industrial Relations* 50 (3), January 2015, pp. 361–371; National Portal of India, "Building Atmanirbhar Bharat and Overcoming Covid-19," Government of India, at https://www.india.gov.in/

spotlight/building-atmanirbhar-bharat-overcoming-covid-19 (accessed October 2, 2020).
93 Press Trust of India, "India-funded oil refinery in Mongolia to be completed by 2022-end: Pradhan," *Business Standard,* September 21, 2019, at https://www.business-standard.com/article/pti-stories/india-funded-oil-refinery-in-mongolia-to-be-completed-by-2022-end-pradhan-119092001148_1.html (accessed October 2, 2020).
94 Marcin Miroslaw Piatkowski and Julian Latimer Clarke, *Mongolia Central Economic Corridor Assessment: A Value Chain Analysis of Wool-Cashmere, Meat and Leather Industries,* Project ID: MN-Mongolia - Trade And Competitiveness Analytical Support -- P164554, Washington DC, World Bank Group, 2019, at http://documents.worldbank.org/curated/en/951491558704462665/Mongolia-Central-Economic-Corridor-Assessment-A-Value-Chain-Analysis-of-Wool-Cashmere-Meat-and-Leather-Industries (accessed October 2, 2020).
95 The World Bank, "Accelerating Mongolia's Development Requires a Shift 'from Mines to Minds'," press release, September 17, 2020, at https://www.worldbank.org/en/news/press-release/2020/09/17/accelerating-mongolias-development-requires-a-shift-from-mines-to-minds-world-bank (accessed October 2, 2020); Jean-Pascal Nganou, Sebastian Eckardt, Luan Zhao, Davaadalai, Undral Batmukh and Katia D'Hulster, *Mines and Minds: Leveraging Natural Wealth to Invest in People and Institutions,* Country Economic Memorandum, Report No. 153064, Washington DC, World Bank Group, 2020, at http://documents.worldbank.org/curated/en/273001600370275964/Mines-and-Minds-Leveraging-Natural-Wealth-to-Invest-in-People-and-Institutions (accessed October 2, 2020).
96 Shah and Rashid, "Economic Analysis of Bilateral Trade: A Case Study of India-Mongolia," pp. 1–6.
97 Here, the 'post-Galwan era' refers to the time after the June 15, 2020 Galwan valley clash in Eastern Ladakh between Indian and Chinese troops. The incident marked the first casualties on the Line of Actual Control in several decades, and has significantly transformed diplomatic, military and economic Sino-Indian ties.
98 India and Australia inked their Arrangement concerning Mutual Logistics Support (MLSA) in June 2020, and India and Japan finalised their Acquisitions and Cross-servicing Agreement (ACSA) in September 2020. See Ministry of Foreign Affairs of Japan, "Agreement Between the Government of Japan and the Government of the Republic of India Concerning Reciprocal Provision of Supplies and Services Between the Self-Defense Forces of Japan and the Indian Armed Forces"; Ministry of External Affairs, "Joint Statement on a Comprehensive Strategic Partnership between Republic of India and Australia," Government of India, June 4, 2020, at https://www.mea.gov.in/bilateral-documents.htm?dtl/32729/Joint_Statement_on_a_Comprehensive_Strategic_Partnership_between_Republic_of_India_and_Australia (accessed October 4, 2020).
99 Ministry of External Affairs, "1st Senior Officials' India-France-Australia Trilateral Dialogue," Government of India, September 9, 2020, at https://mea.gov.in/press-releases.htm?dtl/32950/1st_Senior_Officials_IndiaFranceAustralia_Trilateral_Dialogue (accessed October 4, 2020).
100 For in-depth analysis of these trilaterals, see Priya Chacko and Jeffrey Wilson, *Australia, Japan and India: A trilateral coalition in the Indo-Pacific?* Perth USAsia Centre, Perth, September 2020, at https://perthusasia.edu.au/getattachment/Our-Work/Australia,-Japan-and-India-A-trilateral-coalition/PU-175-AJI-Book-WEB(2).pdf.aspx?lang=en-AU (accessed September 30, 2020); Jagannath Panda, "'JAI', the Quad and China: Understanding the Undercurrents," Working Paper,

SWP, German Institute for International and Security Affairs, November 2019, at https://www.swp-berlin.org/fileadmin/contents/products/projekt_papiere/BCAS_2 019_Panda_Quad_and_China.pdf (accessed October 2, 2020).
101 Jeffrey Reeves, "Sino-Mongolian relations and Mongolia's non-traditional security," *Central Asian Survey* 32 (2), 2013, p. 175, at https://doi.org/10.1080/02 634937.2013.771980.
102 Helen Davidson, "Inner Mongolia protests at China's plans to bring in Mandarin-only lessons," *Guardian,* September 1, 2020, at https://www.theguardian.com/world/2020/sep/01/inner-mongolia-protests-china-mandarin-schools-language (accessed September 30, 2020).
103 "Wang Yi Holds Talks with Foreign Minister Nyamtseren Enkhtaivan of Mongolia," Ministry of Foreign Affairs of the People's Republic of China, September 15, 2020, at https://www.fmprc.gov.cn/mfa_eng/zxxx_662805/t18153 06.shtml (accessed October 6, 2020).
104 Sarah Zheng, "Mongolia: locked between China and the language identity," *South China Morning Post,* September 19, 2020, at https://www.scmp.com/news/china/diplomacy/article/3102103/mongolia-locked-between-china-and-language-identity (accessed October 6, 2020).
105 "Mongolians protest visit of China diplomat as language dispute simmers," *Reuters,* September 15, 2020, at https://in.reuters.com/article/mongolia-china-protests-idINKBN2661S2 (accessed October 6, 2020).
106 Elbegdorj Tsakhia, "Former President of Mongolia (SMHRIC - 20200831)," August 31, 2020, *Southern Mongolia,* video, 5:00, at https://www.youtube.com/watch?v=qNS94Qg7o2A.
107 Alicia Campi, "How North Korea-Mongolia Relations Have Jump-Started the Korean Peninsula Peace Process," *Asia Pacific Bulletin,* 457, 2019, at https://www.eastwestcenter.org/system/tdf/private/apb457.pdf?file=1&type=node&id=3 7013 (accessed October 2, 2020).
108 The first UBD conference was organised in 2014 and the most recent was held in June 2019. Permanent Mission of Mongolia to the United Nations, "Ulaanbaatar Dialogue," at https://www.un.int/mongolia/mongolia/ulaanbaatar-dialogue (accessed October 1, 2020).
109 Embassy of India Pyongyang, "India-DPR Korea Relations," Government of India, February 2020, at https://eoi.gov.in/pyongyang/?pdf4086?000 (accessed October 1, 2020).
110 Jagannath Panda, "What the Trump-Kim Summit Means for India," *The Diplomat,* February 26, 2019, at https://thediplomat.com/2019/02/what-the-trump-kim-summit-means-for-india/ (accessed October 1, 2020).
111 Embassy of India Pyongyang, "India-DPR Korea Relations," Government of India, February 2020, at https://eoi.gov.in/pyongyang/?pdf4086?000 (accessed October 1, 2020).
112 After the imposition of UNSC's sanctions, India's exports fell from US$65.9 million to US$4.17 million; its imports fell from US$54.1 million to US$31.3 million. See data for North Korean exports and imports in 2016 and 2018. North Korea country profile, *The Observatory of Economic Complexity Database,* at https://oec.world/en/profile/country/prk/ (accessed October 1, 2020); United Nations Security Council, *Resolution 2375*, S/RES/2375, September 11, 2017, at https://www.undocs.org/S/RES/2375%20 (2017).
113 The NEAPC consists of three components: the Northeast Asia Peace and Cooperation Platform, the New Northern Policy, and the New Southern Policy. See Ministry of Foreign Affairs, "International Conference on Responsible Northeast Asia Plus Community," Republic of Korea, December 12, 2017, at https://www.mofa.go.kr/eng/brd/m_5676/view.do?seq=319591&srchFr=&amp

%3BsrchTo=&amp%3BsrchWord=&amp%3BsrchTp=&amp%3Bmulti_itm_seq=0&amp%3Bitm_seq_1=0&amp%3Bitm_seq_2=0&amp%3Bcompany_cd=&amp%3Bcompany_nm= (accessed October 7, 2020).
114 Niklas Swanström, *The Case for Multilateralism: The Korean Peninsula in a Regional Context,* Focus Asia: Perspective and Analysis, Series on Peacebuilding on the Korean Peninsula, Institute for Security and Development Policy, Stockholm, 2020, at https://isdp.eu/content/uploads/2020/06/The-Case-for-Multilateralism-FA-02.06.20.pdf (accessed October 7, 2020).
115 For an assessment of ROK's outreach to ASEAN under the NSP's umbrella, see Jaehyon Lee, "Korea's New Southern Policy: Motivations of 'Peace Cooperation' and Implications for the Korean Peninsula," *Issue Brief*, July 2019, The Asan Institute for Policy Studies, Seoul, at http://www.jstor.com/stable/resrep20678 (accessed October 7, 2020).
116 "Presidential Committee on New Southern Policy," Republic of Korea, at http://www.nsp.go.kr/eng/main.do (accessed October 10, 2020). For India-ROK synergy and cooperation under the New Southern Policy, see Yoon Ah Oh, "Korea's New Southern Policy: Progress, Problems, and Prospects," *Asia Pacific Bulletin* 513, 2020, at https://www.eastwestcenter.org/system/tdf/private/apb513.pdf?file=1&type=node&id=37906 (accessed October 10, 2020); Jojin V. John, "India-South Korea Relations Under 'Special Strategic Partnership': 'Act East Policy' Meets 'New Southern Policy'," *India Quarterly: A Journal of International Affairs* 76 (2), 2020, pp. 207–225, at https://doi.org/10.1177/0974928420917798.
117 For a discussion on India's interests in the denuclearisation process on the Korean Peninsula and its potential to play an active role, see Jagannath Panda, "Pyongyang and India: Strategic Choices on the Korean Peninsula," *Asia Pacific Bulletin,* 455, 2019, at https://www.eastwestcenter.org/system/tdf/private/apb455.pdf?file=1&type=node&id=37011 (accessed October 10, 2020).
118 For an argument on how India can harness its ties and play a proactive role in the Korean Peninsula, see Dean J. Ouellette, "A Role for India in the Korean Peace Process: Contemplating Non-Realist Approaches to Broaden Relations with the Korean Peninsula," *Pacific Focus* 34 (3), 2019, at https://doi.org/10.1111/pafo.12146.
119 For an analysis of the visit, see Charles Krusekopf, "North Korea and Mongolia: A New Partnership for Two Old Friends?," Asia Pacific Bulletin 240, 2013, at https://scholarspace.manoa.hawaii.edu/bitstream/10125/30973/APB%20no.%20240.pdf (accessed October 10, 2020).
120 Tsakhia Elbegdorj, "Lecture by President Tsakhiagiin Elbegdorj at Kim Il-sung University, North Korea," November 2, 2013, video, 15:18, at https://www.youtube.com/watch?v=EgTMtgIg5Ic (accessed October 10, 2020).
121 Munkh-Orgil Tsend, "Statement by H.E. Mr. Munkh-Orgil Tsend, Minister of Foreign Affairs of Mongolia, at the General Debate of the 72nd Session of the United Nations General Assembly," Ministry of Foreign Affairs, Government of Mongolia, September 22, 2017, at http://www.mfa.gov.mn/?p=41953&lang=en (accessed October 10, 2020).
122 Tjalling H.F. Halbertsma, "Mongolia and the DPRK at Sixty-Five: Ulaanbaatar's Changing Relations with Pyongyang," *North Korean Review* 10 (2), Fall 2014, p. 23, at https://www.jstor.org/stable/43908939.
123 Julian Dierkes and Mendee Jargalsaikhan, "Mongolia In An Emerging Northeast Asian Region," *The Mongolian Journal of International Affairs* 20, 2018, p. 95, at https://doi.org/10.5564/mjia.v20i0.1026.
124 Permanent Mission of Mongolia to the United Nations, "Ulaanbaatar Dialogue."

Part II
Nuclear challenges in Northeast Asia

7 The relationship of United States-Japan-Mongolia democratic trilateralism to the Indo-Pacific strategy and Korean Peninsular discussions

Alicia J. Campi

Introduction

Trilateralism as a foreign policy strategy gained momentum in 1973, when in the midst of the Cold War the Trilateral Commission, a non-governmental, policy-oriented discussion group of several hundred businesses, government, academia, media, and civil society leaders from Europe, North America, and Japan, was established to foster greater economic and political cooperation. A conceptual framework promoted by the United States (US) banker David Rockefeller and Trilateral Commission Founding Director Zbigniew Brzezinski, the Commission since then has offered,

> a global platform for open dialogue, reaching out to those with different views and engaging with decision makers from around the world with the aim of finding solutions to the great geopolitical, economic and social challenges of our time. Its members share a firm belief in the values of rule of law, democratic government, human rights, freedom of speech and free enterprise that underpin human progress. Members are also committed to supporting a rules-based international system, closer cooperation across borders and respect for the diversity of approaches to policy issues.[1]

The essence of this trilateralism was a strong core alliance among North America, Western Europe, and Japan. This theoretical model in the 1970s was utilised by US President Jimmy Carter to pursue a trilateralist foreign policy which prioritised cooperation and collaboration with European and Japanese allies. He placed 25 members of the Trilateral Commission, including Vice President Walter Mondale, National Security Adviser Zbigniew Brzezinski, and Secretary of State Cyrus Vance, in key policymaking posts in his administration. According to policy analyst Holly Sklar, these trilateralists, out of concern that growing economic and political rivalries would damage the Western alliance, were rejecting former US President Richard Nixon's more unilateralist attempt to employ confrontation to reassert US hegemony over Western Europe and Japan. These trilateralist policymakers advocated an increasingly

DOI: 10.4324/9781003148630-7

"interdependent" world economy, prioritised negotiation and détente, and acquiesced to maintaining nuclear parity among the existing nuclear states.

With the Ronald Reagan administration in 1980, this trilateralist policy was rejected by many Americans as appeasement, although some observers considered that a hard-line trilateralism of limited containment in fact was promoted during the Reagan years by Vice President George Bush, Federal Reserve Chief Paul Volcker, and Secretaries of State Alexander Haig and George Shultz, and Secretary of Defense Caspar Weinberger. During the 1980s, it was postulated that a renovated trilateralism, wherein annual summits would be important for building consensus, negotiating trade-offs, and gaining momentum for controversial international policies, was dominant. Such meetings would become known as Strategic or Policy Summits to facilitate development issues such as trade, finance, and aid as well as security, defence, and arms control policies. Policymakers promoted the concept of shared international responsibilities among the trilateral countries but ran into serious contradictions over how the big powers would share resource distribution and decision-making with smaller states instead of blatantly imposing their own will.[2]

Since the financial crisis of 2008, scholars of international relations again began to focus on "trilateralism as a prism and tool of analysis which could explain interactions in across a range of economic, political and cultural dimensions of international relations."[3] For example, in a conference devoted to examining the trilateral mechanism in Germany in 2011, attention was paid to trilateral and triangular dynamics interacting with the Great Powers in the region of South Asia and the Indian Ocean. The attendees examined whether a "trilateralism perspective" contributes to the analysis of the intractability of the India-Pakistan conflict and limited opportunities for regional integration, Sino-Indian, and US-Indian relations. Also discussed was comparing trilateralism in Asia with trilateralism in Europe.

Twenty-first century trilateralism has been viewed as evolving from "growing interdependence" to "globalisation", yet there has been recognition that, since the 2008 financial crisis, confidence has been shaken in the global system as a whole as new powers have risen to contend for leadership roles. Mini-triangular relationships have sprung up on different continents, mimicking the role played by alliances hundreds of years ago. Often this form of trilateralism is tied to specific national interests at a specific time or to overcoming a specific regional challenge. They may or may not include a superpower nation, but the value of anchoring at least one superpower in the triangular alliance appears to increase the efficacy of the relationship and is judged by the superpower as a cheaper modern form of alliance-building. At the same time, since the superpower adds both stability and instability to the relationship for the smaller nations, this foreign policy strategy increases the management burden upon the junior partners.

A small nation such as Mongolia, geographically situated on a very populous and economically dynamic Eurasian continent which has very different cultures and religions than its own, has promoted trilateral relations in the past 10 years to strengthen its national security and connect its economy to the Northeast Asian dynamism which surrounds it. One of the foreign policy concepts it is now employing is to create different forms of trilateralism. This analysis will explore how this strategy arose and meshed well with the Indo-Pacific policies of the US and Japan. Mongolian policymakers adroitly leveraged the trilateral relationship as a way for these two superpowers to engage a hostile North Korea in hopes of bringing greater stability to the Northeast Asian region. Mongolia has sought to convince these powerful nations that they need Mongolian assistance with the Democratic People's Republic of Korea (DPRK), and thus the Mongolian image around the globe has been greatly enhanced.

Origins of "democratic trilateralism" of United States, Japan, and Mongolia

The Trump administration's Indo-Pacific policy has stimulated new cooperative mechanisms between the US and Japan. One of the more innovative and less recognised manifestations is the growing trilateral cooperation among the US, Japan, and Mongolia, which emerged from Mongolia's attempts since the fall of communism in 1990 to strengthen ties to "Third Neighbours"[4] to balance its historical economic and political dependence on its two border neighbours of China and Russia. Faced with serious economic challenges because of its landlocked status and limited trade partner options, Mongolia in the Twenty-first Century has sought to develop its mineral-based economy and participate in Eurasian economic growth through transportation integration. Mongolia's trilateralism strategy meshes well with the Japanese objective to find new reliable energy sources since the 2011 Fukushima crisis and the US' desire to re-engage with the Indo-Pacific world to offer alternatives to aggressive actions by China.

The democratic trilateral policy dates to March 2013, when Prime Minister Abe Shinzo made a state visit to Mongolia. Abe was committed to invigorating Japan's foreign policy to strengthen its international and security interests in reaction to China's rise as a revisionist power that sought to realign the regional security architecture by dominating the Asia-Pacific.[5] The Prime Minister and Mongolian President Tsakhia Elbegdorj agreed in principle to pursue a regular trilateral dialogue with the US, but its implementation was slow to develop.[6] With the announcement of the One Belt, One Road policy (now entitled Belt and Road Initiative (BRI)) by Chinese President Xi Jinping on September 7, 2013,[7] both Japan and Mongolia felt that they were omitted from its original continental and maritime economic grand design that looked westward across Eurasia, and so interest was revived in finding another cooperative mechanism.

For Mongolia, concern was intensified by the rapprochement between Chinese President Xi and Russian President Vladimir Putin. Strategically

144   *Alicia J. Campi*

speaking, this challenge could not be met by the "Third Neighbour" principle which had guided Mongolia's foreign policy for 25 years. Concerned that a "great game" to create a new version of the Eurasian Silk Road which seemed to exclude Mongolia was being played out, President Elbegdorj used the celebrations around the commemoration of different anniversaries[8] in Sino-Mongol and Russo-Mongol relations in 2014 to formulate a new strategy called "trilateralism", so that his two powerful neighbours did not proceed with Eurasian transportation and energy cooperation without including a role for Mongolia. Elbegdorj recognised that the Chinese-Russian political rapprochement, which is based on economic self-interest, could only profit Mongolia if Mongolia had a seat at the negotiating table and participated in drafting new regional transport and energy growth models. Mongolian policymakers decided that they needed a longer-term strategy to revive Russian economic investment in Mongolia, build domestic transport infrastructure northward to link into the Trans-Siberian rail system to Pacific partners, as well as south to China, and promote Mongolia as a reliable and cheaper "Economic Corridor" alternative within the greater Eurasian transit zone for Sino-Russian transit traffic. Thus, the trilateralism policy at first just focused on deepening Mongolian, Russian, and Chinese transnational infrastructure development and economic cooperation through annual summits at the presidential level. These summits have been held on the sidelines of the Shanghai Cooperation Organisation (SCO), beginning at Dushanbe, Tajikistan on September 11, 2014.[9]

However, Mongolia's new trilateralism strategy with Russia and China caught many in the foreign investor community off guard. Although the subsequent plethora of Mongolian agreements with the two border nations to improve Eurasian transportation connections through Mongolia also could assist many other countries such as Turkey, Japan, South Korea, and in Europe to become stronger regional trade partners, foreign governments were concerned that Mongolia was reverting to the orbit of its non-democratic neighbours which controlled over 90 per cent of Mongolia's trade. When a Mongolian delegation visited New York City and Washington in connection with President Elbegdorj's speech to the United Nations (UN) General Assembly in late September 2014, its members were met with a barrage of questions from US officials about the future of Mongolian allegiance to its "Third Neighbour" policy.

American foreign policymakers believed that the preservation of Mongolian democracy after the end of the Cold War was the single most important achievement of the US-Mongolian partnership. Yet two decades later, the bilateral relationship appeared insecure since it was not based on trade and economics but on a newly established values-driven partnership. The US government, including its embassy in Ulaanbaatar, did not support the concept of a trilateral summit in 2014 among Mongolian President Elbegdorj, Russian President Putin, and Chinese President Xi. This was a non-public position held not only by the US but also by its close allies, especially Japan. American authorities thought that China might receive some special considerations in the lucrative Mongolian minerals market for renewable and traditional power generation to the disadvantage of American companies. Japan was concerned about being locked out of the Mongolian mineral sector and also that the publicity in the region prior to the "celebration" of the seventy-fifth anniversary of the joint Soviet-Mongolian victory over the Japanese army at Khalkhin Gol (aka Nomonhan) might encourage the Chinese and Koreans to engage in a new round of Japan-bashing.

In response to this unease from Japan and the US towards Mongolia's new trilateralism with Russia and China, Mongolian foreign policy specialists such as Bulgaa Altangerel, Mongolian Ambassador to the United States (2012–2017), called for the formalisation of another type of trilateralism—this one among the US, Japan, and Mongolia.[10] One could argue that this informal "democratic trilateralism" already had existed since the early 1990s when the US encouraged and coordinated Japanese leadership in crafting donor assistance policies for Mongolia to make its transition to democracy and the free market.[11] US-Japanese collaboration with Mongolia on the prioritisation and funding of this transition was carried out very openly, and a pattern developed whereby the US took the lead in organising privatisation and democracy-building institutions, while Japan became the prime mentor and guide for establishing the economic mechanisms, including banking, that were necessary for Mongolia's free market to function. Over the years, this informal cooperation morphed into an active policy of US-Mongolian military cooperation paralleling, but not competing, with Mongolia-Japanese joint investment in major domestic construction projects from hospitals to roads to airports and power stations. Japan in the last 10 years has established a strong economic bilateral relationship with Mongolia to diversify its economy beyond natural resources and to strongly advance people-to-people exchanges.

Although some observers believed "the rise of the trilateral between the three democracies is also yet another manifestation of the more active role Mongolia is seeking to play in the region and world" under President Elbegdorj,[12] the public reason given by the Mongols in 2015 for formalising the US-Japan-Mongolia trilateral relationship was centred around including Mongolia in a multilateral framework to approach North Korea. Japanese diplomatic sources indicated that for Japan, the first trilateral foreign ministerial talks with the US and Mongolia were conducted in order "to tap into Mongolia's close ties with North Korea and settle a host of issues involving Pyongyang."[13] As an Australian observer noted, "Mongolia has displayed a willingness to play a mediating role between North Korea and the international community. It has been suggested that Mongolia is one of the only countries Pyonyang likes and actually trusts."[14]

A longstanding dispute between Japan and the DPRK has been the matter of Japanese citizens kidnapped from the shores of Japan to be held in North Korea for decades. The Japanese government officially lists 17 citizens as having been abducted by North Korean agents and suspects Pyongyang's involvement in other disappearances of Japanese nationals.[15] In March 2014, despite years of stalemate in the Six Party Talks, the Mongolian government had successfully assisted the Japanese government in arranging an abductee meeting in Ulaanbaatar. In July 2015 Mongolian President Elbegdorj sent a letter through an aide to North Korean leader Kim Jong-un proposing to move forward on the abduction issue. When a high-ranking Mongolian government official in Ulaanbaatar met with an aide of Prime Minister Abe Shinzo later that month, it was agreed to first hold a senior-level meeting with the US. The Japanese hoped that by drawing Mongolia into a multilateral framework that included the US, it could assist in helping to facilitate the resumption of the stalled Six Party Talks on Pyongyang's nuclear programme and continue progress on resolving the issue of North Korea's abductions of Japanese nationals in the 1970s and 1980s.

As a result, the US, Japan, and Mongolia announced that trilateral foreign ministerial talks in the fall of 2015 would be held "to tap into Mongolia's close ties with North Korea and settle a host of issues involving Pyongyang."[16] This new "democratic" trilateralism mechanism was justified as non-threatening towards Mongolia's border neighbours because relations would be at the foreign ministerial level rather than the presidential summit level of the China-Russia-Mongolia trilateral relationship. Furthermore, it was decided to convene the trilateral foreign ministerial on the fringes of international conferences through 2016.

The inaugural trilateral meeting among Mongolia, the US, and Japan that was held on September 29, 2015 in New York City pioneered a consultation mechanism in a trilateral format that aims to promote the exchange of views on a broad range of issues of mutual interest. At the first meeting, the three sides discussed some topics "to deepen regional security cooperation and expand economic relations."[17] Mongolian Foreign Minister Lundeg Pürevsüren, US Assistant Secretary of State for the Bureau of East Asian and Pacific Affairs Daniel Russel, and Director General for the Asian and Oceanian Affairs, Bureau of the Ministry of Foreign Affairs of Japan Ihara Junichi met on the sidelines of the opening of the UN General Assembly. The Mongolian government statement emanating from this exchange explained that the new framework "laid the foundation for an important dialogue mechanism with our Third Neighbors—the United States and Japan—to exchange views on a broad range of regional and global security and economic issues, and on how to coordinate actions at the regional and global levels that reflect shared interest."[18] A Mongolian observer later called this first trilateral meeting "a Mongolian base medium" for exchanging cooperation and integration perspectives on the regional as well as the multilateral level with Mongolia's key third neighbours.[19] There was little international coverage of the event, but an Indian commentator noted that, although this trilateralist mechanism lacked publicly released specifics, it had "value in creating an institutionalised, regular setting for partners to exchange views, coordinate actions and increase comfort in the way they deal with each other. This can help lay the foundation for greater co-operation further down the line."[20]

Trump administration ties trilateralism to its Indo-Pacific policy

The US-Japan-Mongolia trilateral remained a low-key dialogue forum throughout the rest of the Obama administration. There was no formal meeting among the three countries in 2016. However, the Trump administration within months of coming into power took steps to regularise the trilateral conference into an annual event. In the August 30, 2017 meeting in Ulaanbaatar, not two months after the election of new Mongolian president Khaltmaa Battulga, the importance of US-Japan-Mongolia trilateralism was underscored as a foundational mechanism for Mongolia and its two "Third Neighbours" to exchange views on multilateral cooperation and economic integration. While the focus of the 2017 meeting was on the threat posed by North Korea, all the parties agreed to promote trilateral and multilateral security and find ways to increase trade.[21]

From the initial enunciation of the Trump national security policy on the Indo-Pacific Japan had been given prominence. It was called the US' "critical ally" in the new administration's 2017 National Security Strategy, while Mongolia was never mentioned at all.[22] The Japanese Ministry of Foreign Affairs in April 2017 had affirmed its own "Free and Open Indo-Pacific Strategy,"[23] which had no reference to trilateralism with the US and Mongolia. However, as the Trump administration fleshed out its Indo-Pacific strategic thinking, especially under the direction of Secretary of State Mike Pompeo, a new role for Mongolia was reflected in both nations' foreign policy rhetoric. In 2018, Mongolia and the trilateralism dialogue it had established with the US and Japan grew dramatically in importance in American eyes. This is revealed in the joint statement published during the visit of Mongolian Prime Minister Ukhnaa Khürelsükh to Washington in September 2018, wherein Mongolia is labelled "an important Indo-Pacific partner,"[24] and in December 2018 comments in Ulaanbaatar of United States Chargé d'Affairs Manuel Micaller about "how central Mongolia is in the United States administration's Indo-Pacific Strategy."[25]

The connection of the United Sates-Japan-Mongolia trilateral relationship to the Indo-Pacific strategy was manifested clearly in the third trilateral meeting in Tokyo on April 26, 2018. Integration of trilateralism cooperation was explained as firmly interwoven in the Indo-Pacific policy of the two larger powers:

> During the meeting, the United States and Japan detailed their vision for a peaceful and prosperous Indo-Pacific region in which all countries are free from coercion and can maintain their sovereign right to choose their own paths. Japan and the United States reaffirmed their commitment

to their increased bilateral relationships with Mongolia in line with Mongolia's "third neighbor" policy, and the three countries discussed potential avenues of cooperation to promote connectivity, good governance, and a rules-based international order throughout the Asia-Pacific region.[26]

While the April meeting also prominently mentioned Korean Peninsula developments and the agreement of all three parties to maintain pressure on the DPRK to secure denuclearisation, a new aspect of the trilateral cooperation emerged in the security field and was expressed as the "shared intent to promote trilateral and multilateral security and peacekeeping cooperation."[27] Specifically mentioned were pledging increased cooperation in multilateral institutions and coalitions, including the Community of Democracies and the UN Human Rights Council, because the three nations had shared values. On the US side, there were concrete indications that the Trump administration continued to have a significantly different view of Mongolia's potential in its overall Indo-Pacific foreign policy. The Congressional Research Services noted that the US government viewed Mongolia as an "emerging partner" and as a country with which it may cooperate to achieve a "shared vision of rules-based order in the Indo Pacific." Furthermore, it cited the Department of State's Congressional Budget Justification for Foreign Operations, FY2019, which described US assistance priorities in Mongolia as: "The primary goals of United States assistance to Mongolia are to ensure the United States remains a preferred partner over geographical neighbors Russia and China and to give Mongolia greater latitude to chart an independent foreign and security policy."[28]

Concurrently, there was a dramatic increase in bilateral contacts that were stimulated by the fact that Foreign Minister Damdin Tsogtbaatar visited Washington three times in 2018 to meet with US Secretary of State Mike Pompeo and US congressional representatives. The flurry of diplomatic activity was centred on developing a plan for promoting President Battulga's efforts to increase Mongolian cashmere and textile exports to the US through the Congress-authorised Mongolia Third Neighbour Trade Act.[29] Tsogtbaatar finalised the terms of the $350 million Second Millennium Challenge Compact,[30] which was officially signed by Prime Minister Khürelsükh on a mid-September 2018 visit to Washington, DC. During Khürelsükh's meeting with Secretary Mike Pompeo, they discussed a "Roadmap for Expanded Economic Partnership between the United States of America and Mongolia" and specific measures to expand economic relations.[31] The Prime Minister the next day met with Vice President Mike Pence to promote the upgrading of the bilateral relationship to an "Expanded Comprehensive Partnership."[32]

The year 2019 was important for the US-Mongolia bilateral relationship. Although developments in the bilateral relationship overshadowed the trilateral partnership, at the same time it can be argued that strengthening the US-Mongolian side made the entire trilateral relationship stronger and more

US-Japan-Mongolia democratic trilateralism 149

balanced. The previous year's visits by the Mongolian foreign minister and prime minister laid the groundwork for the state visit of Mongolian President Battulga to Washington at the end of July 2019, which was the first presidential-level visit between the two countries since 2011.[33] Battulga had an Oval Office meeting with President Trump and signed a new Strategic Partnership Agreement, which brought the bilateral relationship to a level that Mongolia only had with Russia, China, Japan and India and making Mongolia only the seventeenth country to have such an agreement with the US.[34]

The Trump-Battulga meeting was focused on trade and security with President Trump's goal to support friendly countries surrounding China as a backdrop to the intensifying US-China trade dispute.[35] Mongolia hoped to increase both military and economic ties to avoid being pressured by its landlocked geographical location in Eurasia and to potentially lessen dependency on China by finding trade routes that did not involve Beijing.[36] One Mongolian observer emphasised that the trip was "an important milestone for not only United States-Mongolian relations, but also for Mongolian foreign policy" in that Mongolia was "recognized as a close ally and respected friend of Uncle Sam."[37] The idea for the partnership originally came from the Mongolian side several years previous, so why in 2019 was it accepted by the US? Although the key element appears to be Mongolia's record of assisting the US and Japan in being a bridge to North Korea, another major factor was that the Trump administration sought to indicate, especially to China, that it was not ceding Northeast Asia to growing Sino-Russian cooperation through the BRI or the Shanghai Cooperation Organization. In addition, it must be recognised that Mongolia, since 2003, had constructed a strong record of fighting terrorism through the deployment of thousands of Mongolian military personnel to UN Peacekeeping and NATO-led missions. This concrete commitment over decades laid the "trust foundation" for the bilateral diplomatic and military discussions on strategic partnership.

Following on the heels of the success of the President's trip was the surprise visit of newly appointed US Secretary of Defense Mark Esper to Ulaanbaatar not one week later. *The Washington Post* described Mongolia as a natural partner for the US and noted that Secretary Esper included Mongolia on his first international trip to deepen US ties:

> At first glance, the visit might seem like an unusual destination for a Pentagon chief's first official trip—especially at a time of escalating tensions elsewhere in the world. But his stopover is just the latest signal that the Trump administration is eager to maintain a strong partnership with the East Asian country of 3 million people that has served as a longtime United States defense partner.[38]

Esper grouped Mongolia with emerging US partners Vietnam and Indonesia, which were: "like-minded countries who believe in a free and open Indo-Pacific, who share the values we do and who believe in respecting one another's sovereignty."[39] This new attitude towards Mongolia and the elevation of its status in the minds of American policymakers was reflected by a senior US defence official who commented that "They have been a good ally that punches above its weight, and I think Secretary Esper wants to acknowledge (that) and see if there are ways to grow the partnership further."[40] However, the official denied that the trip was about promoting any specific initiative, but rather claimed that the US was keen to look at expanding ties, potentially in areas such as military training.

The Voice of America (VOA) news service, an arm of the US government, when describing Esper's visit, pointed out that Mongolia is considered by US defence officials to be a "net exporter of security," and thus was acting as a strong Washington partner ever since Ulaanbaatar signed its first military-to-military agreement in the 1990s to contribute to international peace-keeping missions and training. Commenting that Mongolia is not a traditional destination for US secretaries of defense, VOA quoted Rudy deLeon, a defence policy expert with the Center for American Progress and a former deputy secretary of defense, as explaining that Mongolia is situated between China and Russia and so located in a "neighborhood that has a lot of mischief going on around its perimeter," which was a major reason why Mongolia has had a "pretty consistently upward" trajectory of importance to the US.[41] The VOA report tied the Esper trip to the Trump administration's National Defense Strategy (NDS), which since 2018 has aimed to cultivate more robust partnerships to expand the US' network of allies. On his trip, Esper publicly said that Mongolia is among the "key countries in the Indo-Pacific" where he hopes to build military relationships at a "more senior level" and "given its location, given its interest in working more with us...all those things are a reason why I want to go there and engage."[42]

The 2019 trilateral meeting amongst the three countries could not be arranged until January 2020, when it took place on the sidelines of the annual US-Mongolia bilateral meeting. Held on January 10 in Washington, DC, the dialogue was not at the foreign ministerial level, but rather hosted by General David Stilwell, Assistant Secretary of State for East Asian and Pacific Affairs, and co-chaired by Damdinsuren Davaasüren, State Secretary of the Mongolian Ministry of Foreign Affairs, and Takizaki Shigeki, Director-General of the Japanese Foreign Ministry's Asian and Oceanian Affairs Bureau. In June 2017 Takizaki had met in Ulaanbaatar on the sidelines of the Ulaanbaatar Dialogue on Northeast Asian Security (UBD) with Ri Yong Pil, deputy head of the North Korean Foreign Ministry's Institute for American Studies, to urge Pyongyang to return all abducted Japanese nationals.[43] In the joint statement that emerged, "The United States and Japan reaffirmed their commitment to strengthening their bilateral relationships with Mongolia in line with Mongolia's "third neighbor" policy and the three sides' visions for a free and open Indo-Pacific."[44] Topics discussed included regional development, including in the Indo-Pacific, with emphasis on how the three sovereign, independent, and democratic states could cooperate to ensure a prosperous and peaceful future.

The importance of the North Korean situation to fostering the trilateral relationship was evident in the time they devoted to exchanging views on the DPRK and then reiterating in the concluding document that North Korea must cease provocations such as launching ballistic missiles. The three partners insisted that North Korea abide by its obligations under UN Security Council Resolutions and engage in substantive negotiations, as it had committed to do at the 2018 Singapore summit. Mongolia, despite its close, more than 70 year-long relationship with Pyongyang, was willing in the joint statement to call for full implementation of the relevant UN resolutions seeking "the final, fully verified dismantlement of the DPRK's weapons of mass destruction and ballistic missile programs."[45] Furthermore, the joint statement emphasised that all three countries were concerned about humanitarian conditions inside North Korea and particularly mentioned the necessity for the immediate resolution of the Japanese abductions issue.

During the trilaterals, the US and Japan agreed to support Mongolian efforts to fight anti-money laundering and develop its capacity in line with the recommendations of the Financial Action Task Force. They all agreed to deepen their economic partnership and highlighted enhanced collaboration in the areas of energy development, the digital economy, and cybersecurity. Discussions also included specific ideas to develop transparency, predictability, and legal enforcement within Mongolia's business climate, and thus enhance Mongolia's ability to attract greater US and Japanese investment. In the security sphere, the three nations reviewed the new US strategic partnership with Mongolia and discussed ways to strengthen their trilateral strategic relationship. The next trilateral meeting should be held in Mongolia later in 2020 or early 2021, but due to the coronavirus pandemic and change of administration, it is likely to be held virtually or postponed.

Japanese views of trilateralism with the United States and Mongolia

The story of Mongolia's "Third Neighbour" foreign policy strategy also is closely interwoven with its bilateral relations with Japan. To redesign its political and economic system in the democratic era to meet its post-Cold War national security and globalisation challenges, Mongolia from the early 1990s believed it needed Japanese massive investment. Japan early on promoted the idea of a US-Japan-Mongolian trilateral relationship as a counterweight to China and Russia, and agreed with the Mongols that Japan would be the best nation to work in concert with the US to stabilise Mongolia's economy. Japan has a great interest in Mongolian energy minerals and expects to realise sizeable trade volumes if transportation connectivity within Northeast Asia is achieved. The growing relationship of

152 *Alicia J. Campi*

Mongolia with Japan was welcomed by the US as a way to lessen the financial burden of the US during Mongolia's democracy-building decades and to provide investment capital to counter Chinese investment inflows. Much of the friendly feeling between Mongolia and Japan has built up from Japan's continuing generosity both in Official Development Direct Investment (ODA) managed by the Japanese government and in people-to-people educational assistance, including hundreds of scholarships for Mongolia students.[46] Mongolian Foreign Minister Tsend Münkh-Orgil in March 2005 acknowledged how crucial this assistance was by noting that Mongolia received 70 per cent of its ODA from Japan from 1991 to 2005.[47]

In 2013, Mongolian-Japanese relations were strengthened due to the state visits of the prime ministers of both nations, and concrete contracts in the power and construction fields were signed under very long-term low-interest loans including for a new capital airport and Ulaanbaatar's metro system. Three months after assuming office, Japanese Prime Minister Abe Shinzo travelled to Mongolia in March 2013 to meet Mongolian President Elbegdorj.[48] The trip was spurred by his desire to seek greater cooperation in energy and trade relations, especially since the March 2011 Fukushima Daiichi nuclear power plant accident had shut down Japan's nuclear power plants and left Japanese authorities seeking other forms of energy such as coal, which Mongolia had in abundance. Although the two nations had established a "strategic partnership" in 2010, Abe offered to deepen the bilateral relationship through (1) Cooperation in Politics and Security, (2) Further Development of Economic Relations, and (3) Revitalising People-to-people and Cultural Exchanges. He explained his reasons were "common values not only in terms of bilateral relations but also with regard to regional and global issues."[49] This cooperation was labelled "vitality" or *erch* or *erch khuch* in Mongolian. Over the next three years, Prime Minister Abe made three state visits (totalling six in all) to Ulaanbaatar, and President Elbegdorj made nine visits to Abe. Their working relationship, coined "Abe and Ebe," was one of the strongest among Asian leaders.

A Mongolian researcher claimed that it was during the March 2013 visit that Prime Minister Abe launched Mongolia-Japan-US trilateralism.[50] Although there has been no indication from other Japanese or Mongolian sources that the Mongolian leadership adopted the democratic trilateral concept from Japan, it is clear that the idea of deeper cooperation with the US regarding DPRK and Northeast Asian matters was discussed. On that first state visit, Abe was seeking Mongolian assistance in negotiating with North Korea over the Japanese abductee issue. Mongolia subsequently became a conduit for negotiations between Japan and North Korea since Japan has no diplomatic ties with the North. The Japanese press revealed that Abe discussed the abductions during the mid-September visit of Mongolian Prime Minister Altankhuyag in Tokyo[51] and likely again during an overnight stay by President Elbegdorj in Abe's private residence on September 29.[52] These negotiations bore fruit a year later when in March

2014 the parents of a Japanese abductee named Megumi Yokota were allowed by the North Koreans to meet secretly with the abductee's daughter, Kim Eun Gyong, in Ulaanbaatar.[53]

President Elbegdorj at a July 2016 summit with Abe promised to increase closer cooperation in the international arena, support a seat for Japan in the UN Security Council and promote the US-Japan-Mongolia trilateral dialogue. Abe responded that Japan would continue its economic cooperation and emphasise defence and security collaboration. The two nations signed a Midterm Program (2017–2021) on Strategic Partnership in March 2017 during the visit of Mongolian Foreign Minister Mönkh-Orgil.[54] This closer form of bilateral partnership agreement indicated that Japan saw an advantage in promoting the idea of a formal US-Japan-Mongolia trilateral relationship as a counterweight to China and Russia activities in the Northeast Asian region.

After 2017, Japanese Prime Minister Abe, who had forged a strong economic partnership with Mongolian president Elbegdorj, quickly built a working bilateral relationship with Elbegdorj's successor, President Battulga. Abe and Battulga first met in Vladivostok in September 2017, on the sidelines of the third Eastern Economic Forum. Abe pledged Japan's support for Mongolia's policy to secure access to international waters and proposed expanding defence cooperation and working to settle the Korean Peninsula and other Northeast Asian issues.[55] In their second summit, on September 11, 2018, also in Vladivostok, during the fourth Eastern Economic Forum,[56] North Korea and its impact on Northeast Asia's security was high on the agenda. Prime Minister Abe raised the necessity for both nations to support the US-North Korean process and to realise complete, verifiable, and irreversible dismantlement (CVID) by North Korea of all weapons of mass destruction and ballistic missiles of all ranges. In addition, the two leaders agreed to continue to work closely together toward the early resolution of the abductions issue.[57]

Mongolian views of United States-Japan-Mongolia trilateralism

As noted by Mongolian foreign policy expert Dr. Sharad Soni, "Within the framework of its "multi-pillared" and "multi-dimensional" foreign policy, Mongolia has been pursuing a viable relationship with global and regional powers in order to seek their support especially in recovering the sluggish economic growth being experienced since 2012."[58] It is evident that Mongolia's interest in trilateralism, particularly its persistent approach to "democratic" trilateralism, has evolved from its "Third Neighbour" strategy and its vision of economic development. Yet to date, there has not been a lot of analysis by Mongolian scholars on the democratic trilateral mechanism among the US, Japan, and Mongolia. Most of the focus of Mongolian scholarship has been on the Chinese-Russian-Mongolian trilateral relationship, which emphasises the efficacy of transport and energy corridors to Mongolia's economic development and perhaps strategic peril. This lack of analytical research can be interpreted as an expression by Mongolian foreign policy experts that the neighbourly trilateral relationship is more important now for Mongolia than democratic trilateralism.

In early 2016 a Mongolian security analyst Bolor Lkhaajav pointed out that "U.S.-Japan-Mongolia trilateralism is making its way into the policy framework, providing a complement to plans for a Mongolia-Russia-China economic corridor in Northeast Asia."[59] However, a more most detailed commentary was presented by Dr. G. Baasanhuu at the School of International Relations and Public Administration (SIRPA) within the National University of Mongolia (NUM). Dr. Baasanhuu labels the collaboration with the US and Japan as Mongolia's Trilateral "Third Neighbour Policy" in Northeast Asia, and also ties it to evidence of his country's unique nomadic mindset.[60] According to his interpretation, the major impetus for the 2017 trilateral meeting among the Trump administration, Japan, and Mongolia was to develop a united response to the most concerning topic at the time—the threat of DPRK's nuclear and ballistic rocket programme and the desire of the three countries to seek a denuclearised DPRK. This concern was triggered by the launch of a ballistic missile over Japanese territory on August 29, 2017, which threatened regional and global security. In order to respond to the destabilisation of the power structure and security balance in Northeast Asia, the three countries concluded that they should take responsibility for this matter in accordance with their promises made in the 2005 Joint Statement on Six Party Talks held in Beijing to remind Pyongyang of its obligations. In this context, Baasanhuu argues, the three parties agreed to a position of developing trilateral, as well as a multilateral, security and defence measures in the region. They called upon all the UN member states to take responsibility for reining in the DPRK and solving the nuclear threat and issue of Japanese abducted citizens.

Despite acknowledging the importance of the North Korean denuclearisation issue to the development of the democratic trilateral alliance, Baasanhuu sees mutual economic benefit as the real motivating force behind the growth of the relationship. Noting that Mongolia benefited from the partnership with the US and Japan for its sustainable energy projects and support for its agricultural industry, he opined that all three nations understood that mutually beneficial economic cooperation is the cornerstone of the trilateral relationship, and so they were willing to exchange opinions on how the Mongolian government could strengthen its market in terms of transparency and creation of a stable legal, as well as political environment, for American and Japanese businesses and investors with the simple goal of increasing the volume of trade among the three states.

Baasanhuu's analysis is unique because he ties the political theory of the trilateral mechanism to Mongolia's traditional nomadic culture of three-family-camp lifestyle. This is a reference to the old Mongol herding unit, called *xot-ail* (camp family), consisting of two or three related households which pasture animals communally.[61] According to Baasanhuu, Mongolian foreign policymakers today favour the trilateral approach because of their confidence in the positive attributes of collective arrangements based upon three partners. However, Baasanhuu's reference may be more romantic than realistic, since this three-camp form of nomadism was prevalent only in central and western Mongolia, but rare in the one-third of the country covered by the Gobi. Furthermore, there is evidence that prior to the Eighteenth century the Mongols nomadised in much larger groups than did those observed by travellers and ethnographers in recent centuries.[62] Nonetheless, he concludes that this nomadic tradition has influenced the creation of Mongolian foreign policy strategy.

One could counter this argument by noting that Mongolia is a Buddhist country, and that since the number "3" represents the Three Jewels (the *Triratna*) that Buddhists take refuge in, Mongols are trying to find some way to express or manifest the relation between the pristine, longed-for unity with the reality of worldly diversity by embracing trilateralism in all things. However, the number 3 is common to many belief systems not just Buddhism. Religions are full of trinities, like the Christian trinity, so such a theoretical concept would be difficult to attach solely to Mongolian philosophy.

There may be greater merit in another point which Baasanhuu advances. He asserts the fact that Mongolia's geographic location between two enormous neighbours predicated his country's interest in forming trilateral relations: "the state's security and stability is hugely dependent on the regional state of relations, which therefore pushes Mongolia to implement an active and in some cases, experimental policies to reach its objectives."[63] It might be interesting for political scientists to examine the foreign policy strategies of other countries which face a geographical situation similar to Mongolia—countries such as Poland (between Russia and Germany) or Finland (between Sweden and Russia) or Nepal (between China and India)—and their utilisation of the trilateral mechanism.

Conclusion

The US-Japan-Mongolia trilateral relationship developed out of a Mongolian initiative to find a new mechanism to balance its trilateral geographical relationship with China and Russia. This form of triangular cooperation with the US and Japan is called "democratic trilateralism" because it emphasises the fact that all three countries have shared democratic values. Shared values are not a part of China-Russia-Mongolia trilateralism. Rather, those three countries do not attempt to assert that they have an ideological commonality, but rather are content to acknowledge that their geographical proximity is the basis for seeking to improve economic links and to work together to solve common environmental, transport, and energy problems.

There is a strong element of national security interest motivating the Mongols to forge a US-Japan-Mongolia trilateral relationship. On the surface, the main stimulant appeared to be the attempt to find a peaceful solution to the nuclear programme of the DPRK and to contribute to bringing political stability to the Korean Peninsula. If successful, North Korea's integration into the region would provide Mongolia with new transport alternatives, including a seaport for new clients for its mineral and animal-derived products. Thus, Mongolia's promotion of democratic trilateralism with the US and Japan has thrived, particularly during the Trump administration, due to a key dimension of the trilateral dynamic—the emergence of a renewed emphasis in the Trump era on seeking peace and denuclearisation in Northeast Asia. This goal has enabled Mongolia, a country with a long history of good relations with North Korea, to play a more substantial role in the international relations of its region and continent, which for many decades had been monopolised by superpower gamesmanship.

When examining the US rationale for accepting the trilateralism formula proposed by Mongolian policymakers, we must remember the economic climate preceding the establishment of this mechanism. During the George W. Bush second term (2004–2008) of constructive partnership towards China, which included a November 21, 2005 state visit to Ulaanbaatar, and under the Asian Pivot rebalancing policy of the Obama administration (2009–2016), Mongolia did not economically profit. The US' share of overall trade and investment in Mongolia plunged from 2005 to 2015. In 2004 the US exported to Mongolia only US$28.1 million worth of products while importing US$239.2 million of mostly textile products. However, by 2010, imports had fallen to a meagre US$11.6 million—a level comparable to the very early 1990s. Since 2009, US annual exports to Mongolia vastly outnumbered Mongolian exports to the US. The latest 2019 statistics continued this pattern with US exports to Mongolia valued at US$192.7 million while Mongolian exports to the US stood at only US$24.8 million.[64]

Thus, despite the very vocal claims of US support for Mongolian democracy and free enterprise and praise of Mongolia as an example for development for emerging economies throughout the Eurasian continent, the contracting bilateral economic relationship in the early years of the Twenty-first century evidenced a US retrenchment away from Mongolia. This reality damaged the public reputation of the US by increasing the sense of abandonment in the minds of the Mongolian citizenry and in official circles. For strategic reasons closely tied to the economic rise of China and Chinese-Russian cooperation throughout the Northeast Asian region, the US government reluctantly agreed to a limited, mostly formulaic form of trilateral relations starting in 2015. However, during the Trump years, the American foreign policy apparatus quickly saw that Mongolia could be very useful in communicating with North Korea and thus was willing to support democratic trilateralism as a key part of its overall strategy for the Indo-Pacific and denuclearisation of the Korean Peninsula.

US-Japan-Mongolia democratic trilateralism 157

The Japanese government under Prime Minister Abe, on the other hand, has supported a form of trilateralism with Mongolia and the US ever since 2013. There was a strong economic component to Japanese interest since it was in search of new supplies of energy minerals after the 2011 Fukushima disaster and decades of disruption of oil supplies from the Middle East. Moreover, the Japanese were very sensitive to Chinese economic penetration of Northeast Asia, which was a reflection of Japanese weakness and loss of economic influence in a region fundamental to Japan's national security. But, the North Korean situation also was a strong catalyst motivating Japanese interest in democratic trilateralism. Originally, this was manifested by the realisation that Mongolia could assist in resolving the very significant domestic issue of the return of Japanese citizens abducted decades earlier by the DPRK. With the cessation of the Six Party Talks as a conduit for communication and negotiation, the importance of Mongolia as a reliable, confidential channel to Pyongyang became more evident. Enlisting the US into the trilateral relationship was perceived as strengthening Japan's hand when talking to the North Koreans.

The elections of President Battulga and President Trump successfully energised the US-Mongolian bilateral security relationship as well as burnished the image of Mongolia as a bridge for the US and Japan to North Korea. The vitality of the two bilateral relationships has had the unexpected result of greatly strengthening the interest in and potential effectiveness of trilateral cooperation, not only as regards Northeast Asian security but in broader economic and social areas. Mongolia's promotion of its deeper integration into US and Japanese calculations of overall Indo-Pacific strategic cooperation allows Mongolia to achieve its own foreign policy goals of strengthening its democratic and economic institutional ties to the US and Japan. Thus, it can act as a successful example of democracy and the free market to other ex-authoritarian Asian nations and develop a more dynamic counterbalancing triangular mechanism to the even more important Sino-Russian-Mongolian version of trilateralism.

Notes

1 Website of The Trilateral Commission, at http://trilateral.org/page/3/about-trilateral (accessed April 18, 2020).
2 Holly Sklar, "Trilateralism Renovated for the 1980s," *North American Congress on Latin America*, September 25, 2007, at https://nacla.org/article/trilateralism-renovated-1980s (accessed April 17, 2020).
3 "Trilateralism & Triangular Dynamics in International Relations. Implications for International Relations Theory," Heidelberg, Germany, July 8–9, 2011, University of Warsaw Faculty of Political Science and International Studies, at http://www.ism.uw.edu.pl/wp-content/uploads/2011/10/dokumenty_konferencja_w_heidelbergu-7_lipca_2011.pdf (accessed April 17, 2020).
4 Mongolia's "Third Neighbour" policy is the concept of reaching beyond its two border neighbours to selected developed nations within and outside the Asian

158 *Alicia J. Campi*

region so as to integrate into the world economy. This terminology was first suggested by United States Secretary of State James Baker in August 1990.
5 Piyush Singh, "The Architect: How Abe Redesigned Japan's Foreign Policy," *The National Interest*, March 17, 2016, at https://nationalinterest.org/blog/the-buzz/the-architect-how-abe-redesigned-japans-foreign-policy-15522 (accessed November 13, 2020).
6 William Sposato, "Japan Seeks Stronger Mongolia Ties," *Wall Street Journal*, March 30, 2013, at https://www.wsj.com/articles/SB10001424127887324685104578392123216653156 (accessed November 13, 2020).
7 "President Xi Jinping Delivers Important Speech and Proposes to Build a Silk Road Economic Belt with Central Asian Countries," September 7, 2013, PRC Foreign Ministry, at https://www.fmprc.gov.cn/mfa_eng/topics_665678/xjpfwzysiesgjtfhshzzfh_665686/t1076334.shtml (accessed April 22, 2020).
8 The 75th anniversary of the Russian-Mongolian joint victory over Japanese armed forces in Khalkhin Gol in 1939 and 65th anniversary of PRC-Mongolian diplomatic ties in 1949.
9 Alicia Campi, "Transforming Mongolia-Russia-China Relations: The Dushanbe Trilateral Summit," *The Asia-Pacific Journal* 12 (44, 1), November 10, 2014.
10 Private conversation with the author in 2015.
11 Japan was the largest aid donor to Mongolia. From 1991 to 2003, Japan provided 36,126 billion yen in loans, 68,810 billion yen in grant aid, and 23,342 billion yen in technical cooperation, or a total of 128,278 billion yen—amounting to almost 70 per cent of all bilateral aid to Mongolia. Government of Japan, *Country Assistance Program* (November 2004), 24, Japanese Ministry of Foreign Affairs, at http://www.mofa.go.jp/policy/oda/assistance/pdfs/e_mongolia2004.pdf (accessed February 2, 2020).
12 Prashanth Parameswaran, "US, Japan and Mongolia: Don't Forget Asia's Other Trilateral," *The Diplomat*, October 6, 2015, at https://thediplomat.com/2015/10/us-japan-and-mongolia-dont-forget-asias-other-trilateral/ (accessed April 5, 2020).
13 "Japan, US, Mongolia mull first trilateral foreign ministerial talks," *Kyodo News*, August 14, 2016, at https://www.japantimes.co.jp/news/2015/08/14/national/politics-diplomacy/japan-u-s-mongolia-mull-first-trilateral-foreign-minister-talks/#.XpVV3ndFycw (accessed April 14, 2020).
14 Sinclaire Prowse, "Mongolia—Neutrality and Anxiety," *Asia Society Australia*, at https://asiasociety.org/australia/mongolia-neutrality-and-anxiety (accessed April 22, 2020).
15 "Mongolian minister pledges to explore way for Japan-N. Korea dialogue," *Kyodo News*, February 23, 2018, at https://english.kyodonews.net/news/2018/02/122653c8bfb9-mongolian-minister-pledges-to-explore-way-for-japan-n-korea-dialogue.html?phrase=ufj&words= (accessed April 20, 2020).
16 "Japan, US, Mongolia Mull First Trilateral Foreign Ministerial Talks."
17 "Ambassador Talks to the Mongolian Observer. Mongolia-USA Relations Have Been Elevated to Comprehensive Partnership," Mongolian Embassy in US, June 1, 2016, at http://mongolianembassy.us/2016/06/ambassador-talks-to-the-mongolian-observer/#.XGrbyXdFycw (accessed April 11, 2020).
18 "The First Mongolia-US-Japan Trilateral Meeting Was Held in New York," *Mongolian National Broadcasting*, September 15, 2015, at http://www.mnb.mn/i/64855 (accessed April 11, 2020).
19 G. Baasanhuu, "Impact of National Identity on Modern Mongolian Foreign Policy," Powerpoint presentation, 2019, at http://www.humanities.mn/fileman/Uploads/C_TR_2018-2019/OUXNCC/8%20Mongolian%20Identity%20on%20Their%20Modern%20Foreign%20Policy%20Baasankhuu.pdf (accessed April 14, 2020).
20 Parameswaran, "US, Japan and Mongolia."

21 "Joint Statement from Mongolia-US-Japan Trilateral Meeting," Ministry of Foreign Affairs of Mongolia, August 30, 2017, at http://www.mfa.gov.mn/?p=41580&lang=en (accessed April 15, 2020).
22 "National Security Strategy of the United States," December 2017, 46, *nssarchive.us,* at http://nssarchive.us/wp-content/uploads/2017/12/2017.pdf (accessed April 1, 2020).
23 "Priority Policy for Development Cooperation FY 2017," April 2017, Japanese Ministry of Foreign Affairs, at https://www.mofa.go.jp/files/000259285.pdf (accessed April 15, 2020).
24 "Joint Statement on the Expanded Comprehensive Partnership Between the United States and Mongolia," US Embassy in Mongolia, September 20, 2019, at https://mn.usembassy.gov/2018-joint-statement-pm-khurelsukh-sec-pompeo/ (accessed April 22, 2020).
25 "Remarks by Chargé d'Affaires a.i. Manuel P. Micaller at the New Year Celebration of the Mongolian Association of State Alumni," US Embassy in Mongolia, December 20, 2018, at https://mn.usembassy.gov/2018-cda-remarks-masa-new-year/ (accessed February 2, 2020).
26 "Joint Statement of the 2018 United States-Japan-Mongolia Trilateral Meeting," US Department of State, April 27, 2019, at https://www.state.gov/r/pa/prs/ps/2018/04/281266.htm (accessed April 5, 2020).
27 Ibid.
28 "In Focus–Mongolia," *Congressional Research Service,* July 1, 2019, at https://fas.org/sgp/crs/row/IF10926.pdf (accessed April 5, 2020).
29 "US, Mongolia Celebrate Signing of $350 Million MCC Compact to Address Impending Water Crisis," *Millennium Challenge Corporation,* September 20, 2018, at https://www.mcc.gov/news-and-events/release/release-092018-us-mongolia-joint-declaration (accessed April 20, 2020).
30 In September 2018, the Government of Mongolia and Millennium Challenge Corporation (MCC), an independent US government agency, signed a non-refundable US$350 million MCC Water Compact aimed at improving the water supply of Ulaanbaatar city. This is the second MCC Compact to be implemented in Mongolia. The first was for US$285 million. T. Baljmaa, "MCC Water Compact with USD 350 million investment introduced," *Montsame.gov,* October 4, 2019, at https://montsame.mn/en/read/202791 (accessed April 20, 2020).
31 "Joint Statement on the Expanded Comprehensive Partnership Between the United States and Mongolia," US Embassy in Mongolia, Media Note, September 20, 2019, at https://mn.usembassy.gov/2018-joint-statement-pm-khurelsukh-sec-pompeo/ (accessed April 4, 2020).
32 "Prime Minister Khurelsukh And Vice President Pence Affirm The Upgrade Of Mongolia-United States Relations Into The Level Of Expanded Comprehensive Partnership," Mongolian Ministry of Foreign Affairs, September 19, 2018, at http://www.mfa.gov.mn/?p=47918&lang=en (accessed April 4, 2020).
33 Dulguun Bayarsaikhan, "Mongolia and USA declare strategic partnership," *UB Post,* August 2, 2019, at https://theubposts.com/mongolia-and-usa-declare-strategic-partnership/ (accessed April 5, 2020).
34 Bolor Lkhaajav, "US Becomes Mongolia's 5th Strategic Partner," *The Diplomat,* August 5, 2019, at https://thediplomat.com/2019/08/us-becomes-mongolias-5th-strategic-partner/ (accessed April 5, 2020).
35 "Trump Welcomes Mongolian President Battulga to White House," *Associated Press,* July 31, 2019, at https://www.voanews.com/usa/trump-welcomes-mongolian-president-battulga-white-house (accessed April 6, 2020).
36 Members of the Mongolian delegation mentioned this privately to the author in early August 2019.

37 D. Sayan, "A 'victory' for Mongolian foreign policy," *The Mongol Messenger*, August 9, 2019, at https://montsame.mn/en/read/197374 (accessed April 6, 2020).
38 Dan Lamothe, "Pentagon chief gets a gift horse in Mongolia while pursuing deeper relations to counter China," *The Washington Post*, August 8, 2019, at https://www.washingtonpost.com/national-security/2019/08/08/pentagon-chief-gets-gift-horse-mongolia-while-pursuing-deeper-relations-counter-china/ (accessed April 8, 2020).
39 Carla Babb, "New US Defense Secretary Visits Mongolia," *VOAnews.com*, August 7, 2019, at https://www.voanews.com/south-central-asia/new-us-defense-secretary-visits-mongolia (accessed April 8, 2020).
40 Idrees Ali, "With an eye on Russia, China and a horse, Pentagon chief visits Mongolia," *Reuters*, August 7, 2019, at https://www.reuters.com/article/us-usa-mongolia/with-an-eye-on-russia-china-and-a-horse-pentagon-chief-visits-mongolia-idUSKCN1UX2HP (accessed April 8, 2020).
41 Babb, "New US Defense Secretary Visits Mongolia."
42 Ibid.
43 "Mongolian minister pledges to explore way for Japan-N. Korea dialogue."
44 "Joint Statement on the U.S.-Japan-Mongolia Trilateral Meeting," *Media Note*, Department of State, January 10, 2020, at https://www.state.gov/joint-statement-on-the-u-s-japan-mongolia-trilateral-meeting/ (accessed April 4, 2020).
45 Ibid.
46 In 2014 there were 1,000 Mongolians studying in Japan. Although the statistics differ, there are now about 25,000 Mongolians living and working in Japan. See Mendee Jargalsaikhan, "What's Next For American And Japanese Partnerships With Mongolia?," August 20, 2014, at https://dc.linktank.com/event/beyond-the-quagmire-the-future-of-mongolia-s-united-states-and-japan-partnerships-event9932 (accessed April 19, 2020).
47 Edgar A. Porter, "Mongolia, Northeast Asia and the United States: Seeking the Right Balance," *Asia Pacific University Journal*, November 8, 2005, p. 9, at https://www.apu.ac.jp/rcaps/uploads/fckeditor/publications/journal/RJAPS_V26_PorterE_df.pdf (accessed April 20, 2020).
48 William Sposato, "Japan Seeks Stronger Mongolia Ties, *Wall Street Journal*, March 30, 2013, at Japan Seeks Stronger Mongolia Ties - WSJ, https://www.wsj.com/articles/SB10001424127887324685104578392123216653156 (accessed May 19, 2021).
49 "Prime Minister Abe's Article contributed to four Mongolian Newspapers," *Speeches and Statements by the Prime Minister, japan.kantei.go.jp*, March 29, 2013, at http://japan.kantei.go.jp/96_abe/statement/201303/29_mongol_e.html (accessed April 19, 2020).
50 Lkhaajav Bolor, "Far East Affairs: Mongolia and Japan, *The Diplomat*, March 10, 2017, at https://thediplomat.com/2017/03/far-east-affairs-mongolia-and-japan/ (accessed April 19, 2020).
51 "Chongryon HQ Sale Decision Delayed," *Japan Property Central.com*, October 24, 2013, at https://japanpropertycentral.com/2013/10/chongryon-hq-sale-decision-delayed/ (accessed April 22, 2020).
52 This is the first time that the Prime Minister of Japan Abe Shinzo, had invited a leader of a foreign country to his home. "Shinzo Abe invites President Ts. Elbegdorj to his home," *montsame.gov.mn*, September 30, 2013 and October 2, 2013, at http://english.news.mn/content/157777.shtml (accessed April 20, 2020).
53 Rob York, "Parents of abducted Japanese girl meet granddaughter," *NK News*, March 16, 2014, at https://www.nknews.org/2014/03/parents-of-abducted-japanese-girl-meet-granddaughter/ (accessed April 20, 2020).

54 At that time Japan agreed to a US$820 million soft loan and sought Mongolian cooperation in implementing synthetic gas and fuel production projects using Mongolian coal and Japan's technology. Bayarbat Turmunkh, "Japan to grant an 850 million USD soft loan to Mongolia," *theubpost.mn*, March 31, 2017, https://www.pressreader.com/mongolia/the-ub-post/20170331/281479276254326 (accessed April 22, 2020).
55 "Prime Minister of Japan Shinzo Abe Pays Courtesy Call on President of Mongolia Kh. Battulga," *President of Mongolia website*, September 6, 2017, at https://president.mn/en/2017/09/06/prime-minister-of-japan-shinzo-abe-pays-courtesy-call-on-president-of-mongolia-kh-battulga/ (accessed April 10, 2020).
56 "Meeting with Shinzo Abe, Prime Minister of Japan," President of Mongolia website, September 11, 2018, at https://president.mn/en/2018/09/11/meeting-with-shinzo-abe-prime-minister-of-japan-eef2018/ (accessed April 10, 2020).
57 "Japan-Mongolia Summit Meeting," Ministry of Foreign Affairs of Japan, September 11, 2018, at https://www.mofa.go.jp/a_o/c_m1/mn/page3e_000919 (accessed April 20, 2020).
58 Sharad K. Soni, "The Geopolitical Dilemma of Small States in External Relations: Mongolia's Tryst with 'Immediate' and 'Third' Neighbours," *Mongolian Journal of International Affairs* 20, 2018, p. 32.
59 Bolor Lkhaajav, "Mongolia's Third Neighbor Policy Blooms," *The Diplomat*, March 29, 2016, at https://tribunecontentagency.com/article/mongolia039s-third-neighbor-policy-blooms/ (accessed November 13, 2020).
60 Baasanhuu, "Impact of National Identity on Modern Mongolian Foreign Policy."
61 Caroline Humphrey, "Pastoral Nomadism in Mongolia: The Role of Herdsmen's Cooperatives in the National Economy," *Development and Change*, SAGE, London and Beverly Hills, Volume 9, 1978, p. 152; David Sneath, "Kinship, Networks and Residence," in *The End of Nomadism?*, Caroline Humphrey and David Sneath (eds), Duke University Press, Durham, NC, 1999, pp. 159–161.
62 Christopher Atwood, *Encyclopedia of Mongolia and the Mongol Empire*, Facts on File, Inc., New York, 2004, p. 16.
63 Baasanhuu, "Impact of National Identity on Modern Mongolian Foreign Policy."
64 "Trade in Goods with Mongolia," US Census Bureau, at https://www.census.gov/foreign-trade/balance/c5740.html (accessed April 19, 2020).

8 Why Asia should lead a global push to eliminate nuclear weapons—the role for Mongolia

Michael Andregg

Introduction

The purpose of this chapter is to explicate reasons why Asia is especially well-positioned to lead a global push to eliminate, or greatly reduce, nuclear weapons inventories worldwide, and why Mongolia might be catalytic to that effort. The threat of any general thermonuclear war is existential to civilisation itself. No one understands that better than Japan. North Korea and South Korea want to unify, but they cannot while they are clients of opposing major powers, China and the United States (US). Nuclear weapons tragically complicate this, at great expense and risk to everyone. Meanwhile, Pakistan is destabilising, which scares everyone in South Asia and many worldwide, because of its long feud with nuclear-armed India that has included four conventional wars. The risk that Pakistani nuclear explosives could find their way to Islamic terrorist groups terrifies other nations. Many analysts, therefore, consider South Asia the most likely place for a nuclear war to start today.

Russia is a declining power and is frightened by both NATO and a fast-rising China. China has considerable capital it could devote to a noble, global cause like nuclear arms control. Israel is a wild card, which motivates Iran to be one too. The former has a complete nuclear triad, and Iran could build nuclear weapons in the next several years if allowed. Meanwhile, the US is paralysed on this topic by its weapons industry (among other factors), and everyone who now possesses nuclear weapons is modernising. Europe, in general, is quite alarmed by US' abandonment of the Intermediate-Range Nuclear Arms Treaty (INF)[1] and by Russian threats to use "small" nuclear weapons in tactical situations.[2] Therefore, the European Union (EU) probably would support any Asian effort to bring sanity to this situation before any more large wars get fought over their territories. No European nation wants to become a battleground for major powers fighting with nuclear weapons. This chapter will discuss some solutions, well aware that the countries that already possess nuclear weapons are extremely reluctant to eliminate or even to limit them.

DOI: 10.4324/9781003148630-8

Existential threats and the law of low probabilities

Almost all educated people recognise that a general thermonuclear war would destroy human civilisation itself, perhaps permanently. Nonetheless, some "experts" still toy with "smaller" scenarios of limited nuclear strikes. Why they think those "limited" nuclear conflicts would not escalate is somewhat mysterious. If worst-case scenarios came true, such as nuclear winter,[3] deliberate distribution of radioactive materials, and even clandestine use of biological weapons, human survival itself could be at risk, not just civilisation. Yet, most of the current nuclear powers seem content to sleepwalk on, as though fear of nuclear weapons being used means that they will never be used.

Very few weapons created by people have "never been used." And very few nations at war surrender without using their most powerful weapons. Some nations have accepted lesser defeats during Cold War proxy wars, however. The proxies always suffered most, and some of them lost millions of people killed. Watching that carnage, there always are other people who wish to join the "nuclear club." It buys respect and attention, no matter how immoral. For instance, there is Iran, ever threatened by Israel.[4] Iran threatens Israel too, so both have valid fears. But, if Iran gets nuclear weapons, Saudi Arabia will surely want them too, and so on and on. North Korea's recent testing prompts others, like Japan, South Korea, and Taiwan, to rethink their current bans on creating or using nuclear weapons.

One way or another, all of these countries depend on a theory developed during the earliest days of the nuclear crisis after World War II. This is called the *deterrence theory*, and it was refined during the Cold War. However, nuclear deterrence theory has a critical flaw, an embedded assumption called the "rational actor" assumption.[5] Simply stated, this assumption concludes that if total destruction of any nation were guaranteed, no matter how skillfully it conducted a secret "first strike" against its nuclear enemy(s), no leader would ever order a first strike, because leaders are assumed to be "rational" in their thinking at all times. Hence, the common acronym, "MAD" for Mutual Assured Destruction.

There is a critical difference here between the words "most" and "all". Yes, most national leaders appear to be "rational" most of the time, but a clear-eyed reading of history quickly reveals that not ALL leaders are ever rational, much less always rational. Even wise, moral, intelligent, and clear-headed leaders can be injured, get disease (like brain tumours), and all of them get old (if they are lucky). Each of these factors can diminish "rationality", however that is defined. Furthermore, cultures differ much more than many people realise on what they regard to be "rational".

Crisis situations reduce the validity of the rational actor assumption even more. In crises, people get tired, literally irritated, and are often confused. Information gets distorted, strange things happen, communications may be scrambled, computers can fail, radars can break, officers in the field can "go rogue," and the "fog of war" can make even the simplest things hard to do or even to understand. All of these factors further reduce the validity of the rational actor assumption during crises.

Finally, there are "third parties" in this world who would love to start a nuclear war between "great powers", which they see as mortal enemies. Some call such parties "terrorists", but they do not apply this term to themselves. They call themselves "freedom fighters" or similar noble terms for people trying to protect their small nations or weak communities from ruthless others. One of the nightmare scenarios is for some terrorist group to acquire two nuclear warheads by any one of many possible methods, then smuggle one into Moscow and the other into Washington, DC to be set off simultaneously.

Should such a scenario unfold, with launch-on-warning protocols, several hundred or even thousands of nuclear warheads could be heading towards targets minutes later, no matter how "rationally" the doomsday system was conceived and created.[6] A similar, smaller nightmare scenario, for example, requires only one nuclear explosive, delivered somehow to Tel Aviv. Twenty Islamic capitals could be attacked within thirty minutes if the Israelis were not restrained in response, which few analysts predict they would be.

This brings us to the law of low probabilities. Gamblers know that even very rare events often occur eventually, if they are possible, such as winning a lottery despite multi-million odds against any individual winning one. Someone always does win, eventually. Or, getting hit by lightning despite million to one odds against this. Dozens of such events do occur each year. Mathematician Siméon Denis Poisson figured out some relationships between the probability of a rare event and the time for it to occur.[7]

A concrete example would be, *if* the probability of a triggering event that would set off a general nuclear war is 1 per cent per year, the half-life of human civilisation would be approximately 69 years. That is, if the annual risk is 1 per cent, over 69 years the probability of such a war erupting would be 50 per cent (counterintuitive, but true). If the rare event did not occur, the probability of it occurring during the next 69 years also would be 50 per cent, making the statistical odds of the war occurring over 138 years equal to 75 per cent. That rises the more years one takes that risk, asymptoting to a probability of 99.99999 per cent that the rare event will occur. The practical point is that, if you wait long enough and do not change the core conditions, the rare event will almost certainly happen.

Realising this, some of the brighter minds that helped create deterrence theory and/or implement its weapons and doctrines (including Henry Kissinger, George Schultz, William Perry, and Sam Nunn) have advocated in recent years for getting rid of ALL nuclear weapons.[8] Having stumbled into the nuclear arms race with the Soviets/Russians with the best of intentions, then having dodged close calls like the Cuban Missile Crisis of 1962, and a lesser-known but equally risky crisis in 1983 in Europe (which led to the INF Treaty), these American statesmen and one former Secretary of Defense directly involved in nuclear weapons research, Dr. William J. Perry, realised that reducing the probability of nuclear war was not enough to avoid catastrophe unless the probability is reduced to zero. Rare events happen, and crazy leaders pop up in the strangest places, all too often. In addition, accidents happen, radars and computers fail, and third parties can and often do weird things for perverse reasons. These "wise men's" words of nuclear restraint fly against a tide of vested interests that make much money off the current system today. The weapons businesses and the politicians who support them seldom think ten years ahead much less hundreds of years or millennia. Quarterly profits and next elections usually dominate their very short time horizons compared to civilisations.

Asian nuclear countries and their relevant histories

Having presented some basics, let us discuss a few details of nuclear weapons' history and doctrines in Asia in order to present an argument that Asian leadership is essential, if we are to avoid a nuclear catastrophe in the long term. The nine nations currently known to possess nuclear weapons are Russia, the US, China, France, Great Britain, Pakistan, India, Israel, and North Korea. Among these, five are Asian nations. The US and Israel also are very concerned about developments in Asia, which leads to some targeting of capitals and military forces in Asia. France and Britain have smaller arsenals and are mainly concerned about European threats, but they too have global targeting capability.

The nuclear weapons age began in Asia on August 6, 1945, when the first nuclear weapon used in war was detonated over Hiroshima, Japan. That killed about 100,000 people promptly, and tens of thousands more died over decades due to injury and long-term effects of radiation. Three days later, a second nuclear attack on Nagasaki effectively ended World War II and annihilated more than 100,000 lives there. These attacks, arguably, also saved a half-million allied forces lives, which were assembling for a land conquest of Imperial Japan, and an uncountable number of Japanese civilians and soldiers. So, allied war goals were achieved, but profound effects from these attacks on Japan still linger to this day. Of particular relevance to nuclear issues is Article Six of the Japanese Constitution (written by the American military occupiers), which prohibits both nuclear weapons and any offensive use of Japan's minimal Japanese Self-Defence Forces.

Deterrence advocates justifiably have observed that no one has used a nuclear weapon in war since. However, 75 years without a nuclear holocaust is much less than forever. Nuclear deterrence theory actually requires that to be valid. The presence of such weapons has certainly not ended wars. For example, wars involving the US have killed about six million people since then, largely on the Korean Peninsula and in Vietnam, Cambodia, Laos, and Iraq, along with smaller numbers of people in dozens of other formal and informal war zones scattered across the Middle East, Africa, Asia, and Latin America.

Most of the world was quite relieved when the worst war in history ended in 1945. However, the shock of those first nuclear detonations also stimulated an arms race among other nations to acquire some of their own nuclear bombs. Spies did their jobs,[9] and the Soviet Union was next to detonate its own nuclear weapons in tests that included the largest weapon ever created, a 50-megaton behemoth (called "Tsar Bomba" in the west) on October 30, 1961.[10] The US shared its nuclear technologies with World War II allies Britain and France. Not long after, now communist China (PRC) built its own nuclear "deterrent", and the global nuclear arms race was on.

Another side effect (to some) of the sudden end to World War II was a division of the Korean Peninsula into a communist North and capitalist South. The Korean War of 1950–1953 was not, of course, a side effect to Koreans. But, it was the first example of nuclear patrons backing down and accepting defeat in a proxy war without using them during the engagement. The Soviet Union chose not to use its nuclear weapons to defend North Korea, even though Chinese allies lost at least 150,000 troops there and possibly a great many more.[11]

The peninsula division persists to this day, with a four-kilometre Demilitarised Zone (DMZ) separating North Korea from South Korea. Since peace was never formally declared, small hostile incidents have continued between the two states.[12] Meanwhile, the South's economy has grown 40 times larger than communist North Korea's.[13] Insecurity in the North and uncertainty regarding how far its patrons would go in its defence finally led to the development from 2006 to 2017 of nuclear weapons by the Pyongyang government, which has frightened much of the rest of East Asia.[14] This has come to the attention of the US since it is formally committed to defending both South Korea and Japan from nuclear (or any) attack by adversaries.

Britain, France, and China have opted for "minimal deterrence" out of belief that a few hundred nuclear weapons with reliable delivery systems[15] would be enough to deter aggressors and that "winning" "limited" nuclear wars is impossible. The Soviet Union and the US, however, spent vast sums on research over the succeeding years for new designs, development, and eventually production of over 30,000 nuclear warheads each. This resulted in a global peak of over 60,000 nuclear warheads in 1985.[16] They created scores of different types that are associated with hundreds of delivery systems from ICBMs to artillery to "suitcase bombs."[17] Yields ranged from less than 1 kiloton to over 10 megatons on deployed delivery systems, a range of over 10,000-fold in explosive power.

India conducted its first nuclear weapons test in 1974 but yielded to global diplomatic pressure and public opinion by not publicly developing an offensive arsenal for many years. India at the same time won occasional conventional wars with Pakistan.[18] This situation did not please Pakistan's military, which then devoted billions of dollars from its very scarce resources to close that technology gap. In May 1998, India conducted a series of five nuclear weapons tests, and these were followed promptly by nuclear tests in Pakistan. This proved that both had been conducting secret nuclear weapons research programmes for decades. A South Asian nuclear arms race was now openly on. The two nations rapidly built arsenals that exceeded 100 deliverable warheads each. In 2020, India has at least 135 deliverable warheads and Pakistan 145. It is postulated that Pakistan probably builds more new warheads every year than any other nation.

As noted earlier, many intelligence analysts consider these two nuclear-armed adversaries to be the most likely to use nuclear weapons in anger next, because they are so focused on each other and have such a long history of conventional strife during the last more than 70 years.[19]

Israel is not an Asian nation, but some of its targets are. Israel probably developed its first functional nuclear warhead in 1968, but that story is murky because of its refusal to sign the pivotal nuclear Non-Proliferation Treaty (NPT) of 1970. The NPT requires extensive disclosure of nuclear weapons facilities and materials, numbers of weapons, and international inspections for those states outside of the original nuclear club (US, USSR/ Russia, United Kingdom, France, and China).

The International Atomic Energy Agency (IAEA), an entity within the United Nations system, is central to undertaking those inspection and verification methods that reassure other frightened nations. It has been accepted internationally that requiring intrusive verification of nuclear systems is one principal benefit of international arms control measures, regardless of whether or not they result in quantitative reductions or qualitative limitations on weapons.

At least two other currently non-nuclear Asian nations, in addition to Japan, should be mentioned because they could become nuclear weapons nations much faster than most understand. Either nation also could also become flashpoints for war between major nuclear powers. Those states are Taiwan (Republic of China) and South Korea. So far, they both rely on security guarantees by the US and occasional reassurance that the American "nuclear umbrella" protects them too. But, they worry if the US is now reliable. Meanwhile, Japan has the technologies required for a very fast "nuclear breakout", if North Korea or China were to gravely threaten it. Japan also retains very large quantities of plutonium, a critical, expensive, and hard to acquire element necessary for the larger yield thermonuclear explosives, due to Japan's reprocessing capability that supports its still very large nuclear power industry.

Special importance of Northeast Asia, especially Mongolia

It has been noted how catalytic North Korea could become in this tangled mess of WMDs and threats to use them. Their recent development of both fission and fusion nuclear weapons and ongoing development of ever better delivery missiles with ever longer ranges has woken up both near neighbours and superpowers half a world away. But, there is another small nation in Northeast Asia which is trying to be catalytic, albeit in a positive, peacemaking kind of way. That nation is Mongolia, which tries very hard to maintain good relations with all of the relevant parties, instead of joining one block or another in exclusive alliances. Almost all small nations try to maintain good relations with large neighbours, but Mongolia is probably unique in its devotion to that goal regardless of ideological, religious, and economic divisions. North Korea's list of friends, by contrast, is quite short, but Mongolia is undoubtedly among them. It has invested considerable diplomatic effort in trying to broker better relations in particular between North Korea and South Korea.

Surrounded by Russia and China, Mongolia simply must maintain good relations with these two nuclear giants. Since 1990, very early in its young democracy, it recognised that it also must cultivate good relations with some other major powers to balance those autocratic states. The US was an obvious candidate, and it did indeed help them a lot in the difficult years after the Soviet Union broke up.[20]

Mongolia is special in another way. One hundred fourteen nations have declared themselves "Nuclear Weapons Free Zones" (NWFZ) through six international treaties that declared some continents to be weapons-free (such as Africa and South America) and other large areas that included dozens of countries. Wedged between two huge nuclear powers, Mongolia could not join an area coalition, although it did try. Mongolia's Ambassador to the United Nations, J. Enkhsaikhan, described years of his and others' labour in a paper presented at a conference on these topics at Mongolia's Foreign Ministry in September, 2019. As Dr. Enkhsaikhan noted: "In the mid-1990s, a proposal was made to establish such a zone (a NWFZ) which would include two Koreas, and Japan, to which the United States, Russia, and China would provide security assurances. Due to lack of trust, it was a nonstarter."[21] However, visionaries in Mongolia's new democratic government determined to press ahead with a 12-year effort to gain NWFZ status, which eventually was recognised by the United Nations and by many specific nations. Equally as important to Mongols were bilateral agreements with all of the main nuclear weapons states (the original five, as recognised in the NPT) to preserve their territorial integrity and to promise to never to transit Mongolia with nuclear weapons or otherwise to abuse its strategic space by placing nuclear arms or any of their delivery enablers on Mongolian territory.

There is another potential factor to consider about Mongolia, before discussing much larger and more powerful neighbours such as China and Japan. Mongolia, while developing rapidly, is still only two generations away from a predominantly nomadic, herdsman culture. Its small population is intimate with nature. Even today, only about 3 million people live there on a vast land, only 1 per cent of which can be farmed. Nature knows that indiscriminate destruction, such as WMD cause, damages the "seventh generation" which often is referred to in indigenous cultures in the Americas.[22]

Therefore, Mongols do not try to prevail in disputes by brute force, especially if that would mean destruction of the ecosystems that support us all. The spirituality of people with feet firmly on the ground and spirits in the blue sky also tends to be more inclusive of others, near or far away. So, it can be speculated that there is a spiritual dimension to Mongols that also motivates their approach to nuclear weapons policy.

The economic behemoths of Northeast Asia are obviously China and Japan. One is nuclear-armed and the other is pacifist by constitution, if not by history. Both countries have financial and technical resources that will be sorely needed to implement any agreement to rethink global security on such a large scale. As noted earlier, Japan also has a unique moral claim to leadership of any significant drive to change nuclear realities on earth today. If nuclear China cannot pledge to work towards a nuclear-free world, then all the other nuclear states likely will dig in their heels to obstruct such mammoth change. This is why Chinese support or even leadership is essential.

This then leads to consideration of North Korea and South Korea. North Korea is another relatively small nation bounded by economic giants, China and Japan. Of course, North Korea is preoccupied with South Korea and its superpower patron, the US. Its current dynastic leader, Kim Jong-un, has an especially wicked reputation for killing close relatives and anyone else with insufficient devotion to his police state. But, Kim also is young and has shown that he can rethink current arrangements in possibly catalytic and revolutionary ways, if so inclined. South Korea remembers millennia of common peninsula history and prays for peace. It also has very large resources necessary to manage reunification if and when that becomes possible.

If Mongolia and newly nuclear North Korea could form one axis of peacemaking, representing the smaller nations of the earth, then perhaps China, Japan, and South Korea could form another, an axis of economic powerhouses that recognise that all the money in the world will be worthless if a nuclear war occurs on their lands. Who might start that war would be irrelevant, but it is likely to occur if we wait long enough. Surrounding one's home with huge explosives to "deter" bad people is a formula for long-term pain. This then is fertile ground for visionary leaders in all five of these Northeast Asian nations to reflect upon today.

Major successes and failures of nuclear arms control

In 2019, the world had about 15,000 usable nuclear warheads.[23] About 14,000 of those were owned by Russia and the US, with the remaining thousand scattered among the seven other nuclear weapons nations named above. This reduction from the peak of well over 60,000 nuclear warheads is due entirely to successes in a cluster of nuclear weapons arms control treaties that started with the NPT treaty of 1970.

However, that comprehensive set of restraints is rapidly unravelling today for many reasons.[24] Several of these treaties dealt with numbers of nuclear warheads and delivery systems deployed by the US and the Soviet Union, now Russia. At least as important as warhead numbers were required systems of verification including inspections that came with each treaty. Other treaties prohibit any nuclear weapons in specific areas, like outer space, Antarctica, and among countries that oppose the global nuclear arms race.

Therefore, listed below are the most important among those treaties, ranked roughly by the time of signature or "entry into force."[25] The most salient strengths or weaknesses of each will be noted, and why some failed to gain ratification or even symbolic force of international law.

Antarctic Treaty, 1961

This was the earliest treaty, which established the Antarctic continent as a place exempted from all military activity, not just nuclear weapons. The goal was to foster scientific collaboration in a place safe for all. This treaty has been quite successful.

Partial Test Ban Treaty, 1963

After radioactive isotopes were discovered in baby teeth and mothers' milk, women complained about testing nuclear weapons in the air, which spreads radiation worldwide. Because of this treaty, almost all nuclear tests since then have occurred underground, where most of those radioactive isotopes can be much better contained, so this treaty has been remarkably effective.

Outer Space Treaty, 1967

This treaty prohibits the placement of nuclear weapons in space and generally bans military activity in space that threatens the earth in any way. The treaty can be judged moderately effective since no known nuclear weapons are in space today. However, several countries, including the US, China, and Russia desire other military capabilities in space, and there are movements in that direction. Of particular importance is development of weapons to attack satellites.[26]

Non-Proliferation Treaty (NPT), 1970

"More countries have signed and adhered to the NPT than any other arms limitation and disarmament treaty, a testament to the treaty's value."[27] The basic agreement here was that the early nuclear weapons' nations would share nuclear power technology with the rest of the world in return for non-nuclear nations choosing not to develop nuclear weapons. They also agreed to allow intrusive inspections of reactors and fuel reprocessing facilities to prevent proliferation of weapons technology or materials. However, Article 6 of the NPT also *requires* the nuclear nations to conduct good faith, ongoing negotiations to *eliminate* nuclear weapons *entirely*. Therefore, the most prominent nations not in full compliance with this treaty today are Russia and the US. Some analysts conclude that it is "Time to Ditch the NPT" in favour of the more comprehensive 2017 Treaty on Prohibition of Nuclear Weapons.[28]

Anti-Ballistic Missile Treaty (ABM), 1972

This treaty only involved the US and the Soviet Union, until the Soviet Union disintegrated into Russia and 14 other independent states. Its purpose was to limit creation of defences that could undercut the Mutual Assured Destruction strategy. That worked fairly well at its stated goal, but when the US withdrew in 2002 to build new-generation missile defence systems, Russia also withdrew, so the ABM treaty now is defunct.

Seabed Arms Control Treaty, 1972

This prohibited placement of nuclear weapons on or under seabeds around the world. One of many nightmare scenarios thus averted was creation of tsunami waves by nuclear detonations underwater that could travel thousands of kilometres and harm innocents far removed from the parties to a conflict.

SALT I, 1972

This was the first of a series of bilateral agreements between the US and the Soviet Union (later Russia). The acronym SALT stands for "Strategic Arms Limitation Treaty." This treaty established strict inspection and verification measures for the two "superpowers" and called for continuing negotiations.[29] This was succeeded by SALT II, START, SORT, and finally New START treaties, each of which set lower limits on both deployed warheads and associated delivery systems, such as ICBMs, sub-launched ballistic missiles, bombers, and cruise missiles. Unfortunately, this series of treaties requires ongoing ratification to remain in force, and no talks have been scheduled for several years to continue this process. These have another significant weakness. China has never signed nor ratified any of these bilateral treaties and does not abide by some other treaties like the Intermediate-Range Nuclear Forces Treaty (INF). A recurring theme in weak arms control systems is the failure of the most important nations, the ones who maintain strategic nuclear arsenals, to sign, ratify, or obey them.

Intermediate-Range Nuclear Forces Treaty (INF), 1988

This bilateral treaty banned delivery systems for nuclear weapons with ranges of 500 to 5,500 kilometres (km). It resulted from much discussion in the early 1980s about winning "limited nuclear wars" which might be waged over Europe. Talk was followed by deployment of many types of such missiles by the Soviet Union and the US in Europe. European nations were not generally pleased, so this treaty represented progress. Regrettably, Russia later was accused of developing and deploying a non-compliant, ground-based cruise missile, so the US declared its intention to withdraw from the treaty on October 20, 2018.[30] This decision was finalised on August 2, 2019.[31] It bears mentioning that "Two weeks after abrogating the INF Treaty, the US military ground launched a Tomahawk cruise missile on 18 August, which flew more than 500 km."[32] This illustrates how quickly nuclear nations that want new attack capabilities can create them. It is fear of such "breakout" capabilities that fuels the nuclear arms race cycle, which must be escaped before the "system" detonates. President Donald Trump also has complained that China never signed this treaty. Although this is true, and getting China to do so could be complicated by conflicts with India and Pakistan, if China wanted to lead a new effort on nuclear arms control resurrecting the INF or joining a new one would be a good place to start.

Comprehensive Nuclear Test Ban Treaty (CTBT), (1996)

This was adopted by the UN General Assembly in 1996 and for a time looked like great progress for the world. It would have banned all nuclear explosions (underground as well as in the atmosphere or in the oceans) and established a large international system of test detection technologies.[33] A true and total ban on testing would, over time, reduce everyone's confidence in the old nuclear arsenals and reduce the probability of "first strikes." Unfortunately, the CTBT also required signatures and ratification by all nuclear nations known at that time and by many states that could make them in the future. US President Bill Clinton signed this treaty in 1999, but a hostile US Senate declined to ratify it. This doomed the project, although some detection systems have been deployed, and most nations have refrained from explosive nuclear testing to this day. North Korea is the most recent exception. As of 2016, eight "Annex 2" nations including China had not ratified the treaty, and three nuclear nations had not even signed it by 2020 (India, North Korea, and Pakistan). Therefore, China could lead here too, if it so wished.

Regional Nuclear Weapons-Free Zone Treaties (1961 to 2009)

There currently are seven nuclear-weapons-free zones that cover some very large areas, including Antarctica, Latin America and the Caribbean, South Pacific, Southeast Asia, Africa, Central Asia, and Mongolia. These represent efforts by the many non-nuclear weapons countries to pressure the nuclear nations to stop threatening the entire world with their doomsday arsenals. The central conundrum of this system is exposed again. So long as most nations that have nuclear arsenals will not agree to constrain them, the half-life of human civilisation remains short, and doomsday clocks tick on.

Treaty on the Prohibition of Nuclear Weapons (2017)

Recognising these dilemmas and led by smaller countries, the UN General Assembly voted for a truly comprehensive ban on nuclear weapons on July 7, 2017. The vote was 122 in favour, 1 against, and 1 abstention, with 69 nations not voting, among them all of the nuclear weapons states and all NATO members except The Netherlands.[34] Therefore, despite great efforts and high aspirations on behalf of most of human civilisation, the nuclear weapons arms control treaties must be judged as having been only partly successful.

Why Asia must lead at this time

Today, the nuclear arms race is more qualitative than quantitative, but it still is moving in the wrong direction, if survival of civilisation is a primary goal. Asia must lead nuclear disarmament efforts today because the US will not, Europe cannot, and both Russia and Israel feel surrounded by mortal enemies. Asia must lead because it includes half of the declared nuclear powers (China, India, Pakistan, and North Korea) while Russia is both European and Asian. Moreover, Asia should lead, because it includes Japan, the only country to suffer the full horrors of a nuclear attack.

Mongolia has been leading by hosting a special, APHA/ISCSC conference[35] on nuclear and other issues that challenge survival of our civilisations. Like so many other neutral countries, Mongolia lies between large nuclear powers that could utterly devastate it should they wage a nuclear war over Mongolia's territory. It appears that Mongolia has the courage to point out how bad this system is for all of human civilisation in the long run. Mongolia also is one of the few countries on earth that has good relations with all of the most relevant powers in Northeast Asia and South Asia.

The belief among some people and nations that a few countries can hold the rest of humankind hostage to nuclear terror forever without anyone ever using those weapons is an illusion. Unfortunately, powerful forces that profit from nuclear weapons systems exert daily pressure on governments to block rethinking the fatal assumptions that underlie nuclear deterrence theory today.

Therefore, steps should be taken in international and national laws to prohibit nuclear weapons among civilised nations, similar to the bans on biological and chemical weapons. Such bans have worked reasonably well in the past, and "reasonably well" is much better than no restraints at all. Of course, such solutions are not perfect, but perfection has never been a realistic goal in either law or statecraft. Laws against murder are never perfect either, yet every nation has them. Norms matter. For example, almost no one has been killed by biological weapons since the biological weapons convention was established. Soldiers threw plague-infested bodies over fortification walls in Europe[36] and gave smallpox-infected blankets to Native Americans they wanted to kill.[37] The modern biological weapons convention is not perfect, but we are all safer because of it. We also have much better disease surveillance, research, and response capabilities today, because of that legal taboo and its enabling institutions.

One can follow the examples of the International Committee to Abolish Nuclear Weapons (co-winner of the 2017 Nobel Peace Prize) and of the United Nations to implement the goal of eliminating nuclear weapons. However, a nation also can lead. Therefore, Asian nations should consider their special abilities to do so now in the service of humanity at large.

Notes

1 Reuters, "EU is extremely worried about future of INF nuclear treaty," November 20, 2018, at https://mobile.reuters.com/video/2018/11/20/eu-extremely-worried-about-future-of-inf?videoId=484149671&videoChannel=117759 (accessed October 7, 2020).
2 Christopher Woody, "Russia reportedly warned Mattis it could use nuclear weapons in Europe, and it made him see Moscow as an 'existential threat' to the US," *Business Insider*, September 14, 2018, at https://www.businessinsider.com/russia-warned-mattis-it-could-use-tactical-nuclear-weapons-baltic-war-2018-9 (accessed October 7, 2020).
3 "Nuclear Winter" is a theoretical effect of the burning of many cities in a large or general nuclear war. All those cities with petroleum products and other materials burning at once could create clouds thick and persistent enough to compromise agriculture thousands of miles away. Since this has never been observed directly and no one wants to test it, "nuclear winter" remains a theory today. See "Nuclear Winter," *Encyclopaedia Britannica*, https://www.britannica.com/science/nuclear-winter (accessed October 7, 2020).
4 At least four and possibly more Iranian scientists associated with Iran's nuclear research programme were assassinated by agents of Israel between 2010 and 2012. More data on that can be found in Ronen Bergman's exceptional book, *Rise and Kill First: The Secret History of Israel's Targeted Assassinations*, Random House, New York, 2018, or *Wikipedia*, at https://en.wikipedia.org/wiki/Assassination_of_Iranian_nuclear_scientists (accessed October 6, 2020).
5 Alex Minz, *Understanding Foreign Policy Decision Making*, Cambridge University Press, London, 2010, Chapter 4. In this chapter on "The Rational Actor Model," Minz discusses pros and cons of this critical assumption about behaviours of state leaders.
6 One of the earliest and most enthusiastic rationalists for nuclear deterrence theory, Herman Kahn, was quoted in the most recent US guidance on "Nuclear Operations," in *Joint Publication 3-72* by US Department of Defense (DOD), as the epigraph to Chapter 3 on "Planning and Targeting." Kahn wrote: "My guess is that nuclear weapons will be used sometime in the next hundred years, but that their use is much more likely to be small and limited than widespread and unconstrained." This document was briefly available on the DOD's website, then withdrawn, but it can be found at the Federation of American Scientists, at https://fas.org/irp/doddir/dod/jp3_72.pdf (accessed October 7, 2020).
7 A detailed description of Poisson math distributions and how they work can be found at https://www.umass.edu/wsp/resources/poisson/ (accessed October 7, 2020).

8 Two of these authors were former Secretaries of State, one a Secretary of Defense and Ph.D. nuclear physicist, and Sam Nunn, who was a long-serving US senator who co-authored the "Nunn-Lugar Act" that helped the USSR reduce its nuclear vulnerabilities when it disintegrated into Russia and 14 other independent countries. The point is that even many architects of the nuclear weapons age developed deep misgivings about its long-term wisdom. A thorough review of highly informed skeptics would have to include Albert Einstein and Robert Oppenheimer among others. See George P. Shultz, William J. Perry, Henry A. Kissinger, and Sam Nunn, "A World Free of Nuclear Weapons," *The Wall Street Journal*, January 4, 2007, at https://www.wsj.com/articles/SB116787515251566636 (accessed October 7, 2020).

9 Klaus Fuchs is the best known and possibly the most important spy to leak nuclear secrets to the Soviet Union during the 1950s, but a longer list is available at *Wikipedia*, at https://en.wikipedia.org/wiki/Atomic_spies (accessed October 7, 2020).

10 "Tsar Bomba" is described in a history page of the Atomic Heritage foundation: "50 megatons" yield means the equivalent explosive force of 50 million tons of TNT detonated simultaneously. See https://www.atomicheritage.org/history/tsar-bomba (accessed October 7, 2020).

11 Xu Yan and Li Xizo-Bing (Translator) (1993) "The Chinese Forces and their Casualties in the Korean War: Facts and Statistics," in *Chinese Historians*, 6 (2), May 25, 2017, pp. 45–58, at https://www.tandfonline.com/doi/citedby/10.1080/1043643X.1993.11876905?scroll=top&needAccess=true (accessed October 10, 2020).

12 Simon Rogers, "North Korea vs. South Korea: Mapping every incident from 1958 to 2013," *The Guardian*, April 11, 2013, at https://www.theguardian.com/news/datablog/2010/nov/23/north-korea-yeonpyeong-island-incidents-map (accessed October 7, 2020).

13 Prableen Bajpai, "North Korean vs. South Korean Economies: What's the Difference?" *Investopedia*, April 14, 2019, at https://www.investopedia.com/articles/forex/040515/north-korean-vs-south-korean-economies (accessed October 7, 2020).

14 "North Korea Nuclear Timeline Fast Facts," *CNN Library*, May 6, 2019, at https://www.cnn.com/2013/10/29/world/asia/north-korea-nuclear-timeline---fast-facts/index.html (accessed October 7, 2020).

15 It was thought that in 2018 the United Kingdom had about 215 nuclear warheads, France about 300, and China about 280. See "2018 Estimated Global Nuclear Warhead Inventories," Arms Control Association fact sheet, at https://www.armscontrol.org/factsheets/Nuclearweaponswhohaswhat (accessed October 5, 2020).

16 The 60,000 warheads figure is a minimal estimate. Many references claim the real peak of nuclear weapons was over 70,000. Many factors affect such estimates such as whether one includes "tactical" with "strategic" weapons, or "deployed" with "in reserve" and such, along with continuing secrecy by nations like Israel, India, and Pakistan. The real total number is practically insignificant because any of the larger nuclear inventories could potentially destroy the entire earth (for humans). See Robert S. Norris and Hans M. Kristensen, "Global nuclear weapons inventories: 1945-2010," *Bulletin of Atomic Sciences* 66 (4), November 2015, pp. 77–83, at https://www.tandfonline.com/doi/full/10.2968/066004008 (accessed October 10, 2020).

17 The myriad of nuclear weapons designs from that era included even "man-portable nuclear demolitions" (the US term) and "suitcase bombs" (a Soviet term for warheads designed to look like suitcases) for smuggling to targets.

18 These include wars of 1947 (original partition after WW II), 1965 (when Pakistan lost control of what is now Bangladesh), 1971, and 1999 (the last two were about issues of who controls which parts of Kashmir). The stability of this conflict dyad

was further reduced when India's PM Modi revoked the special, semi-autonomous status of Indian-controlled Kashmir on August 5, 2019. See "Indo-Pakistani wars and conflicts," *Wikipedia*, at https://en.wikipedia.org/wiki/Indo-Pakistani_wars_and_conflicts (accessed October 7, 2020).

19 Annie Waqar, "Nuclear War between India and Pakistan? An expert assesses the risk," *The Conversation,* March 6, 2019, at http://theconversation.com/nuclear-war-between-india-and-pakistan-an-expert-assesses-the-risk-112892 (accessed October 7, 2020).

20 Alicia Campi, *Mongolia's Foreign Policy: Navigating a Changing World*, Lynne Rienner Publications, 2019, especially Chapter 4 on "Building a New Economy Through Donor Aid."

21 J. Enkhsaikhan, "Denuclearizing the Korean peninsula: a broader approach is needed," Asian Political History Association (APHA) conference on, "Challenges Confronting Asia Today: Nuclear Proliferation, Environment, Political-Economic and Civilizational," Ulaanbaatar, Mongolia, September 26–27, 2019.

22 The Seventh Generation takes its name from the Great Law of the Haudenosaunee, the founding document of the Iroquois Confederacy. It is based on an ancient Iroquois philosophy that: "In our every deliberation, we must consider the impact of our decisions on the next seven generations." Seven Generations International Foundation, "7th Generation Principle" explained, at http://7genfoundation.org/7th-generation/#:~:text=The%20Seventh%20Generation%20takes%20its,living%20participatory%20democracy%20on%20Earth (accessed October 10, 2020).

23 These figures do not include undeployed strategic warheads, warheads waiting for disposal or maintenance, or the many tactical nuclear warheads that both Russia and the US maintain. Israel almost certainly has some also, including "suitcase bombs," while China was estimated to have about 150 "tactical" nuclear weapons in 2015. See, *The Nuclear Threat Initiative*, at https://www.nti.org/learn/countries/china/nuclear/ (accessed October 7, 2020).

24 Oliver Thränert, "New Challenges in Nuclear Arms Control," *CSS Analysis in Security Policy* 232, October 2018, at https://css.ethz.ch/content/dam/ethz/special-interest/gess/cis/center-for-securities-studies/pdfs/CSSAnalyse232-EN.pdf (accessed October 7, 2020).

25 The dates of international arms control treaties often are complicated by a date of signature, followed by a date when the treaty "entered into force," which often requires ratification by some number of relevant nations. For simplicity, the single dates on this list will be those years most commonly used in citations about that treaty.

26 It bears emphasis here that while China stopped "destructive" testing in orbit due to the global outcry regarding over 900 fragments resulting from their first kinetic test against their own satellite, it has not stopped testing nor development of its anti-satellite weapons. Neither has the US nor Russia. They have just become more careful about not leaving vast debris clouds in space that could wipe out the international space station or any number of other valuable items in low earth orbit. See Leonard David, "China's Anti-Satellite Test: Worrisome Debris Cloud Circles Earth," *Space.com,* at https://www.space.com/3415-china-anti-satellite-test-worrisome-debris-cloud-circles-earth.html (accessed October 7, 2020).

27 United Nations Office for Disarmament Affairs, "Treaty on the Non-Proliferation of Nuclear Weapons (NPT)," at https://www.un.org/disarmament/wmd/nuclear/npt/ (accessed October 8, 2020).

28 Joelien Pretorius and Tom Sauer, "Is it time to ditch the NPT?," Bulletin of the Atomic Scientists, September 6, 2019, at https://thebulletin.org/2019/09/is-it-time-to-ditch-the-npt/?utm_source=Newsletter&utm_medium=Email&utm_campaign=Newsletter09092019&utm_content=NuclearRisk_DitchNPT_09062019 (accessed October 7, 2020).

29 John G. Behuncik, "Examining SALT Violations and the Problems of Verification," Heritage Foundation, at https://www.heritage.org/defense/report/examining-salt-violations-and-the-problems-verification (accessed October 7, 2020).
30 Tom Nichols, "Mourning the INF Treaty: The United States is not better for withdrawing," *Foreign Affairs*, March 4, 2019, at https://www.foreignaffairs.com/articles/2019-03-04/mourning-inf-treaty (accessed October 7, 2020).
31 Michael R. Pompeo, "U.S. Withdrawal from the INF Treaty on August 2, 2019," press release, US Department of State, at https://www.state.gov/u-s-withdrawal-from-the-inf-treaty-on-august-2-2019/ (accessed October 7, 2020).
32 Scott Howe, US Department of Defense, as cited in *Jane's Defence Weekly* 56 (35), August 28, 2019.
33 "How the International Monitoring System Works," paper of the Comprehensive Nuclear Test Ban Treaty Organization, at https://www.ctbto.org/verification-regime/ (accessed October 7, 2020).
34 United Nations Office for Disarmament Affairs (UNDOA), "Overview of the Treaty on the Prohibition of Nuclear Weapons," at https://www.un.org/disarmament/wmd/nuclear/tpnw/ (accessed October 7, 2020).
35 APHA stands for the Asian Political History Association, and ISCSC is the International Society for Comparative Study of Civilizations. These two academic groups partnered with the Mongolian Foreign Ministry, the Blue Banner Society, and Clarewood University in the United States to co-sponsor a special conference in Ulaanbaatar, Mongolia from September 26–28, 2019.
36 Thomas J. Johnson, "A History of Biological Warfare from 300 B.C.E. to the Present," American Association for Respiratory Care, at https://c.aarc.org/resources/biological/history.asp (accessed October 10, 2020).
37 Jeffrey Amherst was commanding general of British forces in North America during the final battles of the French and Indian War of 1754–1763. Amherst Massachusetts and Amherst College were both named after him. His reputation is now tarnished by accusations of biological warfare against native populations using blankets from smallpox wards. This episode is described in Johnson's history of biological warfare above. Also, the University of Massachusetts maintains a detailed academic record of this subject, "Jeffrey Amherst and Smallpox Blankets," at https://www.umass.edu/legal/derrico/amherst/lord_jeff.html (accessed October 7, 2020).

9 Nuclear non-proliferation in Northeast Asia and Mongolia's policy

Jargalsaikhan Enkhsaikhan

Introduction

Since the dawn of the nuclear age, reducing and eliminating the nuclear threat has become one of the pressing international issues. This issue has been grabbing headlines ever since the end of World War II. With the end of the Cold War in the early 1990s, it was thought that the nuclear-weapon states (NWS) would be able to halt and reverse the nuclear arms race and gradually reduce and eliminate its role in their security policies. Besides the nuclear danger, the Twenty-first century world is facing many other global level challenges as well, especially climate change, COVID-19 virus, and other possible pandemics, as well as the increasing income differences among rich and poor peoples and countries. It is estimated that less than one per cent of global GDP is needed to fund the Paris Climate agreement that would slow and halt climate change and around five per cent of global GDP to fund the United Nations' Sustainable Development Goals (SDGs) by 2030. Therefore, there is a growing realisation and trend to emphasise human security over national security, and it is believed that nuclear disarmament can lead to redirecting funds to financing the SDGs and the Paris Climate Agreement.

This chapter discusses the nuclear weapons threat in Northeast Asia (NEA), and how these issues seriously affect Mongolia's security and well-being. Although progress in nuclear non-proliferation is very slow, as attested by the situation on and around the Korean Peninsula, there are a number of activities now done at the civil society and academic level to address the issue of denuclearising the Korean Peninsula and establishing a Northeast Asian nuclear-weapons-free zone (NEA-NWFZ). As a result, there is a role for small states, such as Mongolia, to play in the discussion of conceptual issues of deterrence, the nuclear umbrella, and alliance commitments.

Mongolia's foreign policy vision, especially in Northeast Asia

Geopolitical reality

Geographically and physically, Mongolia is one of the most vulnerable developing states. It borders on two historical adversaries that also happen

DOI: 10.4324/9781003148630-9

to be veto-wielding permanent members of the United Nations Security Council (UNSC) and recognised NWSs. As a land-locked state, Mongolia has no independent access to the oceans, and hence to world markets, although it works with its two neighbours to exercise its right to access to seaports, as proscribed by the 1982 United Nations Convention on the Law of the Sea. Northeast Asia, with which Mongolia identifies its future, has no multilateral security mechanism or arrangement to properly channel or address great-power rivalry or relations among states of the region.

Lessons of the Cold War period

Mongolia has registered its opposition to nuclear weapons since it became a democracy in 1990. One of the lessons it learned during the East-West Cold War and Sino-Soviet ideological and territorial disputes was that alliance with a NWS and hosting the latter's military bases can be perilous, since the hosting state becomes a nuclear target of the opposing nuclear-weapon power. Linking a country's security with the security or perceived security of an ally, especially of a great power, is a double-edged sword: protection under a "nuclear umbrella" and at the same time a possible target of the ally's rival NWS(s).

Especially between the mid-1960s and mid-1980s, Mongolia felt it was being drawn into the Sino-Soviet confrontation. Mongolia was considered by the Soviet bloc as an important stronghold of socialism in Asia,[1] and its territory was expected to play a strategic role in a possible Sino-Soviet confrontation. At its height during the border conflict in 1969, when armed clashes occurred along some sections of their common border, Moscow possessed over 10,000 nuclear weapons and China already had around 50 nuclear weapons.[2] At that time Moscow had around 60,000–75,000 troops, including two tank and two motorised rifle divisions, and unspecified air force units stationed in Mongolia. Some of the troops were equipped with dual-use intermediate range-ballistic missiles and aircraft. Chinese garrisons also were stationed along the Chinese-Mongolian border. This situation eventually eased; however, the nature of Soviet-Mongolian "alliance" meant that the ultimate decision to use force, including perhaps even nuclear weapons and other weapons of mass destruction, would have been taken by the Soviets themselves, without real consultation with the Mongolian side.

Disintegration of the Soviet bloc and of the Soviet Union itself, as well as complete Russian troop withdrawal from Mongolia, provided Mongolia with a unique opportunity to withdraw from the Soviet "nuclear umbrella" and by doing so to ensure that no nuclear weapon of another NWS would be targeted on any part of the country. The lesson is that such a dangerous situation should never recur again. Now there is a qualitatively new geopolitical situation around Mongolia. Mongolia should not be used as a springboard to threaten others, but rather as a source of stability, predictability, and bridge-building.

Pragmatic foreign policy

Mongolia believes that in this interdependent world, security and prosperity of all states, big and small alike, increasingly are intertwined. Therefore, all states without exception, based on their geographic location or comparative advantage, can make practical, pragmatic contributions to promoting common security and mutually beneficial cooperation. In the post-Cold War geostrategic environment, Mongolia, unlike in the past, is pursuing a multi-pillared foreign policy and working to diversify its foreign relations beyond its immediate neighbours. This major pragmatic turn was reflected in the national security and foreign policy concepts adopted by Mongolia's parliament (the State Great Khural) in June 1994 and updated in 2010 and 2011, respectively. These concepts declared that Mongolia's policy would be based on political realism, non-alignment, and pursuit of its own national interests, and that its priority goal would be to safeguard its security and vital national interests primarily by political and diplomatic means, rather than through alliance with a great power.[3]

Political and diplomatic means of ensuring national security have their limits. History knows many examples when powerful states would abandon their smaller and weaker "allies" to accommodate other stronger powers. Mongolia remains sceptical that others, even its neighbours or other close partners, would actually risk their own core interests to assist Mongolia in times of danger. That is why part of the foreign policy challenge is to identify its own "red lines".[4] Creating situations that would threaten national security need to be avoided altogether through effective preventive diplomacy. This means, first and foremost, the prohibition of the use of its territory by other states to harm the legitimate interests of others, and not allowing itself to be used as a Trojan horse by any other state or group of states. Mongolia's national security concept sees disputes and conflicts between the neighbouring two states as major potential threats to its national security, which is why Mongolia pursues a policy of promoting mutual confidence by establishing a stable and reliable system of maintaining overall peace and security in Asia and the Pacific, particularly in NEA.

Mongolians have a saying that the "duck is calm when the lake is calm." Hence, it believes that the effective way of ensuring national security is through regional trust-building and conflict prevention to avoid being drawn into bilateral or regional conflicts in this interconnected world. Therefore, since the early 1990s, Mongolia has called for regional security dialogue and establishing a regional security mechanism. A new element in Mongolia's post-Cold War foreign policy is promoting a "third neighbour" policy.[5] That approach means reaching out to other states or groups of states with which it shares common democratic values and which are economically developed.

Nuclear Weapons and the Non-Proliferation Treaty

It is a well-known premise that nuclear war cannot be won and must never be fought. That is why the idea of nuclear disarmament and establishing a nuclear-weapon-free world always has enjoyed broad popular support, though the sense of optimism gradually is weakening due to the fact that the NWSs are not thinking of parting with their weapons. Thus, even in 2019 the world spent US$1.9 trillion for arms purposes, of which around US$100 billion was for nuclear arms expenses. It is expected that in the next decade the NWSs will spend over one trillion dollars for nuclear weapons upgrades and modernisation. The use of just a small fraction of today's nearly 13,400 nuclear weapons would lead to devastating catastrophic consequences for the world, as noted at the three conferences on the Humanitarian Impact of Nuclear Weapons held in Oslo, Nayarit, and Vienna in 2013 and 2014. The five NWSs—the United States (US), Russia, China, United Kingdom, and France, known as the P5—officially are recognised *de jure* as such by the 1968 Treaty on the Non-proliferation of nuclear weapons (NPT). These and the *de facto* nuclear-weapon states—Israel, India, Pakistan, and the DPRK (North Korea)—despite their rhetoric to the contrary, are not contemplating any serious steps to reduce nuclear weapons, let alone banning them.

On the contrary, the P5 are intent not only on keeping their weapons but making them even more useable by reducing the punch power of some of their weapons and lowering the threshold of their use, which might make them more likely to be used. The US, although it has reduced its nuclear weapons arsenal by almost 85 per cent, is now modernising its "aging" nuclear triad. In 2018 its unilateral withdrawal from the 1972 Anti-Ballistic Missile (ABM) treaty and 1987 Intermediate-range Nuclear Forces Treaty (INF), together with placement of land- and sea-based missile defences close to Russian and Chinese territories, have compelled the latter two countries to take countermeasures and strengthen their nuclear deterrent and enhance offensive capabilities. The testing of a new land-based version of the American Navy's Tomahawk cruise missiles, hypersonic glider warheads, underwater nuclear drones, and nuclear-powered cruise missiles are all signs of further nuclear arms "improvements".

Russia's deterrence policy, updated in 2020, broadens the possible use of nuclear weapons in cases when overwhelming conventional forces are used.[6] It has announced that it was equipping its navy with hypersonic nuclear strike weapons, Poseidon underwater drones, and deploying Tsirkon hypersonic cruise missiles on surface ships. The speed (at five times the speed of sound) and manoeuvrability of their hypersonic missiles and other "improvements" would make them difficult to trace and intercept, further increasing mutual distrust and tension. The issue of extending the 2010 New START treaty, which many think served both sides well and contributed to nuclear stability, is expiring in February 2021. There is a chance that this treaty, that limits deployed nuclear weapons to 1,550 and deployed missiles, submarines, and bombers of both sides to 700, and envisages mutual on-site inspections to verify compliance, will be extended by a year with the understanding that both sides would freeze all their nuclear warheads, including the tactical weapons, and use the period to hold bilateral talks. The Russians also would include the issue of missile defence systems.

China's nuclear weapons are much fewer that those of the US and Russia, and thus it is not interested in joining their nuclear arms reduction talks. It is believed to be focusing on updating its arsenal by focusing on long-range missiles with multiple warheads, air-launched ballistic missiles, strategic nuclear submarines and developing intercontinental hypersonic glide missiles. However, its top concern, like that of Russia, is the US' missile defence system that could neutralise China's ability to deter nuclear attacks. In that sense, it sees deployment of a US Terminal High-Altitude Area Defense (THAAD) missile defence system in South Korea as designed primarily to protect that country from China's long-range missiles.

Common sense says that the more nuclear weapons are perfected, the less secure the world would become. If this trend continues, other nuclear-capable and aspiring states might choose to go nuclear. There also is the danger of terrorists getting ahold of nuclear weapons technology, if not the weapons themselves. Even acquisition of so-called "dirty bombs" would increase tension and reduce security. Conclusion of the NPT in 1970 was a landmark event aimed at halting proliferation of these weapons horizontally to non-nuclear-weapon states (NNWSs) and increasing the numbers and types of nuclear weapons vertically in the arsenals of the NWSs. It was based on the so-called grand bargain between NWSs and NNWSs both to prevent the proliferation of nuclear weapons and to require the P5 to pursue negotiations in good faith to end the nuclear arms race at an early date and to achieve nuclear disarmament.

Although the treaty was able to prevent proliferation of nuclear weapons to 20–25 countries, today, there are nine states that have nuclear weapons. One of the pillars of the International Atomic Energy Agency (IAEA)'s comprehensive safeguard system[7] was to exert political pressure and "convincing" arguments from the P5, especially from the US, on many nuclear-capable states to join the NPT. Some US allies were provided with its "nuclear umbrella" to protect them in order to agree to refrain going nuclear. The NPT's non-proliferation commitments, export controls, and IAEA's safeguards have played a positive role in preventing horizontal proliferation. However, some states such as Iraq, South Africa, and Libya, made use of the IAEA's weak safeguards system to develop clandestine nuclear weapons programmes. This weakness was addressed in the early 1990s by the adoption of an additional protocol to the IAEA safeguards regime that it is not legally binding unless ratified. That is why some nuclear-capable states have only signed, but chosen not to ratify, it.

On the positive side, four states, have become non-nuclear-weapon states parties to the NPT while receiving security assurances from the NWSs. South Africa, a former *de facto* nuclear weapon state, voluntarily abandoned its nuclear weapons programme and destroyed its weapons, while three states that were once a part of the Soviet Union (Ukraine, Belarus, and

Kazakhstan) turned over their weapons to the Russian Federation. In short, it can be said that the overall performance of the NPT is a mixed one, with the increasing risk of further weakening of the non-proliferation regime due to technological developments, existing loopholes in the treaty regime, and P5 determination not only to keep their weapons but also to pursue vertical proliferation by modernising their arsenals.

Although quantitatively there is near-universal membership in the NPT, there are a number of reasons for the weakening of its regime. First and foremost, the P5 have not lived up to their promises, according to NPT's Article VI, to negotiate nuclear disarmament and "bring those negotiations to a conclusion and achieving nuclear disarmament in all its forms."[8] The US, defying the spirit of non-proliferation, provides its nuclear umbrella to 30 states through the NATO alliance, and justified by bilateral alliance treaties with Australia, Japan, and the Republic of Korea, keeps nuclear weapons on territories of some of them, maintains nuclear sharing arrangements with some, and involves them in nuclear planning and training.

Nuclear-weapon-free zones (NWFZ)

An analysis of the geographical location and history of establishing these zones shows that so far they have been established in geographical areas with regional political structures and where the NWSs did not have much geopolitical stake.[9] However, as practice also demonstrates, establishing NWFZs in areas where the NWSs or great powers have geopolitical stake or interest is much more difficult, for example, in the Middle East, Northeast Asia, or Europe. Mongolia supports establishing NWFZs in various parts of the world as a regional approach to strengthening the global nuclear non-proliferation and disarmament regime until nuclear weapons are eliminated globally.

The history of establishing the five NWFZs demonstrates that each zone is a product of specific regional circumstances and is recognised as such by the UNGA.[10] Establishment was based on the prevailing historical circumstances, the existing regional mechanisms of promoting peace and security, and confidence-building. They formed part of the first wave of NWFZs. Yet, it is well recognised that NWFZs are of greater importance in regions with tensions, lack of regional peace and security mechanisms, elevated geopolitical interests of established NWSs, and actual or suspected existence of nuclear capabilities.

First-generation NWFZs

Throughout the Cold War, the NNWSs have not been mere passive observers of the nuclear arms race and the increase in nuclear danger, but have been taking measures to outlaw nuclear weapons on their respective territories by raising concerns at all levels and establishing NWFZs. The first

NWFZ was established in the 1970s in Latin America. Today, there are 115 nations in five NWFZs: Latin America and Caribbean (the 1967 Treaty of Tlatelolco); the South Pacific (the 1985 Treaty of Rarotonga); Southeast Asia (the 1995 Treaty of Bangkok); Africa (the 1996 Treaty of Pelindaba); and Central Asia (the 2006 Treaty of Semipalatinsk)[11] covering the major part of the Southern hemisphere. These zones have three common characteristics: 1) prohibition of development, testing, manufacturing, production, possession, acquisition, stockpiling, and transportation of nuclear weapons anywhere within the zone; 2) prohibition of the use or threat of use nuclear weapons against states and areas within the agreed zone and provision of security assurances by the P5; and 3) establishment of an agreed mechanism to ensure compliance with the NWFZ treaty.

In 1975 a United Nations report was issued that underlined that the "obligations relating to the establishment of nuclear-weapon-free zones may be assumed not only by groups of states, including entire continents or large geographical regions, but also by small groups of states and even individual countries."[12] Some considered it as an attempt to impose a set of guidelines on states or require that zones to conform to a specific form or pattern. Yet, encouraged by the establishment of NWFZs in Southeast Asia and on the African continent, in January 1997 the UNGA asked the United Nations Disarmament Commission (UNDC) to help promote the creation of additional zones and to develop an updated group zone guideline. This revised guideline was adopted in 1999, but out of respect for divergent views, the guideline underlined that each NWFZ was the product of the specific circumstances of the region and that it needed to be regarded as a non-exhaustive list of generally accepted observations in the development of NWFZs.[13]

Early proposals to establish a Northeast Asian NWFZ

One of the geographical regions that demands the serious attention of the international community is NEA, which represents an important crossroad of strategic and economic interests of the United States, China, Russia, and Japan.[14] Establishing a NEA-NWFZ is not a totally new idea. It has been proposed by some states of the region since the 1970s, although the Cold War mindset and ideological rivalry did not allow giving such proposals all the seriousness that they may have deserved.[15] The main reason given was that although the idea was indeed a noble one, the conditions were not ripe nor were the states ready to seriously talk disarmament. Today, the issue of establishing a NEA-NWFZ is being discussed, although on an informal basis at the level of regional think tanks and disarmament non-governmental organisations (NGOs). Until very recently, talks were held to denuclearise North Korea through the Six Party Talks, but ultimately failed due to a too narrow focus, and the presence of US nuclear weapons in Japan and South Korea and in the nearby seas were looked at with suspicion by Russia, China, and North Korea.

The end of the Cold War in Europe, US-Russian steps to reduce tension in East Asia, the US withdrawal of its tactical weapons from the Korean Peninsula, and the 1992 joint declaration of the two Koreas on the denuclearising the peninsula[16] were very encouraging signs for not only denuclearising the peninsula but also starting the discussion about establishing a NEA-NWFZ. The multilateral negotiations underway in the mid-1990s on establishing NWFZs in Southeast Asia and on the entire African continent raised hopes that the proliferation of nuclear weapons in the sensitive NEA region also might be prevented.

In the early 1990s, American professor John Endicott proposed establishing a limited NWFZ in NEA (LNWFZ-NEA), where "limited" meant both in respect to geography and weapons. Unfortunately, the NWSs were not supportive.[17] In the mid-1990s, Dr. Hiromichi Umebayashi of Peace Depot (Japan) suggested establishing a NWFZ covering the two Koreas and Japan[18] with the three NWSs providing appropriate security assurances to them, known as the 3+3 formula.[19] Additionally, Dr. Seongwhun Cheon and Tatsujiro Suzuki proposed a Tripartite NWFZ that would have involved the three NWSs at some appropriate stage of negotiations.[20] In 1995 Andrew Mack of the Australian National University proposed a NWFZ involving not only the two Koreas and Japan but also Taiwan.[21] Because of lingering great power suspicions such proposals all were non-starters. A year later, Dr. Kumao Kaneko of Japan proposed establishing a so-called "circular" NWFZ, which consisted of a circular area with a 2,000-kilometre radius from the Korean DMZ in which non-nuclear-weapon and nuclear-weapon states would have to negotiate commitments.[22] This too was not accepted.

In 2011 Dr. Morton Halperin of the Nautilus Institute in California proposed a comprehensive approach to the issue by concluding an agreement on peace and security in NEA.[23] Based on this broader approach, the Research Center for Nuclear Weapons Abolition (RECNA) in Nagasaki organised a number of workshops.[24] Some concrete ideas were explored which needed follow-up 1.5 track discussions[25] by governmental officials, but there was no reaction from the countries of the region and the US. The United Nations Advisory Board on Disarmament Matters in July 2013 recommended to the UN Secretary-General to take action towards establishing a NEA-NWFZ.[26] That September at the United Nations High-Level Meeting on Disarmament, Mongolian President Tsakhia Elbegdorj stated that his country was "prepared, on an informal basis, to work with the countries of NEA to see if and how a NWFZ could be established in the region. Though we know well that that would not be easy and would require courage, political will and perseverance, it is doable."[27]

Although no tangible action was taken to follow-up on the recommendation of the United Nations Advisory Board on Disarmament Matters since then, Blue Banner, a Mongolian NGO devoted to promoting full institutionalisation of Mongolia's nuclear-weapon-free status, has been working with RECNA. RECNA's Nagasaki process[28] is aimed at facilitating a political movement towards peace and security in NEA by establishing a NEA-NWFZ through involving experts from the region and other relevant countries and international organisations in its panel on Peace and Security of Northeast Asia (PSNA). The Asia-Pacific Leadership Network for Nuclear Non-Proliferation and Disarmament (APLN),[29] an advocacy group of former political, diplomatic, and military leaders, senior government officials, scholars, and opinion leaders of the 16 countries of the Asia-Pacific region, also raises awareness on the threats of nuclear weapons and promotes eventual elimination of these weapons among the general public, especially high-level policymakers.[30]

Factors negatively impacting a Northeast Asian NWFZ

NEA is one of the world's most militarised regions, where the 1950–1953 Korean War officially is not over. It is also a seat of a number of territorial disputes, as well as of historical animosity and deep distrust. On the other hand, economically, it is one of the most dynamic regions of the world and, whereby 2030, the strong economic growth in the region could, if all goes well, double or even triple. However, deployment of nuclear-weapon-capable forces, including land and sea-based missiles, elements of destabilising missile defence systems, and of non-strategic nuclear weapons on mobile platforms could lead to a nuclear arms race in the region and increase mutual suspicion, all of which negatively affecting the political climate, economic development, and free flow of people and capital.

The US' proposed Guidance for Development for Alliances and Partnerships (GDAP) is aimed at bringing "likeminded democracies" of the Indo-Pacific region closer together and isolating China and Russia by easing and expanding US' arms sales, including critical weapons systems and speeding up approvals.[31] In the military area, in June 2020 the Japanese Government decided to abandon plans to deploy a ground-based interception Aegis Ashore system against ballistic missile attacks. Instead, discussion is underway to improve deterrence by acquiring the ability to block missile attacks "even within the enemy's territory,"[32] including perhaps by using cruise missiles, and thus preparing ground to acquire attack missiles in contravention of the spirit of the Japanese Constitution and the declared three non-nuclear principles. China on a number of occasions has opposed US' deployment of its intermediate-range missiles in the region and warned US allies about embracing this American policy. Another military-based development is US ally South Korea's decision to acquire aircraft carriers to be equipped with short take-off and vertical landing F-35B fighter jets and helicopters.[33] The abovementioned actions surely will affect the overall geopolitical climate and structure in the world.

Strengthening regional confidence and cooperation

Both the Cold War and the Korean War have not yet ended on the Korean Peninsula. Also, past historical problems and territorial disputes among the

Mongolia's policy 187

states of the region remain and flare up from time to time. Absence of a regional mechanism involving all states to address issues of common concern or interest is still felt. Therefore, there is a deficit of multilateral cooperation that is recognised by all the states of the region. This deficit is due partially to the fact that some of the states formed Cold War-era bilateral alliance relations with the US and make decisions on strategic and security relations in close coordination with the latter. Russia and China have their own geopolitical interests and policies regarding peace and security issues in the region. At times their views diverge; however, today when the US' influence in the region is still predominant, their interests on many issues coincide. North Korea has its own interests and pursues a policy of its own, based on its specific political and economic system. The newest member of the region, Mongolia, which has no territorial or border problems with its neighbours, tries to pursue active, non-aligned, and neutral policies, and has offered proposals to develop confidence-building measures supported by economic cooperation.

A small, yet positive step in promoting confidence in the region was the adoption in 1998 by the UNGA of a resolution welcoming Mongolia's unique nuclear-weapon-free status. In 2012, the P5 signed a joint declaration acknowledging Mongolia's national legislation to define this status, and declaring that they would respect it and would not contribute to any act that would violate it. This shows that, if there is a goodwill, there is a way to effectively address even complicated and thorny issues concerning the interests of the great powers, but the P5 so far have declined to recognise Mongolia as a single-state NWFZ.

Denuclearising the Korean Peninsula

The geopolitical issues in Northeast Asia are intertwined closely, so, when one wants to consider the issue of the NEA-NWFZ, one finds that it cannot be seriously addressed if the situation on the Korean Peninsula is ignored. The challenges of inter-Korean relations must be examined, while the issue of South Korean policy cannot be considered without understanding the latter's alliance relations with the US. In turn, American policy cannot be understood without considering relations with China, Russia, Japan, and South Korea. In that sense, the Northeast Asian security issue is a closely intertwined one that may be as complex as the Middle East.

Many issues need to be addressed such as formally ending the Korean War and conclusion of a peace treaty, normalising of US-North Korea relations, freezing of North Korean nuclear weapons programme, and easing of UNSC and bilateral sanctions against North Korea. Another issue is agreeing on the priority or sequence of issues to be addressed. The US and its allies demand that North Korea first eliminate its nuclear weapons, while North Korea believes that this CVID (complete, verifiable, and irreversible dismantlement) is a non-starter because it is an attempt to unilaterally disarm it. Instead, it believes that a step-by-step approach needs to be taken starting with complete normalisation of US-North Korean relations.

In 2003–2009 the states of Northeast Asia, minus Mongolia, established the Six Party Talks (SPT), a regional negotiating forum to discuss the issues connected with North Korea's nuclear programme. In September 2005 Pyongyang agreed in principle to abandon its nuclear weapons programme under certain conditions but this was not realised due to the Banko Delta Asia affair.[34] Meanwhile, North Korea continued its nuclear weapons development programme. Although China tried to reinvigorate the talks, attempts ended to denuclearise North Korea through multilateral negotiations.

By the mid-2010s, it was evident that North Korea was on its way to reach mainland US by miniaturising its warheads to fit on a missile and survive any ballistic trajectory and by developing synthetic materials for the warheads to survive re-entry. The fact that a country with the world's fourth-largest army possesses not only tactical intermediate range but even intercontinental ballistic missiles (ICBMs) raised many nuclear security concerns and delicate geostrategic issues, especially for the US. North Korea's main demands were that the US stop all hostile activities against it, establish normal relations with it, and withdraw bilateral and UNSC-imposed sanctions. It was clear that years of US' strategic patience policy did not change North Korea's pursuit of its nuclear weapons policy.

In 2017 US-North Korean relations sharply deteriorated, yet it was hoped that the 2018 Winter Olympics on the Korean Peninsula could provide an opportunity to reverse the dangerous trend. Several months later in Singapore, the first-ever US-North Korean summit meeting ended with the adoption of a four-point, joint statement of US President Donald Trump and Chairman Kim Jong-un of the DPRK. The two sides committed in principle to establish bilateral relations, join efforts to build a stable peace regime on the Korean Peninsula, and North Korea reaffirmed its earlier pledge to work towards complete denuclearisation of the peninsula. However, in the 2019 follow-up summit in Hanoi, both sides were not able to agree on the degree of sanctions' relief and dismantling of some part of North Korea's nuclear facilities, and so the American President cut short the summit. It became obvious that not much more would be done before the US presidential election in November 2020.

Thus, in October 2020 in a military parade North Korea displayed a larger ICBM missile with payloads that could have the first-strike capability with multiple warheads or mixture with dummy warheads, the Hwasong 15, a new solid-propellant submarine-launched ballistic missile Pukkuksong-3 SLBM (submarine-launched ballistic missiles), and mobile missile transporters.[35] Besides demonstrating its increased nuclear capability to threaten the US, the military parade also was meant to demonstrate the North Korean belief that, in time of crisis, the US would first and foremost think of its own security rather than that of its Northeast Asian allies.

The author believes that it is inevitable to recognise North Korea as a *de facto* nuclear weapon state without delay and start serious negotiations to resolve the issue. Such acceptance to some extent will be a political gain for North Korea and at the same time weaken further the entire non-proliferation regime by showing that with will and perseverance, a state can become a *de facto* NWS. On the other hand, North Korea also knows well that once it has proven that it possesses a credible nuclear arsenal, it would need to look for ways to leverage this to overcome its virtual economic isolation and obtain international sanctions relief. Politically, it would need to compete with South Korea in economic and social areas that only can be achieved through open international cooperation and by integrating into the region's promising economic development.

Mongolia establishes a single-state NWFZ

With the withdrawal of Russian bases from Mongolia and in response to the lessons of the Cold War and a new Sino-Russian pledge not to use territories of bordering third states against each other, Mongolia in September 1992 declared its own territory a NWFZ. Mongolian President Punsalmaa Ochirbat, the first democratically elected president of post-socialist Mongolia, took this step at the UNGA session and underlined that his nation would work to have that status internationally guaranteed.[36] Despite the difficulty of the task, the President considered the initiative as an expression of an independent foreign policy act to strengthen the country's security. In January 1993 Mongolia's nuclear-weapon-free wish found recognition and reflection in the country's Treaty on Friendly Relations and Cooperation signed with Russia, in which the latter pledged to respect its policy of not permitting the deployment on and transit through its territory of foreign troops and nuclear and other weapons of mass destruction.[37] A year later China made a statement in which it pledged to respect Mongolia's policy of turning its territory into a nuclear-weapon-free zone.[38]

The Ochirbat initiative was in line with the trend of NNWSs to promote reduction of regional tensions and nuclear non-proliferation. Mongolia relied on UNGA Resolution 3472 (XXX) which stated that "even individual states" may establish NWFZs.[39] Mongolia's initiative was widely welcomed as contributing to regional stability and confidence-building; however, P5 support was limited to welcoming it only as a declaration of intent. This lack of full support grew out of concern that Mongolia's act might set a precedent with unpredictable political and military consequences and might discourage establishment of regional zones. In order to gain stronger support, in 1997 Mongolia proposed that the United Nations Disarmament Commission (UNDC) consider establishing single-state NWFZs (SS-NWFZs) in parallel with establishing group zones in cases when, due to geographical location or for some other valid reason, a state cannot form part of a traditional zone.

Many developing countries believed that Mongolia's initiative was a novel way to approach the issue of establishing NWFZs, and the Non-Aligned Movement underlined its support for Mongolia to "institutionalize its status as a nuclear-weapon-free zone."[40] However, the P5 argued that Mongolia was an exceptional case, so it would be improper to consider the issue together with establishing a guideline for new group zones. The unanimous support of the Non-Aligned Movement in 1995[41] convinced it to employ multilateral diplomacy at the UNGA. Mongolia held numerous talks with the representatives of the P5, and as a result the General Assembly adopted in 1998 a resolution entitled "Mongolia's international security and nuclear-weapon-free status." This welcomed the decision of Mongolia to declare its territory a nuclear-weapon-free zone and invited member states, including the P5, to cooperate with it in taking the necessary measures to strengthen the country's independence, sovereignty and territorial integrity, the inviolability of its borders, its economic security, its ecological balance, and its nuclear-weapon-free status as well as its independent foreign policy.[42] In February 2000, Mongolia adopted legislation defining its NWFZ at the national level and criminalising acts that would violate the status.[43]

One of the main goals of Mongolia was to acquire credible security assurances from the P5, especially from its border neighbours, that it would not be pressured by any state to violate its nuclear-weapon-free status. After talks with the P5, Mongolia received their acceptance in a joint statement that called Mongolia a state with special nuclear-weapon-free status, although not a full-fledged zone.[44] Although Mongolia officially welcomed the P5 joint statement as an important step in institutionalising its status, unofficially it complained that content-wise, the statement did not reflect the actual good relations that it had with each one of the P5 nations. Discussions continued for almost a decade until all parties agreed in September 2012 to sign parallel declarations. It was agreed that Mongolia would not press for the conclusion of an international treaty providing security assurances of its new status, while the P5 agreed to respect Mongolia's nuclear-weapon-free status and would not contribute to any act that would violate it.

Need for a "Second Wave" of "softer" NWFZs

The establishment of future NWFZs can be considered as the "Second Wave" of NWFZs that needs the development of confidence-building measures (CBMs) and of regional political mechanisms to address the region's specific political, strategic, and other circumstances. This "Second Wave" NWFZs also should include establishment of single-state zones in places where, due to geopolitical circumstances or for some political reasons, establishment of regional zones is impossible. There should not be "blind spots" or grey areas in the yet to be established nuclear-weapon-free world.

There are valid reasons to believe that other SS-NWFZ cases could arise in South Asia. It might be a possibility for Nepal, which is trapped between nuclear India and Pakistan, or Sri Lanka. In Bangladesh, there is a draft bill in parliament to establish a NWFZ. Beyond the South Asian region, there are around 40 United Nations member NNWSs, as well as a dozen non-members, that are not part of political-military alliances or established NWFZs might decide to acquire P5 assurances to respect and honour their NNWS status. These NNWSs or territories may not necessarily require legally based assurances from the P5 on the non-use or threat of use of nuclear weapons against them but a solemn declaration in the Security Council that they would not station nuclear weapons-serving infrastructures in those NNWS and territories reflecting the demands of the Twenty-first century. That would make them part of softer NWFZs at the time when the nuclear arms race is turning from quantitative to a qualitative one. This "softer version" of NWFZs would contribute to reducing the geographical areas of nuclear-weapon-related activities, including placing supporting structures such as surveillance, tracking, or homing devices, or part of command-and-control systems to serve the nuclear weapons systems. It would ensure that they would not use NNWSs as "grey areas" contributing to the arms race.

Mongolia's possible role in security dialogue mechanisms for NEA

Mongolia believes that in this interdependent world all states need to become contributors to security and not only its consumers. It tries to contribute to regional peace and security. In NEA, there are many untapped reserves for trust- and peace-building that could contribute to productive negotiations and political objectives. States can play useful roles based on their comparative advantages. Mongolia, which pursues a proactive foreign policy, has the political advantages that it has no territorial or border problems with its neighbours, no hidden political agenda regarding the Korean Peninsula, and good relations with both Koreas, so it can act in a trust-building role through promoting greater regional confidence and dialogue. It believes it could be useful to some extent in the talks on denuclearising the Korean Peninsula or establishing a NEA-NWFZ.

Mongolia also is willing to be active in other security areas. Its inspectors in the past have been part of IAEA inspection teams in Iran and the DPRK, so it could be useful in developing and executing new inspection and verification mechanisms. Mongolia's successful and effective participation in various international peacekeeping operations (PKOs) has demonstrated that its representatives can be both effective and impartial. Although its armed forces rank 128th in size in the world, it is the 27th largest recognised contributor to PKOs.

Ulaanbaatar Dialogue on Northeast Asia Security

Since the 1980s, Mongolia has advocated greater confidence and dialogue in the region. In 2001, it called for establishing a formal multilateral mechanism to consider the region's post-Cold War pressing issues. In 2003, NEA's main stakeholders had launched the Six Party Talks (SPT) to address the DPRK's nuclear weapons programme, but these have been stalled since 2009. In response to the stalemate, Mongolia in 2014 launched the so-called Ulaanbaatar Dialogue on Northeast Asia Security (UBD), a 1.5 track regional dialogue among the states of the region and other important stakeholders, which meets annually and is attended by representatives of both Korean states. As Dr. Alicia Campi has underlined in her book, *Mongolia's Foreign Policy: Navigating a Changing World*, UBD's objective is to contribute to mutual understanding and greater confidence in order to achieve both "formal and practical security cooperation and consultation."[45] However, UBD also focuses on soft security, economic, and infrastructure development issues in the region. Mongolia is prepared to serve as an honest facilitator among the parties and is willing to share with the DPRK its experience in making a peaceful transition to democratic governance and a market economy, as well as creating a unique internationally recognised NWFZ that would obtain P-5 support. Since its founding, there have been six annual UBD meetings and four of these included DPRK participants.

Blue Banner initiatives

Another dialogue mechanism has been promoted by the Blue Banner NGO. Established in 2005 to promote the goals of nuclear non-proliferation and nuclear disarmament and to turn Mongolia into a single-state NWFZ, Blue Banner is a Mongolian private organisation, independent from governmental financial support. Blue Banner works closely with the NEA network of the Global Partnership to Prevent Armed Conflict (GPPAC) on issues of promoting confidence and peacebuilding on and around the Korean Peninsula and increasing the role of civil society in the states of the region. It also collaborates with such international NGOs as ICAN, IPPNW, and IPB. In 2015, in partnership with GPPAC-NEA, Blue Banner launched a track 2 civil society dialogue,[46] known as the Ulaanbaatar Process (UBP) that creates a political space and venue for the region's civil society organisations to discuss freely issues of common concern and search for common grounds for fruitful cooperation. UBP has produced publications on regional peace and security topics.[47]

Since 2007, Blue Banner has participated in or hosted a number of informal meetings that discussed a NWFZ. In 2017, it suggested recognising the DPRK as a *de facto* nuclear-weapon state and working with DPRK representatives when considering the issue of establishing a NEA-NWFZ. Blue Banner thereupon undertook a yearlong study on the possibility of establishing a NEA-NWFZ from the point of view that if the Korean Peninsula is not properly denuclearised and a NEA-NWFZ not established, a nuclear arms race would follow.

2020 International Policy Forum

On September 30, 2020 the International Policy Forum, co-sponsored by Blue Banner, the Global Peace Foundation (GPF), Action for Korea United, and One Korea Foundation, held two parallel roundtables concerning establishing a NEA-NWFZ and promoting inclusive regional economic development. Some 35 security experts, economists, and political scientists from South Korea, China, Japan, Great Britain, Finland, Russia, India, Mongolia, and the US examined approaches to ending the 74-year division of the Korean Peninsula. The forum decided to erect a regional secretariat to promote further the concept of establishing a NEA-NWFZ.

At this NWFZ roundtable, 19 papers were presented on topics such as the possibility of the three regional NWSs adopting non-nuclear deterrence and no first use pledge policies in the region, providing security assurances to the two Koreas and Japan, and granting international economic assistance to North Korea (a mini-Marshall plan) to help integrate it into regional economic development. Blue Banner underlined that Russian and Chinese security assurances would be important in convincing North Korea that a NEA-NWFZ could be legally binding and politically credible.

At the first roundtable former chief US negotiator during the 1994 North Korean nuclear crisis Dr. Robert Gallucci pointed out that if the issue of NEA-NWFZ is to be pursued, it should address North Korea's concern about the potential threat from US weapons as well as the US' alliance commitments and security interests. He added that a clear understanding of the term "denuclearisation" and issues such as fissile materials and their production facilities needed to be addressed. Dr. John Endicott said that any concept of a limited NEA-NWFZ zone must be a process over time in order to build mutual trust and friendship. The forum also discussed "no first use pledge" and "sole purpose" policies of NWSs, and the necessity for a radical change in approaches to North Korea and developing a reliable regional security mechanism that could include a NEA-NWFZ. The second roundtable considered economic opportunities and examined prospects for regional economic development by discussing Mongolia and Vietnam's transitions from a centralised command economy to a free market. John Dickson, president of the World Trade Partnership, noted that governments and large multilateral institutions move slowly, so it was imperative to develop contingency plans for a peaceful, mutually productive framework for the economic integration of the Korean Peninsula.

Conclusion

The four inter-Korean and the three DPRK-US summit meetings held in 2018 and 2019 have shown that there is political interest on all sides to denuclearise the Korean peninsula. However, both the post-Singapore and post-Hanoi meetings have demonstrated that there was a wide conceptual gap in clearly defining the notion of "denuclearising" the Korean Peninsula that needed to be addressed. Hence, working-level negotiations, when they start, should provide the opportunity to discuss openly the basic elements of denuclearising the Korean Peninsula rather than demanding upfront unilateral denuclearisation of the DPRK.

Mongolian experts at the Blue Banner NGO believe that a novel, mutually acceptable and doable, conceptual approach to the issue of denuclearising not only the Korean Peninsula but of Northeast Asia needs to be developed. Therefore, the bilateral DPRK-US talks need, at some stage, to be expanded to include other former parties to the Six Party Talks, especially South Korea. As things stand today, it would almost take a miracle to convince the DPRK to agree to fully denuclearise itself by parting with its nuclear weapons and its nuclear weapons infrastructure.

A logical question is whether or not Japan or the Republic of Korea, both technologically nuclear-capable states, would allow a *de facto* nuclear DPRK as their neighbour. Will they allow the US to accept the DPRK as a *de facto* nuclear-weapon state, as long as the latter would not threaten directly US territory, which means the US would tolerate DPRK's weapons that might threaten its two allies? Would the *de facto* recognition of DPRK as a nuclear weapon state embolden it in regards to Japan and the Republic of Korea? On the other hand, would the DPRK be satisfied with a security assurance from the US? The DPRK might feel more assured by acquiring additional assurances from its allies, Russia and China. There also is the issue of how to ensure that the talks on economic assistance and investment in the DPRK's economy would be realised.

Finally, there is the broader question of how all these developments might affect the NPT regime as a whole, without setting a dangerous precedent for other nuclear-capable states. A sole purpose nuclear weapons use declaration by the three NWSs would play a positive reassuring role in the region. Deterrence that excludes nuclear weapons would retain the basic bilateral security commitments of the US to Japan and the Republic of Korea, as well as constrain them from pursuing their own nuclear weapons. "Non-nuclear" deterrence can become part of a larger solution since it would contribute to greater predictability and stability, and could avert a possible uncontrollable chain reaction or domino effect resulting in a regional nuclear arms race.

It should be remembered that the question of declaring Mongolia a NWFZ coincided with the country's search for its place in the newly emerging post-Cold War world. Mongols learned about the peril of an alliance with a great power, especially if that was at the expense of its relations with other countries, and that any security risk needed to be removed as early as possible so that it does not turn into a threat in the future. Although Mongolia might not be directly threatened with nuclear weapons, as long as there are nuclear weapons and great power rivalry, there could always be the risk of the use of nuclear weapons. The most effective way to mitigate the situation is to outlaw nuclear weapons and totally eliminate them, and Mongolia is ready to participate in this effort.

Notes

1 Most of the time this notion of "socialism in Asia" excluded China.
2 Robert S. Norris and Hans M. Kristensen, "Global nuclear weapons inventories, 1945–2010," *Bulletin of Atomic Scientists*, July-August 2010, p. 81.
3 The National Security Concept of 1994 stressed that it was necessary to "strictly observe the policy of not allowing the use of the country's territory against other States" and "ensure the nuclear-weapon-free status of Mongolia at the international level and make it an important element of strengthening the country's security by political means." See Para. 23, One.5.
4 A red line that Mongols draw for themselves beyond which they might affect the legitimate interests of other states, including the neighbours.
5 See Alicia Campi, *Mongolia's Foreign Policy: Navigating a Changing World*, Lynne Rienner Publishers, Denver, 2019.
6 See "Foundations of State Policy of the Russian Federation in the Area of Nuclear Deterrence," Moscow, June 2, 2020.
7 The three pillars of IAEA's activities are Safety and Security, Science and Technology, and Safeguards and Verification.
8 See "Legality of the Threat or Use of Nuclear Weapons," International Court of Justice, July 8, 1996, at https://web.archive.org/web/20171018153630if_/http://www.icj-cij.org/en/case/95 (accessed November 13, 2020).
9 Michael Hamel-Green, *Regional Initiatives on Nuclear and WMD-Free Zones: Cooperative Approaches to Arms Control and Non-Proliferation*, UNIDIR/2005/19, Geneva, 2005, at https://vcdnp.org/wp-content/uploads/2018/03/NWFZ-TF-Report-final-1.pdf (accessed October 30, 2020); *Nuclear-weapon-free zones in the 21st century*, edited by Pericles Gasparini Alves and Daiana Belinda Cippolone, UNIDIR/97/37, Geneva, 1997; Oluyemi Adeniji, *The Treaty of Pelindaba on the African Nuclear-Weapon-Free Zone*, UNIDIR/2002/16, Geneva, 2002.
10 UNGA resolutions 3472 B (1975) that defined the concept of NWFZs and annex to UNGA resolution A/48/42 on guidelines and recommendations for regional approaches to disarmament within the context of global security.
11 Alves and Cipollone, *Nuclear-weapon-free zones in the 21st century*; Hamel-Green, *Regional Initiatives on Nuclear and WMD-Free Zones: Cooperative Approaches to Arms Control and Non-Proliferation*.
12 "Comprehensive Study of the Question of nuclear-weapon-free zones in all its aspects," *UNGA document Official Records of 30th session*, Document No. 27A (A/10027/ADD.1), New York, 1975, p. 310.
13 See *Official Records of the General Assembly. Fifty-fourth Session. Supplement No. 27 (A/54/27)*, New York, 1999–2000.
14 See Yong-Sup Han, "Nuclear Disarmament and Non-Proliferation in Northeast Asia," in *Nuclear Policies in Northeast Asia*, Andrew Mack (ed.), UNIDIR/95/16, Geneva, January 9, 1995, pp. 35–38, at https://www.unidir.org/publication/nuclear-policies-northeast-asia (accessed November 14, 2020).
15 John Simpson, "Nuclear capabilities, Military Security and the Korean Peninsula: A Three-Tiered Perspective from Europe," *The Korean Journal of Defense Analyses*, IV (2), Winter 1992; Tae-Hwan Kwak and Seung-Ho Joo, "The Denuclearization of the Korean Peninsula: Problems and Prospects," *Arms Control Today*, 14 (2), 1993; Michael Mazarr, "North Korea at the Crossroads: Nuclear Renegade or Regional Partner?" *Arms Control Today*, May 1993; Alexander Y. Mansurov, "The Origins, Evolution and Current Politics of the North Korean Nuclear Programme," *The Non-Proliferation Review*, Spring 1993; Shinichi Ogawa, "The Nuclear Security of Japan, and South Korea: A Japanese view," *The Korean Journal of Defense Analyses*, IX (1), Summer 1997; Mark Byung-Moon Suh, "Progress and Prospects of Nuclear-Weapon-Free Zones in

East Asia," paper presented at the Pugwash Workshop on Eliminating Nuclear Weapons, New Delhi, 1998.
16 Jeffrey Lewis, "Why the 1992 Joint Declaration on Denuclearization of the Korean Peninsula Still Matters," *38North.org*, March 18, 2011, at https://www.38north.org/2011/03/1992-joint-declaration/ (accessed November 10, 2020). For the text of the joint declaration in which the parties have agreed not to test, deploy or use nuclear weapons, nor to possess nuclear reprocessing and uranium enrichment facilities, see "Joint Declaration of the Denuclearization of the Korean Peninsula," United States Department of State, at https://2001-2009.state.gov/t/ac/rls/or/2004/31011.htm (accessed November 14, 4020).
17 John E. Endicott, "A Limited Nuclear-Weapons-Free Zone in Northeast Asia: A Track-II Initiative," *Acronym Institute for Disarmament Diplomacy*, 35, March 1999, at http://www.acronym.org.uk/old/archive/35nwfz.htm (accessed November 8, 2020).
18 It should be underlined that when one talks about NEA-NWFZ, it is meant as a zone encompassing the two Koreas and Japan.
19 Hiromichi Umebayashi, "Nuclear weapons can be eliminated," *Chugoku Shimbun*, April 13, 2009, at http://www.hiroshimapeacemedia.jp/?p=19762https%3A%2F%2Fwww.msn.com%2F%3Fpc%3DSK2D&ocid=SK2DDHP&osmkt=en-us (accessed November 11, 2020).
20 Cheon Seongwhun and Tatsujiro Suzuki, "The Tripartite Nuclear-Weapon-Free Zone in Northeast Asia: A Long-term Objective of the Six-Party Talks," *International Journal of Korean Unification Studies* 12 (2), 2003, pp. 41–68.
21 Andrew Mack, "A Northeast Asian Nuclear-Free Zone," in Andrew Mack (ed.), *Nuclear Policies in Nuclear Policies in Northeast Asia*, UNIDIR, Geneva, 1995, pp. 114–117, ibid.
22 Kumao Kaneko, "Japan Needs No Umbrella," *Bulletin of Atomic Scientists*, March/April 1996, pp. 46–51, at https://www.tandfonline.com/doi/abs/10.1080/00963402.1996.11456608 (accessed November 10, 2020).
23 Morton Halperin, Peter Hayes, Chung-in Moon, Thomas Pickering, and Leon Sigal, "Ending the North Korean nuclear threat by a Comprehensive security settlement in Northeast Asia," *Nautilus.org*, June 28, 2017, at https://nautilus.org/napsnet/napsnet-policy-forum/ending-the-north-korean-nuclear-threat-by-a-comprehensive-security-settlement-in-northeast-asia (accessed November 9, 2020).
24 Fumihiko Yoshida, Haksoon Paik, Michael Hamel-Green, and Peter Hayes, "Policy Proposal "From Peace on the Korean Peninsula to a Northeast Asia Nuclear Weapon Free Zone," Research Center for Nuclear Weapons Abolition (RECNA), September 8, 2019, at https://www.recna.nagasaki-u.ac.jp/recna/bd/files/Policy-Proposal-2019.pdf (accessed November 10, 2020).
25 Track 1.5 discussion means talks that include government officials that participate in their personal capacity and not representing a state or government.
26 "Work of the Advisory Board on Disarmament Matters. Report of the Secretary-General," United Nations, A/68/206, July 26, 2013, at https://www.un.org/ga/search/view_doc.asp?symbol=a/68/206&Lang=E (accessed November 10, 2020).
27 "Statement of President Ts. Elbegdorj of Mongolia at UN High-level meeting on disarmament," UNGA document A/68/PV.11, September 26, 2013, p. 7, at https://www.un.org/en/ga/68/meetings/nucleardisarmament/pdf/MN_en.pdf (accessed November 10, 2020).
28 "Panel on Peace and Security in Northeast Asia. Nagasaki Process Framework Document," Research Center for Nuclear Weapons Abolition (RECNA), November 16, 2016, at https://www.recna.nagasaki-u.ac.jp/recna/psnanews/15327 (accessed November 14, 2020).

29 Chung-in Moon, "The Next Stage of the Korean Peace Process–Why Seoul Remains Optimistic After Hanoi," *Asia-Pacific Leadership Network*, March 14, 2019, at http://www.apln.network/activities/activities_view/The_Next_Stage_of_the_Korean_Peace_Process_-_Why_Seoul_Remains_Optimistic_After_Hanoi (accessed November 10, 2020).
30 For an important analysis touching upon the main political and legal issues involved, see Michael Hamel-Green, "An Alternative to Nuclear Deadlock and Stalled Diplomacy–Proposals, Pathways, and Prospects for the Northeast Asia Nuclear Weapon Free Zone," *Research Center for Nuclear Weapons Abolition (RECNA)*, October 20, 2020, at https://www.recna.nagasaki-u.ac.jp/recna/psnanews/26106 (accessed November 9, 2020).
31 Todd C. Lopez, "Defense Security Cooperation Agency Sees Growing Interest in Partnerships." DOD News, May 6, 2020, at https://www.defense.gov/Explore/News/Article/Article/2177634/defense-security-cooperation-agency-sees-growing-interest-in-partnerships/ (accessed November 10, 2020).
32 Michael Unbehauen and Christian Decker, "Japan Cancels Aegis Ashore: Reasons, Consequences, and International Implications," *Journal of Indo-Pacific Affairs* 3 (3), Fall 2020, at https://www.airuniversity.af.edu/JIPA/Display/Article/2361398/japan-cancels-aegis-ashore-reasons-consequences-and-international-implications/ (accessed November 10, 2020).
33 Joseph Trevithick, "South Korea Considers Building Large Aircraft Carriers As Country Prepares To Buy More F-35s," *the drive.com*, October 11, 2019, at https://www.thedrive.com/the-war-zone/30347/south-korea-considers-building-large-aircraft-carriers-as-country-prepares-to-buy-more-f-35s (accessed November 13, 2020).
34 Banko Delta Asia is a bank based in Macau that the US Treasury viewed as a primary money laundering bank for North Korea's illegal financial activities. See Press Center, "Treasury Designates Banco Delta Asia as Primary Money Laundering Concern under USA," PATRIOT Act, US Department of the Treasury, September 15, 2005, at https://www.treasury.gov/press-center/press-releases/pages/js2720.aspx (accessed November 14, 2020).
35 H. I. Sutton, "North Korea Reveals New SLBM: Pukguksong-4," *Naval News*, October 15, 2020, at http://www.hisutton.com/North-Korea-Pukguksong-SLBM.html (accessed November 8, 2020).
36 "H.E. Mr. Ochirbat Punsalmagiin, President of Mongolia. Statement in the general debate of the General Assembly at its 44th session," UNGA document A/47/PV.13, October 6, 1992.
37 Article 4 of the "Treaty on Friendly Relations and Cooperation between Mongolia and the Russian Federation," January 20, 1993. See *Mongolia's NWFS: documents speak (basic documents 1992–2015)*, Ulaanbaatar, 2015, p. 7.
38 "Statement by Chinese Delegation at the Second Session of the Preparatory Committee for the 2020 NPT Review Conference on Nuclear-Weapon-Free Zones and Nuclear Issues in the Middle East," Foreign Ministry of the People's Republic of China, April 30, 2018, at https://www.fmprc.gov.cn/mfa_eng/wjb_663304/zzjg_663340/jks_665232/kjfywj_665252/t1611765.shtml (accessed November 9, 2020).
39 "Comprehensive Study of the Question of nuclear-weapon-free zones in all its aspects," UNGA document, "Official Records of 30th session, Document No. 27A (A/10027/ADD.1)," New York, 1975, p. 310.
40 Paragraph 62 of the final document of "XII Ministerial Conference of the Movement of Non-Aligned Countries," New Delhi, April 4–8, 1997, Research and Information System for Developing Countries, at http://ris.org.in/others/NAM-RIS-Web/NAM%20Declaration%20%26%20Docs/NAM-12 MinisterialConf-delhi-Apr4-8-1997-min.pdf (accessed November 9, 2020).

41 Paragraph 86 of the "Final document of the 11th Heads of State Summit Conference of the Movement of Non-Aligned Countries," Cartagena, Colombia, 1995, *Research and Information System for Developing Countries,* at http://ris.org.in/others/NAM-RIS-Web/NAM%20Declaration%20%26%20Docs/NAM%20Summit-11Cartegena-11-16%20Sep-1995-Final%20Document%20-Cartegena-Declaration-min.pdf (accessed November 9, 2020).
42 Paragraph 5, "Mongolia's International Security and Nuclear-Weapon-Free Status," UNGA resolution A/RES/53/77 D, January 12, 1999, at https://undocs.org/en/A/RES/53/77 (accessed November 10, 2020).
43 "Law of Mongolia on its nuclear-weapon-free status," *General Assembly and Security Council documents* A/55/56, S/2000/160, February 29, 2000, at https://www.ctbto.org/fileadmin/user_upload/pdf/Legal_documents/national_provisions/Mongolia_Lawonnuclearweaponfreestatus_030200.PDF (accessed November 9, 2020).
44 This political understanding formed the basis of the 1998 General Assembly resolution 53/77 D entitled "Mongolia's international security and nuclear-weapon-free status." In it, the UNGA welcomed Mongolia's declaration of its nuclear-weapon-free status and expressed conviction that such a status would contribute to enhancing stability and confidence-building in the Northeast Asian region. In their statement supporting the UNGA resolution, the P5 stated that their commitments reflected in Security Council resolution 984 (1995) providing security assurances to NNWSs parties to the NPT applied to Mongolia.
45 Campi, *Mongolia's Foreign Policy: Navigating a Changing World,* Lynne Rienner Publishers, Denver, 2019, p. 235.
46 Track 2 dialogue is the practice of non-governmental, informal, and unofficial organisations or individuals, known as the non-state actors, to discuss issue of mutual interest or concern for the purpose of arriving at some understanding or joint action.
47 See *Reflections on Peace and Security in Northeast Asia: Perspectives from the Ulaanbaatar Process (compilation of articles),* Uragsh-Orgil Company, Ulaanbaatar, 2018; *Perspectives on Peace and Security: Voices from Civil Society and the Ulaanbaatar Process (compilation of articles),* Uragsh-Orgil Company, Ulaanbaatar, 2019.

10 The changing regional dynamics in Northeast Asia: Russia's North Korean conundrum and the case of Mongolia

Nivedita Kapoor

Introduction

The region of Northeast Asia (NEA) occupies a key position in Russian foreign policy—defined in terms of its political, economic, and strategic interests. The post-Soviet period necessitated a complete re-working of its relations with Northeast Asian states, where Russia's overall economic and geopolitical position remains weak. The enunciation of the policy of pivot to the East, which was driven by needs for economic development of its Far East and the strategic imperative to become a stronger player in the rapidly developing Asia-Pacific, has made Moscow focus on NEA more closely in recent years. It considers maintenance of stability on its strategic rear a matter of vital national interest, especially since several ongoing disputes between key NEA states make the situation precarious.

Given the shared border and the economic and strategic considerations, the North Korean nuclear issue remains the key challenge for Moscow in the region. It supports multilateral efforts to deal with the situation and remains in opposition to United States' unilateral sanctions policy. While its position has aligned with China in recent years, Russia has indicated that it is interested in following a multi-vector policy[1] in the region. This would help it avoid over-dependence on rising China through engagement with various regional players and strengthen its position as an influential stakeholder. In this context, the importance of NEA countries like Japan, South Korea, and Mongolia can hardly be denied. This has been reflected in the increased focus of Russia in building its ties with Mongolia, especially as the latter pursues an active policy of diversifying relations with other major NEA powers. Apart from a shared interest in building ties with North Korea, the two countries also are interested in multilateral efforts to bring North Korea to the negotiating table. This chapter will seek to examine the success and limitations of Russia's policy towards North Korea within the broader paradigm of its position in NEA. In this context, it also will trace the evolution of Russian-Mongolian relations and examine possibilities and challenges regarding engagement on North Korea, which remains one of the leading security challenges for Russia in NEA.

DOI: 10.4324/9781003148630-10

Russia in Northeast Asia

The fact of geography places Russia firmly in Northeast Asia, a region defined by its myriad political, economic, and strategic complexities. For Russia, it is not only important as a key partner for the economic development of its Far Eastern territories and as a market for its natural resources, but also for establishing its geopolitical presence as a key player in rapidly developing Asia. The impact of regional territorial disputes, concerns about developments in the Taiwan Straits, and, most importantly for Russia, the North Korean nuclear issue right on its doorstep make NEA an area of concern in strategic terms.

The post-World War II period has seen the rise of the United States (US) as a preeminent power in NEA, a position that is steadily being challenged by China in the Twenty-first century. The US, despite not being geographically present in NEA, exercises its influence through its long-term defence presence and its network of alliances with Japan and South Korea, as well as other bilateral partnerships. It is this Sino-US competition, further heightened by the COVID-19 pandemic, that is expected to define the future regional balance of power in NEA.

These developments outlined above have led to a realisation in Russia that as the centre of global politics and economics shifts to Asia, Russia will have to make efforts to align its future with the region as well.[2] The Russian pivot to the East had been fuelled since it held the APEC summit in Vladivostok in 2012. However, a series of events, beginning with the 2014 Ukraine crisis, have plunged Russia-West relations to new post-Cold War lows. Russia believes the situation will be long-term in nature, which further enhances the importance of NEA for Russia policymakers. Apart from the economic need to integrate with NEA, the "security interdependence of its eastern provinces"[3] with the region remains high. This has led Russia to call for the establishment of an "effective mechanism for strengthening peace, security, mutual trust, and mutually beneficial cooperation in Northeast Asia."[4] Here, the key security concern for Russia remains North Korea, given its opposition to nuclear proliferation, fears of a conflict on its borders, and concern over US' missile defence plans in the region.

The involvement in the North Korean issue and the broader NEA also gives credence to Russian declaration of itself as a unique Eurasian power that has interests spanning both the continents of Europe and Asia. It also ties with its aim of establishing a multipolar world, leading Moscow to propose the idea of setting up a multilateral security framework for the region. Russia now faces the task of furthering its influence in a region not only beset by US-China rivalry, but also the presence of other powerful stakeholders like South Korea and Japan. At present, Russian economic integration in NEA remains low, and there is also a lack of defence networks[5] that affect its ability to be a rule-setter in the region.

North Korea in Russia's foreign policy

North Korea had joined the Non-Proliferation Treaty (NPT) in 1985, which meant it was not allowed to produce nuclear weapons. With the end of the Cold War, talk between the two Koreas in 1992 led to a pledge for denuclearisation of the peninsula. However, the International Atomic Energy Agency (IAEA) accused the North Korean regime of not complying with provisions of the NPT and raised fears that it was enriching plutonium to make bombs. During the first nuclear crisis of 1994, the US, fearing heavy casualties if it used force, negotiated a settlement in return for Pyongyang freezing its nuclear programme and permitting IAEA inspections. In 1999, in return for the relaxing of US sanctions, Pyongyang declared a moratorium on long-range missiles.

The first Korean summit in 2000 called for peaceful reunification and resulted in the reunification of some families, improved economic ties and continued negotiations. However, Washington accused North Korea of having a clandestine nuclear programme, named North Korea as part of axis of evil alongside Iran and Iraq, and re-imposed sanctions. Whereupon in 2002, North Korea, arguing that the weapons were necessary for its self-defence, admitted that it indeed had a secret uranium enrichment programme, withdrew from NPT in 2003, and expelled IAEA inspectors, As the situation grew more precarious, the Six Party Talks (United States, Russia, Japan, China, South Korea, North Korea) were launched in 2003, but it took two years for Pyongyang to agree to give up its nuclear programme. In 2006, North Korea test-fired seven ballistic missiles, and later in the year claimed it had tested its first nuclear weapon, which led to United Nations Security Council (UNSC) sanctions. A 2007 deal through the Six Party Talks led to North Korea again agreeing to halt its nuclear programme in return for foreign aid. When a new South Korean government took a hard line on the North a year later, talks broke down over North Korea's refusal to allow full and unhindered access to inspectors. In 2009, Pyongyang announced a second nuclear test, but in 2012, soon after a change of North Korean leadership to Kim Jong-un, IAEA inspectors were allowed in and a moratorium on testing was declared in return for economic aid. However, this moratorium was brief. Another nuclear test was conducted in 2013, which resulted in the US tightening sanctions in hopes of forcing the North Koreans to return to the Six Party Talks. More nuclear and missile tests followed in 2016 and 2017. Despite the three summit meetings in 2018–2019 between new US President Donald Trump and Kim Jong-un, the two sides still have not reached a deal.

Russia believes that one of the leading issues that threatens strategic stability in NEA is the ongoing North Korean nuclear crisis. Moscow directly relates the resolution of the nuclear issue on the Korean Peninsula to the achievement of "lasting peace and stability in north-east Asia."[6] As a permanent member of the UNSC and sharing a border with North Korea,

Russia has its strategic and economic interests in the region intertwined with the resolution of this issue. While acknowledging that denuclearisation is a difficult goal to achieve, Russia remains concerned about the ongoing nuclear and ballistic missile programme of North Korea and its impact on the global non-proliferation regime.[7] This explains its support of the UNSC sanctions, despite being unsure about their efficacy in containing nuclear proliferation.[8]

Russia has had to rebuild its ties with North Korea in the post-Soviet period to accommodate a situation where it is neither a security guarantor to the North Korean regime nor a key economic partner. In the 1990s, Russian focus was on developing relations with South Korea; since 2000, the former superpower has sought to build ties with North Korea as well. This began with the signing of the Treaty on Friendship, Cooperation, and Good Neighbourly Relations in 2000 and a military cooperation agreement. This was followed by the visit of Kim Jong-il to Russia in 2001 and 2002. The following year, Russia participated in the Six Party Talks after reports emerged of Pyongyang pursuing a nuclear weapons programme. In fact, it was North Korea that insisted that Russia be brought into the talks as a counterbalance to the US, and Moscow saw it as an avenue to boost its regional presence.[9] The talks could not prevent North Korea's 2006 nuclear test, its withdrawal from the talks three years later, or its resuming its nuclear enrichment programme.

Meanwhile, interactions between the two states continued, and in 2014, Russia wrote off the Soviet-era debt. While Chinese ties with North Korea became strained around this time due to its repeated nuclear and missile tests, Russia continued its engagement and 2015 was declared the Year of Friendship between the two countries. However, international sanctions, in response to North Korean nuclear tests in 2016, led to a cooling of ties to a certain extent, but Russia did not block UNSC sanctions despite wanting them watered down.

Russian-North Korean trade relations remain limited, with bilateral trade in 2019 amounting to just US$47.9 million. There are prospects of this improving through trilateral projects which include South Korea, but sanctions so far have prevented any effective development on this front. Some of the proposed projects include a gas pipeline, a railway link, and electricity transmission. Russia employed significant North Korean labour in its construction sector, with workers sending millions in remittances back home, which were a vital source of revenue for the regime.[10] However, the passage of UNSC Resolution 2397 of 2017 in response to Pyongyang's launch of an ICBM meant that this revenue has now ended. Russia has limited financial capacity to invest significantly in North Korea and Russia's economic model of exporting natural resources is not very compatible with North Korea's low level of economic development.

China, in contrast, is North Korea's largest trade partner, even though trade volumes have suffered in recent years due to strict United Nations

(UN) sanctions. It also provides aid to Pyongyang and has important strategic interests for keeping the regime afloat, which involve preventing a US-dominated peninsula, averting destabilisation, and promoting non-proliferation. North Korea is open to improving relations with Russia to avoid over-dependence on China. However, cognisant of Moscow's limited strength as an independent player on the Korean Peninsula, Pyongyang has been focused more on balancing through the other major powers of the US and South Korea.[11]

Despite an uptick in political and economic engagement between the two sides since 2014, the first summit between Russian President Vladimir Putin and North Korean leader Kim Jong-un only took place in 2019, underscoring the decline in influence of the former superpower when it comes to the Korean Peninsula.[12] The 2018 Panmunjom Declaration[13] only mentions trilateral meetings with the US or in quadrilateral format with the addition of China. It does not mention Russia or reflect any proposal to include other players in resolution of the nuclear issue. The Trump administration in the last four years has engaged directly with North Korea or done so in a trilateral format with South Korea. In contrast, Russia would prefer multilateral efforts to deal with the situation, given that it cannot deliver results working independently. Like the now suspended Six Party Talks, this format suits Moscow's goals in that its membership cemented its position as an important player.

However, driven by economic, military, and diplomatic interests in NEA, especially in North Korea, Moscow has revived its efforts in the region in recent years.[14] A shared border, need for stability in its backyard and an interest in being an influential player through diplomacy together have defined recent Russian actions on North Korea. It also cannot deny further proliferation by the communist regime leading to a regional nuclear race only will strengthen American military presence—a scenario it would loath to see materialise. Already, the revelation of North Korea ballistic missiles led to the American proposal to set up THAAD missile defence. This, Russia fears, could form part of a larger missile defence plan by the US across Europe and the Asia-Pacific that will affect Moscow's ability to strike against its Cold War rival and thus imperil its overall security[15] and endanger strategic stability.[16] It has the economic interests, including trilateral projects, of the Russian Far East in mind in promoting trade with both Koreas, while also wanting to prevent instability arising out of any regime collapse. The current UNSC sanctions prevent the trilateral projects from being implemented. These goals mean it has an interest in North Korea refraining from further nuclear proliferation. While not opposed to reunification of the two Koreas, Moscow does not want it to happen as a result of unilateral US policy or through violent actions resulting in refugee flow across its borders. It also has called for North Korea's legitimate concerns to be respected regarding security guarantees and regime change.[17]

Over the years, efforts to denuclearise the Korean Peninsula have been unsuccessful and North Korea has argued that its nuclear weapons are a bulwark against regime change. Currently, both South Korea and Japan rely on the American nuclear umbrella and also host US troops on their soil as a means to stabilise the region, which Pyongyang says are a "threat to its existence."[18] The safety of troops stationed in South Korea and Japan is one of the key concerns for the US, as well as the security of its two alliance partners in NEA. Japan favours a strong US position on North Korea, while South Korea has been more cautious. These countries have, in addition to the UNSC sanctions, imposed additional sanctions to pressure North Korea into giving up its nuclear weapons.

This approach has been opposed by both Russia and China, both of whom argue that these actions push North Korea towards further proliferation. A 2017 joint roadmap by Russia and China called for a "suspension for suspension", in which the North Korean side would suspend its nuclear and missile programme in return for US/South Korea refraining from large-scale military exercises. This would be done alongside a parallel approach towards denuclearisation and conducting talks to address all issues of concern.[19] In fact, this joint statement was indicative of close coordination between Moscow and Beijing on the Korean issue. Then in October 2018, the first-ever meeting at the deputy foreign minister-level of representatives from Russia, China, and North Korea took place.

Russia and China have found that their positions broadly coincide on other related issues as well, including deployment of THAAD and "possible outcomes of regime change" in Pyongyang.[20] They have also worked to dilute the sanctions to some extent by threatening to use their veto power in the UNSC.[21] Neither Moscow nor Beijing wants Korean reunification to lead to a pro-US peninsula or American troops on the Russian-Korean border[22] or chaos resulting from collapse of the ruling communist regime. However, China sees North Korea as a buffer state on its border and is thus a lot more wary of reunification than Russia, which sees economic benefits accruing from direct access to the developed South Korean market, as well as connectivity projects as a result of a unified state. But, as noted earlier, if unification is seen as tilting the balance in favour of the US, Russia is likely to be in opposition to such a move.

The breakdown of the Six Party Talks has led to limits on the role of Russia because, despite being an important stakeholder, it does not play a decisive role.[23] Recent years have seen Russia allow China to take the lead in dealing with the North Korean issue. This was reflected in it not opposing Beijing from taking a harsher stand on sanctions against Pyongyang. While the Chinese-North Korean relationship remained strained between 2013 and 2018, Moscow did not attempt to take advantage of the situation for its benefit.[24] This is also a reflection of the qualitative improvement in Sino-Russian ties that have made China the leading strategic partner of Russia. Both countries see benefits in limiting US' influence in the region and on the

Korean Peninsula; their ideas have been in broad agreement. This is not to say that their concerns are exactly identical, but the divergences are not wide enough to prevent their coming up with the joint roadmap.

Moscow is aware that China has the economic influence over the North Korean regime and its own leverage is low.[25] This situation leads Russia to focus on using diplomatic manoeuvres to keep its diplomatic channels open while giving China the lead.[26] It also has to deal with a sense that Russian ambition to play an important role in resolving the issue is not backed by real deeds.[27] In order to change that perception, it would have to significantly strengthen its economic and political presence in NEA through engagement beyond Beijing with Seoul and Tokyo, which has had limited success until now.[28] Its worsening relations with the US since the 2014 Ukrainian crisis and the subsequent rapprochement with China also have impacted development of bilateral ties with American allies in the region. In order to avoid an over-dependence on China and establish its independent position on the North Korean issue, Moscow will need improved relations with all the regional stakeholders—both big and small. It is in this context that Mongolia enters the picture.

Russia's policy towards Mongolia in Northeast Asia and the case of North Korea

In 2018, Russian deputy foreign minister Igor Morgulov said that it was possible Mongolia could become a part of the Six Party Talks.[29] While the format itself has been stalled since 2008, Russia has consistently supported its revival. Regardless of the status of the forum, it is relevant to examine why Russia considered it appropriate to back this idea. The reason for this seems to be two-fold: an improvement in Russia-Mongolia ties as well as the latter's efforts to be a part of solution to the Korean Peninsula issue.

During the Cold War period, Mongolia was a satellite state of the Soviet Union, although not absorbed into the USSR. The USSR's collapse led to a free fall of relations with post-Soviet Russia in the 1990s and stabilised only in the Twenty-first century. The signings of the Ulaanbaatar declaration in 2000, the Moscow declaration in 2006, and the bilateral strategic partnership declaration in 2009 set the stage for an expansion of political, economic, and military ties. Since 2014, when Russia's relations with the West broke down as a result of Ukrainian crisis, the former superpower has turned its focus more sharply than before towards Asia.

This also has found reflection in its relations with Mongolia, whose economy is still closely tied to Russia's in specific ways. It imports 90 per cent of its oil and gas from Russia and the latter is a co-owner of the trans-Mongolian Ulaanbaatar Railway, and until 2018 was co-owner of the key copper extraction operation (and largest Mongolian budget contributor) in Erdenet. In 2014, Mongolia did not join western condemnation of Russia over its annexation of Crimea but instead looked to improve economic ties with the former superpower and promote Ulaanbaatar as an important connectivity link.[30] That same year saw Russia giving a green light to visa-free travel to Mongolia and enhanced military-to-military cooperation.[31] In 2015, Mongolia participated in the 70th anniversary victory day celebrations in Moscow. The 2019 visit of Russian President Vladimir Putin to Mongolia saw the relationship raised to the level of comprehensive strategic partnership. The two sides had signed an intergovernmental agreement on transit rail transportation in 2018 which gave Mongolia access to Russian Far Eastern seaports. Mongolia also has expressed its intention to sign a free trade agreement with the Eurasian Economic Union.[32]

In addition, the 2004 intergovernmental agreement providing for military-technical assistance to Mongolia on a grant basis resumed in 2019.[33] Russia supplies most of Ulaanbaatar's defence supplies and the two sides have conducted regular military exercises called "Selenga" since 2008. Despite the coronavirus pandemic, their militaries met in November 2020 for this annual exercise. Mongolia also participated in Vostok military exercises in 2018 in Russia, which included China. This remains part of Moscow's efforts to maintain "neutral, stable, and peaceful" countries on its borders.[34] These measures also help it preserve its influence despite acknowledging rising Chinese power in its traditional areas of influence in the neighbourhood.

A landlocked country wedged between China and Russia, Mongolia faces the challenge of pursuing a balanced foreign policy to avoid over-dependence on any one partner. In fact, some experts note that good relations with Russia are important for Mongolia's balanced approach towards foreign policy and provide a way to "offset China's influence."[35] The value of China for Mongolia can hardly be denied, which is why in 2014, the two sides raised their relations to a comprehensive strategic partnership. China is a rising power that is shaping the economic landscape of the region through its various initiatives, including the BRI, and other financial initiatives, and critical for Mongolian connectivity across Asia. This has become important as Mongolia's economic dependence on China has risen, with the latter emerging as its key trade partner for 90 per cent of its exports. In contrast, Russia is the destination for only 1 per cent of Mongolian exports. About 34 per cent of Mongolia's imports come from China with Russian share at 29 per cent. Other key import partners include Japan, South Korea, United States, and Germany.[36]

In an effort to balance "Sino-Russian rivalry towards Mongolia," Ulaanbaatar has become an enthusiastic participant in several trilateral mechanisms.[37] Since their first meeting in 2014, the leaders of China, Russia, and Mongolia now meet regularly on the sidelines of the Shanghai Cooperation Organisation (SCO) summit. While Mongolia is an observer at SCO, it has not yet moved towards becoming a full member. This has been interpreted as its desire to maintain a certain level of neutrality. Currently, two major projects are in process that would strengthen Russia-Mongolia-China linkages. One is the Power of Siberia 2 pipeline that would pump natural gas from Russia to China; its feasibility study has begun in order to decide on the final route and pricing considerations. If the route via Mongolia is chosen, it would be an important collaboration for the two countries. The other relates to the China-Mongolia-Russia Economic Corridor that forms part of Beijing's BRI. The progress on this particular BRI corridor has been slow,[38] and the Heihe-Blagoveshchensk Bridge over the Amur River that would play an important link in the transit between three countries by connecting into the Trans-Siberian rail network was only completed in 2019.[39] The fulfilment of these projects will contribute towards realisation of Russian foreign policy goals vis-à-vis Mongolia that include furthering economic ties, establishing its presence as an important player, and ensuring security in its near-abroad.[40]

Mongolia, which has sought to position itself as a key to regional connectivity, is expected to benefit from the realisation of these projects. By positioning itself as a bridge, it is given the opportunity to enhance its own economy by building relevant infrastructure and increased investment as well as gaining access to distant markets. There also is the potential to integrate the BRI with Mongolia's own domestic Steppe Road Plan announced in 2014 that seeks to develop the local economy through becoming a key transportation link and improving infrastructure.[41]

In the midst of this delicate balancing act between Russia and China, Mongolia understands that it needs multiple partners not just for strategic autonomy but also to ensure economic growth. For instance, in an effort to maintain balanced investment ties with multiple partners, it enacted a law in 2010 declaring that no foreign country can have more than one-third proportion of the total foreign direct investment (FDI) in any state-owned mineral deposit.[42] The costs of over-dependence on one country were driven home in 2016 when amidst financial difficulties in order to secure a loan, the Mongolian foreign minister had to pledge to China that the Dalai Lama would not be invited again to the country where 53 per cent of people practice Buddhism.[43] In this case, Japan took charge and secured over US$5 billion for the beleaguered country, highlighting the importance of Mongolia's "Third Neighbour" policy it has followed for years now.[44]

Mongolian foreign policy and its outreach to North Korea

The Third Neighbour policy is part of Mongolia's efforts to pursue an independent foreign policy and involves building relations with a wide variety of regional stakeholders beyond Russia and China—including the US, Japan, South Korea, India, and European Union (EU), to name a few.[45] In addition to the Russia-Mongolia-China trilateral, Mongolia also is promoting a Mongolia-US-Japan trilateral.[46] Mongolia has cultivated close ties with the US, with the relationship being upgraded to a strategic partnership in 2019. It has sent peacekeepers to both Iraq and Afghanistan, and it was the 2003 deployment of its troops to Iraq that played a role in Russia "intensifying its political and military exchanges" with Ulaanbaatar.[47] Mongolia's annual peacekeeping UN training exercise, Khaan Quest, involves the active participation of the US Pacific Command and at the same time involves several dozen countries, including China.[48] A total of 38 countries participated in the exercise in 2019. These efforts have been pursued at a time when the regional order in NEA is in a flux. As a result, improving ties with Japan and the two Koreas has followed as a natural corollary.

Ulaanbaatar has developed its relations in such a way that it today enjoys good relations with both Korean governments as seen in its growing economic and cultural engagement.[49] On the one hand, Mongolia's relations with North Korea stretch back to the Soviet period; it was one of the first countries to recognise the establishment of the communist state in 1948. Mongolian President Tsakhia Elbegdorj visited North Korea in 2013, not long after Kim Jong-un took charge as the leader. In 2018 the North Korean foreign minister visited Mongolia to celebrate the establishment of 70 years of diplomatic relations. A few thousand North Korean workers were employed in Mongolia until 2019, and Mongolia was able to use the Rason, North Korean port for trial coal shipments. The two countries also maintain regular contacts at the military level, as well among civilians like medical professionals, businesspeople, and sportspersons.[50]

On the other, Ulaanbaatar's relations with South Korea are active in the political and economic domains, with regular high-level visits on both sides. Mongolia also is named as a key partner in Seoul's New Northern Policy (NNP) that seeks to promote its engagement with the countries to the north of Korean Peninsula which also includes Russia and Central Asian states. Mongolia has been intent on using its small country diplomacy and non-nuclear-weapon state status positions as a possible peacemaker in NEA.[51] The idea has been to use its various relationships to position itself as a potential player in dealing with contentious issues in the region and providing its services as a neutral meeting ground. Mongolia has been laying the groundwork for such a role for quite some time. In 2007, it played host to Japan-North Korea talks to normalise relations and in 2012 to provide a venue for meeting between families of Japanese abductees by North Korea. The US held track 1.5 talks with North Korea in Ulaanbaatar in 2014.[52] These efforts, despite not always yielding optimum results, raised Mongolia's regional profile in its attempts at presenting itself as an impartial partner that can contribute to development of peace and security in NEA.[53] Such moves also are aimed at compensating for a situation where Mongolia has limited influence to exercise, which constraints its overall geostrategic impact.

The launch of Mongolia's Ulaanbaatar Dialogue (UBD) in 2014 has led some scholars to look at it as complementing Seoul's Northeast Asia Peace and Cooperation Initiative (NAPCI) initiative.[54] The UBD focuses on track 1.5 and track 2 efforts[55] and seeks to build mutual understanding and trust among the various stakeholders. NEA has many historical and territorial disputes that make it one of the most volatile regions prone to conflict, so Mongolia offers itself as a country with good relations with all regional players that is uniquely positioned to be a venue for a regional security dialogue, including discussions on the North Korean nuclear issue.[56] Key participants in the UBD include Mongolia, North Korea, South Korea, China, US, Russia, and Japan. Moscow has extended its support for this initiative, seeing Mongolia as a neutral player. While North Korea did not attend the UBD in 2019, its representatives have attended three out of six annual meetings, thus it is seen as an opportunity to keep lines of communication open with North Korea.

Shared interests: Russia and Mongolia in North Korea

As has been noted earlier, Russia considers the situation in the Korean Peninsula to be critical for the overall security of NEA. While it has steadily worked to improve relations with North Korea, the 2018 Panmunjeon Declaration makes no mention of Russia and seeks to resolve conflict through the involvement of both the Koreas, the US, and China. The breakdown of the Six Party Talks also has had a negative impact on Russia's influence, even though it still has a say due to its position as a permanent member of the UNSC. If Moscow is to continue to play a significant role in the North Korean issue, it will have to do more than simply improve relations with the communist regime. It will have to become a more important player in the broader region of NEA, where its focus on China has led to a neglect of other relationships. A diversified portfolio of ties is critical to improve Russia's regional power projection that would further its position and help realisation of its pivot to Asia. In this case, relations with regional stakeholders like South Korea, Japan, and Mongolia become important.

At first glance, Mongolia is a much smaller player in the grander scheme of things in NEA, wedged as it is between Russia and China and trying to diversify its relations with other powers to avoid being enmeshed between the two big powers. This would lead some to argue that Mongolia as a small player does not exercise significant geopolitical importance for Russia. However, as discussed earlier, Mongolia is one of the few powers that has cordial relations with both the Koreas and by carrying on sustained economic and political engagement has never closed off its interactions with Pyongyang. Russia is deeply interested in preventing any conflict on the Korean Peninsula and, while it has allowed China to take the lead on the issue in recent years, it would prefer to have a seat at the table in any discussions regarding the Korean Peninsula.[57]

Mongolia's efforts to act as a neutral party in the North Korea issue and sustained pursuit of multilateral engagement has its benefits, as evident in its hosting of the UBD, as well as delicate secret talks on its soil of Japan and the US with North Korea. While experts agree that its mediation alone might not lead to resolution of the nuclear issue, its value as an "effective channel...for increasing communication, finding common ground, and beginning to ease tension"[58] can hardly be denied. Given that Mongolia emphasises multilateral interaction to deal with NEA security concerns rather than just a club of a few members, it ties into the Russian narrative in a region where Russia is no longer the rule-setter. Moscow also has indicated its openness to other multilateral initiatives being promoted by Mongolia like the Northeast Asian Nuclear-Weapon-Free Zone, "which calls for security guarantees to non-nuclear states by nuclear-capable nations."[59]

Moscow realises its relative weakness in NEA and seeks to diversify its ties to become an influential regional power while avoiding an overdependence on China. Therefore, it is not surprising that Mongolia, despite not being a major power, figures in its equation—both in the case of North Korea and in the case of the broader NEA. However, Russian and Mongolian efforts to play roles on the North Korean nuclear issue are hardly expected to be smooth. The breakdown of the Six Party Talks stalled any organised multilateral engagement on the nuclear issue. This was evident in recent years when the US and North Korea directly engaged with each other or with the involvement of South Korea. The Panmunjom Declaration also only mentioned the two Koreas, the US, and China, leaving out other regional stakeholders. While Russia continues to have its role as a UNSC permanent member, it does not have enough leverage to impact the action of either the US or North Korea.[60]

For Mongolia, it will be a significant challenge to promote its initiatives with North Korea to a level that makes it a key player. The presence of multiple major powers in the region will make it very difficult for Mongolia to make a mark on an issue that is of critical concern to those powers. The absence of an established security architecture in NEA also disproportionately benefits the leading powers, as they set the rules of the game while the middle and smaller powers struggle to establish their influence. The evolving regional balance of power makes this situation even more acute, as a growing US-China rivalry squeezes the space available to other middle-level powers on critical issues involving NEA security.

This situation also has consequences for Russian policy for the Korean peninsula, which faces the choice of either following a more independent path or choosing to align with Beijing.[61] As Vassily Kashin explains, the increase of Chinese influence on North Korea and its attempts to weaken the US-South Korea alliance through the "three no's agreement"[62] will generate a response from the Americans. Russia, which has recently been siding with China on the North Korean issue, still wishes to have a diversified East Asia policy. But its ongoing conflict with the US has made this proposition difficult and led to ever closer Sino-Russian engagement. A policy that continues on this line will lead only to further polarisation along US-China lines, reducing space for multilateral engagement on North Korea. However, a more independent policy by Russia at a time when it is yet to succeed in establishing close relations with other key stakeholders in NEA will put it in a weaker position amidst heightened US-China bipolarity. Apart from their individual limitations, Russia and Mongolia together do not add significantly to each other's strengths on the North Korean issue, given their lack of leverage on Pyongyang. This situation could worsen as a result of the emerging regional order.

Conclusion

Russia sees the North Korean nuclear issue through the prism of political, economic, and strategic consequences. It wants to be seen as a major power in Asia, reap the benefits of economic cooperation with both Koreas, and prevent conflict on its borders to preserve regional security. Ideally, it would prefer a multipolar NEA, instead of a region dominated by either the United States or China, wherein it can be a critical player.[63] However, the breakdown of Russian ties with the West has tilted its foreign policy towards China, a factor which also is reflected in its North Korea policy.

At present, Russia's key strengths on the issue come from its permanent seat at UNSC and its relatively cordial relations with the North Korean regime. Given the state of its ties with the West and its overall weak political, economic, and defence linkages in NEA, Sino-Russian cooperation on North Korea is likely to continue. While this means that Russia remains relevant in the Korean Peninsula, it does not play a decisive role due to a lack of effective leverage over key players.[64] Russia's efforts to play a constructive role also are thwarted by the breakdown of the multilateral format of talks that at present show no signs of revival. This potentially puts a spanner in the role of Mongolia, whose position would benefit from inclusion of other regional stakeholders to talks on the nuclear issue. While Mongolia has a role as a neutral party, the rise of bipolar rivalry between the US and China raises the danger of major powers taking control of the issue, leaving out other middle and smaller powers from contributing effectively despite their stakes in the issue.

In other words, while both Russia and Mongolia have the potential to contribute constructively to the North Korean nuclear issue in a multilateral format, their ability to do so independently remains limited. Furthermore, if NEA continues to proceed along the same path of heightened US-China bipolar rivalry in the aftermath of the coronavirus pandemic, the goals of Moscow and Ulaanbaatar will be harder to achieve than ever before.

Notes

1 In the post-Soviet period, Russia has presented itself as a power with interests in both the East and the West, owing to its geographical location that stretches from Asia to Europe. This balance in pursuit of national interest and building bilateral and multilateral relationships with foreign countries from both these geographies is what has been characterised as a multi-vector foreign policy.

2 "Foreign Policy Concept of the Russian Federation," Ministry of Foreign Affairs of the Russian Federation, February 18, 2013, at https://www.mid.ru/en/foreign_policy/official_documents/-/asset_publisher/CptICkB6BZ29/content/id/122186 (accessed October 20, 2020).
3 Tula Kahrs, "Regional Security Complex Theory and Chinese Policy towards North Korea," *East Asia* 21 (4), 2004, pp. 64–82.
4 Foreign Policy Concept of the Russian Federation.
5 "Asia Power Index: Country Profile–Russia," Lowy Institute, 2020, at https://power.lowyinstitute.org/countries/russia/ (accessed October 20, 2020).
6 "Joint Statement by the Ministry of Foreign Affairs of the Russian Federation and the Ministry of Foreign Affairs of the People's Republic of China on the Korean Peninsula Issues," IAEA, August 14, 2017, at https://www.iaea.org/sites/default/files/publications/documents/infcircs/2017/infcirc922.pdf (accessed October 24, 2020).
7 Artyom Lukin, "Thinking Beyond China When Dealing with North Korea: Is There a Role for Russia," Foreign Policy Research Institute, April 4, 2017, at https://www.fpri.org/article/2017/04/thinking-beyond-china-dealing-north-korea-role-russia/ (accessed October 23, 2020).
8 Alexander Gabuev, "A Russian Perspective on the Impact of Sanctions," Carnegie Moscow Center, August 3, 2017, at https://carnegie.ru/2017/08/03/russian-perspective-on-impact-of-sanctions-pub-72723 (accessed October 27, 2020).
9 "North Korea-Russia Relations: A Strained Friendship," International Crisis Group, December 4, 2007, at https://d2071andvip0wj.cloudfront.net/b71-north-korea-russia-relations-a-strained-friendship.pdf (accessed October 26, 2020).
10 "Russian Trade With North Korea Increased 40% In 2019," *Moscow Briefing*, March 18, 2020, at https://www.russia-briefing.com/news/russian-trade-north-korea-increased-40-2019.html/ (accessed November 21, 2020).
11 Jaewoo Choo, Youngjun Kim, Artyom Lukin, and Elizabeth Wishnick, "The China-Russia Entente and the Korean Peninsula," The National Bureau of Asian Research, March 29, 2019, p. 14, at https://www.nbr.org/wp-content/uploads/pdfs/publications/sr78_china_russia_entente_march2019.pdf (accessed November 3, 2020).
12 Artyom Lukin, "Why Russia Is Still Playing Second Fiddle in Korean Geopolitics," Valdai Discussion Club, August 21, 2018, at https://valdaiclub.com/a/highlights/russia-second-fiddle-in-korea/?sphrase_id=1156047 (accessed November 4, 2020).
13 "Panmunjom Declaration," United Nations General Assembly, April 27, 2018, at https://kls.law.columbia.edu/sites/default/files/content/pics/Panmunjom%20Monitor/-Panmunjom%20Declaration.pdf (accessed November 3, 2020).
14 Gabuev, "A Russian Perspective on the Impact of Sanctions."
15 Alexander Gabuev and Li Aixin, "Can Russia and China Join Efforts to Counter THAAD," Carnegie Moscow Centre, March 27, 2017, at https://carnegie.ru/2017/03/27/can-russia-and-china-join-efforts-to-counter-thaad-pub-68410 (accessed November 2, 2020).
16 Ian E. Rinehart, "Ballistic Missile Defense in the Asia-Pacific Region: Cooperation and Opposition," Congressional Research Service, 2015, p. 15, at https://fas.org/sgp/crs/nuke/R43116.pdf (accessed November 5, 2020).
17 "Joint statement by the Ministry of Foreign Affairs of the Russian Federation and the Ministry of Foreign Affairs of the People's Republic of China on the Korean Peninsula Issues."
18 Eleanor Albert, "What to Know About Sanctions on North Korea," Council on Foreign Relations, July 16, 2019, at https://www.cfr.org/backgrounder/what-know-about-sanctions-north-korea (accessed October 27, 2020).
19 "Joint statement by the Ministry of Foreign Affairs of the Russian Federation and the Ministry of Foreign Affairs of the People's Republic of China on the Korean Peninsula Issues."

The changing regional dynamics 213

20 Albert, "What to Know About Sanctions on North Korea."
21 Choo et al., "The China-Russia Entente and the Korean Peninsula," p. 6.
22 Ibid., p. 15.
23 Alexander Gabuev, "Bad Cop, Mediator or Spoiler: Russia's Role on the Korean Peninsula," *The Moscow Times*, April 24, 2019, at https://www.themoscowtimes.com/2019/04/24/bad-cop-mediator-or-spoiler-russias-role-on-the-korean-peninsula-a65369 (accessed November 6, 2020).
24 Choo et al., "The China-Russia Entente and the Korean Peninsula," p. 24.
25 Scott Snyder, "Where Does the Russia-North Korea Relationship Stand," Council on Foreign Relations, April 29, 2019, at https://www.cfr.org/in-brief/where-does-russia-north-korea-relationship-stand (accessed November 1, 2020).
26 Gabuev, "Bad Cop, Mediator or Spoiler."
27 Gleb Ivashentsov, "Putin-Kim Summit: A Long Overdue Event," Valdai Discussion Club, April 23, 2019, at https://valdaiclub.com/a/highlights/putin-kim-summit-long-overdue-event/ (accessed November 8, 2020).
28 Paul Stronski and Richard Sokolsky, "The Return of Global Russia: An Analytical Framework," Carnegie Moscow Center, December 14, 2017, at https://carnegieendowment.org/2017/12/14/return-of-global-russia-analytical-framework-pub-75003 (accessed November 7, 2020).
29 "Mongolia may join talks on Korean Peninsula denuclearization," *TASS*, October 21, 2018, at https://tass.com/world/1027010 (accessed November 5, 2020).
30 Sergey Radchenko, "Mongolia Hangs in the Balance: Political Choices and Economic Realities in a State Bounded by China and Russia," in Gilbert Rozman and Sergey Radchenko (eds), *International Relations and Asia's Northern Tier: Sino-Russia Relations, North Korea, and Mongolia*, Palgrave Macmillan, 2018, p. 131.
31 Mendee Jargalsaikhan, "Mongolia's Dilemma: A Politically Linked, Economically Isolated Small Power," in Gilbert Rozman and Sergey Radchenko (eds), *International Relations and Asia's Northern Tier: Sino-Russia Relations, North Korea, and Mongolia*, Palgrave Macmillan, 2018, p. 161.
32 "Press statements following Russian-Mongolian talks," *The Kremlin*, September 3, 2019, at http://en.kremlin.ru/events/president/transcripts/61435 (accessed November 9, 2020).
33 "Russian-Mongolian talks," *The Kremlin*, September 3, 2019, at http://en.kremlin.ru/events/president/news/61429 (accessed November 9, 2020).
34 Mendee, "Mongolia's Dilemma: A Politically Linked, Economically Isolated Small Power," in Gilbert Rozman and Sergey Radchenko (eds), *International Relations and Asia's Northern Tier: Sino-Russia Relations, North Korea, and Mongolia*, Palgrave Macmillan, 2018.
35 Jeff Reeves, "Russo–Mongolian Relations: Closer than Ever," *Russian Analytical Digest*, January 30, 2015, at https://css.ethz.ch/content/dam/ethz/special-interest/gess/cis/center-for-securities-studies/pdfs/RAD-161-2-5.pdf (accessed November 8, 2020), p. 4.
36 "Investment in Mongolia," *KPMG*, 2019, at https://assets.kpmg/content/dam/kpmg/mn/pdf/investment-in-mongolia-2019.pdf (accessed November 6, 2020).
37 See Alicia Campi, "Mongolia's Response To Increasing U.S.-China-Russia Rivalry In Asia," East West Center, August 7, 2020, at https://www.eastwestcenter.org/publications/mongolia%E2%80%99s-response-increasing-us-china-russia-rivalry-in-asia (accessed November 6, 2020).
38 Elizabeth Wishnick, "Mongolia: Bridge or Buffer in Northeast Asia," *The Diplomat*, June 19, 2019, at https://thediplomat.com/2019/06/mongolia-bridge-or-buffer-in-northeast-asia/ (accessed November 7, 2020).
39 Gaye Christoffersen, "Sino-Russian Local Relations: Heihe and Blagoveshchensk," *The Asan Forum*, December 10, 2019, at http://www.theasanforum.org/sino-russian-local-relations-heihe-and-blagoveshchensk/ (accessed November 6, 2020).

40 Sergey Radchenko, "Sino-Russian Competition in Mongolia," in Gilbert Rozman and Sergey Radchenko (eds), *International Relations and Asia's Northern Tier: Sino-Russia Relations, North Korea, and Mongolia*, Palgrave Macmillan, 2018, p. 115.
41 The Steppe Road Plan, introduced in 2014 by Mongolia, is a wide-ranging initiative that seeks to improve trans-border trade and develop the local economy. This is aimed to be done via construction of a road link across Mongolia, connecting China to Russia, as well as development of new railway lines, oil and gas pipelines, and an upgrade of the electricity grid.
42 David Caprara, Katharine H.S. Moon, and Paul Park, "Mongolia: Potential Mediator between the Koreas and Proponent of Peace in Northeast Asia," *Brookings East Asia Commentary*, January 20, 2015, at https://www.brookings.edu/opinions/mongolia-potential-mediator-between-the-koreas-and-proponent-of-peace-in-northeast-asia/ (accessed November 12, 2020).
43 "China says hopes Mongolia learned lesson after Dalai Lama visit," *Reuters*, January 24, 2017, at https://www.reuters.com/article/us-china-mongolia-dalailama-idUSKBN158197 (accessed November 21, 2020).
44 Yiyi Chen, "China and Japan's Investment Competition in Mongolia," *The Diplomat*, August 1, 2018, at https://thediplomat.com/2018/08/china-and-japans-investment-competition-in-mongolia/ (accessed November 8, 2020).
45 "Mongolia's 'Third Neighbor' Foreign Policy," *Asia Society*, June 18, 2013, at https://asiasociety.org/korea/mongolias-third-neighbor-foreign-policy (accessed November 21, 2020).
46 Campi, "Mongolia's Response To Increasing U.S.-China-Russia Rivalry In Asia."
47 Mendee, "Mongolia's Dilemma: A Politically Linked, Economically Isolated Small Power," in Gilbert Rozman and Sergey Radchenko (eds), *International Relations and Asia's Northern Tier: Sino-Russia Relations, North Korea, and Mongolia*, Palgrave Macmillan, 2018.
48 Mark Minton, "A Stronger Korea-Mongolia Link in a Changing Northeast Asia," in Gilbert Rozman and Sergey Radchenko (eds), *International Relations and Asia's Northern Tier: Sino-Russia Relations, North Korea, and Mongolia*, Palgrave Macmillan, 2018, p. 150.
49 Mendee Jargalsaikhany, "A Potential Breakthrough in Mongolia's Relations With North and South Korea," Jamestown Foundation, *Eurasia Daily Monitor*, March 2, 2015, at https://jamestown.org/program/a-potential-breakthrough-in-mongolias-relations-with-north-and-south-korea/ (accessed November 6, 2020).
50 Julian Dierkes and Otgonbaatar Byambaa, "Japan's Mongolian connection in North Korea," *East Asia Forum*, November 5, 2013, at https://www.eastasiaforum.org/2013/11/05/japans-mongolian-connection-in-north-korea/ (accessed November 5, 2020).
51 Bolor Lkhaajav, "Mongolia's Small Country Diplomacy and North Korea," *The Diplomat*, September 29, 2016, at https://thediplomat.com/2016/09/mongolias-small-country-diplomacy-and-north-korea/ (accessed November 9, 2020).
52 Alicia Campi, "Ulaanbaatar Dialogue on Northeast Asian Security," Jamestown Foundation, *Eurasia Daily Monitor* 11 (126), July 11, 2014, at https://jamestown.org/program/ulaanbaatar-dialogue-on-northeast-asian-security/ (accessed November 6, 2020).
53 Minton, "A Stronger Korea-Mongolia Link in a Changing Northeast Asia," in Gilbert Rozman and Sergey Radchenko (eds), *International Relations and Asia's Northern Tier: Sino-Russia Relations, North Korea, and Mongolia*, Palgrave Macmillan, 2018, p. 152.
54 Caprara et al., "Mongolia: Potential Mediator between the Koreas and Proponent of Peace in Northeast Asia," *Brookings East Asia Commentary*.
55 Track 1.5 refers to engagement between government officials (in an unofficial capacity) and other subject experts that exist outside the official channels to

discuss, debate, and seek solutions on specific issues. Track 2 is the engagement without any government/official participation that takes place between academicians, people, NGOs, and the like.
56 "Ulaanbaatar Dialogue," Foreign Affairs Ministry of Mongolia, Mongolian Ministry of Foreign Affairs, 2015, at http://www.mfa.gov.mn/wp-content/uploads/2015/12/Ulaanbaatar-Dialogue.pdf (accessed November 12, 2020).
57 Vassily Kashin, "Russia's Dilemma on the Korean Peninsula," Carnegie Moscow Center, October 30, 2020, at https://carnegie.ru/commentary/83076 (accessed November 12, 2020).
58 Caprara et al., "Mongolia: Potential Mediator between the Koreas and Proponent of Peace in Northeast Asia," *Brookings East Asia Commentary*.
59 Lukin, "Why Russia Is Still Playing Second Fiddle in Korean Geopolitics."
60 Gabuev, "Bad Cop, Mediator or Spoiler."
61 Kashin, "Russia's Dilemma on the Korean Peninsula."
62 In 2017, China imposed economic sanctions on South Korea in response to the latter agreeing to install the US THAAD missile defence system. Seoul signed the "three-nos agreement" with Beijing in return for lifting of the sanctions, which included no deployment of additional THAAD; no cooperation in the US-led missile defence system; and no trilateral security alliance with Japan and the US.
63 Artyom Lukin, "Russia's Role in the North Korea Conundrum: Part of the Problem or Part of the Solution," *FPRI*, March 4, 2016, at https://www.fpri.org/article/2016/03/russias-role-in-the-north-korea-conundrum-part-of-the-problem-or-part-of-the-solution/ (accessed November 11, 2020).
64 Gabuev, "Bad Cop, Mediator or Spoiler."

Part III
Socio-economic, environmental, and civilisational challenges in Northeast Asia

11 Environmental security issues in Northeast Asia and cooperation among Russia, China, and Mongolia

Elena Boykova

Introduction

In the modern world, there are three main categories of security threats: military, economic, social-environmental. Environmental threats include changes in the composition of the atmosphere and their consequences, pollution of natural fresh waters and waters of the seas and oceans, deforestation and desertification, soil erosion, risks associated with the development of biotechnology, environmental pollution, etc. According to experts, the danger of environmental disaster in the world as a whole and in Northeast Asia (NEA) in particular is increasing. From this aspect, it can be interpreted as an aggravating threat. However, despite the progressive trends of recent years, insufficient attention is still paid to environmental problems. Threats to environmental security are not perceived as a priority.[1] Moreover, this problem requires the adoption of urgent measures that inextricably are linked with increasing responsibility of government authorities and society towards the formation of modern environmental culture.

Some experts consider that the traditional paradigm of national security has given way to such new paradigms as global security, regional security and trans-regional security.[2] It is from the point of view of regional security that this chapter considers the issue of protecting the environment in NEA and the participation of Russia, China, and Mongolia in this process.

Environmental security is a combination of natural, social, and other conditions that ensure safe life and activity of a population located in a given territory. Environmental safety is understood as the state of protection of the natural environment and vital environmental interests of human beings from possible negative impacts of economic and other activities, emergencies and their consequences. Broadly speaking, it is an ability to stand against threats towards life, health, well-being, basic human rights, livelihoods and social order.

In the era of global interdependence, environmental security is becoming an integral part of human consciousness. Environmental policy has become a necessary area of activity for almost any state. Inability to solve global

DOI: 10.4324/9781003148630-11

environmental problems through the efforts of one country has contributed to the inclusion of the environmental aspect in foreign policy priorities of many states and environmentalisation of international relations. Nowadays in the world, there are more than 500 international ecological organisations. Environmental issues are included in the action programmes of almost all authoritative organisations on the global level. Participation in international environmental cooperation is seen as a necessary element in strengthening security of almost any country. Besides, it is also a question of a state's international political prestige and reflection of its ability to quickly and adequately respond to planetary changes.[3]

Permanent technocratic changes in the external environment caused by intensification of economic activity give rise to new challenges—pollution of the atmosphere and water resources, transboundary transfer of pollution and environmental degradation in large cities and urban areas. Intensive economic development has led to the emergence of a new danger—technogenic and natural, associated with the intensification of human economic activity (induced seismicity, flooding, sinking of the Earth's surface). Anthropogenic environmental pollution as a result of excessive pressure occurs in those regions where there is an intensive growth of industrial potential, and environmental requirements are not sufficiently taken into account. The situation is aggravated due to the occurrence of natural hazards—climatic: hurricanes, typhoons, dust storms, droughts, hydrological floods; geological and geomorphological: earthquakes, rockfalls, landslides, mudflows.

An important task of multilateral cooperation in the field of environmental protection in NEA is to solve problems such as the impact of human society on the environment as a whole, interaction of ecology and economy, as well as organisation of rational environmental management using market leverage. In the future, it will be possible to consider the issues of correlation of legal regulation of the economy with the aim of strengthening environmental safety and bringing environmental standards of different countries into uniformity.

The impact of environmental processes on safety manifests itself in different ways: traditionally, as a direct cause of internal and international conflicts, and more broadly, as an interconnection of environmental problems, development, and safety.[4] In the latter case, an environmental crisis destabilises socio-economic and political development of a country, which aggravates internal problems that can create a real threat to national, regional and global security.

In solving environmental problems, a significant role belongs to politics. First, it is a state's interest in development of the national economy and, accordingly, the environmental impact of this process; second, regional interests; and third, globalisation, which has been increasing more and more recently. The global nature of environmental problems determines the need to solve them on both international and regional, as well as on national levels.

Northeast Asia and environmental security

In the field of environmental protection in NEA, two main tasks are clearly outlined: domestic-political, which combines interests of the nation and its society, and foreign policy, which coincides with the national interests of other states and their common environmental interests in the region. Regional cooperation in NEA in the field of environmental protection particularly is driven by common environmental interests of the states of the region, as well as by the type and severity of regional environmental problems.

The necessity of constantly monitoring the changes in the environment both at national and regional levels is recognised by almost all nations of the region, which leads to the construction of not only bilateral but also multilateral agreements on environmental issues. International cooperation in NEA on an equal basis is important especially for solving long-term environmental protection problems, such as protecting the atmosphere from pollution, as well as the migration of birds, mammals, and fish across national borders, and regulating the use of water resources that cross borders. From this point of view, it is particularly important to carry out joint research with the aim of identifying and evaluating the complex of environmental hazard factors in the region.

Issues related to environmental security are quite serious both in Russia, China, and Mongolia. In each country, this problem has its own peculiarities; however, the affiliation of all three countries to the NEA region makes it necessary to form a multilateral cooperation mechanism in this area. These environmental security problems seemingly do not cause controversy among Russia, China, and Mongolia. Therefore, they could become areas for trilateral cooperation, such as in preservation of natural flora and fauna ecosystems; protection of rare and endangered species of plants and animals; preservation of natural monuments; organisation of special reserves; and, environmental education.

Cooperation between Russia and China in the field of ecology and environmental protection is carried out within the framework of the sub-commission on environmental protection of the Russian-Chinese Commission through the preparation of regular meetings of the heads of government of the two countries. The main document that regulates environmental relations between China and Russia was signed in 1994 entitled "Agreement between the government of the Russian Federation and the government of the People's Republic of China [PRC] in the field of environmental protection."[5] A number of protocols were concluded later, such as an "Agreement on joint protection of forests from fires" (1995), "Agreement on cooperation in joint development of forest resources" (2000), and "Agreement on rational use and protection of transboundary waters" (2008). In 2006, Russia and China created an environmental committee, which has become a new model of international cooperation.[6] A permanent dialogue is being held at the level of the Minister of Natural Resources and Ecology of Russia and Minister of Ecology and Environment of the PRC.

The Russian-Mongolian Joint Commission on environmental protection was established in 1994 in accordance with an agreement between the government of the Russian Federation and the government of Mongolia on cooperation in the field of environmental protection. In 2010, the Republic of Buryatia within the Russian Federation and Mongolia, which share a common border, signed an agreement on cooperation in the field of environmental protection, rational use of natural resources and tourism. This document provides for the implementation of special efforts to prevent cross-border forest-steppe fires, as well as attracting human resources, equipment, technologies and communication links to extinguish them. In addition, issues related to the joint processing and use of wood materials, development of production of fuel briquettes, creation of centres for breeding seedlings of deciduous and coniferous trees, implementation of state sanitary and epidemiological control of the Selenga river and transboundary water bodies are considered in the document.[7] In the field of tourism, several large-scale joint projects are planned within the framework of the "Baikal-Khubsugul"[8] and "Great Tea Road"[9] projects.

Lake Baikal in Russia and Lake Khubsugul (aka Khuvsgul) in Mongolia are among the most popular tourist destinations in their countries. The Russian-Mongolian project is based on three tourist routes that are to contribute to the development of cultural, environmental, conference and sports tourism, increase the tourist flow, enhance business and other contacts, attract investment into the economy, and develop the tourist infrastructure of the Baikal-Khubsugul region. In 2016, Russia, China, and Mongolia signed an agreement on the Great Tea Road interregional tourism project, which is a part of the One Belt, One Road initiative. The main goal of the project is to create, develop and promote an international tourism brand of the same name. The project helps to strengthen international relations, expand tourism exchange and increase the contribution of tourism to the economy and social sphere. Currently, the project involves the Republic of Buryatia, the Trans-Baikal territory, the Irkutsk region, the Chinese provinces of Fujian, Jiangxi, Hunan, Hubei, Henan, Hebei, Shanxi, the Inner Mongolia Autonomous region, and the capital region of Mongolia. Russia and Mongolia's attention to improving cooperation in the field of ecology also is evidenced by the fact that in 2018, the Resource Centre for Russian-Mongolian cooperation in education, science, youth policy and ecology was established at Baikal State University in Irkutsk.[10]

In 1990, China and Mongolia signed an intergovernmental "Agreement on cooperation in environmental protection," in which they agreed to cooperate on many issues, including the prevention and control of soil weathering and erosion, the implementation of measures for the protection, research, and reproduction of wild animals and plants in border areas, and the prevention of environmental pollution.[11] The two countries in 2012 signed a "Memorandum of cooperation in the field of environmental protection." As a result, there were regular meetings of experts in the field of ecology who exchanged information on topical issues related to the state of the environment.[12]

Since 2007, Mongolia and Japan have been cooperating in the sphere of environmental protection in the framework of the Mongolian-Japanese dialogue between the ministries of environmental protection of the two countries. The purpose of the dialogue is the exchange of information and discussion on cooperation in this field. Over recent years, several bilateral dialogue events have been held. At them were discussed the elements of the two countries' environmental policy and specific measures taken, bilateral cooperation in the field of protection from dust and sand storms, Mongolia's experience in creating environmental zones, problems of climate change, and development of bilateral cooperation in the field of ecotourism and other issues.

As evidence of their continuing to develop, strengthen and deepen their strategic partnership in all areas, Mongolia and Japan signed a "General agreement on the implementation of the environmental protection" project under assistance to be provided by the Japanese side in March 2019. Within the framework of the project, joint scientific research with Japan providing the necessary equipment will be conducted to protect the unique nature of Mongolia and maintain ecological balance in the country. A grant of US $1.8 million also will be spent on developing Mongolia's water resources.[13] In this regard, experts from the Japan International Cooperation Agency (JICA) will visit Mongolia and make a decision about how the funds will be used.

Cooperation in the environmental sphere between Mongolia and South Korea is developing. In accordance with an agreement signed in 2014, the Korea International Cooperation Agency (KOICA) has built an environmental research centre in Ulaanbaatar. This centre will ensure the implementation of environmental projects and conduct assessment and research on natural resources, as well as create an environmental education system.

China-Mongolia-Russia economic corridor and ecology

In 2015, China, Russia and Mongolia started to develop the programme to construct an economic corridor. On the sidelines of the Shanghai Cooperation Organisation (SCO) summit in Tashkent, the leaders of the three countries agreed to create the China-Mongolia-Russia Economic Corridor. At the same time, a work plan for creating the Economic Corridor was signed. This project is one of the most dynamically developing projects in NEA and in Asia as a whole. The Economic Corridor is a unique project that combines a variety of fields of multilateral cooperation. A new model of international partnership is being formed by strengthening bilateral and multilateral regional mechanisms and structures aimed at joint sustainable development and ensuring stability in the NEA region and in the world. The road map of the China-Mongolia-Russia Economic Corridor provides for the launch of more than 30 trilateral investment projects, implementation of which will contribute to the further development of trade and economic cooperation among the three countries and their interaction in other spheres.

However, the realisation of large-scale economic projects in the boundary regions of the three countries will inevitably have an impact on the ecosystems and economy of neighbouring countries and create a serious burden on the natural environment of the region. In this regard, the most important places in the economic corridor project are given to environmental cooperation among the three countries and search for ways to solve a number of major environmental problems, such as the creation of transboundary special protected natural areas (SPNA), preservation of water basins, and establishing an ecological culture. Of particular importance is the necessity to develop a mechanism for trilateral cooperation in the ecological field, which would meet not only the national interests of each country but also the common interests of Russia, China, and Mongolia.

As Chinese researchers X. Zhang and S. Zhang have written, "with the strengthening of economic and trade relations between China and Russia, the environmental needs and environmental technology cooperation has become increasingly urgent."[14] These words can be rightly attributed to Mongolia since its trade and economic relations with Russia and China will develop within the framework of the economic corridor project that will require strengthening cooperation in the field of environmental security with Mongolia's neighbours.

Throughout the economic corridor project, optimisation of forms of interaction among the three countries in the field of environmental protection, rational use of natural potential, and reproduction of natural resources are becoming more and more relevant. In addition to activities related to trade and economic cooperation among the three countries, such as the development of transport infrastructure and integrated connectivity, improvement of trade and transport conditions, arrangement of border checkpoints, improvement of customs control, financial and investment spheres, energy, agriculture, tourism and humanitarian exchanges, the development of the China-Mongolia-Russia Economic Corridor includes many other issues of ecology and environmental protection. Examples of these are cooperation in the field of biodiversity; in activities concerning specially protected natural territories; in protection of wetlands; forest fire control; combating desertification; expansion of cooperation in the fields of prevention and elimination of the consequences of natural disasters; and in the organisation of effective exchange of information during environmental disasters, manmade accidents, transboundary forest and steppe fires, and, especially, dangerous infectious diseases and natural hazards.[15]

Ecological security and national interests

When developing and implementing specific projects that address environmental issues, it is important to avoid taking unilateral actions that can cause significant environmental and economic damage to partners. Here are just two examples. At the meeting of the leaders of Russia, China, and Mongolia in June 2016 in Tashkent, President Vladimir Putin spoke about questions of environmental cooperation. He said that "we are witnessing very positive changes in the field of cooperation the environmental in sphere of the entire region"[16] and then touched on a very complicated problem related to Mongolia's project to build a hydroelectric dam in the Selenga river basin, which might create certain risks for the ecology of Lake Baikal.

> We would like very much to most carefully study this question with our Mongol friends and with the People's Republic of China....As to the energy deficit of Mongolia, it is a serious question...Of course, we need to think about this, and this problem needs to be solved. Nevertheless, it can be solved by various means, and above all–by developing the energy complex of the region. For instance, Russian stations could increase the supply of electricity they generate to the northern regions of Mongolia.[17]

In December 2016, a meeting of the Russian-Mongolian intergovernmental commission was held in Ulaanbaatar, where the issue of the Mongolian Minis project, which involved the construction of hydraulic structures in the Selenga river basin, was discussed. The parties agreed to create a joint working group for comprehensive consideration of environmental questions. In 2018, the first meeting of the Russian-Mongolian working subgroup was held on the "Scientific support for the development of materials for the comprehensive review of the questions related to the planned construction of hydraulic structures on the water-collecting territory of the Selenga River in Mongolia." The participants in the meeting discussed questions of energy, water supply and water safety in Mongolia, as well as the environmental assessment on the impact of the construction of hydropower plants in the Selenga basin and Baikal Lake. That meeting revealed that the problem was far from being solved and even had political overtones. On some issues related to the implementation of the Minis project, the Russian and Mongolian sides had quite serious disagreements. Among the issues of concern, economic and environmental ones dominated but in some cases the domestic political situation affected interstate strategy and partnership. Russia objected to the project to build a hydroelectric power station on the Selenga River and its tributary the Egiyn-Gol because it considers that the proposal could cause significant damage to the vulnerable ecosystem of Lake Baikal.

The Russian side relied on an agreement signed in 1995 between the governments of Russia and Mongolia on the protection and use of transboundary waters, which states that "the term 'negative impact' means any significant harmful effects on the environment, people and material objects resulting from changes in the state of transboundary waters caused by human activities, the physical source of which is located on the territory of the other party."[18] In 2017, public hearings had been held in the Irkutsk region and in Buryatia on the terms of reference for the regional environmental assessment of the Minis project's facilities. As a result of this hearing, the draft terms of the reference were not supported by the Russian side. As for Mongolia's position on this issue, the problems of hydroelectric power and providing drinking water to the country's residents, especially the population of the southern Gobi regions, came to the fore. It also was taken into account that Mongolia is facing the problem of rapid land desertification, which requires more regulation of water reservoirs.

In 2017, the Inspection Commission of the World Bank, which is financing the "Minis" project, started its work in the Baikal region. Specialists of this organisation studied the environmental risks associated with the possible construction of a hydroelectric generating station on the Selenga River and its tributaries in Mongolia. The general regional environmental expert assessment, the analysis of the environmental impact and social consequences, as well as the position of the World Bank all became obstacles to the engineering and construction of the Egiyn-Gol project. Russia and Mongolia in 2018 then agreed to include the Egiyn-Gol Hydroelectric Power Plant (HPP) in the regional environmental assessment of projects for the construction of hydraulic structures in the basin of the main tributary of Lake Baikal, although previously the Mongols had refused to do so.

After several years of studying the problem, the Mongolian side in 2019 decided that the construction of the Selenga HPP would not be carried out, and it refused to build the Shuren hydroelectric power station and the Orkhon drainage system within the framework of the Minis project. At the same time, Russia and Mongolia agreed to work together actively in the field of renewable energy in Mongolia. That same year the governments of the Russian Federation and Mongolia signed an agreement on cooperation in the field of electric power. The document provides for the implementation of "joint projects in the field of power generation, export and import of electric energy to Mongolia (from Mongolia), [and] development of the power grid of Mongolia,"[19] but also which will avoid the construction of hydroelectric power stations on the Selenga and its tributaries.

One problem was solved, but a new threat of natural disaster soon arose. On the border between the Trans-Baikal territory and Mongolia, an environmental conflict is brewing. In the summer of 2020, construction of a dam began in Mongolia on the Uldza River (Ulz Gol), which flows in northeast Mongolia and partially in the Trans-Baikal territory. It is planned to block the river with a dam 700 metres long and 9-12 metres high to create a reservoir with a capacity of 27 million cubic metres to "prevent the river from drying out."[20] The Uldza River is the main source of water for the UNESCO-protected cross-border territories in Russia and Mongolia.

In 1994, the lakes were included in the list of wetlands of international importance.[21] Torey Lakes are filled with water or dry up completely, depending on the wet or dry periods that last for several years.[22] According to Russian experts, the construction of the dam may endanger the existence of the Torey Lakes.[23] These lakes are a system of lakes located in southeastern Transbaikalia and consists of two connected drainless lakes—Barun-Torey and Zun-Torey, which are the largest lakes in this region. The southwestern part of Barun-Torey lake is located in Mongolia. The peculiarity of these lakes is the unstable water regime, which in dry years cause the lakes to almost completely dry up. The Uldza and Imalka rivers flow into Barun-Torey; Zun-Torey is fed by the flow of water from Barun-Torey along the channel connecting them. The two lakes are the core of the protected area of the Dauria nature reserve. The Mongolian part of Barun-Torey Lake is included in cluster "A" of the Mongol Daguur nature reserve. Now the wet period has begun, and the lakes are filled with the waters of the Uldza River, which the Mongolian side has begun to block with a dam.

This construction is of particular concern to the staff of the Dauria reserve and environmentalists who believe that great damage could be caused to the Russian-Mongolian UNESCO World Heritage Site "Landscapes of Dauria." Life in this vast natural area depends on the fullness of the Torey Lakes. For the ecosystem of Dauria, the construction of a dam on the Uldza River could have disastrous consequences. A significant part of the ecosystem will be threatened primarily for millions of migratory and nesting birds. The situation is aggravated by the fact that the Russian side was not involved in the discussion on the dam project and in the bilateral assessment of the dam's impact on the ecosystem of Torey Lakes basin.[24]

Members of the international ecological coalition "Rivers without Borders," which includes both Russian and Mongolian ecologists, sent an official appeal to the UNESCO World Heritage Committee outlining the threat to the Russian-Mongolian site caused by the dam and linking it to new mining.[25] The coalition called on the Mongolian authorities to stop the construction of the dam on the Uldza River and conduct an environmental impact assessment of the project: "we have no doubts about the real purpose of building the new hydroelectric complex. This is due to the fact that about 80 per cent of water users in the Uldza River basin are Mongolian mining enterprises. In other words, a unique World Natural Heritage site will lose its main source of water only for the sake of increasing the volume of mining and processing of minerals."[26] These experts expressed the concern that in the future Mongolia may intensify dam construction projects at the heads of other transboundary rivers.

In connection with extension of Russian-Chinese economic ties, including in the development of natural resources in Siberia and the Far East, cooperation in the field of ecology is becoming more and more relevant. An important part of Russian-Chinese relations is cross-border environmental cooperation. One of the most serious problems in this field is the problem of using cross-border reservoirs, primarily the Amur, Ussuri and Argun rivers. Basically, the claims of the Russian side come down to the fact that the Chinese side, when using its sections of the transboundary rivers, often makes the decision to transfer those rivers into areas bordering Russia and develops these projects on an unilateral basis without coordinating its actions with the Russian side. In 2007–2008, the construction of a canal was completed to transfer a part of the water runoff from the 669 kilometre Chinese section of the Argun (aka Hailar) river to the Inner Mongolia Autonomous Region, where desertification of lands and drying up of Lake Dalai occur. Water also is required for the operations there in a molybdenum copper deposit and local tourist resort. This project was called Hailar–Dalai.

According to experts, the water intake at the source of the Argun River, as calculations show, has been a catastrophe to the ecosystem of the whole region within Russian territory. The population of the Russian border villages standing on the Argun River bank have been deprived of floodplain meadows for forage, which creates problems for animal husbandry in the entire Trans-Baikal territory.[27] According to Russian researchers, additional water consumption in the Chinese part of the Argun River basin likely will cause significant consequences to the hydrological regime.[28] The project of artificial redistribution of part of the flow of the Argun (Hailar) River to Dalai Nor-Lake might result in a range of environmental, economic, social, and political problems in the zone of common interests of Russia, China, and Mongolia.

After the project was completed in 2009, the Chinese side took into account the opinion of the Russian side. Water withdrawal capacities in this project were to be reduced to 390 million cubic metres per year. However, according to media reports, when the canal was put into operation at least until 2011, the canal shutters never were closed, so water from the Hailar River continuously flowed into the drainage channel.[29]

Russia-China-Mongolia ecological cooperation

Despite some emerging problems in cooperation in the field of ecology, there are a number of examples of successful bilateral and trilateral cooperation in the field of environmental protection among Russia, China, and Mongolia.

Since 2015, Russia and Mongolia have been implementing a joint programme to protect the Altai mountain sheep or *argali* in the cross-border zone of Russia and Mongolia. The objective of the programme is to restore this species in the region in order to recreate a sustainable wild population. In 2017, Russia and Mongolia signed a programme for monitoring the Altai *argali* in the cross-border zone. Every year, experts of the two countries organise a joint counting of the *argali* population, specify the boundaries of its habitat, and adjust environmental plans. One of the tasks of Russian and

Mongolian specialists, together with the authorities of the two countries, is to counteract the illegal turnover of *argali* derivatives. Thanks to the protection activities of Russian and Mongolian specialists, the *argali* population now is constantly increasing.

Russia and Mongolia have joined forces in developing a joint programme for conservation and monitoring cross-border snow leopard (*irbis*) groupings. The questions of their study and monitoring are of particular importance for the restoration of this predator both in Russia and in Mongolia. As stated in the "Strategy for the conservation of the snow leopard in the Russian Federation (2014)": "the survival of the snow leopard in Russia largely depends on the preservation of spatial and genetic relationships of its Russian groups with the main population core of this species in Mongolia, as well as with large groups in Eastern Kazakhstan and North-Western China."[30]

In this regard, the task of effectively preserving two stable populations of snow leopards on the border between Russia and Mongolia has become of particular importance. As a result of cooperation between the two countries on the study and preservation of cross-border populations of snow leopards, the number of key groups has been maintained at a stable level. Recent researches have confirmed the reality of the existence of a cross-border Russian-Mongolian group of snow leopards on the Tsagaan Shibetu and the Tsagaan Shivuut mountain ranges in Mongolia. The tasks of the experts involve the establishment and expansion of transboundary Russian-Mongolian protected areas to ensure sustainable populations of snow leopard on the ridges Chikhacheva in the Altai on the border between Russia and Mongolia; on Tsagaan Shibetu in Southwest Tuva and Northwest Mongolia; and on Saylyugem, which is on the border between the Republic of Altai and Mongolia. Their responsibilities include the transboundary Russian-Mongolian reserve "Saylyugem", which consists of the Russian national park "Saylyugemskiy" and the Mongolian national park "Silkhemin Nuruu" in Bayan-Olgii aimag.

In 2015, the Russian-Mongolian intergovernmental agreement on the creation of the specially protected natural transboundary area called "The Heads of the Amur" (Istoki Amura) was signed. This area includes the Sokhondinsky State Natural Biosphere Reserve in Russia and the Onon-Baldzh National Park in Mongolia. This cross-border specially protected natural area preserves not only the sources of the Amur River but also the sources of Lake Baikal. This project provides international support for the development of a protected area along the borders of the two countries. The creation of the Russian-Mongolian transboundary reserve "The Heads of the Amur" gives additional opportunities for the conservation of biological and landscape diversity of the southern Trans-Baikal region in the basins of the headwaters of the Amur River and in northeastern regions of Mongolia, and for the promotion of scientific research and environmental monitoring.

Russia and China cooperate in the frame of the "Amur Green Belt" international programme initiated by the World Wildlife Fund (WWF). The programme is aimed at creating a comprehensive network of specially protected natural areas (SPNA) linked by ecological corridors and buffer zones. The programme focuses on transboundary ecosystems. As part of the development of the programme, a memorandum was signed in 2016 on the formation of a Russian-Chinese network of cross-border nature reserves in the Amur basin. The parties established cooperation among 16 Chinese SPNAs and 12 Russian SPNAs located directly along the border of Russia and China along the Amur and the Ussuri rivers. The total area of these partner environmental reserves is 1.9 million hectares.

In 2017, Russia and Mongolia decided to create the Tunka-Khubsgöl cross-border reserve. From the Russian side, it will be administered as the national park "Tunkinsky", while the Mongolian section will be called the Mongolian national park "Khubsgöl". The implementation of this project will create additional opportunities for the conservation of biological and landscape diversity in the basins of Lake Baikal and Lake Khubsgöl, as well as contribute to the development of scientific research, environmental monitoring and educational tourism.

Mongolia and China cooperate in solving common environmental problems for the two countries, such as the prevention of desertification and dust storms. Desertification is considered one of the main environmental threats in Mongolia. This problem is comparable in its scale and consequences to such problems as climate change, loss of biological diversity, environmental pollution, etc. According to experts, more than 76 per cent of the country's territory is desert or affected by degradation.[31] Over the past 75 years, the average annual surface air temperature in Mongolia has increased by 2.1 degrees Celsius, and annual precipitation has decreased by about 7 per cent.[32] Droughts have become more frequent, and water and wind damage to the soil has increased. All this is a consequence of desertification in Mongolia.

China, which is severely affected by desertification, began to combat this problem in the 1950s. The efforts of the Chinese government, in particular to restore vegetation in arid areas, have reduced the rate of desertification and soil erosion in some regions of the country, where the area of degraded land has decreased and the level of poverty in desert areas has decreased. According to China, desertification is a challenge to all mankind, and therefore it is necessary to fight the onset of deserts on a global scale. China is willing to share its experience and technologies and to expand cooperation with various countries, especially with Mongolia, since the problem of desertification and dust storms afflicts their border regions. The joint project "Monitoring and evaluation of dust storms, desertification conditions in the neighbouring regions of Mongolia and China" was launched in February 2016, and $600,000 has been allocated for the project, all funded by the PRC government.[33]

In Mongolia, the severity of the problem is indicated by the fact that, compared to 2014, in 2016 the size of deteriorated pastureland decreased from 65 per cent to 57 per cent but the area experiencing desertification enlarged. In particular, pastureland deterioration increased in entire territories of Selenge, Arkhangai, Khuvsgul, Tuv and Khentii aimags and northern parts of Bayankhongor and Uvurkhangai aimags. Major part of severely deteriorated pasture areas belongs to Sukhbaatar and Dornogobi aimags.[34]

In 2003, the Russian-Mongolian cross-border reserve "Uvs Nuur basin," was designated as a UNESCO World Heritage site. It includes the territories of the Russian state natural biosphere reserve "Ubsunurskaya hollow", located in the south of Tuva, and the Mongolian state natural biosphere reserve "Uvs Nuur". The reserve was created for the purpose of protecting and studying the nature of the Uvs Nuur basin, conducting joint scientific research, carrying out environmental monitoring of natural environmental conditions as well as developing eco-tourism and environmental education. Special attention is being paid to the protection of habitats and monitoring of cross-border groups of two flag species of the region, such as the snow leopard and the Altai mountain sheep (*argali*). On the territory of the reserve, joint parallel surveys are conducted on snow leopards, cross-border groups of *argali*, monitoring of animals, birds, and mountain ecosystems, as well as on the state and quality of cross-border water bodies. On the basis of the reserve, an international Russian-Mongolian ecological school entitled "World of the Uvs Nuur basin" is held regularly, and children's ecological tourist exchanges are carried out. In 2011, the "Petroglyphic Complexes of the Mongolian Altai" were further included in the UNESCO World Heritage List.

The Russia-China-Mongolia International Protected Area "Dauria" (DIPA), established in 1994, is an example of successful trilateral environmental interaction. It is run by a trilateral commission, members of which are representatives of Russia, China, and Mongolia. This international project plays an important role in preserving the nature in the Dauria eco-region. The reserve is one of few tripartite protected areas in the world. It includes the Daursky state natural biosphere reserve in Trans-Baikalia (Russia), the Dalainor biosphere reserve in Inner Mongolia (China), and the Mongol Daguur Strictly Protected Area (Mongolia).

The Daurian steppes are a vast region (about 300,000 sq. kilometres) located at the junction of the borders of Russia, Mongolia and China. The plant communities formed here are unique, rich in endemics, and, unlike other steppe regions of the planet, largely have retained their original appearance. The abundance of Daurian small salt lakes rich in food attracts millions of birds migrating to the north from Australia and South Asia. About 360 species of birds, of which more than 25 are listed as globally vulnerable or threatened on the International Union for

Conservation of Nature Red List, pass through or nest here. For many species, the Daurian steppes are key habitats. The steppes are inhabited by more than 50 species of mammals. In 2000, the World-Wide Fund for Nature (WWF) included the Daurian steppes among the 200 ecoregions of the planet that are of particular importance for the conservation of life on the Earth. Over the years of existence of DIPA, more than 70 joint expeditions have been conducted to study the flora and fauna of the region, and work continues to preserve rare species of animals and plants.

There are thousands of Mongolian antelope, *dzeren*, in the protected area. Thanks to the successful activity of the Dauria International Reserve, the threat of the disappearance of *dzerens* in the border regions of Mongolia and Russia has been reduced. One of the most significant results of the international reserve's activities has been the return of the *dzeren* to Transbaikalia. In the early 1990s, the number of antelopes that constantly inhabited the Daursky reserve was only 15 to 20 species. In 2016, about 7,400 of these animals already were living in the Daursky reserve and the Dzeren Valley reserve. A second herd of almost 500 *dzerens* was formed in the protected area of the Sokhondinsky reserve.[35] Currently, there is an urgent need to preserve such rare bird species as the Daurian and Japanese crane, bustard, and dry-nosed goose, whose populations are critically endangered.

One of the challenges facing the DIPA is the expansion of its territory in each of the three countries, including the creation of bilateral cross-border sectors in the floodplain of the Argun River and in the region of Lake Buir Nur. In 2019, at the suggestion of the Russian side, the study of the possibility of creating a "green zone"—a kind of buffer ring around DIPA—was started. An equally important task that corresponds to the place and role of the region in preserving the planet's biosphere is the creation of one whole transboundary biosphere reserve and an entire wetland of international significance. It is planned that the DIPA will be included in the World Network of Biosphere Reserves under UNESCO's Man and the Biosphere Programme and in the UNESCO World Heritage List.

In 2017, the Russian-Mongolian territory "Landscapes of Dauria" received the status of a UNESCO World Heritage site. The site includes several protected areas in the northern part of the vast Daurian steppe eco-region, which is transitional between the taiga and the desert. It includes a variety of steppe ecosystems: the Daursky state natural biosphere reserve, its protected area and section of the federal reserve "Dzeren Valley" (Russia) and the strictly protected natural area "Mongol Daguur" with its buffer zone (Mongolia). All the above-mentioned cooperation between Russia and Mongolia, as well as Russian-Mongolian-Chinese trilateral interaction in the organisation of cross-border nature reserves, are unique examples of successful and fruitful environmental cooperation in the world.

Conclusion

Changes in traditional worldviews, including an ecological one, are typical for the peoples of many countries. Revival of ecological traditions, national ecological consciousness, as well as improvement of environmental education are of particular importance nowadays. In recent decades, the situation in the world, including in the economic sphere, is rapidly changing, new types of economic activity and professions that have no roots in the economic culture of specific peoples are emerging. Under these circumstances, the psychological characteristics of young people, their traditional worldviews, and economic consciousness have changed, and so it is in Russia, Mongolia and China. Now, it is necessary to develop a special strategy of interaction with nature that preserves the customary unity of man and nature in the mind and rejects consumer attitudes towards nature that are not associated with recognition of its self-worth. Of particular importance is the formation of modern environmental awareness and training of careful attitude towards nature and adaptation to the eco-cultural situation.

Common interests in preserving the region's natural environment and using natural resources unite Russia, China, and Mongolia. Approaches to solving the problem of environmental safety in each country may be at variance, depending on their national interests. However, the absence of unsolvable contradictions among the three countries gives hope that by joining their forces China, Russia, and Mongolia in the future can come closer to finding solutions for this problem and make a serious contribution to strengthening environmental safety in the NEA region. From this point of view, it is necessary to develop a special programme of trilateral environmental and economic cooperation by identifying the main areas: 1) quality monitoring and protection from pollution of transboundary bodies of water, river, and forest biological resources; 2) prompt response to environmental emergencies; and 3) management of transboundary (international) reserves.

Cooperation among Russia, China, and Mongolia in addressing nature security issues can be considered not only as an activity to protect the environment at the regional level but also as a search for ways to create a mechanism for trilateral cooperation. It is understood that cooperation in the field of environmental security, due to the common interests of the states of NEA, as well as the severity of regional problems in this area, objectively is necessary. Environmental issues in the region should occupy an important place in the system of interstate regional relations. For the NEA countries, ensuring environmental safety is directly related to furthering economic and social growth. Economics and ecology are closely interconnected; therefore, economic stability is not possible under environmental instability. A stressful environmental situation significantly narrows the possibilities for transformations in the economic, social, demographic and even political spheres, and reduces their effectiveness.

The dynamics of interaction in the field of ecology shows that bilateral cooperation will prevail over multilateral cooperation for a long time due to its greater specificity and efficiency. At the same time, the need to constantly monitor the condition and changes of the environment, both at the national and regional levels, is recognised by almost all NEA states, which implies the conclusion of not only bilateral but also multilateral agreements on environmental protection. Sooner or later, the states of the region will come to an understanding of the necessity of systematic multilateral cooperation. It is only a matter of time before a coordinated regional environmental policy is developed.

Notes

1. E.V. Gamerman, "Politicheskie aspekty ekologicheskoi bezopasnosti v Severo-Vostochnoi zii" ["Political aspects of environmental security in Northeast Asia"], *Teorii i problem politicheskikh issledovanii* [*Theories and Problems of Political Studies*] (in Russian), 8 (6A), 2019, p. 213.
2. V.N. Lukin and T.V. Musiyenko, "Traditsionnyye i novyye paradigmy bezopasnosti: sravnitel'nyy analiz" ["Traditional and new security paradigms: a comparative analysis"] (in Russian), *Credo New* 4, 2006, at http://credonew.ru/content/view/589/31 (accessed April 4, 2020).
3. V.N. Morozova, *Mirovaya ekologicheskaya politika i mezhdunarodnoye ekologicheskoye sotrudnichestvo* [*World environmental policy and international environmental cooperation*] (in Russian), Voronezh, 2007, p. 4.
4. N.G. Rogozhina, "Ekologicheskaya bezopasnost' stran Vostochnoy Azii" ["Ecological safety of the countries of East Asia"], *Aziya i Afrika segodnya* [*Asia and Africa today*] (in Russian), 12, 2015, p. 49.
5. *Elektronnyy fond pravovoy i normativno-tekhnicheskoy dokumentatsii* [*Electronic Fund of legal and regulatory and technical documentation*], 1994, at http://docs.cntd.ru/document/1900388 (accessed April 28, 2020).
6. V.M. Klantsov, "Intensivnoye ekonomicheskoye razvitiye Kitaya: ekologicheskiye posledstviya dlya Rossii" ["China's intensive economic development: environmental consequences for Russia"], *Rossiya v Azii: problemy vzaimodeystviya* [*Russia in Asia: problems of interaction*] (in Russian), Moscow, 2006, pp. 380–381.
7. "Buryatiya i Mongoliya podpisali dogovor o sotrudnichestve v sfere prirodopol'zovaniya i turizma" ["Buryatia and Mongolia signed an agreement on cooperation in the field of nature management and tourism"] (in Russian), *fedpress.ru*, April 12, 2010, at https://fedpress.ru/article/839898 (accessed September 16, 2020).
8. A.P. Sukhodolov, "Mezhdunarodnyy turistskiy marshrut Baykal–Khubsugul" ["International tourist route Baikal-Khubsugul"], *Rossiya i Mongoliya* [*Russia and Mongolia*] (in Russian), 8, 2010, pp. 24–25; P. Amarjargal, "Proyekt Baykal – Khubsugul" ["Baikal – Khubsugul project"], *Molodoy uchenyy* [*Young scientist*] (in Russian), 29 (133), 2016, p. 624.
9. S.V. Dikhtyar, "Velikiy chaynyy put' kak innovatsionnyy turistskiy proyekt" ["The Great tea road as an innovative tourist project"] (in Russian), Eurasiatourism, at http://eurasiatourism.org/1145/1152/index.phtml (accessed October 28, 2020).
10. "V Baykal'skom gosuniversitete otkrylsya rossiysko-mongol'skiy resursnyy tsentr" ["Russian-Mongolian resource center opened at Baikal State University"] (in Russian), *rsr-online.ru*, June 9, 2018, at https://www.rsr-online.ru/press/publikatsii/v-baykalskom-gosuniversitete-otkrylsya-rossiysko-mongolskiy-resursnyy-tsentr/ (accessed September 21, 2020).

Environmental security issues in Northeast Asia 235

11 "Zhōnghuá rénmín gònghéguó zhèngfǔ hé ménggǔ rénmín gònghéguó zhèngfǔ guānyú bǎohù zìrán huánjìng de hézuò xiédìng (qiāndìng rìqí 1990 nián 5 yuè 6 rì)" ["Agreement on cooperation in environmental protection between the Government of the People's Republic of China and the Government of the People's Republic of Mongolia" (date of signing May 6, 1990)] (in Chinese), at http://pkulaw.cn/fulltext_form.aspx?Gid=100664340&Db=eagn (accessed September 21, 2020).
12 B. Bold, "BNKhAU-yn BOYa-tai khamtyn ajillagaany myekhanizm bii bolgokhyg zorij baina" ["We intend to create a mechanism for cooperation with the Ministry of nature and environment of the PRC"] (in Mongolian), *Montsame*, November 13, 2018, at https://www.montsame.mn/mn/read/170988 (accessed August 6, 2020).
13 B. Ariunbayar, "Mongoliya i Yaponiya podpisali soglasheniye o realizatsii proyekta v oblasti okhrany okruzhayushchey sredy" ["Mongolia and Japan signed an agreement on the implementation of a project in the field of environmental protection"] (in Russian), *Polpred*, March 12, 2019, at https://polpred.com/?ns=1&ns_id=2940127 (accessed August12, 2020).
14 Xiujie Zhang, Sichen Zhang, "China-Mongolia-Russia economic corridor and environmental protection cooperation," *R-Economy* 3 (3), 2017, p. 163, at https://journals.urfu.ru/index.php/r-economy/article/view/2972 (accessed September 14, 2020).
15 "Programma sozdaniya ekonomicheskogo koridora Kitay–Mongoliya–Rossiya" ["China-Mongolia-Russia Economic Corridor Program"] (in Russian), Russian Ministry of Industry and Trade, September 1, 2015, at http://minpromtorg.govrb.ru/rus-ch-mn.pdf (accessed September 14, 2020).
16 "Vstrecha [Prezidenta RF Vladimira Putina] s Predsedatelem KNR Si Tszin'pinom i Prezidentom Mongolii Tsakhiagiyn Elbegdorzhem, 23 iyunya 2015 goda" ["[President of the Russian FederationVladimir Putin's] meeting with President of the PRC Xi Jinping and President of Mongolia Tsakhiagiin Elbegdorj" (in Russian), June 23, 2016, at http://kremlin.ru/events/president/news/52211 (accessed August 6, 2020).
17 Ibid.
18 "Zhōnghuá rénmín gònghéguó zhèngfǔ" ["Agreement on cooperation in environmental protection between the Government of the People's Republic of China and the Government of the People's Republic of Mongolia"].
19 *Elektronnyy fond pravovoy i normativno-tekhnicheskoy dokumentatsii.*
20 D. Jargal, "UNESCO-guiin өviig suitgeh dalang mongolchuud barj bayna" ["Mongols are building a dam to destroy UNESCO's heritage"] (in Mongolian), *Montsame*, September 25, 2020, at https://montsame.mn/mn/read/237612 (accessed September 28, 2020).
21 "The List of Wetlands of International Importance (Ramsar List)," November 11, 2020, at https://www.ramsar.org/sites/default/files/documents/library/sitelist.pdf (accessed October 21, 2020).
22 O.K. Kirilyuk, V.Ye. Kirilyuk, O.A. Goroshko, "Dinamika ekosistem zapovednika i ikh sovremennoye sostoyaniye" ["Dynamics of ecosystems in the reserve and their current state"], in *Biosfernyy zapovednik «Daurskiy»* [*Biosphere reserve "Daursky"*] (in Russian), O.K. Kirilyuk (ed.), Ekspress-izdatel'stvo, Chita, 2009, pp. 61–63.
23 O. Korsun, "Dve strany – odna reka?" ["Two countries – one river?"], *Chitinskoye obozreniye* [*Chita Review*] (in Russian), October 10, 2020, at http://obozrenie-chita.ru/article/reka-uldza (accessed October 21, 2020).
24 Yu. Skornyakova, "Osipov napravil v Minprirody i MID RF obrashcheniya v zashchitu Toreyskikh ozyor" ["Osipov sent appeals to the Ministry of Natural Resources and the Ministry of Foreign Affairs of the Russian Federation in defense of Torey Lakes"], *Novosti Chity [Chita News]* (in Russian), October 8,

2020, at http://chita-news.net/society/2020/10/08/31551.html (accessed October 23, 2020).
25 Jargal, "UNESCO-guiin өviig suitgeh dalang mongolchuud barj bayna" ["Mongols are building a dam to destroy UNESCO's heritage"] (in Mongolian).
26 G. Byambasuren, "Ekologichid Mongol Uls dalan barij baigaag esergüütsen UNESCO-d khandjee" ["Environmentalists have invoked UNESCO with a protest against the construction of the dam in Mongolia"] (in Mongolian), *Shuud.mn*, September 24, 2020, at http://www.shuud.mn/a/522844 (accessed October 22, 2020).
27 K.G. Muratshina, "Rossiya–Kitay: riski sotrudnichestva v sfere ispol'zovaniya transgranichnykh vodoyemov" ["Russia–China: the risks of cooperation in the field of transboundary water bodies"], *Ural'skoye vostokovedeniye. Mezhdunarodnyy al'manakh* [*Ural Survey of Oriental Studies. International almanac*] (in Russian), 6, 2015, p. 91.
28 M.V. Bolgov and N.L. Frolova, "Vodnyy rezhim reki Argun' i ozera Dalainor v usloviyakh antropogennogo vozdeystviya" ["Water regime of the Argun River and Lake Dalainor under anthropogenic impact"], *Geografiya i prirodnyye resursy* [*Geography and natural resources*] (in Russian), 4, 2012, pp. 26–27.
29 HuoWei, "Zhěngjiù běifāng dì yī dàhú: Shuǐmiàn 10 nián wěisuō 520 píngfāng gōnglǐ" ["Save the largest lake in the North [of China]: its water surface area has decreased by 520 square kilometers in 10 years"] (in Chinese), January 24, 2011, at http://green.sina.com.cn/news/roll/2011-01-24/112721865817.shtml (accessed September 12, 2020).
30 "Strategiya sokhraneniya snezhnogo barsa v Rossiyskoy Federatsii" (18 avgusta 2014 goda) ["Snow Leopard Conservation Strategy for the Russian Federation" (18 August 2014)] (in Russian), *rulaws.ru*, at https://rulaws.ru/acts/Rasporyazhenie-Minprirody-Rossii-ot-18.08.2014-N-23-r/ (accessed September 11, 2020).
31 D.A. Darbalayeva, V.S. Batomunkuyev, E.D. Sanzheyev, and D. Ts.-D. Zham'yanov, "Otsenka vliyaniya protsessov opustynivaniya na uroven' zhizni naseleniya aymaka Orkhon" ["Assessment of the impact of desertification processes on the standard of living of the population of the Orkhon aimag"] (in Russian), *Fundamental'nyye issledovaniya* [*Fundamental research*] (in Russian), 9 (5), 2014, pp. 1047–1051.
32 G. Erdenebat, "Mongol orny tsöljilt, gazryn doroitlyn 56 khuvi ni baigaliin üzegdeltei kholbootoi" ["56% of desertification and land degradation in Mongolia are related to natural phenomena"] (in Mongolian), *Montsame*, June 17, 2020, at https://www.montsame.mn/mn/read/228574 (accessed September 17, 2020).
33 G. Battsetseg, "O sotrudnichestve s KNR v oblasti okruzhayushchey sredy" ["On cooperation with China in the field of the environment"] (in Russian), *Montsame*, February 26, 2016, at https://www.montsame.mn/ru/read/153433 (accessed September 20, 2020); "Mongoliya i Kitay dogovorilis' sovmestno borot'sya s ekologicheskimi problemami" ["Mongolia and China agreed to work together to combat environmental problems"] (in Russian), *BaikalInform*, February 28, 2016, at https://baikalinform.ru/ekologiya/mongoliya-i-kitay-dogovorilisb-sovmestno-borotbsya-s-ekologicheskimi-problemami (accessed September 20, 2020).
34 M. Unurzul, "Pasture deterioration and desertification research underway," *Montsame*, January 3, 2019, at https://montsame.mn/en/read/176060 (accessed October 28, 2020).
35 O.K. Kirilyuk, O.A. Goroshko, V.Ye. Kirilyuk, *Mezhdunarodnyy zapovednik "Dauriya": 10 let sotrudnichestva* [*Dauria International Protected Area: 10 years of cooperation*] (in Russian and English), Ekspress-izdatel'stvo, Chita, 2006, pp. 23–24.

12 Asia and beyond: organised environmental crime

Lynn Rhodes

Crimes against the environment in Asia and beyond have serious repercussions affecting society, legal development, economies, biodiversity, human rights, and civilisation. Environmental crime is often transnational or transboundary in nature with links to organised criminal entities. Organised, transnational networks, particularly in East Asia, which are involved in exploitation of natural resources, wildlife poaching and trade, illegal unregulated fishing, and illegal exploitation of and trafficking in minerals and precious stones are being funded by such activities. Money generated from environmental crimes degrades and harms the environment and keeps sophisticated, international criminal networks in business, fuelling insecurity around the world.

For both developed and developing countries, environmental crime is increasing exponentially and poses a serious threat in the Northeast Asian and Asia Pacific regions and globally. It undermines conservation efforts, harms economies and livelihoods, and compromises systems on which humans depend. The impacts reach beyond the environment and biodiversity but deep into our societies and civilisation and, ultimately, threaten basic survival.

Worldwide, governments have varying enforcement capacities and laws. The transnational nature of environmental crimes and increasing involvement of organised criminal groups, along with varying degrees of governmental capacities and limited administrative infrastructure, often permit criminality and exploitation by default. These issues increasingly are relevant for comprehensive and cooperative security, also known as enhanced law enforcement and coordinated enforcement action across boundaries. Criminal justice systems often are challenged to meet the multi-level threats presented by the transnational nature of environmental crimes.

Many international commissions and agencies actively have reinforced efforts to develop projects and direct support in response to the protection of the environment, environmental crimes, threats to civilisation and security. Numerous resolutions encourage and assist in cooperation for bilateral, regional and international entities to prevent, combat and eradicate many forms of environmental crimes. This chapter explores threats, risks,

DOI: 10.4324/9781003148630-12

and opportunities relating to organised, transnational, transboundary crime, environmental protection, and civilisation, including in Northeast Asia.

There is no universally agreed upon definition of "environmental crime". There is no single answer. It is most commonly understood as a collective term to describe illegal activities harming the environment and aimed at benefitting individuals or groups or companies from the exploitation of, damage to, trade, or theft of natural resources, and includes serious crimes and transnational organised crime.[1] Environmental crime is recognised as the fourth largest criminal enterprise in the world, after drugs, counterfeiting and human trafficking, and it is increasing 5–7 per cent every year. Over 1,000 protected-area officers[2] have been killed worldwide and many more injured over the last 13 years.[3] Nearly 900 were killed from 2009 to 2018.[4]

> Vast sums of money generated from environmental crimes not only harm the environment and threaten protected-area officers, but the funds keep sophisticated international criminal gangs in business, fuelling insecurity around the world. Armed and unarmed groups worldwide, use environmental crimes as a low-risk high-profit source of revenue: depriving governments of revenues while threatening peace, development and security. The economic loss due to environmental crime is estimated at up to $258 billion annually. Weak laws and poorly funded security forces enable international criminal networks and armed rebels to profit from a trade that fuels conflicts, devastates ecosystems and is threatening species, including us, with extinction.[5]

Species are going extinct at a faster than historic rate. If ecosystems collapse, human existence and some civilisations, as we know them, may become impossible or extinct. A global system collapse is possible, and with it the world's economic and political systems face systematic risks because of their intricate and interconnected natures.[6] Researchers agree that more work needs to be done to clarify what parts of the system(s) could collapse and destroy civilisation. A civilisational collapse is a drastic decrease in human population size and political/economic/social complexity, both globally and for an extended time. The environment provides the foundation of sustainable development, our health, food security, and our economies. Ecosystems provide clean water supply, clean air, and secure food, and ultimately both physical and mental well-being. Natural resources also provide livelihoods, jobs, and revenues to governments that can be used for education, health care, development, and sustainable business models.

Diversity of environmental crimes has grown, and the impacts go beyond those thought of as traditional crimes. Environmental crimes impede our ability to have and retain a sustainable and healthy planet. They add to the cost and impact on the environment and the cost to future generations.

Deforestation, chemical dumping, and illegal fisheries cause loss of ecosystem services, such as clean air and clean water, extreme weather mitigation, and cause food, health, and well-being insecurity. They also deprive governments of critical revenue and undermine legal businesses.

Northeast and Southeast Asia: collaboration matters

The Northeast Asia region is no exception to the world of transnational organised crime affecting the environment. The threats are woven into this and neighbouring regions. The trafficking and exploitation of products such as wood, timber, wildlife, waste, and other resources increase risks to security and stability of all affected countries. Millions of tonnes of hazardous waste and harmful chemicals are transported to and within Asia, with resulting negative effects for both the environment and the human population.

Due to the demand for goods, resource-rich environments, and low prosecution risk, environmental criminal markets are flourishing. Northeast Asia and Southeast Asia have long-established trade and transportation routes which lend themselves to ease of transport and illicit use of such methods, markets, and delivery (Figure 12.1).

Since many of these environmental crimes and issues are transnational or transboundary in nature, it requires the entire region to work together to address the problems. Over the past few decades, several cooperative frameworks and mechanisms have been established to deal with these issues. The Northeast Asian Sub-regional Program for Environmental Cooperation (NEASPC) was established in the early 1990s to deal with many of the transboundary issues and help provide collaboration on numerous projects including mitigation of transboundary air pollution often coming from power plants in China and coal-burning stoves in Mongolia. The Asian Network for Prevention of Illegal Transboundary Movement of Hazardous Wastes is another network which works with authorities of the Basel Convention in Asia, assisting countries in capacity-building of affiliated countries for best management, information, movement, export, and import of hazardous waste. "The intention is to provide the best understanding of specific criminal markets in order to develop evidence-based strategic and programmatic responses."[7]

The 2019 report *Transnational Organized Crime in South East Asia: Evaluation, Growth and Impact* by the United Nations Office on Drugs and Crime (UNODC) describes how the situation has contributed to illicit wildlife and timber networks, which are among the world's largest markets. Supply chains for these goods operate at all levels from the source to the market to the consumer. Examples are commercial illegal logging, timber processing, paper and pulp manufacturing, and extensive timber transport. At the lowest level of the criminal activity are small-scale individuals who are easily recruited, in part, because they are vulnerable and attempt to acquire basic subsistence income.

240 *Lynn Rhodes*

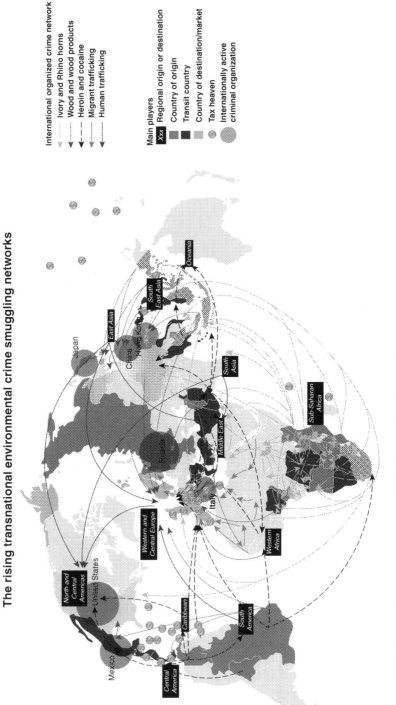

Figure 12.1 Transnational Environmental Crime Smuggling Networks.

Weak governance of forest resources, unclear forest tenure, corruption in timber supply chains, and the region's proximity to Chinese consumer markets and timber processing industries attract the criminal networks that value Asia's timber species. Although a number of Southeast Asian governments have enacted logging bans and other timber sector regulations to reduce illegal timber trafficking, these same efforts together with persistently high demand continue to inflate prices, so that trade in alternative species that could be introduced by more vulnerable Southeast Asian source countries is difficult to establish.[8]

Enhanced or otherwise known as coordinated and collaborative law enforcement-response can help address these trends. The responses can be either formal or informal and can help put responses into context for effective action. Enforcement cases show an increase in the scale and organisation of environmental crimes. Those who have been prosecuted and found guilty, for example, for illegal logging and laundering of hundreds of millions of dollars dwarf the resources that would otherwise be available for enforcement, investigation, and prosecution.

Financially, the large and growing scale of environmental crimes requires new and collaborative responses. It requires international cooperation including international jurisdictions and collaboration across borders. The UNODC works with member states in the Asia Pacific region for the Global Program for Combating Wildlife and Forest Crime by providing expertise for policy-strengthening, legislative, and regulatory frameworks. Importantly, they provide training and direct assistance in order to guide and help implement regulations and laws.

Training

Training relating to environmental crimes is unique, specialised, and requires advanced coordination and investigative techniques. Part of the specialised training reinforces capacity-building of involved parties which includes enforcement and customs officers, rangers, natural resource officials, and prosecutors. Specialised training includes a range of expertise specific to environmental crimes and networks. Key subjects include Anti-Smuggling; Intelligence Gathering; Crime Scene Management; Risk Profiling; Electronic Surveillance; Controlled Delivery; Financial Investigations (aka money laundering); Wildlife Forensics and the specialty of prosecuting Wildlife Cases.[9]

Since the first joint United States (US) and China meeting in 2007, the US Environmental Protection Agency (EPA) and China's Ministry of Ecology and Environment (MEE) have established a long-standing partnership, which advances the environmental protection capacities in both the US and China and focuses on key areas. In 2019, the EPA hosted a delegation of 22 environmental enforcement officials and inspectors from the Chinese MEE and provincial environmental protection bureaus for specialised training and exchange on US' enforcement and compliance of environmental laws. EPA shared its experience and lessons regarding administrative, civil, and criminal enforcement of environmental laws; the inspection process; federal, state, and local coordination; and the use of advanced monitoring tools and data analytics to target compliance. The delegation from China presented specifics on developments and improvements to China's environmental enforcement and compliance assurance abilities based on lessons jointly learned from exchanges with EPA.[10]

The ability to coordinate effectively and help control environmental crimes is more important today because of their direct threats to peace, security, and civilisation. Worldwide, armed terrorist and non-state groups are benefiting financially from these crimes to fund their activities, such as the smuggling of drugs, guns, oil, antiques, migrants, and anything for profit. Environmental crimes provide a relatively low-risk, high-profit source of revenue compared to other forms of revenue and effective, coordinated response is essential.

Three examples of effective coordinated responses

1. Project Predator, which unites 13 countries in Asia, including China and Vietnam, was coordinated through INTERPOL in 2011. It unites the efforts of police, customs, and wildlife officials in the specified countries where wild tigers can still be found. The partnership under the Global Tiger Initiative brings together officials from the 13 tiger range countries, the United States Agency for International Development (USAID), the United Kingdom's Department for Environment, Food and Rural Affairs (DEFRA), World Bank, Smithsonian Institution, and INTERPOL. The Project has provided capacity building to law enforcement agencies to combat tiger and other wildlife crimes and has strengthened their ability to work with wildlife officials using advanced, intelligence-led methods of investigation. The Project encourages countries to establish such task forces and environmental crime programmes and demonstrates their effectiveness and interrelated ecosystems. Project Predator's long-standing relationship with USAID has resulted in vital law enforcement developments and achievements across Asia between 2010 and 2015. The collaborative project led to 560 arrests and to the seizure of more than a hundred large cats, 2,500 turtles and tortoises, and 12.6 tonnes of ivory.[11]
2. The overarching Montreal Protocol played, and continues to play, a role in reducing illegal trade in ozone-depleting substances with several coordinated programmes including "Informal Prior-Informed Consent" coordinated with the United Nations Environmental Programme (UNEP). Because of this and related projects, over 800 tonnes of ozone-depleting substances called chlorofluorocarbons (CFCs) were seized from 2006 to 2010. The scale of illegal trade in CFCs has been reduced as a

result of a global agreement on phasing out these substances, which also has affected criminal markets. These types of programmes demonstrate how implementing environmental rule of law with global agreements such as the Stockholm, Rotterdam, and Basel Conventions can meet environmental goals and reduce illicit global trade in these goods or commodities by not allowing safe haven for the activities and by helping to close criminal markets.

3. In 2017 the Environmental Crimes Committee of the International Association of Chiefs of Police (IACP) developed an online tool to assist field and safety professionals in their response to investigations of environmental crimes. The application is called *ChemSafety* and is readily available online. Its effectiveness is supported with the following statistics: in one month (April–May 2018) data show over 71,000 sessions, 171,427 views, and over 50,000 individual users. The application guides field and safety professionals through the S.A.F.E. acronym in response to environmental crimes:

S: Safety and health for the law enforcement officer
A: Acute and chronic chemical, biological, and radiation exposures
F: Forensic evidence protection and preservation
E: Environment, human health, and wildlife impacts

This web application is intended to enhance the abilities of law enforcement officers and other safety professionals to safely respond to incidents of potential or suspected environmental crimes and hazardous materials incidents by providing information and best practices in the key areas for safe, effective response to and investigations of environmental crimes.[12]

Table 12.1 and Figure 12.3 illustrate the major environmental crimes, annual economic loss, their drivers, and their resulting impacts. Beginning at Figure 12.2's centre hub, primary key drivers of environmental crime show the nexus and scale of these drivers: corruption; corporate crime; conflicts; domestic and international demand; lack of law enforcement at the national and international levels; lack of legislation; and both international and national mafias.

The UNEP-INTERPOL 2016 *Rapid Response Assessment Report* (RRAR) describes ecosystems as providing a range of services and providing the very foundations of our economy, human health, livelihoods, and well-being. Those can include clean air, water supply, extreme weather mitigation and storm protection, food security, and pollination, to list a few. It describes the environmental impacts of illegal trade in wildlife. However, there is no current assessment of environmental impacts for the wider range of environmental crimes and their full implications for sustainability and development goals. For both developed and developing countries, environmental crime is accelerating. The impacts reach beyond the environment and biodiversity and deep into our societies and ways of life.

Table 12.1 Different forms of environmental crimes and their approximate estimated scale summary from UNEP-INTERPOL RRAR 2016

Environmental Crime	Annual loss of resources pre 2014 estimate (USD)	Annual loss of resources 2016 estimate (USD)	Sources or reviews
Illegal logging and trade	30–100 billion	50.7–152 billion	New sources: UNEP 2014 (10–30% updated by FAOSTAT 2014: Roundwood including wood-fuel: 3.7 b m3 average export unit price of 37 USD/m3=global wood trade of USD 507 b. With 10–30% possibly illegal this accounts for USD 50.7–152 billion
Illegal, Unreported and Unregulated fisheries	11–30 billion	11–23.5 billion	MRAG and UBC 2008 (10–23 billion) UNODC 2011 and Agnew 2009 (12–23%) of global trade). Does not include illegal open sea discard of approx. 1/3rd of global catch. Discards may account for tens of billions of USD in addition.
Illegal extraction and trade in minerals/mining	12–48 billion	12–48 billion	Estimated as only 11-4% of by industry of the global trade (GFI, 2011; GA 2021). New source GI 2016 indicates 28–90% of mined gold was illegal in five South America counties, accounting alone for 7 billion USD on gold in five countries, suggesting this is a gross underestimate. However it has been kept as this for now as more research is needed.
Illegal trade and dumping of hazardous waste	10–12 billion	7–23 billion	USDOJ 2000 (10–20 billion): GA 2012. New source UNEP 2015 (unaccounted or illegally traded E-waste alone accounted for 12.2–19 billion USD in 2015)
Illegal trade and poaching of plants and other wildlife	7–23 billion	7–23 billion	Wyler and Sheik 2008 (5–20 billion). Haken 2011. (7.8–10 billion). US Government agencies 2000 cited OECD 2012 (USD 6–10 billion excluding wood and fish). New estimates

Asia and beyond 245

Sum of environmental crime	70–21.3 billion	UNODC including mainly endangered species cf. CITES. Separate section on growth in environmental crimes.
	91–259 billion (30–22% higher i.e., 26% on average	All converted to 2016 USD
Drugs	344 billion	UNODC 2005 (cannabis herb and resin USD 142 billion). UNODC 2011 (2009 cocaine 85 billion + opiates/heroin 68 billion)
Human trafficking (excl. recent migrant to Europe)	157.1 billion	International Labour Organisation 2014 (forced labour generates USD 150 billion in illegal profits per year. 2/3 is from sexual exploitation the rest other economic exploitation) EUROPOL-INTERPOL.2016 (Recent migration wave Europe USD 5.5 billion)
Counterfeit crimes	288 billion	OECD 2007 and UNODC (USD 250 billion) does not include domestically produced and consumed products or non-tangible digital products.
Small arms illegal trafficking	1.5–3 billion	10–20% of illicit small arms trade, which is USD 10-3 billion incl. parts and sights per year (Small Arms Survey 2012) Ammunition USD 4.2 b. per year (Janes Intelligence Review 2013).

Estimates derived from published reports, UN statistics on legal trades and estimates from criminal intelligence through INTERPOL on the extent based on reporting from National Central Bureaus in member states given that criminals do not report statistics on their activities. Hence wide ranges are provided.

Crimes, jurisdictions, prosecution

An environmental crime can only be prosecuted if the specific jurisdiction decides the offence is to be governed by way of law. Often, simply identifying the environmental crime as a criminal offence can be leveraged to help enforce environmental law. Jurisdictions worldwide have different abilities and approaches to carry out enforcement. Approaches from varying jurisdictions come with different penalties and sanctions. Even with strong environmental laws, if a jurisdiction does not have the full capacity to enforce the laws, it cannot be effective. These issues are increasingly relevant for comprehensive and cooperative security also known as enhanced law enforcement and coordinated enforcement actions across boundaries. Criminal justice systems are often challenged to meet the multi-level threats presented by the transnational nature of environmental crimes.

Mongolia

Three times larger than the country of France, Mongolia is the most sparsely populated country in the world, with a population of approximately 3 million people. Its ability to protect the country's vast natural resources was challenged especially in its transition from a historically pastoral to a market-driven economy.[13] Nevertheless, Mongolia has instituted strong environmental laws, and environmental protection is embedded in the constitution and laws of the land. Articles 1–3 of Mongolia's environmental laws are outlined below.

> Article 1. The PURPOSE of this law is to regulate relations between the State, citizens, business entities and organizations in order to guarantee the human right to live in a healthy and safe environment, an ecologically balanced social and economic development, the protection of the environment for present and future generations, the proper use of natural resources and the restoration of available resources.
> Article 2. LEGISLATION. Legislation on environmental protection: 1. The legislation on environmental protection is comprised of the Constitution of Mongolia, this law, and other relevant legislative acts issued in conformity with them. 2. If an international treaty to which Mongolia is a party is inconsistent
> with this law then the provisions of the international treaty shall prevail.
> Article 3. RESOURCES. Resources protected by law and relevant definitions:
> 1. This law shall protect the following conservation resources from any adverse effects in order to prevent ecological imbalance: (1) land and its soil; (2) underground resources and mineral wealth; (3) water; (4) plants; (5) animals; (6) air.

Asia and beyond 247

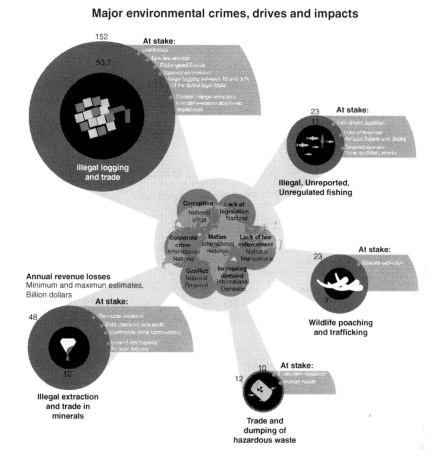

Figure 12.2 Environmental Crimes Illustrated. Courtesy UNEP-INTERPOL RRAR 2016.

It is known that the capacity to monitor, enforce, and prosecute environmental crimes varies from country to country. Furthermore, with countries having varying capacities and resolve for monitoring and response to transnational environmental crime threats, it is not surprising that organised criminal groups are targeting countries with lower capacity and political will to implement and enforce robust countermeasures.[14] For example, while Mongolia has enacted strong environmental laws, it has experienced an explosion of mining projects, wildlife poaching, development, and other resource threats endangering the environment. Mongolian protected-area officers patrol vast areas of open space far removed from modern infrastructure and legal support systems. Even with good laws and good officers,

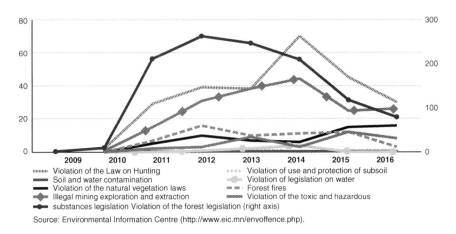

Figure 12.3 Environmental Crimes and Offenses. Mongolia 2009–2016.
Source: UNEC Mongolia Performance Review 2018 (scale zero to 300).

the nation's enforcement capacity needs improvement in order to show substantial results in regards to enforcement of existing environmental laws. A large percentage of Mongolia is classified as under protected status, increasing the stress level, capacity, and demands on protected-area officers, and the ability of these officers and the courts to prosecute environmental crimes.

Mongolia's Criminal Code was amended in 2017 by chapter 24 to include environmental crimes. Criticisms of many specified environmental violations in the code indicate that the laws have not been generally enforced in practice. However, according to the 2018 *Mongolia Environmental Performance Review*, a new "Law on Violation" was passed in May 2017 which gives the force of law for all violations of laws that are not considered a crime. This provision provides some enforcement opportunities which would give authority commensurate with enforcement and prosecution capacity. Figure 12.3 illustrates the types and frequency of environmental crimes in Mongolia in the last 10 years.

China

Under President Xi Jinping since 2012, China has increased prioritisation to address longstanding environmental problems in order to help resolve environmental crime. China's courts and enforcement agencies have focused efforts specifically on addressing environmental crime, with heightened focus on polluters. They reported arresting 15,095 people for environmental crimes in 2018. The figure was 51.5 per cent higher than the previous year according to China's top prosecuting body, which has been trying to better utilise their enforcement officers and judicial authorities to address environmental damage done to the overall environment. During the same period, the number of prosecutions reached 42,195, up 21 per cent. In addition to pollution and waste crimes, offences included illegal deforestation and land occupation, illegal mining, and fishing, according to Zhang Zhijie, a senior prosecutor with China's Supreme People's Procuratorate. According to Zhang, China prosecutes environmental crimes with the purpose not only to impose simple criminal punishments on the suspects and defendants but to repair social relations, restore environmental damage and demonstrate a favourable course of development.[15]

It is important to identify criminal offences so that they can be incorporated into legal responses, prosecution, and restoration, where possible. Simply identifying offences as criminal acts has the ability at times, to serve as a deterrent and allows for collective education on environmental law. Globally, however, the varying degrees to which crimes are identified, incorporated into law, listed, and subsequently prosecuted allow for criminal elements to hedge the differences amongst countries and states for their benefit. International commissions, organisations, and agencies actively have reinforced efforts to develop projects and policies, and provide direct support in response to environmental crimes, threats to civilisation, security, and systematic risks. Resolutions and "toolkits" encourage and actively assist in the cooperation for bilateral, regional, and international entities to prevent, combat, and eradicate the many forms of environmental crimes and transnational criminal networks.

One such example occurred in November 2019 when representatives of both customs and law enforcement agencies met in Shenzen, China regarding a joint operation called Operation Thunderball[16] involving large-scale seizures of ivory, timber, plants, animals, and African pangolin scales. The operation was coordinated by INTERPOL and the World Customs Organization and involved over 100 counties. The operation was indicative of improvements in building capacity to coordinate, investigate, prosecute and begin a restoration process. Also participating in the meeting were members of the International Consortium for Combating Wildlife Crimes. This large effort demonstrated an effective model of enhanced law enforcement and response in combating environmental crime.

Environmental security and criminal networks

In 2014, the INTERPOL General Assembly passed a resolution in response to emergency threats in environmental security. In that resolution, instead of defining environmental crime, it focused on environmental security by recognising the impact environmental crime can have on a nation's political stability, environmental quality, natural resources, biodiversity, and economy. It also recognised that criminal networks engaging in financial crime, fraud, corruption, illicit trade, and human trafficking are active in or facilitating environmental crime.[17]

Earlier in 2010, the 79th INTERPOL General Assembly adopted an environmental crime resolution that acknowledged the need for a robust international environmental enforcement response. It identified a criminal convergence around the environment, biodiversity, and natural resources sectors maintained by organised crime. Suppressing criminal activity that converges around these sectors is a critical contributing factor to assist in the maintenance of national security and good governance. As governments adopt varying responses to environmental crimes and environmental security, international cooperative organisations are used to help address shared environmental vulnerabilities and enhanced law enforcement and prosecutorial response. A number of strategic goals in support of environmental security and threats have been identified. In the 2017–2020 INTERPOL Strategic Plan, two of those goals specifically address such support in order to:

1. identify and dismantle transnational criminal networks, including criminal operating models and unlawful influences that threaten environment, biodiversity, and natural resource security.
2. address criminal threats, illegal trade, and trafficking in environmentally sensitive goods, biodiversity, and natural resources. The Plan identifies key objectives and many areas of direct assistance to countries experiencing major incidents of environmental crime and threats.

Increasingly, illegal use of natural resources is driving armed conflicts, in addition to becoming a nexus of organised crime, so the emphasis on security for the environment is needed more than ever. Encouraged by the United Nations (UN) Security Council, UN member states are being asked to work together to both collect, analyse and share information intelligence to help prevent terrorism and transnational organised crime. To increase effectiveness, a broader definition of environmental crime is needed in addition to referring to environmental crime as a serious crime. Several categories can be used as a reference umbrella to help understand this broad definition. They include crimes such as: illegal logging; dumping and trade in hazardous waste; smuggling of ozone-depleting substances; illegal fishing and trade; illegal trade in conflict diamonds; and illegal trade and poaching of wildlife and plants. White-collar crimes that work in concert with environmental crimes include forgery; tax fraud; money laundering; terrorism; and involvement in organised crime.

The United Nations Environmental Program (UNEPA) Governing Council plays a key role in maintaining focus and awareness on legislative efforts across vested interests in order to support the rule of environmental law. These efforts are driven largely by the increase in organised criminal groups trafficking in hazardous waste, wildlife, and illegal timber harvesting (see Figure 1.5). The UNEP Governing Council recognises that environmental crime undermines environmental goals and effective governance. Its decision 27/9, in part, emphasised the strengthening of environmental governance and expertise for prosecutors, judges, and law enforcement.[18]

In April 2016, the International Union for Conservation of Nature (IUCN) World Environmental Law Congress met in Rio de Janeiro. Several forward-thinking actions resulted from the congress. Included among them were core principles to strengthen collective efforts involving implementation and enforcement strategies; laws that *can* be enforced; implementation and accountability; coordination of roles; and the importance of treating environmental crimes as serious crimes. An informal network of international organisations necessary for effective collaboration include INTERPOL, UNEP, CITES/ICCWC, Rotterdam, Stockholm and Basel Conventions, World Bank, UNDP, the Montreal Protocol, and others. Together they investigate and combat forgery, money laundering, terrorism, associations with organised crime, tax fraud, and threat finance relating to environmental crime. The networks investigated have extensive global traffic routes.[19] Statistics for environmental crimes are difficult to measure due to the sheer volume and diversity of underground activity. However, it is generally recognised that progress in combating individual cases grows along with the realisation these crimes are a significant threat to peace, civilisation, society, health, security, and development.

In addition to many forms of wildlife poaching and illegal timber harvesting, the impact of global waste and pollution is valued at US$410 billion per year. The global waste sector takes several forms including legal industry, environmental protection, unregulated business, and trafficking in hazardous waste and chemicals by organised crime.[20] The links of environmental crimes to white-collar, organised criminal networks continue to be low risk with high-profit margins. They harm our collective environment and security while exploiting natural resources to fund their illegal activities. At least 40 per cent of global internal conflicts in the last 60 years have links to natural resources.[21]

Causes of environmental crime: response and restoration

Poverty, demand, and a permissive environment are root causes enabling environmental crime.

- Poverty is a driver of environmental crime because the poor are often vulnerable and easy to recruit at entry levels of activity.
- Demand for goods derived from natural resources such as wood, timber, wildlife, and waste disposal drive criminal activity due to readily available profits.
- Underfunding and lack of capacity to enforce law and regulations lead to crimes occurring almost by inertia or default.

Coordinated international operations and task forces reveal successful case studies to combat wildlife, fisheries, and forestry crime; ozone layer depletion; and pollution. Impacts on a global scale undermine peace for the survival of civilisation and security of the world's people, in addition to both legal business, development, and trade.

Lester R. Brown, in *PLAN B 3.0*,[22] writes that we are in a race between tipping points in nature and our political systems. Brown offers suggestions to assist countries to stabilise populations and ecosystems before they become failing states. He notes that in order to understand the current environmental dilemma, it is beneficial to look at earlier civilisations that also experienced environmental trouble. Some early societies were able to modify how they lived with the environment in order to avoid collapse or decline but others were not. The question is how we will respond today?

Civilisations—across borders, across states, across oceans—are threatened, due in part to the growing number of violations and sheer scale of organised and transnational environmental crimes that must be curtailed. However, steps being taken globally to reverse these downward trends are being done on an incremental basis. Global and enhanced awareness, strategies, and implementations are needed. When worldwide awareness, strategy, coordination of laws and policies are improved upon, success is possible. Education and awareness about these conditions are necessary first steps. Implementation of goals is next. The low-risk, high-profit margins of organised environmental criminal networks must be curtailed even with small and, hopefully, large gains. Our quality of life and civilisation itself is at stake. Engaged response, sound laws, increased and rapid capacity to monitor, enforce and restore, help to ensure our ability to have clean air and water, the basics of life as we know it, and as we would like to leave for future generations.

Mongolia, China, and Northeast Asia face complex environmental challenges. They are working independently and collectively to combat them locally, nationally, and regionally. It is important to recognise the transboundary nature of these organised environmental crimes and their impacts. Such challenges require reinforced actions and cooperation. Additionally, environmental cooperation continues with multilateral bodies and bilateral projects. The North-East Asian Sub-regional Programme for Environmental Cooperation (NEASPEC) is one such cooperative effort. After agreement from a 1992 conference of the United Nations Economic and Social Commission for Asia Pacific (UNESCAP), NEASPEC was established one year later with the goal of working comprehensively in the region for environmental cooperation. NEASPEC today includes the six member-states of China, Japan, Mongolia, Russia, South Korea, and North Korea, as well as UNESCAP.

Progress is not always rapid and cooperative efforts of this type often come with conflicting priorities which can hinder or slow their joint efforts. The need for transnational, transboundary, innovative solutions including customs, regulations, jurisdictions, and enhanced law enforcement efforts will continue to be needed to address organised environmental crime in the region.

Notes

1 *The Rise of Environmental Crime, A UNEP-INTERPOL Rapid Response Assessment, 2016*, p. 17, at https://www.cms.int/sites/default/files/document/unep_cms_mikt1_inf-5.4.a_the_rise_of_environmental_crime.pdf (accessed October 14, 2020).
2 Employees of a "clearly defined geographical space, recognized, dedicated and managed, through legal or other effective means, to achieve the long-term conservation of nature with associated ecosystem services and cultural values." See *IUCN Definition 2008*, at https://www.iucn.org/theme/protected-areas/about (accessed October 14, 2020).
3 "Park Rangers on the Frontline being Killed at an Astonishing Rate from India to Thailand to Africa, Global Conservation," *Global Conservation*, March 31, 2016, at http://globalconservation.org/news/park-rangers-frontline-being-killed-astonishing-rate-new-solutio/ (accessed October 14, 2020).
4 "World Ranger Day 2017–Ranger Roll of Honor In Memoriam, International Ranger Federation, 2018," International Ranger Federation, at https://www.internationalrangers.org/wp-content/uploads/2018-Honour-Roll.pdf (accessed October 14, 2020).
5 *The Rise of Environmental Crime*, p. 7.
6 Lynn Rhodes, "Verge of Collapse? Survival of Civilization in the Anthropocene," *Comparative Civilizations Review* 72 (72) Article 9, 2015, p. 4, at https://scholarsarchive.byu.edu/ccr/vol72/iss72 (accessed September 10, 2020).
7 "Transnational Organized Crime in South East Asia: Evolution, Growth, and Input," UNODC, *Report 2019*, 2019, pg. 1, at https://www.unodc.org/documents/southeastasiaandpacific/Publications/2019/SEA_TOCTA_2019_web.pdf (accessed October 14, 2020).
8 Ibid., p. 6.
9 John C. Cruden and David S. Gualtieri, "Towards a More Coordinated, Integrated Response to Wildlife Trafficking and other Natural Resource Crime," Penn Law: Scholarship Repository, 2017, at https://scholarship.law.upenn.edu/cgi/viewcontent.cgi?article=1014&context=alr (accessed October 12, 2020).
10 "USEPA Efforts in the Asia-Pacific Region," United States Environmental Protection Agency, January 19, 2017, at https://www.epa.gov/international-cooperation/epa-efforts-asia-pacific-region (accessed October 12, 2020).
11 USAID, "Protecting Tigers with Project Predator," 2016, p. 2, at https://rmportal.net/biodiversityconservation-gateway/resources/research/communities-combating-wildlife-trafficking/protecting-tigers-with-project-predator/view (accessed October 15, 2020).
12 International Association of Chiefs of Police, Environmental Crimes Committee, at http://www.theiacp.org/chemsafety/ (accessed October 13, 2020).
13 Lynn Rhodes, "Civilizational and Environmental Effects of Mongolia's Transition from a Pastoral to a Market-Driven Economy," *Comparative Civilizations Review* 69 (69), 2013, p. 2, at https://scholarsarchive.byu.edu/ccr/vol69/iss69/5 (accessed October 14, 2020).
14 "Transnational Organized Crime in South East Asia," p. 15.
15 "China Environmental Crime Arrests up more than 50% in 2018," *Reuters*, February 14, 2019, at https://www.reuters.com/article/us-china-environment-crime-idUSKCN1Q30ZE (accessed October 14, 2020).
16 INTERPOL, "Wildlife trafficking: Organized Crime hit hard by joint INTEPOL-WCO global enforcement operation," July 10, 2019, at https://www.interpol.int/en/News-and-Events/News/2019/Wildlife-trafficking-organized-crime-hit-hard-by-joint-INTERPOL-WCO-global-enforcement-operation (accessed October 14, 2020).
17 *The Rise of Environmental Crime*, p. 26.

18 "Governing Council of the United Nations Environmental Programme (February 18–22, 2013)," Nairobi, UNEP, March 12, 2013, p. 2 and 10, at https://wedocs.unep.org/bitstream/handle/20.500.11822/17292/K1350945.pdf?sequence=3&isAllowed=y (accessed October 14, 2020).
19 *The Rise of Environmental Crime,* pp. 35, 44, 47–48, 62.
20 Ibid., p. 62.
21 Ibid., p. 67.
22 Lester R. Brown, "PLAN B 3.0," *Earth Policy Institute,* W.W. Norton & Company, New York and London, 2018.

13 When Toynbee's "fossilized" or "arrested" societies are reborn as peripheral states: the cases of Israel, Mongolia, Korea, and Japan

Joseph Drew

The goal of this chapter will be to consider certain societies that the lauded founder of the comparative study of civilisations, Arnold Toynbee, once dismissed as "fossilized", but which like Lazarus abruptly rise from the dead centuries after they were buried and reappear with vigour on the world stage. Several contemporary Asian states appear to qualify: Mongolia, Israel, Japan, and Korea, in particular. If these civilisations were considered to have risen from nothing to greatness once upon a time and then, later and sadly, fallen into desuetude, following a natural and prescribed pattern that scholars from Ibn Khaldun to Spengler have outlined, how can we explain their sudden rebirth, their renewed and resurgent presence in the modern world? Does this really mean that the cyclical theory of civilisations may be accurate in general and that not all societies die completely? Perhaps some hibernate.

Is the reappearance of certain ancient civilisations, now in peripheral status to greater lands but possibly projecting once again a great future, a peculiar phenomenon of the present? What features of history and society and politics have facilitated this? How is it even possible? To look at these examples, we first might note the ideas of non-core peripheral societies and states, a staple of such modern thinkers as Toynbee, the world-systems school of Immanuel Wallerstein, and others, and then benefit by applying the Marginal Man theory of sociologists Robert Park and Everett Stonequist or the "double consciousness" idea of W.E.B. DuBois to these no-longer-dead, now alive civilisations.

The pattern of history—are there patterns?

Unilinear patterns

First, there is a tendency to think that all historical development proceeds in a straight line. They are *unilinear*, all going towards a single goal. Many Christians, for example, believe that their religion tells them that the movement of history is straightforward, towards a desirable end. In their case, the goal of Christianity is the second coming of Christ, the founder of their faith.

DOI: 10.4324/9781003148630-13

When this happens, they say, there will be a major battle, called Armageddon, between the forces of good and evil. Then there will follow the period called the rapture, in which Christians will ascend to heaven and non-Christians will do the opposite by going to hell. Or, as in the Sermon on the Mount, all men will live in harmony, the lions will lie down with the lambs. Either way, what we know as history will come to end, they say.[1]

Second, there are others who advocate a unilinear view of history but a different and troubling one.[2] There are many today who tell us that we are rapidly hurtling towards a horrible end on Earth. For some, it is a socially induced end. The atomic age was ushered in at the end of the Second World War, with the bombing of Hiroshima and Nagasaki, and the United States (US) soon was joined by the Soviet Union in the possession of atomic weaponry. Today, atomic powers include the US, Russia, China, the United Kingdom, France, Israel, India, Pakistan, and North Korea, with Iran possibly *en route* to such a status; perhaps other states are going to possess this awesome weaponry. Then, either hostility between some of these powers will occur, or else terrorists will gain control of atomic bombs. Either way, the end is obvious: mankind will destroy itself. This is a straight line towards an inglorious end, building upon inherent tendencies of destruction that are contained in the human personality.

Third, it is unilinear but physically tragic. These individuals say that history is moving towards environmental disaster. As the world's population consumes more and more of the Earth's fossils for fuel, we have wantonly and in profligate stupidity despoiled our environment, making it inevitable that sooner or later we cannot survive. Our insensitive lack of planning and foresight thus spell our own doom. The oceans, while rising dangerously, are filling up with plastics, which kill the marine life; our burning of coal and oil is generating climate change; the polar ice caps are melting and deserts are expanding; storms increasingly are frightening—we are basically ruining the house we live in. The end is near, as we generate an atmosphere impossible for man to live in.

In addition, there also are a few who see the tendency of history to be leading, regardless of these dangers, to a type of political end. Our political experience is leading us to a status in which Western-style liberal democracy will become the sole system of politics. This, they maintain, is not just the passing of one phase of history but actually the end of history. This view was a widely held belief when the Soviet Union fell. The idea of Francis Fukuyama[3] and others is that societies worldwide will see their structural differences of governance diminish. This view is not as devastating to man's survival as the others but it also is decreasingly popular in our now bleaker age.

Cyclical patterns

However, there are other non-linear ways of seeing the past and future of humanity. Others, for example, follow the writings of Ibn Khaldun, in *The Muqaddimah: An Introduction to History*.[4] To them, history is *cyclical.* This seer described a world in which humans build worlds that ascend slowly in a cycle from meaninglessness to predominance, only to collapse at the end of their good run and then disappear into the sands of time. The Roman Empire rose to world power and, following its period of predominance for many centuries, was reduced to nothingness. The British Empire did the same, and the American Century appears about to be completed. This is man's fate, and we can see history as a succession of triumphs and failures, a story which will have no end. Oswald Spengler and Arnold Toynbee[5] were two modern avatars of Ibn Khaldun's type of approach.

Dialectic patterns

In additional to unilinear and cyclical patterns to history, Georg Wilhelm Friedrich Hegel[6] gave us the idea, with ancient origins, which others call the *dialectic*. This is a third major structure or way of viewing human history and man's ascendancy on this planet. At the basis is a struggle between the thesis and the antithesis, an assertion and its opposite. These two are fundamental to existence. They battle and, in the end, the struggle results in a synthesis; this is a conclusion in which elements of the two somehow coalesce or coexist. However, philosophers point out, that synthesis is itself a thesis. Thus, it proceeds to generate its opposite, an antithesis, and from this battle emerges a solution, a new synthesis. But, of course, this new synthesis is itself a thesis, however, and it creates therefore its opposite, the antithesis. And thus, man's history is laid out in front, for all to see. Thesis, antithesis, and synthesis. Philosophers who have followed Hegel here perceived this dialectical foundation to be leading to an ever-better world, as man's reason moved through history. Reason will govern the world, asserted Hegel, and history "is none other than the consciousness of freedom."[7]

Some have argued that, while history in fact does move dialectically, it is based on materialism, not reason. It rests on economics, and it leads towards the triumph of communism. According to these believers, Karl Marx, who built on Hegel's philosophy, is the correct prognosticator. Karl Marx, a student of Hegel, famously turned his teacher on his head. In his *Theses on Feuerbach*, he said that the "philosophers have only interpreted the world, in various ways; the point, however, is to change it."[8] The dialectic to Marx was not based on the progress of man's reason, but rather it was based on the modes of production and the control of these economic forces by one class or the other. Thus, dialectical idealism (the movement of the idea through history, as it progresses ever forward towards the goals humanity seeks) had become, in Marxist terminology, dialectical materialism.[9]

According to Marxists, there have been and will continue to be a series of revolutions, all of which end the life of one ruling class and, after the struggle, create a new ruling class. This is determined, they argue, by the laws of economics, under which all relations of mankind are regulated, and which are independent of their will. In this view, the final revolution is inevitable. It is one in which the socialists will triumph because they are representatives of the working class gathered into a party that has become known as the vanguard of the proletariat. According to Lenin, writing in *State and Revolution*,[10] this socialist revolution will be followed by a communist one; then, the world will see the withering away of the state and the rise of pure communism. At this time, all men will be brothers, peace and tranquillity will predominate, and prehistory—by which the communists mean this endless cycle of domination and revolutions, one era following the other—is going to end.

A somewhat similar view from the Age of Reason, although not based on the dialectic, was generated by a Frenchman, the Marquis of Condorcet.[11] He saw history as the laying out of tableaux, each of which revealed the progress of the human mind, and each of which was progressive, that is, at a higher level of civilisation than its predecessor. We are advancing, moving forward, with the triumph of reason. Man is emerging from ignorance into a rational state, and the result will be a logical world. Count Saint Simon, Auguste Comte, and many others built on these assumptions during the Age of Reason.

Absurd patterns

But perhaps, thought others, history is *absurd*. The problem vexed German philosophers in the Nineteenth century. After a century of debate, Wilhelm Dilthey wrote his famous work *Pattern and Meaning in History*[12] in order to examine this conflict among thinkers. Was there, in fact, a discernible pattern to history? Perhaps the flow of history cannot be reduced to single explanation, to one type of analysis; the natural and cultural sciences perhaps differed in their subject matter and their approach. Perhaps, we can look backward and discern a pattern, wrote Sartre and Camus in literature, Stanford Lyman,[13] and others in sociology, but we cannot project forward. Man's behaviour patterns are too complex to yield such predictable large trends in history. Life is absurd, going in an endless number of directions, and we have to accept the illogic that finding a master trend entails.

The patterns of civilisation

Four sets of ideas, then, have gained currency as we seek to understand the patterns and meanings of our existence over the past 10,000 years or so of civilisation: unilinear patterns, cyclical patterns, dialectical patterns, no patterns. But what is a civilisation? Samuel Huntington, in his famous book, *The Clash of Civilizations and the Remaking of World Order*, provides a convenient guide to the topic. He writes that "human history is the history of civilizations. It is impossible to think of the development of humanity in any other terms."[14]

He then delineates five central propositions[15] concerning the nature, identity, and dynamics of civilisation, in a chapter entitled "Civilizations in History and Today." Here are the first three significant ones:

1. A distinction exists between civilisation in the singular and civilisations in the plural. Originally, the idea of civilisation, which was generated by French thinkers in the 1700s, was cast as the opposite of "barbarism"; so civilised society was settled, urban and literate. The more the subject was studied, however, the broader the view European and then American scholars took of the topic of civilisation. They saw that there are many civilisations, "each of which was civilised in its own way."[16]
2. A civilisation is a cultural entity. Both "civilisation" and "culture" refer to the overall way of life of a people, the "values, norms, institutions, and modes of thinking to which successive generations in a given society have attached primary importance."[17] Braudel describes a civilisation as "a space", a "cultural area", or "a collection of cultural characteristics and phenomena."[18] To Immanuel Wallerstein, it is "a particular concatenation of worldview, customs, structures, and culture (both material and high culture) which forms some kind of historical whole and which coexists (if not always simultaneously with other varieties of this phenomenon)."[19] For Durkheim and Mauss, it is "a kind of moral milieu encompassing a certain number of nations, each national culture being only a particular form of the whole."[20]
3. Civilisations are comprehensive. None of their constituent units can be fully understood without reference to the encompassing civilisation. A civilisation is the broadest cultural entity. Civilisations are mortal but they can evolve and adapt. Several scholars have laid out the stages which they think civilisations pass through. For Quigley,[21] there are seven, for example. Civilisations are cultural, not political entities.

Over the past several centuries, many scholars have studied civilisations. Among the most prominent have been Oswald Spengler, in his *Decline of the West*. Indisputably, however, one of the greatest students of civilisation, perhaps the most prominent of all to examine the comparative study of civilisations, has been the late Arnold Toynbee. This British scholar, famous for his twelve-volume work, *A Study of History*, sought to discern the nature of civilisations and the pattern of their rises and declines. For him, civilisations have existed for thousands of years among human beings, and they followed upon the predominance of hunter-gatherer societies. Gradually, civilisations arose in certain cradles of civilisation, and eventually civilisation became the predominant structure housing humanity. The problem, he found, is that civilisations themselves co-existed with other civilisations.

What constituted the nature of these civilisations? How did their societies structure themselves? Were there commonalities that could be discerned, allowing us to engage in the comparative study of civilisations? Were all civilisations on a route to coalesce? Was there simply a rise and fall of civilisations? What were their achievements, and did it matter that they were inevitably succeeded by other preeminent civilisations? Toynbee was a believer in the cyclical view of history. He argues that civilisations are the greatest "intelligible fields of study," and he finds that 21 or later 23 great civilisations that have experienced a certain similar pattern of growth and decline. In both his text and in Table V, especially the summary table of civilisations of his abridged edition,[22] Toynbee lists those he finds to be the indisputable *developed* civilisations:

1. Egyptiac;
2. Andean;
3. Sinic;
4. Minoan;
5. Sumeric;
6. Mayan;
7. Yucatec;
8. Mexic;
9. Hittite;
10. Syriac;
11. Babylonic;
12. Iranic;
13. Arabic;
14. Far Eastern—Main Body;
15. Far Eastern—Japanese Offshoot;
16. Indic;
17. Hindu;
18. Hellenic;
19. Orthodox Christian—Main Body;
20. Orthodox Christian—Russian Offshoot; and
21. Western.

According to Toynbee, these civilisations have gone through challenges; a time of troubles; a universal state; a universal peace; and possess certain philosophies, religions, and sources of inspiration for their religions.

Mongolian nomads and Jews: "arrested" civilisations

There is another type of civilisation called "arrested" civilisations. According to Toynbee, there have been five arrested civilisations: the Polynesians, the Eskimos, the Nomads, the Spartans, and the Osmanlis. Why are these civilisations not included on the list of developed civilisations by Toynbee? What does he mean by "arrested" or abortive civilisations? Toynbee determines that some do not grow to manhood. "It is the existence of civilisations which have kept alive but failed to grow."[23]

The Nomads faced the physical challenge of the steppe but "the mastery of the Steppe demands so much of the Nomads' energies that none is left over."[24] Toynbee writes that Nomadism is essentially a society without a history.[25] The Mongols, he claims, are part of a rhythmic alternation between periods of relative desiccation and humidity, which causes alternate intrusions of Peasants and Nomads into one another's spheres:

> The most striking recorded examples of Nomad explosion are the intrusions of the Turks and the Mongols, which occurred in what was probably the last dry period but one.... The relentless pressure of the cultivator is probably more painful in the long run, if one happens to be the victims of it, than the Nomad's savage onslaught. The Mongol raids were over in two or three generations; but the Russian colonisation which has been the reprisal for them has been going on for over four hundred years.[26]

Further, he describes the Nomad's point of view. He says that the rise of peasant power in Russia was seen by nomads to be like a machine. "In its grip the Nomad is either crushed out of existence or racked into the sedentary mold, and the process of penetration is not always peaceful."[27]

Finally, and perhaps most surprising, was the fact that Toynbee felt compelled to offer a very harsh announcement for advocates of these formerly great or these almost civilisations: they are dead. Their great civilisations, or near-developed civilisations, were actually at their end several centuries ago. If their descendants still survive today, they are, in fact, but fossils of a once-thriving civilisation. He lists civilisations which are today "fossilized":

> On closer inspection we can discern two sets of what appear to be fossilized relics of similar societies not extinct, namely: one set including the Monophysite Christians of Armenia, Mesopotamia, Egypt and Abyssinia and the Nestorian Christians of Kurdistan and ex-Nestorians in Malabar, as well as the Jews and the Parsees; and a second set including the Lamaistic Mahayanian Buddhists of Tibet and Mongolia and the Hinayanian Buddhists of Ceylon, Burma, Siam and Cambodia, as well as the Jains of India.[28]

Further, he writes that "we can sort out the 'fossils' and assign them to the extinct societies to which they originally belonged."

> "The Jews and Parsees are fossils of the Syriac Society as it was before the Hellenic intrusion upon the Syriac World....The Lamaistic Mahayanian Buddhists of Tibet and Mongolia correspond to the Nestorians. They represent an unsuccessful reaction against the metamorphosis of Mahayanian Buddhism from its original Indic form to the later shape, molded by Hellenic and Syriac influences – in which it was eventually adopted by the Sinic Society.[29]

The Jews come in for special, even hostile, treatment by Toynbee. They are "manifestly fossils of the Syriac Society." Maurice Samuel wrote that

Toynbee "means that the Jewish people are spiritually and intellectually a fossil, an inert and petrified form devoid of any living juices, a lifeless simulacrum of genuine peoplehood."

Fossils return to life

Arnold Toynbee created a kind of intellectual Procrustean Bed with his assertions, alienating the sensitivities of many, as he sought to shove complex historical events into sweeping generalisations. While we surely are indebted to him for proving that civilisations are intelligible units of history and can be compared, perhaps he committed some gross errors in the process. A particular error is his reference to the fossils among us, especially those in Asia. For example: the Parsis of today have produced outstandingly successful individuals, and their community surely is the most advanced in India. Their ancient faith is quite alive, both itself and in its great contributions to other religions—Christianity, Judaism, and Islam.

A paper by Marvin R. Koller, entitled "The Living Fossil" has argued that applying the fossil metaphor "to Jews and Judaism was a serious distortion of reality and merits refutation."[30] As to the territorial imperative, the author writes that "Judaism can be said to be a civilization that is without territory but is adaptive to all lands. On the other hand, there is an historical and firm connection between Judaism and the land areas associated with the modern state of Israel."[31]

In spite of Toynbee's assertions, the Jews and the Mongols, it may be argued, have emerged from the dead. They are very much alive. Like Lazarus, these societies have risen abruptly from the dead centuries after they supposedly were buried. Their countries—the states of Israel and Mongolia—have emerged once again upon their ancestral homelands. Both are sovereign, both have developed their own culture and language, and both today are very successful.

On a recent online list entitled "Gross Domestic Product Ranked By Country 2019," Israel is ranked at #34 and Mongolia at #129,[32] and they also are successful if comparing GDP per capita. Israel is at #34 and Mongolia at #91 in the International Monetary Fund listing of 2018; they are #32 and #92 in the World Bank listing of 2017; and #37 and #95 in the CIA listing of 2017.[33] When we consider that Israel only was again declared a state when the British mandate ended in 1948, and Mongolia only emerged from Soviet domination and dispensed with the designation of People's Republic when it gained its new democratic constitution in 1992, these are remarkable economic and political achievements.

Clearly, these two societies are neither fossilised nor arrested anymore, and perhaps they never were at all. How can we explain their sudden rebirth, since these countries until recently were considered part of other peoples' empires? If these cultures and their civilisations were considered to have risen from nothing to significance earlier in history and then, later and sadly, fallen into desuetude, how can we explain their sudden rebirth, their renewed, and resurgent presence in the modern world? Does this really mean that while the entire cyclical theory of civilisations may be accurate in general, not all societies die completely? Do some hibernate? Or transmogrify, that is, they change their shapes to adapt to new situations? Is the reappearance of certain ancient civilisations—now in peripheral status to larger nations, but possibly projecting once again great futures, a peculiar phenomenon of the present? What features of history and society and politics have facilitated this?

Sociological theories behind Israel and Mongolia

If the "fossils" of Israel and Mongolia are compared, commonalities are evident: first, they succeeded in throwing off the yoke of conquerors and oppressors, and, second, they also have assumed the status of somewhat peripheral states in the contemporary world. Two writers about civilisations deal with the term "periphery" but not in exactly the same way meant here. First, Phillip Bagby, writing in 1958, differentiated between major and peripheral civilisations.[34] There have been distinct civilisations and secondary, dependent, or peripheral civilisations. His list finds that today only Western civilisation and three peripheral civilisations survive, Eastern, Chinese, and Indian. He parallels, in some ways, Toynbee's concepts of developed, abortive, and arrested civilisations. Bagby criticises Toynbee harshly, however, and he foresees the development of more in-depth comparative study of civilisations. Wei Ruan in his essay entitled "Civilization and Culture" analyses Bagby's definition of civilisation, which rests much of the argument on the size of cities. He concludes that, "Yet, whatever the flaws in Bagby's approach may be, Bagby's definition is workable and has been adopted by some theorists."[35]

Second, from an economics point of view, according to the sociologist Immanuel Wallerstein, civilisation-like entities also can be seen as part of world-systems as a set of mechanisms, which redistributes surplus value from the periphery to the core.[36] To Wallerstein, the core is the developed, industrialised part of the world, and the periphery is the "underdeveloped"—typically raw materials-exporting, poor part of the world. The market is the means by which the core exploits the periphery. Nonetheless, neither Mongolia nor Israel are seen as peripheral by worldsystem theorists. There are significant sociological views on the very concept of peripherality or marginality which might better illustrate the nature of Mongolia and Israel, two "fossils" in the past and today. It also may enable us to include Korea and Japan in the list. Two such sociological views are those of the "leaders from the periphery" and of the "Marginal Man."

Kurt Lewin, writing in his book, *Resolving Social Conflicts*, examined the social distance between people and noted the difference between the central regions of personality and the more peripheral layers. The central regions or nucleus are the more intimate.[37] People who are fleeing from the nucleus, such as in minority groups, and who are successful in their economic or professional status, often are on the margins of the group—in it but not happy about the group and how it is perceived. However, these very individuals, simply because they are the most successful in the eyes of the outside world, frequently are called to leadership posts by their underprivileged group. They become what he designates "leaders from the periphery." They accept the role, making it possible for them to maintain close contact with the majority of the overall society and its leaders, even though they dislike their own people. They exhibit what he calls negative chauvinism, attacking the very group they are putatively to lead, running down their own people.[38]

Just as a social group chooses "leaders from the periphery," by analogy it can be argued that the similar phenomenon can occur for entire societies. Peoples and nations who live on the periphery understand the worldview, the strengths, and the weaknesses of the central power. They may ascend to leadership as leaders from the periphery, precisely because they understand the vulnerabilities or errors of the central civilisation. These societies are of the civilisation or adjacent to it but they also can resent it. They can become the leader from the periphery, perhaps even doing so by shedding some of the vulnerabilities of the leaders of the central power. In other words, they rise to power by being able to see the world through the eyes of the central civilisation.

Moreover, they are on the margins of yet other societies, peoples, and cultures who are not at all part of the central civilisation or who are at the margins themselves of competing civilisations and societies. This location on the social periphery, this geographical distance, gives them special characteristics, enabling them to see the world as quite different neighbours see it. They obtain certain strengths, if perhaps unseen ones, and they may experience the absence of certain vulnerabilities that a "middle kingdom" such as China, or Egypt, or Mesopotamia, might not see in itself. These strengths predispose them to rise to power as "leaders from the periphery," while also enabling them to survive when the core societies or civilisations are washed away by the tides of history.

Max Weber once pointed out that Judea, the land of the Jews, was on an interstitial area, where two major civilisational imprints crossed each other. He wrote that "For as far back as we can go, Palestine was, in historical times, a middleman's country between Egypt and the region of the Orontes and Euphrates and between the Red Sea and the Mediterranean."[39] They saw these civilisations and worldviews, and incorporated parts of them, while rising above other aspects, but their own culture was itself neither of them. Moreover, during the post-Exilic period, the Jews became and remained for many centuries a "pariah people" in the eyes of Christians and Muslims.[40] However, the peripherality of the Jews is what gave them staying power—the ability to see the world through the eyes of several or many other peoples and their cultural assumptions and worldviews.

In his essay entitled "Components of the National Culture", Perry Anderson has argued that Britain, as opposed to Continental Europe, had become intellectually sterile by the mid-Twentieth century: "Britain, the most conservative major society in Europe, has a culture in its own image: mediocre and inert. This culture had failed to provide any intellectual alternative to the status quo [which was] why radicals in Britain found it so hard to think their way out of the system they wanted to overthrow."[41] Great Britain was separated geographically from the main of Europe, and it had not been conquered since 1066. Unlike continental Europe, in which one country after another had superimposed itself upon the whole and thus generate a palimpsest of ideas that contained visible traces of earlier forms, stimulating other more complex ideas and worldviews, Britain for one thousand years had not been ruled by others.

We can observe that the Jews and to a lesser extent the Mongols both had long periods during which they roamed the world. Thus, they absorbed the points of view of many other peoples, other societies, other civilisations. They could see the world as others see it. But, they had a peripheral status to all of these "others", and they eventually recreated themselves in an independent homeland which was still peripheral to the mighty central civilisations. A certain exceptional creativity was the inevitable result.

W.E.B. Du Bois, one of the most well-known African American intellectuals of the Nineteenth century, wrote of a concept he called "double consciousness."

> It is a peculiar sensation, this double-consciousness, this sense of always looking at one's self through the eyes of others, of measuring one's soul by the tape of a world that looks on in amused contempt and pity. One feels his two-ness,—an American, a Negro; two souls, two thoughts, two unreconciled strivings; two warring ideals in one dark body, whose dogged strength alone keeps it from being torn asunder.[42]

Clearly, this concept may be analogised to the level of civilisations. The Mongols and the Jews possessed their own civilisation but participated as well in adjacent ones. They were able to see themselves in the eyes of their neighbours—not equal, perhaps, because not in the central society or civilisation. Thus, they were actually more sophisticated, able to live at least two social or cultural lives.

A similarly fascinating concept was presented by E.V. Stonequist in the book, *The Marginal Man*, especially in the introduction by his famed teacher, Robert E. Park. Park quotes William Graham Sumner, who argued that each small primitive society thinks of itself "in the first person and regards itself as 'the center of everything.'"[43] Park and Stonequist bring up the personality type of the Marginal Man, whose "fate has condemned to live in two societies and in two, not merely different but antagonistic, cultures....In that case, his mind is the crucible in which two different and refractory cultures may be said to melt and, either wholly or in part, fuse.[44]

Park concludes that the "Marginal Man" is "a personality type that arises at a time and a place where, out of the conflict of races and cultures, new societies, new peoples, and cultures are coming into existence....Inevitably he becomes, relatively to his cultural milieu, the individual with the wider horizon, the keener intelligence, the more detached and rational viewpoint."[45] For Park, such a person is always relatively the more civilised human being, and as Spengler has said, grows up at the expense of earlier and simpler cultures.

Resurgent peripheral societies: Korea and Japan

I would argue that two other Northeast Asian civilisations deserve close attention as non-fossilised societies on the periphery, South Korea and Japan. While not an absorbed part of a central major civilisation, they are modern powerhouses. In Toynbee's *A Study of History*, there is no mention whatsoever of Korea and merely nine topics mentioned for Japan. For Toynbee, the main part of Far Eastern Society is China and he declares that China "has prolonged its existence in a petrified form instead of passing expeditiously through disintegration into dissolution by way of a universal state running out into an interregnum."[46]

By contrast, however, he sees both the Russian and Japanese civilisations as experiencing a "radical metamorphosis". Both, he declared, were impressive, as they emerged from these metamorphoses and "must still have been in the full *élan* of growth."[47]

> Instead of undergoing a compulsory process of Westernization at the hands of their Western neighbors—Poles, Swedes, Germans or Americans, the Russians and the Japanese carried through their social metamorphosis with their own hands, and were thus enabled to enter the Western comity of nations as the equals of the Great Powers and not as colonial dependencies or 'poor relations.'[48]

Clearly, Toynbee's view of history reveals that Japanese society was peripheral to the central civilisation of China and believes that the Japanese repelled the Mongol assault in 1281 mostly because of their military efficiency from more than a hundred previous years of internecine struggles.

According to the great scholars Edwin O. Reischauer and John K. Fairbank, Korea and Japan rank as the two most interesting variants of the "Peripheral Areas of East Asian Civilization." They maintain that,

> for more than a thousand years, the higher cultures of Korean and Japan resembled that of China so closely that in many respects they

seemed virtually identical with it....[In Korea], the bulk of literary production is almost indistinguishable from the writings of Chinese authors. In political institutions, in religious and ethical concepts, and in arts and letters, Korea and Japan have long been full-fledged participants in East Asian civilization.[49]

They acknowledge Japan's heavy cultural debt to China, and Korea's even closer cultural similarity but dismiss the possibility that Korea or Japan would be entirely absorbed into China. Even in their habits of daily life, the Chinese, Koreans, and Japanese have developed more distinctive patterns than those of the various national units of Europe.[50] Furthermore, they acknowledge the strong structural similarities among Korean, Japanese, and the Altaic languages of North Asia—not the Chinese language.

Korea's central position in the geography of Northeast Asia has meant that it has served as a meeting ground for civilisations. Korea has served as a bridge in early times for higher civilisation to pass from China to Japan. Korea was on the periphery of not only China but also Japan, and the peoples of the north.

Throughout history it has been a meeting ground for influences and pressures not only from China and Japan but also from the areas to the north. In the early period, the northern influences came from the far-ranging Altaic-speaking nomads – the Mongols and the Tungusic Jürched, Khitan and Manchus; in the modern period, from Imperial and then Communist Russia....The clash of the cultural, political and military forces from these three larger areas have made Korea a strategic zone of contact in East Asian history.[51]

As to Japanese culture and civilisation, "for information about the earlier periods of Japanese history it is usually safer to rely on accounts found in the Chinese dynastic histories than on the native literature."[52] The mainstream of cultural influence on Japan came from the continent by way of Korea. In the first century A.D. "no fixed boundary appears in fact to have existed at the time between the territories of the Koreans and of the Japanese," so, "the rise of powerful dynasties in China and Korea impelled Japan to achieve a unified government if it were not to be overwhelmed."[53]

The early history of Japan paralleled that of Korea but later diverged as its own civilisation matured. "While Korea became an interesting variant of the Chinese pattern, Japan became a country which had much in common culturally with China and Korea but contrasted sharply with them in social and political structure as well as historical experience."[54] It has been noted that geography is a major point of difference between Korea and Japan: "Japan's position as a relatively remote island country may best explain its distinctive role in East Asian history. The parallels with the British Isles, at

268 *Joseph Drew*

the opposite end of the Eurasian landmass, are striking. But the historical isolation of Japan has been considerably greater than that of England."[55]

Climate made Japan the most productive land per cultivated acre in the world with water resources ideally suited for agriculture, and it is surrounded by seas loaded with fish. The emergence of a powerful culture and expanding civilisation was predictable, and even by the First century C.E., contact with China was underway. Additionally, by the Fourth century there was a Japanese settlement on the south coast of neighbouring Korea. People also moved in the opposite direction. Steady immigration from Korea to Japan grew during the fifth and sixth centuries, and from then on, relations with Korea and China were significant. Thereupon, Buddhism moved in from China. By the Sixth century the Japanese consciously were borrowing from China, including the very name of the country. Seen from China, the Japanese islands were Nihon or Nippon, "the Source of the Sun," which is pronounced in Chinese is Zhih-ben, Japan in English.

So, three powerful major societies or civilisations arose on China's borders in Northeast Asia. Can we label all three as civilisations on the "periphery"? Indeed, China was the Middle Kingdom, not only as it saw itself but also as geography blessed it. But the Mongols, the Koreans, and the Japanese were peripheral states which, to various degrees, incorporated the culture and civilisation of the central Chinese civilisation and mixed these with their own, autochthonous institutions. These peripheral states were to rise into world historic importance.

Once fossils now resurgent: marginal societies

This set of sociological and comparative theories from the last half-century may be beneficial to our understanding of the patterns of history, at least as far as the life trajectories of civilisations are concerned. Toynbee, who almost singlehandedly created the discipline known as the comparative study of civilisations, described a cyclical pattern for developed civilisations. He also set aside some civilisations as abortive, others as arrested, and he claimed that some groups today are but fossilised remnants of ancient civilisations.

Such a delineation may be helpful as a starting point, but the facts prove that there are major flaws in this argument. One such flaw is the assertion that fossils exist in social history. Arguably, even if social fossils do exist, this category must be further refined because, as in the cases of Israel and Mongolia, fossilised civilisations never were really fossilised at all. In fact, they are very much vibrant and alive today, albeit perhaps in an existence or shape that likely would not have been foreseen a century ago.

Furthermore, peripheral civilisations have existed and do exist. Toynbee, in my opinion, suffered from a certain intellectual constriction, a form of the Procrustean Bed, in his thinking. Thus, he spent years attacking the Zionist movement and misdescribing or mischaracterising Jewish society in the

Twentieth century. Why? Fossils cannot come alive, and so resurgent political Zionism should not have been possible, according to his theories. But even fossils can be uncovered that have live DNA in them, so does DNA ever die? My theory is that Mongolia, Israel, Korea, and Japan are all, to a major extent, peripheral societies in Asia. They are not part of a central civilisation but they draw from central civilisations on the interstitial areas in which they reside, and, thus, they constitute vital civilisations of their own.

The land of Mongolia was absorbed by China in the past and more recently dominated by Russia for long periods, including during the entire Soviet era. Mongolia also has ruled China. But, that did not mean that Mongolia as a civilisation was ever defunct. Rather, it has existed as a "Marginal Man" in society, a "stranger", a land, and a people that constituted a living palimpsest. It consisted of a people that invaded and occupied much of the world and famously respected and learned from others. It has been a geographical and social entity on the periphery. In all these roles Mongols have absorbed much that is perceptive from other cultures, incorporating many and conflicting worldviews of others. So, too, the Jewish people and their national homeland today, Israel.

Korea often has been dominated by China, the Mongols (who themselves ruled China for many years), and then by the Japanese (who also colonised Manchuria and invaded mainland China). However, it similarly has long been the cultural bridge between and among its neighbours and China. It has, like Mongolia, similarly incorporated the worldview of others while retaining, for most of history, an historic independence and separate identity. Finally, most triumphant of all, Japan, the great rising world power of East Asia in the Twentieth century, peripheral, perhaps to some extent a "fossil" since the Meiji Restoration, now an economic and cultural world centre like the other two, only even more dynamic. These Northeast Asian countries all have emerged, alive and mighty.

Geography has guided the destiny for many in Northeast Asia and in Southwest Asia. Today, Mongolia, an independent state, rests on the periphery, on the crossroads of a powerful Eurasia, and it provides a venue for some of the world's most intractable issues to be resolved. Mongolia, which was exposed to so many cultures during its long sojourn from its own homeland through much of the Asian and European continents and while on its home territory as well, now is able to help resolve conflicts across East Asia because of this unique history. Its near neighbour South Korea is more powerful economically than most countries in the world, and it recently has performed more effectively in fighting the COVID-19 pandemic than the US and Europe.

Similarly, the Jewish people have moved from tribal brotherhood to universal "otherhood", and back again, as Benjamin Nelson[56] has written. In ancient days they were creative in small Judea because their land was peripheral to other great civilisations, especially the Mesopotamians (from whence the patriarch Abraham migrated) and the Egyptians (where the Jews were slaves for centuries). They were occupied by the Assyrians, Babylonians, Greeks, Romans, Arabs, British, and many others. This marginality, this peripherality, enabled a small nation to write the Bible and generate the moral law which formed a basis upon which Western Civilisation rose. After their expulsion by the Romans from their homeland, the Jews wandered the face of the Earth, becoming strangers everywhere. This experience of two thousand years led to great horrors, especially the Spanish Inquisition, the pogroms of Eastern Europe, and then the Holocaust, but it also generated a people who understood how others saw the world. Finally, with the creation of a reborn state of Israel in their ancestral land, the Jews have become a lively, intellectually vigorous, fighting nation once again.

Geographically peripheral, socially marginal, cosmopolitan, world travellers, the Mongols and the Jews were exposed to a host of worldviews, *weltanschauungen*, and as a result today the two represent the triumph of the outsider, the universal others, revivified "fossils" which are running their own countries successfully. South Korea and Japan join their ranks, perhaps the most powerful peripheral civilisations in the world today. None of the four ever really died. Thus, it is possible to conclude that: first, sociological theory is closely related to civilisational analysis and second, Toynbee needs to be seriously updated.

Notes

1 Christian eschatology posits a unilinear history, although there are many schools of thought about the goal and the nature of the outcome. In general, Christian futurism anticipates a rapture, an Antichrist, a great tribulation, and a second coming of Christ. There are many texts on the subject. See, for example, David Fergusson, "Eschatology", in *The Cambridge Companion to Christian Doctrine,* Colin E. Gunton (ed.), Cambridge University Press, Cambridge, UK, 1997, pp. 226–244.
2 For those projections that end sad, in mass destruction, the best approach is via the World Future Society. See https://www.worldfuture.org/ (accessed October 28, 2020).
3 Francis Fukuyama, *The End of History and the Last Man.* Free Press, New York, 1992.
4 Ibn Khaldun, *The Muqaddimah, An Introduction To History*, translated by Franz Rosenthal, Princeton University Press, Princeton, NJ, 1969.
5 See Oswald Spengler, *The Decline of the West* (Vol. 1, "Form and Actuality"; Vol. 2, "Perspectives of World History"), Alfred A. Knopf, New York, 1926 and 1928. Also, for the most accessible abridgment of Arnold Toynbee's work, *A Study of History,* see D.C. Somervell, *A Study of History: Abridgement of Vols I-VI*, with a preface by Toynbee, Oxford University Press, Oxford, UK, 1946.
6 For a review of Hegel's view of the movement of the dialectic, see https://plato.stanford.edu/entries/hegel-dialectics/ (accessed October 28, 2020).
7 https://www.marxists.org/reference/archive/hegel/works/hi/history3.htm (accessed October 15, 2020).
8 https://www.marxists.org/archive/marx/works/1845/theses/theses.htm (accessed October 15, 2020).

9 Karl Marx and Frederik Engels, *Selected Works*, International Publishers, New York, 1970, p. 30. Thus, Marx stated that he turned his teacher on his head. The dialectic exists but to Marx, it was based on materialism, not idealism. For Hegel it was the idea moving through history; for Marx, it was material factors, such as control of production.
10 See, for example, Vladimir Lenin, *State and Revolution: The Economic Basis for the Withering Away of the State*, 2017, at https://www.marxists.org/archive/lenin/works/1917/staterev/ch05.htm.
11 Marquis de Condorcet, *Sketch for a Historical Picture of the Progress of the Human Mind* [French: *Esquisse d'un tableau historique des progrès de l'esprit humain*], 1794. For an English version, see Online Library of Liberty, at https://oll.libertyfund.org/titles/condorcet-outlines-of-an-historical-view-of-the-progress-of-the-human-mind.
12 Wilhelm Dilthey, *Pattern and Meaning in History: Thoughts on History and Society*, Harper and Row Publishers, New York, 1962.
13 Stanford M. Lyman and Marvin B. Scott, *A Sociology of the Absurd*, Appleton-Century-Crofts, New York, 1970.
14 Samuel Huntington, *The Clash of Civilizations and the Remaking of World Order*, Touchstone, New York, 1997, p. 40.
15 Ibid., pp. 40–44.
16 Ibid., p. 41.
17 Ibid., p. 41.
18 Ibid., p. 41.
19 Ibid., p. 41.
20 Ibid., p. 41.
21 Ibid., p. 302.
22 Toynbee, *A Study of History*, pp. 34–35; 566.
23 Ibid., p. 164.
24 Toynbee, see insert at p. 566.
25 Ibid., p. 169.
26 Ibid., p. 170.
27 Ibid., pp. 170–171.
28 Ibid., p. 8.
29 Ibid., pp. 22–23.
30 Matthew Melko and Leighton Scott, *The Boundaries of Civilizations in Space and Time*, University Press of America, Lanham, Maryland, 1987, pp. 291–292.
31 Ibid., p. 292.
32 http://worldpopulationreview.com/countries/countries-by-gdp/ (accessed April 4, 2020).
33 https://en.wikipedia.org/wiki/List_of_countries_by_GDP_(PPP)_per_capita (accessed April 4, 2020).
34 Huntington, p. 43.
35 Wei Ruan, "Civilization and Culture," *Globality Studies Journal: Global History, Society, Civilization*, (24), May 28, 2011, at https://gsj.stonybrook.edu/wp-content/uploads/2011/05/0024Wei.pdf (accessed April 4, 2020).
36 For a review of Wallerstein's views, see Immanuel Wallerstein, *The Modern World-System: Capitalist Agriculture and the Origins of the European World-Economy in the Sixteenth Century*, Academic Press, New York, 1974; Immanuel Wallerstein, *The Modern World-System II: Mercantilism and the Consolidation of the European World-Economy, 1600–1750*, Academic Press, New York, 1980; Immanuel Wallerstein, *The Modern World-System III: The Second Era of Great Expansion of the Capitalist World-Economy, 1730-1840*, Academic Press, New York, 1989.

37 Kurt Lewin, *Resolving Social Conflicts,* Harper and Row, New York, 1948, p. 73.
38 Ibid., pp. 195–197.
39 Max Weber, *Ancient Judaism,* The Free Press, New York, 1967, pp. 21–22.
40 Max Weber, *The Sociology of Religion,* Beacon Press, Boston, 1964, p. 108.
41 Perry Anderson, "Components of the National Culture," *New Left Review,* 1 (50), July–August 1968, at https://newleftreview.org/issues/I50/articles/perry-anderson-components-of-the-national-culture.
42 William Edward Burghardt Du Bois, "Strivings of the Negro People," *The Atlantic,* August 1897, at https://www.theatlantic.com/magazine/archive/1897/08/strivings-of-the-negro-people/305446/ (accessed April 4, 2020).
43 Robert E. Park, "Cultural Conflict and the Marginal Man," in Talcott Parsons, Edward Shils, Kaspar Naegele and Jesse R. Pitts (eds), *Theories of Society: Foundations of Modern Sociological Theory,* The Free Press, New York, 1965, p. 944.
44 Ibid., p. 945.
45 Ibid., p. 946.
46 Toynbee, *A Study of History,* p. 361.
47 Ibid., p. 269.
48 Ibid., p. 269.
49 Edwin O. Reischauer and John K. Fairbank, *East Asia: The Great Tradition,* Houghton Mifflin Company, Boston, 1960, pp. 395–396.
50 Ibid., p. 397.
51 Ibid., p. 399.
52 Wm. Theodore de Bary, Donald Keene, and Ryusaku Tsunoda (eds), *Sources of Japanese Tradition,* Columbia University Press, New York, 1960, p. 3.
53 Ibid., p. 4.
54 Reischauer and Fairbank, *East Asia: The Great Tradition,* p. 450.
55 Ibid., p. 451.
56 Benjamin Nelson, *The Idea of Usury: From Tribal Brotherhood to Universal Otherhood,* Princeton University Press, Princeton, NJ, 1949; 2nd edition, University of Chicago Press, Chicago, Il, 1969.

Index

1956 Declaration 55; "territorial" article of the 55
1972 Anti-Ballistic Missile (ABM) treaty 181
1993 Treaty on Friendly Relations and Cooperation 60
1994 Foreign Policy Concept 36
1994 National Security Concept 36
2005 Joint Statement on Six Party Talks 154
2010 National Security Concept 37
2011 Foreign Policy Concept 37
2011 Fukushima crisis 143, 157
2014 East Asia Summit in Myanmar 106
2014 Sunflower Movement 32
2015 National Intelligence Strategy (NIS) 17, 18
2017 National Intelligence Strategy (NIS) 10–18, 147; economic 13; goals of 16; military and security 13; pillars of 11; Advance American Influence 12; Preserve Peace Through Strength 11; Promote American Prosperity 11; Protect the Homeland 11; political 13; priority actions in the Indo-Pacific 13
2017 Treaty on Prohibition of Nuclear Weapons 171
2018 Singapore summit 78, 151
2018 Winter Olympics on the Korean Peninsula 188
2019 international conference in Ulaanbaatar, Mongolia 2; "Challenges Confronting Asia Today: Nuclear Proliferation, Environment, Economic, Civilisational" 2
2019 National Intelligence Strategy (NIS) 14, 18; National Intelligence Priorities Framework 12
2019 Vietnam Summit 19, 150
2020 Brookings study on Trump policy 15

Abductions issue 151, 153
Abe and Ebe 152
Abe Doctrine 96
Abe Shinzo Japanese Prime Minister 31, 55–6, 85–6, 88, 91, 94–6, 98–9, 106, 143, 146, 152–3, 157; defence policies 99; visit to; Mongolia 143, 152; Russia 55
ACSA 106
Act East Policy (AEP) 17, 106–7, 110, 112, 118
Action for Korea United 193
Activism 76, 103, 112; Chinese 112; diplomatic 103; regional 76
Adventurism 33, 106, 112, 116; Chinese 106; economic 116; ill-effects of 116; North Korean 33; soaring 112
Aegis Ashore system 186
Afghanistan 38, 90, 207; US operations in 90
Africa 50, 97, 165, 168, 172, 182, 184
Age of Reason 258
Aggression 13–4, 34, 103; Japanese 34
Agreement on cooperation in environmental protection 222
Agreement on cooperation in joint development of forest resources 221
Agreement on joint protection of forests from fires 221
Agreement on rational use and

protection of transboundary waters 221
Agreement(s) 5, 13, 15, 23, 32, 38, 40, 50, 53, 55, 57, 63, 77–80, 83, 87, 94, 108–9, 111, 114–6, 122, 144, 148–50, 153, 168–71, 178, 185, 202, 205–6, 210, 221–3, 226, 229, 234, 243, 252; aid 83; bilateral 5, 32, 108–9, 111, 122, 168, 171; trade 13; civil nuclear 109, 115; corporate 50; interagency 50; intergovernmental 50, 206, 229; military-to-military 150; Mongolian 144; multilateral 5, 221, 234; mutual 111; strategic partnership 38
Agriculture 58, 83, 108, 111, 117–8, 224, 268
Air pollution 239
Alignment 103–4, 120; multi- 104; non- 103–4, 120; pointed 104
Alliance-building 142
Alliances and partnerships 3–4, 12–4, 18–9, 23, 30–31, 38–9, 50, 52–5, 59–60, 65, 78–9, 82, 85–8, 90–96, 99–100, 103–6, 109–16, 118, 120–21, 123–24, 141–2, 144, 148–54, 156, 168, 178–80, 183, 187, 191–4, 200, 204–7, 210, 223, 225, 241–2; bilateral 85, 112, 153, 183, 187; treaties 183; Chinese-led quasi- 39; commitments 178, 193; comprehensive 50; constructive 156; diplomatic 52; economic 115; exclusive 168; formal 92; India and Japan 106; international 223; Japan and US 4, 86, 88, 91, 96, 99, 100; military-political 54–5; US-led 30; Mongolian and US 144; political 52, 104, 115; political-military 191; regional 30, 65; security 105, 115; Soviet-Mongolian 179; stability 90; strategic 23, 38, 50, 59–60, 93–5, 99, 104, 110–11, 114–6, 123–4, 149, 151–3, 205–7, 223; bilateral 94, 205; comprehensive 104, 114, 206; global 104, 120; structure 19; triangular 142; trilateral 19, 148, 154; values-driven 144; Western 141
Ally(ies) 9, 11, 13, 15–8, 24–5, 30, 42, 59, 62, 93, 97, 107, 122, 141, 144, 147, 149–50, 166, 179–80, 182, 186–8, 194, 205; Chinese 166; Kurdish 42; Northeast Asian 188; relationships 24; strategic 107; traditional 122

Altai *argali* 228
Altai, Republic of 229
Altangerel, Bulgaa 145
Altankhuyag, Mongolian Prime Minister 94, 152; visit to Japan 152
"America First" policy 3, 12, 15, 18, 25
American Navy 181
American(s) 142, 174, 210, 266; administrations 15; allies and partners 11, 16; economy 11, 90; exports 13; foreign policy 156; interest 17; interests 12; military deployment in the Indo-Pacific 24; military forces 34; military power, retreat of 89; national interests 85; national power 11; national security 9, 18–9; "nuclear umbrella" 167; people 9–12; policy 38, 186–7; policymaking 17; power 11, 15, 17; regional leadership 33; security and prosperity 17; threat to 17; security establishment 14; strategy 17; troops stationed in South Korea 59; way of life 10–11
Amur Green Belt 230
Anderson, Perry 265; Components of the National Culture 265
Animals and plants 222, 232; protection, research, and reproduction of 222
Animosity 186
Antarctica 170, 172
Antarctic Treaty, 1961, 170
Antelope 232
Anti-Ballistic Missile Treaty (ABM) 171, 181
Anti-China coalition 30
Anti-money laundering 151
Antipathy 37
Appeasement 142
"Arc of Freedom and Prosperity" policy 87–8, 96
Arctic 48
Arctic Council 58
Argali 228–9, 231
Armament 86
Arms 51, 162, 171; sales 186
Arms control 60, 66, 142, 162, 167, 169, 171–3; measures 167; nuclear 162, 169, 172; policies 142; weak systems 171
Arms race 164, 166–7, 170, 172–3, 178, 182–3, 186, 191–2, 194; cycle 172
ASEAN and Japan 87
ASEAN and Russia 55

Index 275

ASEAN Defense Minister's Meeting-Plus (ADMM+) 91
ASEAN plus three 85, 91
ASEAN Regional Forum (ARF) 79, 85, 91
ASEAN summit in Singapore in 2002, 87
ASEM 87
Asia 1–6, 9, 14–9, 21–2, 25, 30–33, 36, 38, 42, 47–50, 53–4, 56, 58, 61–5, 76–7, 79–82, 85–100, 103, 105–7, 110–13, 117, 120–23, 142–3, 148–9, 151, 153–4, 156–7, 162, 165–9, 172–3, 178–80, 183–8, 190–92, 194, 199–201, 203, 205–6, 208–11, 219, 221, 223, 231, 237–9, 241–2, 252, 262, 267–9; economic order in 100; foreign policy in 86, 88; Japanese 86, 88; military forces in 165; peripheral societies in 269; regional politics of 1; trilateralism in 142; US; influence in 33; involvement in 87; strategic interest in 106
Asia EDGE (Enhancing Development and Growth through Energy) 18; Asian: economy 76; leadership 165; nuclear countries 165; policy 87, 97, 107, 115, 117; security 92, 157, 187
Asian countries 2, 17, 31–2, 98, 106, 269
Asian Development Bank (ADB) 79, 100
Asian Infrastructure Investment Bank (AIIB) 15, 65, 92, 100
Asian NATO 30
Asian Network for Prevention of Illegal Transboundary Movement of Hazardous Wastes 239
Asian Pivot 156
Asian Political History Association (APHA) 173
Asia-Pacific affairs 65
Asia-Pacific Economic Cooperation (APEC) 9, 85, 87, 91, 200; CEO Summit 9
Asia-Pacific Leadership Network for Nuclear Non-Proliferation and Disarmament (APLN) 186
Asia-Pacific Region 4, 9, 14, 17, 21, 25, 47–9, 54, 61, 65, 77, 79–80, 85–6, 88–92, 95–9, 111, 143, 148, 186, 199, 203, 237, 241, 252; Chinese influence over 99; economic cooperation 49; development of 65; Japan's regional policy towards 89; power vacuum in 89; regional architecture for 86; regionalism in 85–6, 91–92; security architecture in 111; security of 96; policy in 89; US commitment in 86
Aso Taro, Minister of Foreign Affairs (MOFA) 87–8, 95–6; policy 96
Assistance: donor 145; economic 90, 193–4; international 193; educational 152; Mongolian 143, 152; policies 145; priorities 148
Association of Southeast Asian Nations (ASEAN) 18, 23, 55, 79, 85–9, 91–2, 96, 105–6, 121; Singapore summit, 2002, 87
Atal Bihari Vajpayee Centre of Excellence on Information, Communication and Technology (ABVCE-ICT) 109
"Atmanirbhar Barat" 117
Atomic development 66
Atomic energy 57
Atrocity 39
Australia 4, 13, 16–7, 19, 24, 49, 79, 87–8, 96, 98, 105, 113–4, 116, 119–20, 183, 231; Chinese economic retaliation in 113
Australia-Japan-India (AJI) trilateral groupings 119
Australian National University 185
Autonomy 103, 207
Ayres, Alyssa 16

Bae, Lee Sok 58
Bagby, Phillip 263
Baikal-Khubsugul region 222
Baikal State University in Irkutsk 222
Baker, James, US Secretary of State 38, 114; visit to Mongolian 114
Balancing power 105
Ballistic missiles: air-launched 182; attacks 186; intercontinental 188; solid-propellant submarine-launched 188
Bangladesh 18, 108, 191
Banking 145
Banko Delta Asia affair 188
Barun-Torey Lake 227
Basel Convention 239, 243, 251
Bastion missile systems 57
Battulga, Khaltmaa, President of Mongolia 23, 37, 60–61, 111–2, 116, 147–9, 153, 157; election of 157; visit to; India 111–2, 116; US 149

276 *Index*

Belarus 182
Belt and Road Forum for International Cooperation 81
Belt and Road Initiative (BRI) 15, 31–2, 51, 53, 65, 80, 92, 98–9, 143, 149, 206–7
Bhutan 112
Biden, US President 55; comprehensive foreign policy 25
Biegun, Stephen, Deputy Secretary of State 20–21; Bilateral; agreements 5, 32, 108–9, 111, 122, 168, 171; conflicts 180; transactions 86; contacts 148; transactions 86; cooperation 53, 55–7, 93, 223, 228, 234; international 54; cultural 86; economic; cooperation 57–8; relations 22, 156; dialogue 223; free trade agreement 40; infrastructure projects 95; negotiations 83; partnership 112, 153; sanctions 187–8; security 23; strategic; partnership 94, 205; relations 116; synergy 106, 108; talks 182; tension 31, 38; trade 13, 30, 56, 58, 80, 95, 105, 109, 116–7, 202
Bilateral alliance 85, 183, 187; Cold War-era 187; relations 187; treaties 183
Bilateral relations 22–3, 25, 50, 55, 57, 59–62, 91, 93–4, 115, 144–5, 148–53, 157, 188; Japan and Mongolia 150, 153; Mongolia and US 148; security 115; strategic 116
Bilateral ties 103–4, 107–8, 111, 114, 116, 120–21, 123, 205; India and Mongolia 104, 111
Biodiversity 5, 224, 237, 243, 249–50
Biological diversity 230
Biosphere Programme and in the UNESCO World Heritage List 232
Biotechnology 219; development of 219
Blind spots 190
Blue Banner Foundation 2, 185, 192–4; initiatives 192
Bogd Khaan 34, 41; monarchy 34
Bolshevik Russia 34
Bolton, John, National Security adviser 20
Border: checkpoints 224; China and India 33; China and Mongolia 42, 179; China and Russia 230; Chinese 38; common 62, 179, 222; conflict 179; disputed 103; maritime 33; Mongolia and Russia 229; nations 144; neighbours 143, 146, 190; problems 187, 191; security 111, 115; sovereignty of 11
Brazil 50
Brazil, Russia, India, China and South Africa (BRICS) 50
Bridge-building 179
Britain 53, 165–6, 193, 265
Brown, Lester R., 252; PLAN B 3.0 252
Brzezinski, Zbigniew 141
Buddhism 41, 155, 207, 261, 268
Buddhist: connection 108; legacy 104; philosophies 107
Buffer state 114, 120, 204
Buryatia, Republic of 222, 226
Bush, George W., US President 10, 15, 25, 85, 142, 156; visit to Ulaanbaatar 156

Cambodia 165, 261
Canada 114
Capability(ies) 11, 13, 20, 30, 34, 40, 42, 90, 96, 105, 165, 167, 170, 172, 174, 181, 183, 188; ballistic missile 20; economic 40; first-strike 188; military 40, 96, 170; missile 20, 30, 34; nuclear 20, 105, 183, 188; pursuance of 105; nuclear second-strike 30; offensive 181; power projection 34; technological 40
Capacity building 97, 115, 120, 239, 241–2; measures 115; programmes 120
Carafano, James 19, 23
Caribbean 172, 184
Carter, Jimmy, US President 141
Caucasus 88
Center for American Progress 150
Central Asia 17, 21, 31, 38, 87–8, 106–7, 112–3, 172, 184; Chinese links with 31; Japan's policy 87; US foreign policy towards 87–8
Central Asian states 51, 92, 208
Central power 264
Central Russia 48
Chemical dumping 239
ChemSafety 243
Cheon, Dr. Seongwhun 185
Chikura Shobo 89
Chile and Japan 82; Economic Partnership Agreement 82
China, People's Republic of (PRC) 1–5, 10, 13–9, 21–2, 24–5, 30–42, 47–53, 56, 61–66, 76–7, 79–83, 85–6, 88–93,

Index 277

95–100, 103, 106–7, 110–24, 143–6, 148–51, 153–6, 162, 165–73, 179, 181–2, 184, 186–9, 193–4, 199–211, 219, 221–5, 228–31, 233, 239, 241–2, 248–9, 252, 256, 264, 266–9; ability to deter nuclear attacks 182; apprehensions 113; assertiveness 10; attitude towards territorial disputes 92; Beiyang government 34; border 38; capabilities 40; compliance assurance 242; criticism of 17; danger to Mongolia 40; economic clout in Mongolia 118; economic needs 33; environmental enforcement 242; exports to Russian Federation 51; fastrising 162; foreign policy 3, 30, 37; implications for Mongolia 3, 30; in Northeast Asia 3, 30; objectives of 30–33; global trade 51; growing power 37; interests and strategies 76; internal affairs 33; investments 17; language policy 119; Mongolia's economic dependence on 119, 206; northern border 38; nuclear second-strike capability 30; nuclear weapons 182; political discontent in 39; power and intentions 30; power grabbing stance 99; reassertion 32; recognise of 50; regional; "activism" 76; economic leadership 31; security architecture and 92; reunification of 32; revisionist 112, 123; rise of 4, 19, 25, 86, 88, 92, 99, 106–7, 112, 116–7, 123, 156; as a revisionist power 143; economic 25, 156; effects of 4, 99; India's concerns 106–7; military 25; revisionist 112, 123; strategy 32; territorial claims 32; trade strategies 17; US foreign policy towards 88; Xi's regime 2, 32–3
China and India: border 33; discontent 123; post-Galwan era 119; standoff 103
China and Japan 62, 92, 96, 98, 99–100, 267; competition 99; conflict 96; cultural debt 267; First Japan-China Forum on Third Country Business Cooperation 98; joint business 98; relations 92, 100; territorial disputes 62
China and Korea 268
China and Mongolia 3, 34, 37, 40, 42, 62, 77, 80, 179, 207, 223–4, 228, 230–31, 233; Agreement on cooperation in environmental protection 222; border 42, 179; economic influence 40; foreign direct investment (FDI) 40; Memorandum of cooperation in the field of environmental protection 223; relations 34, 144
China and North Korea 31, 90
China and Russia 1–4, 10, 18, 24, 35–6, 38, 42, 49–53, 61, 63–4, 80, 88, 93, 95–6, 107, 113–5, 117, 120, 143–5, 148–51, 153–7, 168, 186–7, 189, 194, 204, 206–7, 209–11, 221, 224, 227–8, 230–31; Agreement on joint protection of forests from fires 221; Agreement on rational use and protection of transboundary waters 221; border of 230; comprehensive partnership 50; cooperation 52, 149, 156, 211, 221, 230; environmental technology 224; military-technical and military spheres 52; software development 52; environmental relations 221; exports and imports 51; intentions 50; joint manoeuvres and exchanges 52; network of cross-border nature reserves 230; partnership 52; pledge 189; political rapprochement 144; relations 36, 49–51, 93, 228; diplomatic 49; economic 224; trade 224; rivalry 3; tension 51; ties, economic 227; trade 51, 95; transit traffic 61, 144
China and South Asian countries relations 98
China and Soviet Union 36, 179; border conflict 179; confrontation 179; disputes 179; split 36
China AND Taiwan economic connections 32
China and US 15–7, 47, 76, 100, 111, 120, 123, 149, 162, 200, 210–11, 241; confrontation 111; friction 15; relations 17; rising hostilities 111; rivalry 120, 200, 210; strategic competitiveness 111; trade; dispute 149; relations 99; war 76
China and USSR 49
China dream 32
China, Japan, and Korea cooperation 79
China, Japan and ROK trilateral summits 65
China-Mongolia-Russia Economic

278 *Index*

Corridor (CMREC) 3, 40, 77, 80–81, 207, 223–4
China-Russia 107, 146, 155; relations 107
China-Russia-Mongolia 157, 206, 233; trilateralism 155; trilateral relationship 146, 153
China's Ministry of Ecology and Environment (MEE) 241
China's Supreme People's Procuratorate 249
China-Taiwan 32, 85; economic integration 32
China threat 15
Chinese: activism 112; adventurism 106; agenda 17; allegation 33; concerns 113; direct investment 41; economic; growth 93; retaliation in Australia 113; retaliation in South Korea 113; economy 116–7, 119; dependency on 116, 119; encroachment 42; exports and imports 51; foreign policy in Northeast Asia 3; geopolitical aspirations 17; government 30, 33, 39, 97, 230; influence over Mongolia 38; integration 51; invasion 36; investment 32, 40, 152; in infrastructure 32; irredentism 32; leadership 31, 41; objectives of 31; links with Central Asia 31; media 34; military expansion 113; objectives 30, 37; paranoia 33; policy(ies) 25, 39, 88, 96; political demands 41; power revisionist 111; preferences 31; security assurances 193; specially protected natural areas (SPNA) 230; strategic sensibilities 34; strategy 92
Chinese Civil War 89
Chinese Communist Party (CCP) 32–3, 35, 38–9, 41
Chinese Ministry of Defence, sanctions on 52
Chinese SPNAs 230
Chlorofluorocarbon (CFC) 242
Christianity 255, 262
Christians 255–6, 261, 264
Christian trinity 155
CITES/ICCWC 251
Civilisation(s) 2, 5, 107, 162–5, 173, 237–8, 242, 249, 251–2, 255, 258–70; abortive 263
ancient 255, 263, 268; arrested 260, 263; central 264–6, 269; Chinese 266, 268; cyclical theory of 255, 263; definition of 263; developed 260–61, 263, 268; cyclical pattern for 268; East Asian 266–7; fossilised 268; history of 258; Japanese 266–7; life trajectories of 268; nature of 259; patterns of 258; rise and fall of 259; Russian 266; study of 5, 255, 259, 263, 268; Western 263, 270
Civilisations, peripheral 263, 268, 270
Civil nuclear agreement 109, 115
Civil nuclear pact 106
Civil society 5, 79, 141, 178, 192
Civil society dialogue 192; track 2, 192
Civil society organisations 192
Civil War 89
Climate change 124, 178, 223, 230, 256; problems of 223
Clinton, William (Bill), US President 89–90, 172
Coalition governments, persistence of 104
Coalition(s) 30, 38, 104, 148, 168, 227; allied 38; American-led 38; ecological 227
Coal-powered thermal power stations 93
Coercion 10, 14, 41, 147; economic 41
Cold War 1–3, 10, 14, 16, 22, 25, 36–7, 42, 88–91, 93, 103–4, 113–4, 141, 144, 151, 163, 178–80, 183–7, 189, 192, 194, 200–201, 203, 205; end of 3, 25, 36, 89, 103, 113, 144, 178, 185, 201; lessons of 179, 189; post 104; proxy wars 163
Communication(s) 21, 51, 60, 78, 117–8, 121, 157, 163, 209–10, 222; external 117; Communism 89, 143, 257–8; fall of 143
Communist ideology 36
Community of Democracies 148
Competition 4–5, 10–11, 14, 16, 23, 42, 53, 99–100, 107, 115, 200; fair 23; geopolitical 11, 14, 16; global 10; China and Japan 99; military 99; resource 5; strategic 4, 11
Complete, Verifiable and Irreversible Dismantlement (CVID) 153, 187
Compliance assurance 242
Comprehensive Nuclear Test Ban Treaty (CTBT), 1996, 172
Comprehensive Partnership agreement 23
Comprehensive Strategic Partnership Treaty of 2019, 60

Comte, Auguste 258
Confidence-building 22, 55, 61, 183, 187, 189–90
Confidence-Building Measure (CBM) 55, 61, 187, 190; military 55
Conflict(s) 1, 5, 12, 25, 62, 86, 90, 96, 98, 107, 142, 163, 171–2, 179–80, 192, 200, 209–11, 220, 226, 238, 243, 250–51, 258, 266, 269; armed 62, 192; bilateral 180; border 179; China and Japan 96; civilisational 1; DPRK and ROK 107; environmental 226; ideological 1; India and Pakistan 142, 172; internal 220; international 220; nuclear 163; prevention 180; regional 86, 90, 180; zones 90
Confrontation 15, 47, 54, 63, 111, 141, 179; Sino-Soviet 179
Congressional Research Services 148
Connectivity(ies) 2, 18, 51, 77, 80, 95, 97, 106–7, 111, 117–8, 124, 148, 151, 204, 206, 207, 224; air 111, 117, 124; development 118; digital 18; energy 80; integrated 224; Japan and Mongolia 95; lack of 117; options 107
Contacts 57, 64, 90, 94, 105, 148, 208, 222; bilateral 148; humanitarian 94; military-to-military 90; people-to-people 94, 105; trilateral 148
Containment 17, 88, 142; limited 142
Continental Europe 265
Cooperation 2–5, 9, 13–4, 16–7, 19, 22–3, 33, 36–8, 47, 49–50, 52–62, 64–6, 77–89, 91–5, 97–9, 104–5, 108–13, 115–6, 118, 120–22, 141, 143–9, 152–7, 180, 186–7, 189, 192, 200, 202, 206, 208, 211, 219–26, 228–30, 232–4, 237, 239, 241, 249, 252; bilateral 53, 55–7, 93, 223, 228, 234; China and Russia 149, 156, 211, 221, 230; ecology and environmental protection 221; cultural 86–7; bilateral 57, 58; deeper 152; defence 14; defense 9; diplomatic 121; ecological 228; economic 9, 16, 49, 54, 57–8, 61–2, 65, 78, 82, 86, 89, 94–5, 98, 109, 111, 141, 144, 153–4, 187, 211, 224, 233; energy 61, 78, 81, 144; environmental 220, 224–5, 228, 232, 239, 252; environmental technology 224; bilateral 54; international 49; multilateral 54; humanitarian 65; informal 145; innovative 52; intelligence 14; international 49, 54,
85, 91, 95, 98, 189, 221, 223, 241; interregional 50; investment 56, 58; law enforcement 14; military 37, 113, 120, 145, 202, 206; military-technical 57; Mongolia and Russia 59; multilateral 49, 147, 187, 220–21, 223–4; multi-level 62; mutually beneficial 49, 54, 180, 200; cooperative conditions for 2; peace 121; policy of 22; political 86, 141; possibilities of 49; quadrilateral 19; regional 13, 22, 49, 82–3, 91, 95, 99, 186, 221; resource 2; ROK-DPRK-Russia 59; Russia, China, and Mongolia 5, 62, 219; Russia and South Korea 59; scientific 52; trilateral 148; security 9, 14, 33, 37–8, 94, 97, 116, 121, 146, 192; strategic 157; technical 52; transportation 80, 144; triangular 155; trilateral 157
Corruption 37, 241, 243, 249
Council of the International Maritime Organization 108
Council on Foreign Relations 16; *Asia Unbound* 16
Counterintelligence 13
Counter-proliferation 12
Counterterrorism 12
COVID-19 crisis 20, 24, 51–2, 76, 99, 106, 114, 116–7, 151, 178, 200, 206, 269; fight against 52; ramifications of 116; spread of 52
Crimea 42, 205
Crime(s) 1, 5, 37, 237–9, 241–3, 246–52; environmental 1, 5, 237–9, 241–3, 246–52; organised 5, 238–9, 250–51; pollution and waste 249; transboundary 5, 238; transnational 5, 238
Criminal gangs 238
Criminal groups 5, 237, 247, 250
Criminality 237
Criminal justice systems 237, 246
Criminal markets 239, 243
Criminal networks 237–8, 241, 249–52; environmental 252; international 237–8
Cross-border: infrastructure 31, 61; zone 228
Cross-Strait Agreement on Trade in Services 32
Cross-Strait economic interdependence 32
Cruise missiles 171–2, 181, 186; nuclear-powered 181

280   Index

Cuban Missile Crisis of 1962, 164
Cultural: bilateral 86; bridge 269; connections 105; cooperation 86–7; debt 267; engagement 122; exchange 87, 108, 152; genocide 119; heritage 104; interaction 112; links 107, 114; security 119; similarity 267; ties 108
Culture(s) 57–60, 65, 96, 107–8, 119, 143, 154, 163, 168, 219, 224, 233, 259, 262–9; ecological 224; environmental 219; herdsman 168; indigenous 168; Japanese 266–7; Korean 266; nomadic 154, 168; refractory 266
Cyber: malicious activities 12; security 111, 115, 151; threat 12
Cybersecurity Partnership 18

Dalai Lama 41, 112, 117, 207
Dalainor biosphere reserve 231
Dalai Nor-Lake 228
Dams 225–7
Damdin Tsogtbaatar 78, 148
Darkhan oil refining facility 95
Dauria eco-region 231
Dauria International Protected Area (DIPA) 227, 231–2
Daursky state natural biosphere reserve 231, 232
Davaasüren, Damdinsuren 150
Debt 40, 98, 117, 202, 267; cultural 267; external 40; trap 40
Defence 9, 11, 13–4, 16, 19, 30, 36, 52, 57, 60, 77, 86, 90, 94, 96, 98–9, 108, 111, 115, 119, 142, 150, 153–4, 166, 171, 182, 186, 200, 203, 206, 211; capability 13; cooperation 9, 14; dialogue 77; missile 11, 13, 19, 30, 171, 182, 186, 200, 203; needs 14; network 13, 30
Deforestation 219, 239, 249
DeLeon, Rudy 150
Demilitarised Zone (DMZ) 24, 166, 185; Korean 24, 185
Democracies 38, 88, 114, 145, 186; likeminded 186; regional 38
Democracy 3, 23, 38, 42, 88, 90, 93, 96, 114, 144–5, 152, 156–7, 168, 179, 256; Central Asian 114
liberal 90, 256; Mongolian 144, 156; multi-party 38; shared values of 114
Democratic: governance 192; links 119; trilateralism 4, 141, 143, 145–6, 153–7; trilateral policy 143; values 24, 38, 104, 110, 155, 180; shared 104, 110, 155
Democratic People's Republic of Korea (North Korea) (DPRK) 1–2, 19–22, 48, 57, 59, 62–6, 76–9, 81–3, 107, 121–3, 143, 145, 148, 151–2, 154, 156–7, 181, 188, 191–4; see also DPRK
Democratic Progress Party 32
Democratic trilateralism, Japanese interest in 157
Democratisation 93, 97, 99
Denuclearisation 2, 4, 10, 13–4, 19–20, 25, 62–4, 78, 120–21, 148, 154, 156, 188, 193–4, 201–2, 204; complete 62, 188; deal 20; dialogue 4; Korean 2, 10, 19, 154; negotiations 4, 121; North Korean 2, 19, 154; roadmap 4
Department for Environment, Food and Rural Affairs (DEFRA) 242
Department of State's Congressional Budget Justification for Foreign Operations 148
Desertification 219, 224, 226, 228, 230–31; conditions 230; problem of 230
Deterrence 19, 22, 163–6, 173, 178, 181, 186, 193–4; conceptual issues of 178; minimal 166; non-nuclear 193–4; policy 181
Deterrence theory 163–5, 173; nuclear 163, 165, 173
Developing countries 83, 114, 190, 237, 243
Development: connectivity 118; domestic 104; economic 2, 25, 31, 47–8, 57, 61, 77, 83–4, 89, 92–3, 97, 111, 153–4, 186, 189, 193, 199–200, 202, 220, 246; industrial 48, 56; infrastructure 40, 58, 97, 118, 123, 144, 192; issues 142, 192; legal 5, 237; mutually beneficial 54; natural resources 48; political 220; regional 80, 150; social 111, 246; socio-economic 48, 220; socioeconomic 47; strategies 80, 81; sustainable 12, 224, 238; technological 183
Development assistance 93
Development Bank of Mongolia 81, 95
Development Road Programme 80
Dialogue diplomacy 121
Dickson, John 193
Digital: economy 151; connectivity 18

Dilthey, Wilhelm 258
Diplomacy 12, 20, 22, 59, 78, 86, 88, 91, 96, 99, 107, 113–4, 120–21, 180, 190, 203, 208; "bromance" 20; dialogue 121; economic 86, 99; failed 20; Indian 107; Mongolian 114; multilateral 91, 190; multi-pillar framework of 114; preventive 180; small country 22, 208; soft 113; value 99; value-oriented 88, 96; "wolf warrior" 113, 120
Diplomatic: activism 103; attitudes 99; efforts 63, 106, 168; endeavours 88; exchanges 108, 113; leverage 33; missions 108; outlook 107; partnership 52; policy 123; pressure 166; process 62, 64; recognition 35; restoration of 53; Russia-South Korea 57; relations 49, 53, 57, 82, 208; techniques 114; ties 105, 108, 121–2, 152; visits 111
Direct foreign investment 49
Direct investment 34, 40–41, 95, 207; Chinese 41
Dirty bombs 182
Disarmament 60, 170, 173, 178, 180, 182–4, 192; nuclear 173, 178, 180, 182–3, 192
Disaster 22, 23, 97, 111, 157, 219, 226, 256; environmental 219, 256; management 22, 111; preparedness 23; relief operations 23
Disaster risk reduction 97
Diseases 105, 224; infectious 105, 224
Disparity 42, 48, 51; economic 51; natural resources 48
Disputed: border 103; islands 50, 55; South China Sea 112; territories 54, 56
Disputes 2, 13, 21, 32, 50, 59, 62, 84, 92, 145, 149, 169, 179–80, 186, 199–200, 209; DPRK and Japan 145; historical 21; island-based 92; maritime 13; peaceful resolution of 13; settlement 62; territorial 13, 21, 32, 50, 62, 84, 92, 179, 186, 200
Distrust 34, 181, 186
Disunity 42
Diversification 11, 56; industrial structure 56
Doklam plateau military stand-off 112
Domestic: construction projects 145; development 104; energy 79; factors 104; growth 104; transport infrastructure 144

Doomsday system 164
Double consciousness 255, 265
DPRK (North Korea) 1–2, 18–22, 48, 57, 59, 62–6, 76–9, 81–3, 107, 121–3, 143, 145, 148, 151–2, 154, 156–7, 181, 188, 191–4; ballistic missile programs, dismantlement of 151; *de facto* nuclear 194; economy 194; nuclear and ballistic rocket programme 156; threat to regional stability 122, 154; nuclear; issue 78; missile programme 62, 64, 121–2; status 64; tests 64; sanctions against 21, 65; self-reliance policy 79; threat 121; Trump policy 20; weapons of mass destruction 151; dismantlement of 151
DPRK and Japan 77, 122, 145; dispute 145
DPRK and Mongolia 82, 122; relations 82; ties 122
DPRK and ROK 19, 107, 123; conflict 107
DPRK and South Korea 62
DPRK and US 62, 63, 122, 193–4; "interim agreement" 63; talks 194
Drainage 226, 228
Bolor, Dr. G. BaasanhuuLkhaajav 154–5
Drones 181
Droughts 220
Drugs 11, 238, 242
Dual-use intermediate range-ballistic missiles 179
Du Bois, W.E.B., 255, 265
Dust storms 220, 230
Dutch disease 117
Dzeren 232

Early Warning System (EWS) 52
Earthquakes 220
East and Central Europe 88
East Asia 19, 21, 64–5, 77, 85–7, 90, 94, 96, 105–6, 111, 166, 185, 210, 237, 239, 269; division of 19; power balance in 96; security 87; stability in 111; tension in 185; transactions in 86
East Asian Community 77, 85, 87–8; Japanese concept of 77
East Asian Summit (EAS) 79, 91
East China Sea 33
Eastern Economic Forum (EEF) 49–50, 55, 57, 153
Eastern Europe 93, 270

282 *Index*

Eastern Kazakhstan 229
Eastern Siberia 54
East West Center 2019 Policy Studies 16
East-West Cold War 179
Ecological: balance 190, 223; coalition 227; consciousness 233; cooperation 228; corridors 230; culture 224; international coalition 227; security 225; traditions 233
Ecology 56, 60, 220–5, 228, 233–4
Economic: adventurism 116; agenda 60; transactions 86; architecture 3; arrangements 31; international 193; assistance 90, 193–4; international 193; benefit 31, 154; busts 118; bilateral 57–8; challenges 141, 143; coercion 41; cohesion 91; connections 32; consciousness 233; cooperation 9, 16, 49, 54, 57–8, 61–2, 65, 78, 82, 86, 89, 94–5, 98, 109, 111, 141, 144, 153–4, 187, 211, 224, 233; crisis 112; culture 233; dependence 36, 59, 119, 122, 143, 206; development 2, 25, 31, 47, 48, 57, 61, 77, 83–4, 89, 92–3, 97, 111, 153–4, 186, 189, 193, 199–200, 202, 220, 246; difficulties 77, 95; diplomacy 86; disparity 51; embargo 30; engagement 122–3, 203; expansion 105; fluctuations 13; Northeast Asian 3, 79; frameworks 33; freedom 23; gains 99; giants 169; growth 2, 10, 23, 82–3, 93, 95, 105–6, 117, 143, 153, 186, 207; inducements and penalties 17; influence 24, 35, 40, 60, 157, 205; integration 3, 21, 32, 76–7, 79, 82–4, 116, 118, 122, 147, 193, 200; global 49; interaction 62, 112, 117; interdependence 32, 77, 81; interests 50, 184, 202–3; investment 144; isolation 48, 189; reforms 104; issues 49, 146; leadership 31, 80; leverage 31, 33, 41; liberalisation 23, 104; liberal principles 24; links 155; management 22; opportunities 12, 193; partnership 3, 96, 151, 153; partnerships 115; policy 77, 104; power 42, 86; powerhouses 169; problems 228; projects 4, 65, 80, 224; Chinese-style 34; market-oriented 36; prosperity 91, 97; order 100; realities 90; recovery 86; reforms 34, 36, 83; regional; development 193; leadership 31; relations 11, 15, 22, 55, 57, 79, 94, 119, 145–6, 148, 156, 224; bilateral 145; imposition of 33; resource 5; retaliation 113; rivalries 141; sanctions 33, 92, 121; security 11, 77, 115, 190; self-interest 144; significance 107; socialist ideals 104; sovereignty 22; stabilisation programme 95; stability 95, 233; threats 219; ties 54, 60, 87, 149, 201, 205, 207, 227; transactions 86, 91; cultural 86; international 49; multilateral 86; transition 83; vitality 90
Economic corridor 3, 40, 61–2, 77, 80, 118, 144, 154, 207, 223–4
Economic Corridor zone 62
Economic development 2, 25, 31, 47–8, 61, 77, 83–4, 92–3, 97, 111, 153–4, 186, 189, 193, 199, 200, 202, 220, 246; China-funded 92
Economic growth 2, 10, 23, 82–3, 93, 95, 105–6, 117, 143, 153, 186, 207; Chinese 93; long-term 95; mid-term 95
Economic Partnership Agreement 82, 93, 95
Economic Partnership Agreements (EPA) 79, 241–2
Economic Research Institute of Northeast Asia (ERINA) 81
Economy 2–3, 5, 11–2, 24–5, 31, 40, 48–9, 58–60, 65, 76–8, 80, 82–3, 86, 88, 90–91, 95–6, 104, 111, 113, 116–9, 124, 142–3, 145, 151, 156, 166, 192–4, 205, 207, 220, 222, 224, 237–8, 243, 246, 249; American 11, 90; Asian 76; Chinese 116–7, 119; digital 151; DPRK's 194; free market 12; giant 80, 111; global 31, 111; green 124; market 2, 78, 83, 88, 192; mineral-based 143; Mongolian 40, 95, 113, 117–8, 151; national 220; Northeast Asian 76; regional 49; resilient 116; Russian 58; strong 11
Ecosystems 169, 221, 224–8, 230–2, 238–9, 242–3, 252; destruction of 169; loss of 239; transboundary 230
Ecotourism 223, 231
Education 39, 59–60, 65, 108, 221–3, 231, 233, 238, 249, 252; environmental 221, 223, 231, 233
Egiyn-Gol Hydroelectric Power Plant 225–6
Egypt 261, 264
Eight-Point Cooperation Plan 56

Index 283

Elbegdorj, Tsakhia, Mongolia's President 22, 39, 61, 77, 80, 94, 119, 122, 143–6, 152–3, 185, 208; lecture at Kim Il-Sung University 122; speech to the United Nations (UN) General Assembly 144; visited Mongolia 94; visited Pyongyang 122
Empire of Japan, collapse of 89
Endicott, John 185, 193
Energy 1–2, 6, 11, 18, 22, 32, 51, 56–7, 60–62, 65, 78, 79–84, 87, 105, 109–11, 115–18, 124, 143–4, 151–2, 154–5, 157, 167, 182, 201, 224–6; atomic 57; connectivity 80; Chinese-led 32; cooperation 61, 78, 81, 144; demands 116; domestic 79; electric 226; imports 83; management 22; mineral 1, 6; needs 117, 124; nuclear 56, 81; regional regime 32; renewable 81, 111, 118, 124, 226; security 2, 32, 65, 81, 105, 115; supplies 32, 79; sustainable 154; unified network 61
Energy Charter Treaty 82
Engagement 5, 9, 15–6, 30, 36, 90, 105–7, 113, 121–3, 166, 199, 202–3, 205, 208–10; cultural 122; economic 122–3, 203; India and Mongolia 107; international 114; people-to-people 106; rules of 30; societal 122
Enkhbold, Miyegombo 37
Enkhsaikhan, J., 4, 168
Environment 2, 4–5, 13, 58, 76, 78, 81, 87, 95, 97, 111, 116, 118, 154, 180, 219–24, 226, 233–4, 237–9, 243, 246–7, 249–52, 256; business-friendly 118; economic 116; effects on 226; external 220; geopolitical 2, 111; geostrategic 180; impact of 220, 238; permissive 251; resource-rich 239; security 4, 76, 78, 81, 97, 116; strategic 13
Environmental: assessment 225–6; challenges 3; conflict 226; criminal markets 239; crisis 220; culture 219; damage 249; degradation 220; disaster 219, 224, 256; education 221, 223, 231, 233; hazard 221; impact 220, 226–7, 243; insecurity 5; interaction 231; interests 219, 221; laws 242, 246–8; management 220; monitoring 229–31; needs 224; policy 219, 223, 234; practices 37; requirements 220; risks 226; safety 5, 219–20, 233; security 5, 119, 219, 221, 224, 233, 249–50;

standards 220; technology 224; threats 230; zones 223
Environmental cooperation 220, 224–5, 228, 232, 239, 252; cross-border 228; international 220; causes of 251
Environmental crime 1, 5, 237–9, 241–3, 246–52; organised 252; training relating to 241; transnational nature of 5, 237, 246–7
Environmental issues 5, 123, 220–21, 225, 233; agreements on 221
Environmental pollution 219–20, 223, 230; anthropogenic 220; prevention of 223
Environmental problems 219–21, 224, 228, 230, 248; global nature of 220; protection 221; regional 221; security 221
Environmental processes, impact of 220
Environmental protection 220–24, 228, 234, 238, 241, 246, 251; problems 221
Environmental Protection Agency (EPA) 241, 242
Equality 53
Esper, Mark, US Secretary of Defense 149–50; visit to Ulaanbaatar 149
Ethnic: identity 40; minority 39; Mongols 42
Euphrates 264
Eurasia 21, 24, 31, 58, 79, 88, 91, 93, 106, 143, 149, 269
Eurasian economic growth 143
Eurasian Economic Union (EAEU) 53, 80, 206; initiatives of 80
Eurasian nations 116
Eurasian Silk Road 144
Eurasian states 92–3
Eurasian transit zone 144
Eurasian transportation 144
Eurasian transportation and energy cooperation 144
Europe 10, 12, 22, 25, 51, 56, 80, 85–6, 88, 90, 93, 120, 141–2, 144, 162, 164, 172–4, 183, 185, 200, 203, 265, 267, 269–70; Chinese exports to 51; trilateralism in 142
European Union and Northeast Asia relations 33
European Union (EU) 33, 61, 84–5, 162, 207
Exchanges 4, 20, 49, 52, 56, 63–4, 77, 79, 87, 96, 98, 108, 111, 113, 115, 145–7, 154, 208, 222–4, 231, 242; cultural 152;

284　*Index*

ecological tourist 231; information 223–4; Ministry of Defence 115; people-to-people 152
Expanded Comprehensive Partnership 23, 148
Expansionism 103
Exploitation, natural resources 5, 237
Explosives 162, 167, 169; thermonuclear 167
Exports and imports 13, 18, 31, 34, 40, 51–2, 55, 58, 60, 80, 83, 104, 111–2, 117–8, 148, 156, 182, 205–6, 226, 239; American 13; cashmere and textile 148; China and Russia 51; Chinese 51; energy 83; market 117; mineral 80; Mongolia and US 148; Mongolia's 40; Russian 51; strategic 112; technology 18
Extremism 115

F-35B fighter jets 186
Fairbank, John K., 266
Far East 3, 35, 47–49, 54, 56, 58, 62, 65, 80, 199, 203, 227; development of 47–8, 56; quality of life of 49
Far Eastern Federal District (FEFD) 48
Federal Customs Service of Russia 51, 58
Finance 55, 60, 118, 142, 251
Financial: difficulties 95, 207; flows 51; institutions 55; pressure 90; relationships 15
Financial Action Task Force 151
Financial crises of 1997 and 2008, 86, 142
Financing 13, 18, 178, 226
Finland 155, 193
First Japan-China Forum on Third Country Business Cooperation 98
Fisheries 58, 239, 251; illegal 239
Fishing 5, 57–8, 97, 237, 249–50; illegal and unregulated 5, 97, 237, 250
Fissile materials 193
Food 87, 121, 220, 231, 238–9, 243
Flora and fauna, preservation of 221, 232
Ford, Lindsey 15
Foreign: aid 106, 201; governments 41, 144; investment 49; policy 38, 148; relationships 36; trade 40, 51, 56, 58, 60, 77
Foreign Affairs 14, 50, 78, 87, 93, 109, 146–7, 150

Foreign Direct Investment (FDI) 34, 40, 56, 95, 117–8, 207
Foreign policy(ies) 3–4, 12, 14, 16–8, 21, 23, 25, 30–32, 37, 47, 50, 53–4, 60–61, 65, 76–7, 83, 85, 86–8, 91, 96, 99, 103–7, 110, 112–6, 120, 122, 141–5, 147–9, 151, 153–7, 178, 180, 189–91, 199, 201, 206–7, 211, 220–21; ambitions 105; approaches 106; Biden 25; challenge 180; Chinese 3, 30, 37; concepts 143, 180; strategy 110; transition 104; contemporary 104–5; ambitions 105; post-Cold War 104; grand strategy 104; Indian 4, 103–6; Indo-Pacific 148; initiatives 105; Japan's 4, 54, 85–6, 88, 143; Mongolian 3, 61, 76–7, 83, 107, 113–5, 122, 144–5, 149, 153–5, 178, 207; "multi-dimensional" 153; "multi-pillared" 153, 180; NEA-oriented 77; objectives 21; options 107; post-Cold War 104, 180; pragmatic 180; priorities, environmental aspect in 220; proactive 191; protocols 122; Russian 50, 60, 199, 207; strategies 3; Third Neighbourhood 103; trajectory 105, 112; transitional 104; trilateralist 141; Trump 17, 23; well-articulated 104; well-defined 104
Foreign Policy Concept of the Russian Federation 47, 54
Foreign relations 14–5, 21, 23, 36, 180; Mongolia and US 23
Forest 48, 221–2, 224, 233, 241; resources 221, 241
Forest and steppe fires 222, 224
Forgery 251
France 15, 119, 165–7, 181, 246, 256
Free and fair economic zone 98
Free and Open Indo-Pacific (FOIP) 4, 23, 95–9, 106, 147
"Free and Open Indo-Pacific Strategy" 97; three pillars of 97
Freedom 13, 19, 23, 40, 88, 96–7, 141, 164, 257; commitment to 13; economic 23; fighters 164; of navigation 19, 97; of speech 141
Free market economy 2
Free Trade Agreement (FTA) 40, 57, 79, 87, 206
Fujian 222
Fukuda Doctrine 86

Fukuda Takeo, Japanese Prime Minister 86; tour of ASEAN 86
Fukushima Daiichi nuclear power plant accident 152
Fundamentalism 85

G7 54
G8 56
Gallucci, Dr. Robert 193
Ganbaatar, Sainkhuu 37
Gas pipeline project 56
Gas production 56, 58
General Customs Administration of the PRC 51
Genocide 119
Geo-economics 107
Geographical: barriers 107; distance 107–8, 264; location 149, 183, 189; location 155, 180; proximity 155; relations 4, 155
Geopolitical: aspirations 17; challenges 141; climate and structure 186; competition 11, 14, 16; environment 2, 111; importance 3, 47; interests 51, 183, 187; issues 187; realities 4, 103, 107, 178
Geopolitics 76, 88, 98, 123
Geostrategic: environment 180; importance 3, 47; issues 188; regions 48; rivalry 5
Gerlain, Pierre 15
Germany 56, 142, 155, 206
Glide missiles 182
Globalisation 104, 142, 151, 220
Globalism 25
Global Partnership to Prevent Armed Conflict (GPPAC) 192
Global Peace Foundation (GPF) 193
Global push 4, 162; to eliminate nuclear weapons 162
Global Tiger Initiative 242
Global Times 112
Gobi 93, 155, 226
Goods 23, 40–41, 51, 61, 96–7, 99, 239, 243, 250–51; manufactured 51; public 97; Russian 51, 61
Governance 12, 16, 32, 53, 148, 192, 241, 250–51, 256; architectures 16; democratic 192; energy, Chinese-led 32; global 53; mechanisms 53; regional 16
GPPAC-NEA 192
Grant /assistance 93

Grassroots aid 93
Great Britain 53, 165, 193, 265
Greater Eurasian Partnership 53
Greater Tumen Initiative (GTI) 81; Consultative Commission Meeting 81; priority projects 81
Great game 2, 144
Great powers 142, 266; interests of 187
Great Tea Road 222
Green zone 232
Gross Domestic Product (GDP) 40, 116–7, 178, 262
Groupings and organisations 25, 85, 119–20, 229; Indo-Pacific 119; regional 85; trilateral 119, 120; multinational 25
Group zones 189–90
Guidance for Development for Alliances and Partnerships (GDAP) 186
Gujral doctrine 105
Gujral, Inder Kumar, Indian Prime Minister 105

Habitats 231–2
Habomai archipelago 54
Habomai group of islands 54
Haig, Alexander 142
Hailar–Dalai 228
Halperin, Dr. Morton 185
Harmony 19, 256
Harris, Admiral Harry 17
Hashimoto Ryutaro, Japanese Prime Minister 87, 90; "Reforms for the New Era of Japan and ASEAN for a Broader and Deeper Partnership" 87
Hazardous waste 239, 250–51
Health 58–60, 76, 111, 118, 219, 238–9, 243, 251; infrastructure 118; crises 76
Hebei 222
Hegel, Georg Wilhelm Friedrich 257
Hegemony 15, 141; US 141
Helsinki dialogue 22
Henan 222
Heritage Foundation 16, 19
Highways 61
Hiroshima, Japan 165, 256
History: dynastic 267; East Asian 267; Japanese 267; patterns of 268; unilinear 255; cyclical 256; dialectic 257; absurd 258
Holocaust 270
Hong Kong 21, 24, 91, 99; crisis in 24

286 *Index*

Hostility 11, 17, 256
Hotel and restaurant business 58
"Hub and spoke" system 85–6, 91
Hubei 222
Humanitarian: aid 52, 121; assistance 23, 108; cargoes 52; contacts 94; cooperation 65; crises 84; exchanges 56, 224; interventions 52; relations 60; ties 54
Humanitarian Impact of Nuclear Weapons 181
Humanity 12, 174, 256, 257, 258, 259
Human: resources 222; rights 5, 22, 38, 88, 90, 96, 141, 219, 237; trafficking 105, 238, 249
Hunan 222
Huntington, Samuel 258; *Clash of Civilizations and the Remaking of World Order, The* 258
Hurricanes 220
Hydrocarbons 56
Hydroelectric power 225–6
Hydroelectric Power Plant (HPP) 225–6
Hydrogen bomb test 64
Hypersonic glider warheads 181
Hypersonic nuclear strike weapons 181

Ibn Khaldun 255, 256, 257; *Muqaddimah: An Introduction to History, The* 256
ICAN 192
Idealism 257
Identity 40, 258, 269; ethnic 40; Mongolian 40; separate 269
Ihara Junichi 146
Immigration 11, 268; Korea to Japan 268
Imperial Japan, conquest of 165
India 1, 4, 9, 14, 16–7, 19, 22, 24–5, 38, 50, 79, 88, 96, 98–9, 103–24, 142, 149, 155, 162, 165–7, 172–3, 181, 191, 193, 207, 256, 261–2; Act East policy 17; AEP 107, 118; ambition as a "leading power 105; concerns of a growing China 106–7; diplomacy 107; diplomatic missions to Mongolia 108; diplomatic outlook 107; disputed border 103; domestic growth 104; economic policy 104; expansive assistance 113; extended neighbourhood policy 107; first nuclear weapons test 166; foreign aid 106; foreign policy 4, 103–6; ambitions 105, 120; initiatives 105; post-Cold War 104; proactive 103; strategy 110; transition 104; global perspectives 105; hegemonic ambitions 105; inclusion in Mongolia's third neighbour policy 113, 115; independence in 1947 108; Indo-Pacific vision 116; interests in Indo-Pacific region 103; international outlook 105; landmark UN Resolution 108; Modi administration 108; Mongolian policy 120; neighbourhood policy 105; Northeast Asian outlook 106, 112; Northeast Asian policy 107, 115, 117; North Korea policy 121; nuclear-armed 162; nuclear capabilities 105; pursuance of 105; nuclear power status 105; nuclear weapons tests 167; outlook 107, 110; participation in world politics 104; policy outlooks 107; politics 106; role of, elevation of 16; shifting political calculations 112; soft diplomacy 113; strategic choices 122; strategic imagination 4, 104
India and Japan: civil nuclear pact 106; partnership 106; relations 106
India and Mongolia 4, 103–4, 107–20, 123, 124; bilateral: agreements and treaties 108–9, 111; cultural exchange projects 108; ties 107, 111; China factor 119; civil nuclear agreement 115; cooperation 120; energy security 115; democratic links 119; diplomatic ties 108; economic integration 116; engagement 107; exports and imports 117; foreign direct investments (FDIs) 117; historical ties 4; historic-cultural links 114; joint economic projects 4; joint military (army) exercises 113; lines of credit and aid 108; relations 103, 108, 110, 118; information and communication technology 118; mining 118; renewable energy 118; security links 113; security partnership 113; shared democratic values 104; shared Indo-Pacific vision 116; spiritual links 114, 119; ties 4, 103–4, 107–8, 111–2, 114, 116; bilateral 104; progress and momentum in 103; reinvigoration of 114; restrictive nature of 108; trade 117; trade; connectivity 118;

partnership 118; training and
assistance to Mongolian defence
personnel 115
India and Pakistan 142, 172; conflicts
142, 172; intractability of 142
India and ROK ties 121
India and US relations 142
India-Bhutan-China tri-junction 112
India-France-Australia dialogue 119
Indian missions abroad 105
Indian Ocean 10, 15, 97, 98, 142; sea
lanes 10
India's Technical and Economic
Cooperation (ITEC) 111
Indochina 89
Indonesia 14, 18, 87, 92, 149
Indo-Pacific region 2–4, 9–10, 12–25, 38,
79, 89, 95–99, 103–4, 106–7, 111, 116,
119–24, 141, 143, 147–50, 156–7, 186;
American military deployment in the
24; concept 104; free and open 9, 18, 38,
95, 97, 106, 149–50; groupings 119;
India's interests in 103; national security
9; policy 3, 14, 16, 99, 143, 147–8;
foreign 148; strategic cooperation 157;
strategic thinking 147; strategies 4, 16,
18, 21, 25, 97, 147; Japan and US 4; US
priority actions in 13
Indo-Pacific Transaction Advisory
Fund 18
Industrial: development 48, 56;
infrastructure 35; production 48
Industrialisation 80
Industrial revolution, fourth 57
Industries 40–41, 118, 241; domestic 41;
mining 40, 115; Mongolian 40
Information, exchange of 223–4
Information Technology (IT) 60,
109–10, 115, 118; parks 118
Infrastructure 1, 11, 13, 16–7, 31–2, 35,
40, 48–9, 51, 56–8, 60–61, 80, 83, 93,
95, 97–8, 106, 117–8, 123, 144, 192,
194, 207, 222, 224, 237, 247;
administrative 237; Chinese
investment in 31–2; connectivity 51;
cross-border 31, 61; development 40,
58, 97, 118, 123, 144, 192; health 118;
high-quality 13; industrial 35;
investments 17; bilateral 95; military
57; projects 31, 80, 93, 95; quality 13,
97; tourist 222; trade 31; transnational
144; transparent financing practices
13; transport 48, 144, 224

Index 287

Infrastructure Transaction and
Assistance Network 18
INF Treaty 164, 172
Inner Mongolia 34, 39, 42, 222, 228, 231
Inner Mongolia Autonomous Region
39, 228
Inner Mongolian Autonomous
province 119
Innovation 11, 57, 86
Insecurity 5, 237–9; environmental 5
Inspection Commission of the World
Bank 226
Instability 1, 19, 142, 203, 233;
regional 19
Insurgency 35
Integration 3, 21, 32, 47, 51, 53, 65,
76–7, 79, 82–4, 92, 95, 99, 106, 113,
116, 118, 122, 142–3, 146–7, 156–7,
193, 200; arrangements 77; Chinese
51; disadvantages of 83; efforts 21;
initiative 51; international 77; political
21; process 21; regional 21, 65, 92, 99,
142; transportation 143; trilateralism
cooperation 147
Intellectual property 11
Intelligence 9, 12–4, 167, 241–2, 250,
266; anticipatory 12; cooperation 14;
current operations 12; cyber threat 12;
foreign 13; strategic 12
Intelligence Community (IC) 12
Interactions 49–50, 57, 59–62, 65–6, 95,
112, 210, 220, 224, 231–4; cultural 112;
economic 62, 117; bilateral 54;
multilateral 54; environmental 231;
international 66; practical 57;
Russian-Mongolian 60; strategic 50;
technological 112; trilateral 232
Inter-Continental Ballistic Missile
(ICBM) 64, 166, 171, 188, 202
Intercontinental hypersonic glide
missiles 182
Inter-Korean rapprochement 123
Inter-Korean relations 187
Intermediate-Range Nuclear Arms
Treaty (INF) 162
Intermediate-Range Nuclear Forces
(INF) 162, 164, 171–2, 181
Intermediate-Range Nuclear Forces
(INF) Treaty 171, 181
Internal affairs 33, 36
International: arms control measures
167; concerns and issues 87; conflicts
220; cooperation 49, 54, 85, 91, 95, 98,

288 *Index*

189, 221, 223, 241; criminal gangs 238; diplomatic cooperation 121; ecological; coalition 227; organisations 220; economic; assistance 193; cooperation 49; engagements 114; forums 52, 87, 108; free market 86; institutions 15, 37; integration 77; interaction 66; price fluctuations in 58; law 13, 23, 53, 64, 116, 170; markets 11, 32, 58, 86; military field exercises 94; multilateral forums 116; order 31, 85, 104, 148; organisations 53, 60, 91, 93, 115, 186, 251; outlook 103, 105, 115–6, 121; partnership 223; peacekeeping operations (PKOs) 24, 150, 191; perceptions 32; planning 114; anomalies in 54; relations 2, 32, 50, 54, 88, 91, 142, 156, 220, 222; responsibilities, shared 142; sanctions 65, 83, 189, 202; security 52, 60, 190; stability 52; strategies 104, 107; talks 22; trade 31; transportation 80; treaties and agreements 114, 168, 190, 246
International Association of Chiefs of Police (IACP) 243
International Atomic Energy Agency (IAEA) 167, 182, 191, 201; comprehensive safeguard system 182; inspection and verification 167, 171, 191; safeguards 182; use of weak safeguards 182
International Committee to Abolish Nuclear Weapons 174
International Consortium for Combating Wildlife Crimes 249
International Court of Justice 108
International Economic Forum 51
International Energy Agency (IEA) 32
International Institute for Strategic Studies-Fullerton Lecture, Singapore 105
International Monetary Fund (IMF) 95, 262
International order 31, 85, 89, 104, 148; liberal 31, 85; *Pax Americana* 104; rules-based 148
International policies 114, 142; controversial 142
International Policy Forum 193
International relations: dimensions of 142; environmentalisation of 220; impacts on 91
International Society for Comparative Study of Civilizations (ISCSC) 173
International Society for the Comparative Study of Civilizations 2
International Solar Alliance (ISA) 115
International Think Tank for Landlocked Developing Countries (LLDC) 81
International Tribunal for the Law of the Sea 108
International Union for Conservation of Nature (IUCN) 251
International Union for Conservation of Nature Red List 231
International waters, access to 153
INTERPOL 242–3, 245, 249–51
INTERPOL Strategic Plan 250
Interregional Cooperation Forum 58
Intrusion 33, 261
Investment 15–9, 23, 32, 34, 40–41, 48–9, 56–8, 60–61, 65, 79, 81, 92, 95–6, 109, 117, 144–5, 151–2, 156, 194, 207, 222, 224; Chinese 32, 40, 152; cooperation 56, 58; direct 58, 117; economic 144; foreign 49; infrastructure 17; mutual protection of 58; trilateral 224
IPB 192
IPPNW 192
Iran 162–3, 191, 201, 256; IAEA inspection teams in 191
Iraq 38, 90, 165, 182, 201, 207; US operations in 90
Irkutsk region 222, 226
Irredentism 32
Islam 262
Islamic fundamentalism 85
Island of Bolshoi 50
Island of Bolshoi Ussuriisky 50
Island of Shikotan 54
Island of Tarabarov 50
Islands: disputed 50, 55; ownership of 55
Islands of Habomai 55
Islands of Iturup 55
Islands of Kunashir 55
Islands of Shikotan 55
Isolation 48, 122, 189, 268; economic 48, 189; infrastructural 48
Isolationism 18
Israel 5, 162–3, 165, 167, 173, 181, 255–6, 262–3, 268–70; first functional nuclear warhead 167

Israel and Mongolia 262-3, 268
Italy 117
Iturup Islands 54
Ivashentsov, Gleb, Ambassador 64
Iwashita Hiroaki 88
Jaishankar, Subrahmanyam, India's Minister of External Affairs 105
Japan 1, 4-5, 13, 16-9, 21-4, 30-31, 33-4, 38, 47-50, 53-7, 61-3, 65-6, 76-7, 79, 81-3, 85-100, 106-7, 114, 116-7, 119-22, 141, 143-7, 149-57, 162-3, 165-9, 173, 183-5, 187, 193-4, 199-201, 204, 206-9, 223, 252, 255, 263, 266-70; abductions of nationals 93, 146; Abe administration 31, 86, 91, 95-6, 98-9; aggression 34; Air Self-Defence Force 97; attacks on 165; Basic Plan for National Defense 56; Central Asian policy 87; concept of East Asian Community 77; defeat in World War II 86; defence costs 86; development assistance 93; donor assistance policies for Mongolia 145; foreign policies 88; foreign policy 4, 54, 85-6, 88, 96, 99, 143; in Post-World War II 86; three pillars of 87; foreign policy in Asia 86, 88; "Free and Open Indo-Pacific" policy 4; government 91, 93, 98, 100, 145-6, 152, 157; Indo-Pacific policies of 99, 143; Russian imports from 55; isolation of 268; Japanese government 186; Koizumi's administration 87; militarism 33; military forces, post-war restrictions on 30; military threats from China 56; national interest 88; national policy 86; non-military role 86; policy towards 93; Asia-Pacific region 89; Mongolia 93; Russia 54; rise of 89; role of 19; Russian exports to 55; security; architecture 88; independence 85; role 87; settlement 268; territorial claims of 57; White Paper on Developmental Cooperation 2018, 93
Japan-America-India (JAI) trilateral groupings 119
Japan and Korea 24, 62, 166, 200, 204, 263, 266-7, 270; difference 267
Japan and Mongolia 82, 94-5, 143, 152, 223; bilateral relations 150, 153; connectivity 95; cooperation 153; defence 153; environmental protection 223; politics and security 152; Economic Partnership Agreement 95,

95; economic stabilisation programme 95; General agreement on the implementation of the environmental protection 223; joint investment 145; mid-term action plan 94; Midterm Programme of Mongolian-Japanese Strategic Partnership for 2017-2021 94, 153; relations 152; strategic partnership 93-4, 223
Japan and North Korea negotiations 152
Japan and ROK 19
Japan and Russia 53-6; cooperation 56; disputed territories 54, 56; Joint Declaration of 1956, 55; joint ventures 56; peace treaty 55; relations 53-6; economic 55; trade 55
Japan and South Korea 24, 62, 166, 200, 204, 266, 270; territorial disputes 62
Japan and US 4, 18-9, 23, 30, 55, 85-6, 88, 91, 96, 99-100, 143, 145, 147, 149, 151-7, 207, 209; alliance 4, 86, 88, 90-91, 96, 99-100; importance of the 4, 99; stronger-than-ever 90; bilateral alliances 85; military-political alliance 55; regional missile defence 30; relationship 18, 23; strategies of 4
Japan and USSR relations 53
Japan Bank for International Cooperation 95
Japanese abductions issue 93, 146, 151-2, 154, 157
Japanese Constitution 165, 186; Article Six of 165; three non-nuclear principles 186
Japanese hostage crisis 87, 145-6
Japan International Cooperation Agency (JICA) 223
Jews 260-62, 264-5, 270; post-Exilic period 264
Jiangxi 222
Job creation 58
Joint Declaration on the Promotion of Tripartite Cooperation 79
Panda, Dr. Jagannath 192; *Mongolia's Foreign Policy: Navigating a Changing World* 192
Judaism 262
Judea 264, 269
July revolution 35

Kazakhstan 116, 183, 229

Kazianis, Harry 20
Khaan Quest multinational exercise 24, 38, 94, 113, 208
Khaltmaa Battulga, Mongolian President 60, 81
Khan, Genghis 39
Khubsgöl 230
Khürelsükh, Ukhnaa, Prime Minister of Mongolia 80, 94–5, 147–8; visit to; Japan 95; US 148
Kim Jong Un 19–20, 62, 78, 82, 122, 146, 169, 188, 201, 203, 208
Kim Yong-chol, South Korean Minister of Unification 63
Kissinger, Henry 164
Koizumi Junichiro, Prime Minister 87
Koji, Murata 100
Koller, Marvin R., 262
Kono Taro, Foreign Minister of Japan 94; visit to Mongolia 94
Korea International Cooperation Agency (KOICA) 223
Korean Peninsula 1–5, 13–5, 19–25, 33, 59, 62–4, 66, 82, 84, 89, 94–5, 104, 120–23, 148, 153, 156, 165–6, 169, 178, 185–8, 191–4, 201, 203–5, 208–11; conflict potential on 62; confrontation on 63; crisis 33, 63; denuclearisation of 14, 19–20, 24–5, 63, 188, 201; denuclearisation talks 19; denuclearising 5, 178, 187, 191, 194; division of 166, 193; economic events on 1; instability on 1; issue of denuclearising 5, 178; nuclearisation on 1; nuclear issue on 82, 201; nuclear problem 62; peace and stability in 4, 104; peace processes on 121; political events on 1; stabilisation of 15; stability issues 2; unification talks for 19
Korean Peninsula Comprehensive Settlement Action Plan 63
Korean rapprochement 122–3
Korean War of 1950–1953 89, 166, 186–7
Koreas 1, 5, 21, 34, 59, 63, 78, 168, 185, 191, 193, 201, 203, 208–11, 266; reunification of 1
Kumao Kaneko, Dr., 185
Kunashir Islands 54
Kuril Island 53–7; Russian possession of 55; Japan's recognition of 55
Kyrgyzstan 116

Labour 38, 48, 65, 82, 168, 202; groups 38; local 38; resources 48; wartime, compensation for 65
Lake Baikal 222, 225–6, 229–30
Lake Dalai 228
Lake Khubsgöl 230
Lake Khubsugul 222
Lakes 180, 227, 231; drainless 227; system of 227
Landlocked Developing Countries (LLDC) 81
Landscapes of Dauria 227, 232
Landslides 220
Languages 20, 39, 107, 119, 262, 267; Altaic 267; Chinese 267; Japanese 267; Korean 267; Mandarin 119; Mongolian 119; policy 119
Laos 165
Latin America 165, 172, 184
Launch-on-warning protocols 164
Lavrov, Sergey, Minister of Foreign Affairs 50, 63
Law of low probabilities 163, 164
Laws: enforcement 5, 14, 97, 237, 241–3, 246, 249–52; environmental 242, 246–8; international 13, 23, 53, 64, 116, 170; objective of 31
Leadership 9, 16, 31, 33, 41, 48, 80, 83, 90, 142, 145, 152, 165, 169, 201, 264; Asian 165; Chinese 31, 41; American 33; economic 31, 80; global 33; Japanese 145; Mongolian 152; regional 33; Russian 48; strategic 33; United States 9, 90
Leffler, Melvyn 14
Legitimacy 41
Lenin 258; *State and Revolution* 258
Lewin, Kurt 263; *Resolving Social Conflicts* 263
Liberalisation 23, 37, 104; economic 23, 104; reforms 104; political 37
Libya 182
Li Keqiang, Chinese Prime Minister 98; visited Japan 98
Limitation and disarmament treaty 170
Limited NWFZ (LNWFZ) 185
Line of Actual Control (LAC) 103
Li Peng, Chinese Premier 36
Livelihoods 219, 237–8, 243
Lkhaajav, Bolor 154
LNG 56
Loans 40–41, 48, 93, 95, 152; low-

interest 152; soft 48, 93, 95; yen-denominated 93, 95
Logistics 58, 119
Look East Policy (LEP) 105–6, 110
Lukin, Alexander 51

Mack, Andrew 185
Major powers 1–3, 5–6, 99, 103, 121–2, 162, 168, 203, 210–11; aspirations 103, 122; foreign policy of 3; inclinations 103; role of 3; security policies of 1; strategies of 3
"Make in India" 117
Malabar exercises 106
Malaysia 14, 87, 92
Manchuria 269
Manchus 267
Manmade accidents 224
Manufacturing 58, 117, 124, 184, 239
Marginality 263, 270
Marginal Man 255, 263, 265–6, 269; theory 255
Maritime 13–4, 25, 33, 97, 112, 143; borders 33; disputes 13; open system 13; partners 14; security issues 13
Maritime order 89; free and open 97
Markets 2, 11–3, 16, 31–2, 36, 48, 51, 58, 78, 82–3, 86, 88, 90, 95, 117, 124, 145, 154, 157, 179, 192–3, 200, 204, 207, 220, 239, 241, 243, 246, 263; developed 48; economy 2, 78, 83, 88, 192; export 117; foreign 31; free 2, 12–3, 86, 145, 157, 193; international 11, 32, 58, 86; price fluctuations in 58; leverage 220; minerals 145; Mongolian 95; open 90; Russian 48, 51
Marquis of Condorcet 258
Marx, Karl 257; *Theses on Feuerbach* 257
Materialism 257
Mattis, Jim, Secretary of Defense 24, 97; Dynamic Force Deployment 24
Ma Ying-jeou, President of Taiwan 32
Media 34, 37, 112, 141, 228; Chinese 34; Chinese official 37; local 37; state-owned 112; uncensored 37
Medical sciences 111
Medicine 56, 59
Mediterranean Sea 264
Meiji Restoration 269
Memorandum of cooperation 94
Memorandum of Understanding (MOU) 57, 61, 80–81, 109–10, 116;

"Power of Siberia 2" 80; Russia AND South Korea 57
Mesopotamia 261, 264
Metamorphosis 261, 266
Metz, Steven 14
Micaller, Manuel 22, 147
Middle East 10, 12, 25, 86, 90, 97, 157, 165, 183, 187
Middle Kingdom 268
Midterm Programme of Mongolian-Japanese Strategic Partnership for 2017–2021, 94
Migration 48–9, 221; loss 48; outflow 49
Mikhanev, Andrei, World Bank Country Manager for Mongolia 118
Militarism 33
Military: build-up 24; capability 96; capacities 76; competition 99; consequences 189; cooperation 37, 113, 120, 145, 202, 206; deployment process 24; efficiency 266; equipment 24, 34; exercises 63, 113, 204, 206; expansion 113; infrastructure 57; manoeuvres 42; operation 90; power 42, 86–7, 89–90, 96–7; US 86, 89; relations 3, 13, 37, 150; spending 90; stability 24; standoff 33; superiority 33; tensions 34; threats 17, 37, 56, 63, 219; ties 149
Military-to-military: agreement 150; contacts 90
Mine-golia 116
Minerals 1, 5–6, 37, 40–41, 51, 56, 61, 80, 83, 111, 115–8, 124, 143, 145, 151, 156–7, 207, 227, 237, 246; endowments 118; exploitation of 5, 237; exports 80; market 145; radioactive 115; raw materials 56; reserves 116, 124; resources 1, 6; trafficking in 5, 237; wealth 41, 118, 246; illegal 5, 237
Mining 40, 82, 115, 117–8, 227, 247, 249; industry 40, 115; defence against 11
Ministry of Foreign Affairs (MOFA) 78, 87–8, 93, 109, 146–7, 150
Missile attack warning system 52
Missile crisis of 2017 63
Missile development programme 64
Missiles 11, 13, 18–20, 30, 34, 36, 52, 57, 62–5, 121, 151, 153–4, 164, 167, 171–2, 179, 181–2, 186, 188, 200–204; attacks 11, 186; ballistic 13, 18, 20, 64, 151, 153–4, 171, 179, 181–2, 186, 188,

201–3; capabilities 20, 30, 34; cruise 171, 172, 181, 186; defence 11, 13, 19, 30, 171, 181–2, 186, 200, 203; deployment of 172; glide 182; hypersonic 181; land and sea-based 186; long-range 182, 201; mobile transporters 188; nuclear 34, 62–5, 121; testing 20
Missionaries 107
Modi, Narendra, Prime Minister of India 103–8, 110–12, 115, 117–8, 123; commitment 106; diplomatic visits 111; domestic initiatives 117; East Asian tour 110; foreign policy approaches 106; perception 110; visit to; Mongolia 104, 110–11, 115, 118; Ulaanbaatar 103
Monarchy 34
Mondale, Walter, US Vice President 141
Money laundering 251
Mongol 37, 42, 115, 144, 154, 225, 227, 231–2, 261, 266
Mongol Daguur Strictly Protected Area 231
Mongolia: 2017 presidential election 37; American support of 22; a non-nuclear weapon state 22; candidature as a non-permanent UNSC 108; central 155; China's danger to 40; China's economic clout in 118; China's trade sanctions 117; Chinese influence over 38; Chinese migrant workers in 37; control over 41; culture 154; democratic revolution in 36; dependence on; China 122; Soviet Union 59; diplomacy 114; diplomatic policy 123; disadvantages of 82; domestic institutions 119; economic; dependence on China 119, 206; development 154; significance of 107; economy 40, 95, 113, 117, 118, 151; dependent on China 117; mineral-based 143; efforts 2, 95, 207, 209; energy minerals 151; entry into the United Nations General Assembly 35; environmental; laws 246; threats in 230; export market 117; exports 40; facilitating talks between Japan and DPRK 122; facilitating talks between the US and DPRK 122; fear and suspicion of China 119; Five Hills military base 24; foreign policy 3, 61, 76–7, 83, 103, 107, 113–5, 122, 144–5, 149, 153–5, 178, 207; independent 189–90, 207; neutrality in 122; Northeast Asia 3; options 107; post-Cold War 180; principles of 3, 76; regional 122; Third Neighbourhood 103; foreign policy vision 178; foreign relations 21; geographic; location 155; position 35, 107; positioning 80; goals of 190; government 21, 37, 41, 80, 83, 95, 117, 146, 154; IMF-led programme in 95; implications of 3, 30; importance of 157, 167, 207; imports from 60; independence of 35, 41, 114; Indian aid 112; Indian diplomatic missions to 108; India's bid for a non-permanent seat on UNSC 108; initiatives 189, 190; interest in trilateralism 153; international policy 114; investment 151; Japanese 151; US 151; Japanese policy towards 93; law 24; market 95; member state of the UN 108; military 36, 38, 145, 149; mineral; reserves 116, 124; market 145; mining industry 115; mountain ranges in 229; nationalism 39, 42; national security 5, 34, 36, 180; concept 180; impact on 5; National Security Concept of 2010 21; northeast 226; northern and southern borders 40; nuclear-weapon-free status 185, 187, 190; institutionalisation of 185; nuclear-weapon-free wish 189; nuclear-weapon-free zone 189–90; ODA from Japan 152; overreliance on China 118; impact of 118; perceptions and challenges for 77; policy 5, 153, 178, 180, 189; policymakers 24, 81, 84, 143–4, 156; policy of cooperation 22; policy trends for 76; post-Cold War 37; problems with China 36; regional security for 61; risks for 30; role 1, 3–4, 22–3, 81, 94, 120, 144–5, 147, 162, 191, 211; in Northeast Asia 3; in security dialogue mechanisms 191; Indo-Pacific 23; Russian investment in 144; Russian troop withdrawal from 179; Russia's exports to 60; security; cultural 119; environmental 119; risk to 40; strategy 36; strategic; advantages 82; directions 77; sustainable growth 93; third neighbour policies 118; third

neighbour policy 113–5, 122, 144, 207; trade sanctions 112; trilateralism strategy 143; United States assistance to 148; unsustainable reliance on China 124; water resources 223; western 155; withdrawal of Russian bases from 189
Mongolia and North Korea 106, 122, 156; cooperation; agricultural 122; economic 122; societal 122; relations 156; ties 122
Mongolia and Russia 5, 21, 37, 59–61, 82, 144, 146, 153, 155, 157, 189, 199, 205–7, 209, 211, 222–3, 225–32; border 229; cooperation 59; interaction 60; memorandum of understanding 80; military relations 37; relations 5, 59–61, 144, 189, 199; strategic partnership 59–60; trade 60; trade and economic ties 60; transboundary reserve 229; working subgroup 225
Mongolia and South Korea cooperation 223
Mongolia and Soviet Union 36, 145, 179; alliance 179; mutual assistance treaty 36
Mongolia and US 23–4, 144–5, 147–50, 157; bilateral; meeting 150; relations 148; cooperation 145; military 145; exports 148, 156; foreign relations 23; military-to-military agreement 150; partnership 144; relations 148–9; security relationship 157; bilateral 157; Strategic Partnership Agreement 149; trade and investment 156; trade 24
Mongolia Environmental Performance Review 248
Mongolia-Japan-US trilateralism 152
Mongolian Armed Forces 24
Mongolian Institute of Northeast Asian Security and Strategy (MINASS) 79, 81
Mongolian Minis project 225–6
Mongolian Parliament 36
Mongolians 38–9, 41, 119, 123, 180
Mongolia-Russia-China economic corridor 154
Mongolia Society, The 2
Mongolia Third Neighbour Trade Act 148
Mongols 22, 36–40, 42, 119, 145, 151, 155–6, 168–9, 194, 226, 260–62, 265, 267–70

Monopoly 24, 40
Montreal Protocol 251
Moon Jae-in, South Korean President 31, 57–8, 62, 78, 121; New Northern Policy 58; peace-building strategy 121; visit to Russian Federation 57
Moscow Declaration 60
Moscow Nonproliferation Conference 63
Most Favoured Nation (MFN) 109
Mudflows 220
Multilateral: agreements 5, 221, 234; cooperation 49, 147, 187, 220–21, 223, 234; engagements 23, 114; international cooperation 54; negotiations 63, 90, 185, 188; security 23, 147–8, 179, 200
Multipolarity 50, 52, 114
Münkh-Orgil, Tsend, Mongolian Foreign Minister 152
Murder 11, 173
Muslims 264
Mutual: agreement 111; assistance 36; beneficial ties 110; concern 13; confidence 87, 180; distrust 181; economic benefit 154; exchange and cooperation 4; interest 59, 146; intertwining 47; on-site inspections 181; recognition 59; respect 41, 53; suspicion 186; threats 17; trust and benefit 65, 76, 79, 87, 193, 200; understanding 51, 62, 77–8, 87, 96, 100, 192, 208
Mutual Assured Destruction (MAD) 163, 171; strategy 171
Myanmar 96, 106

Nagasaki, Japan 165, 185, 256
Nanyang Technological University, Singapore 16
Narasimha Rao, Indian Prime Minister 105
Narcotics 87
National: objectives 10; policy 86; power 11, 32; security 60; self-defence 36; strategies 12; territorial disputes 32
National defense 56, 96, 150; strategy 150
National Defense Program Guidelines (NDPG) 96
National Defense Strategy (NDS) 150
National Development and Innovation Committee (NDIC) 109

294 Index

National economy 220
National Intelligence Strategy (NIS) 9, 12, 14, 18
National Intelligence Strategy (NIS) of 2019, 12
National interests 10, 12, 65, 85, 88, 90, 114, 142, 180, 199, 221, 224–5, 233; Japanese 88
US 10, 85
Nationalism 15, 39, 42; Mongolian 39, 42; non-Han 39
National park 229, 230
National Programme for the Development of the Far East 49
National security 1–6, 9–12, 14, 16–21, 23, 25, 34, 36–7, 56, 77, 86, 96, 114, 116, 141, 143, 147, 151, 156–7, 178, 180, 219, 250; challenges 2, 6; global 3; Indo-Pacific 9; innovation 11; Northeast Asian 2; planning 1; policy 9, 19, 147; strategic principles 23; strategy 3, 9, 17, 25, 96, 147; US 9, 16, 18–9
National Security Concept of Mongolia 2011, 77
National Security Council (NSC) 9, 14, 96, 111
National Security Strategy (NSS) 3, 9–18, 96, 147; 2017 10–18; Bush's 2002 10; Trump Administration's 10
"National Strategy of Engagement and Enlargement" policy 89
National University of Mongolia (NUM) 154
Nations/States 99; "like-minded" 113; Asian 1, 25, 157, 165, 167, 169, 174; autocratic 168; border 144; buffer 114, 120, 204; crisis-hit 112; Eurasian 25, 116; friendly 25; landlocked 112–3, 116, 179; like-minded 12, 149; mineral-rich 111; non-nuclear weapon 22, 172, 185; normal 122; nuclear 142, 169–70, 172, 210; nuclear weapons 167, 169; nuclear-capable 182, 194; nuclear-weapon-free 82; peripheral 5, 255, 263, 268; rationalist behaviour 114; reclusive 121; rogue 20; small 2, 23, 91–2, 142, 164, 168–9, 178, 270; smaller 25, 106, 142, 169; South Asian 25; sovereign 10, 12; spoke 85; superpower 142; trilateral 142; Western 121

Natural: environment 87, 219, 224, 233; biosphere reserve 231–2; disasters 13, 97, 224, 226; environment 87, 219, 224, 233; gas pipelines 31, 81; hazards 220, 224; monuments 221; potential 224
Natural resources: development 48; disparities 48; exploitation of 5, 237; rational use of 222; reproduction of 224
Nautilus Institute in California 185
NEA Exim Banks Association 81
Negotiation(s) 2, 4, 20–21, 23–4, 41, 50, 53, 55, 57, 63–5, 76, 78, 83, 90, 120–21, 142, 151–2, 157, 171, 182–3, 185, 188–9, 191, 194, 201; bilateral 83; denuclearisation 4, 121; failed 78; Japan and North Korea 152; multi-party 4; peaceful 2, 23, 120; prioritised 142; productive 191; Six Party format of 64; strategies 78; to eliminate nuclear weapons 171; working-level 194
Nehru, Jawaharlal, Indian Prime Minister 106, 108
Neighbour: border 143, 146, 190; immediate 115, 180; powerful 83, 144, 168; powerhouse 118; spiritual 124; third 24, 113, 118, 120, 143–4, 146–8, 151, 153–4, 207; virtual 113
Neighbourhood 3, 104–7, 110, 112–3, 115, 150, 206; extended 104, 107; extensive 106; immediate 104, 106, 110
"Neighbourhood First" policy 106
Neighbours plus 36
Neo-conservativism 16
Nepal 18, 155, 190
Netherlands, the 173
"New Asian Security Concept" 92
New Eastern policy 80
New Northern Policy 58, 208
New Pacific Community 90
New Silk Road 31
New Southern Policy (NSP) 31, 121
New START treaty 181
New Zealand 13, 17, 49, 87–8
"Nine bridges" of cooperation 58
Nixon, Richard, US President 141
No first use pledge policies 193
Nomadic Elephant 113
Nomadism, three-camp form of 155
Nomads 260–61, 267

Index   295

Non-Aligned Movement (NAM) 114, 124, 190; principles 114
Nonalignment: ideals 114; strategy 103
Non-Christians 256
Non-governmental exchanges 79
Nongovernmental organisations (NGOs) 79, 184–5, 192, 194
Non-interference 36
Non-nuclear deterrence 193
Non-Nuclear Weapon State (NNWS) 182–3, 185, 189, 191; status 191
Non-profit organisation 79
Non-proliferation 1, 4–5, 13, 60, 63–4, 66, 97, 105, 178, 182–3, 189, 192, 202; objectives 105
Non-Proliferation Treaty (NPT) 167–71, 180–83, 194, 201; Article 6, 170, 183
Non-residential Indians 105
Norov Altankhuyag, Mongolian Prime Minister 94; visit to Japan 94
North America 141
North and South 122
North Asia 267
North Atlantic Treaty Organization (NATO) 19, 23, 30, 38, 149, 162, 173, 183; alliance structure 19; operations 38
Northeast Asia and Mongolia 3, 5, 93, 178
Northeast Asia and Russia 3, 49; relations 3, 49
Northeast Asian Development Bank 79
Northeast Asia (NEA) 1–6, 9–10, 13, 18–25, 30–33, 42, 47–50, 53, 57, 59, 61–66, 76–88, 93, 95, 98, 100, 103, 106–7, 110, 112–3, 115, 117, 120–23, 143, 149–54, 156–7, 167–9, 173, 178–80, 183–8, 191–4, 199–201, 203–5, 208–11, 219–21, 223–4, 233–4, 237–9, 252, 266–9; affairs 9; agreement on peace and security in 185; allies 188; challenges in 3, 6; China's foreign policy in 3, 30; cooperation in 49, 221; economic 62; regional 49, 221; denuclearisation in 4, 156; economic behemoths of 169; influence in 24; integration in 3, 76, 79, 84, 200; penetration 157; economies 76; environmental protection in 220–21; environmental security and 221; environment in 219; geo-economics of 107; geopolitical; importance 3, 47; issues in 187; geostrategic importance 3, 47; growth and development of 6; importance of 167; integration 3, 79; international cooperation in 221; issues 153; Mongolian foreign policy towards 3; national security 2; challenges in 6; non-proliferation regime in 13; nuclear non-proliferation in 5; nuclear weapons threat in 178; policy 107, 115, 117; India's 107, 115, 117; power structure in 76, 154; regional; architecture for 86; cooperation and trust 22; framework 21, 22; order in 85; role of 47; Russian economic influence in 24; Russia's policy 65; security 1, 3, 21, 63, 65–6, 76–79, 95, 120, 150, 154, 157, 187, 191, 192, 210; balance in 154; impact on 153; issues in 5, 187, 219; strategic landscape 2; US's view of 10
Northeast Asian Nuclear Weapons Free Zone (NEA-NWFZ) 5, 178, 184–6, 187, 191–3; issue of 193
Northeast Asian Sub-regional Program for Environmental Cooperation (NEASPC) 239
North-East Asian Sub-regional Programme for Environmental Cooperation (NEASPEC) 252
Northeast Asian Super Grid (ASG) 81
Northeast Asia Plus Community of Responsibility-sharing (NEAPC) 121
Northern Logistics System 61
Northern Sea Route 58
North Korea 2, 4–5, 9, 13–5, 17–22, 30–34, 47, 59, 61–5, 76–9, 82–3, 85, 90, 93, 100, 104, 106, 120–23, 143, 145–7, 149–54, 156–7, 162–3, 165–9, 172–3, 181, 184, 187–9, 193, 199–205, 207–11, 252, 256; *see also* Democratic People's Republic of Korea (North Korea) (DPRK); abductions of Japanese nationals 93, 146; adventurism 33; aggression 13, 14; concern 193; cyber, nuclear, and ballistic missile programmes 18; demands for relief 20; denuclearization issue of 2; dependence on China 122; geographic position 31; hydrogen bomb test 64; military parade 188; missile testing 20; nuclear-armed 18; nuclear capability 188; nuclear facilities 188; nuclear programme 21, 64, 146, 188; dismantling of 21; nuclear weapons

296 *Index*

development programme 188; nuclear weapons policy 188; political gain for 189; provocations by 18; Russia's policy towards 5, 199; UN sanctions 64; US policy on 21
North Korea and Russia 13, 202
North Korea and South Korea 77, 82, 162, 168, 169; tension 82
North Korea and US 4, 64, 77, 153, 187, 210; bilateral discussions 4; dialogue 64; relations 187; normalisation of 188; track 2 level meeting 77
North Korean nuclear crisis 193, 201
North-South dialogues 114
North-Western China 229
Northwest Mongolia 229
Nuclear: and conventional deterrence 19; arms control 162, 169, 172; arms race 164, 166–7, 170, 172–3, 178, 182–3, 186, 191–2, 194; arsenals 171–3; attack 19, 165–6, 173; blackmail 19; bombs 166; pursuance of 105; breakout 167; capabilities 20, 105, 183, 188; actual or suspected existence of 183; catastrophe 165; challenges 3; club 163, 167; countries 165; crisis 163, 193, 201; danger 178, 183; deterrence theory 163, 173; deterrence theory 165; deterrent 166, 181; detonations 166, 171; development 82; disarmament 173, 178, 180, 182–3, 192; disarmament goals of 192; enemy(s) 163; energy 56, 81; explosives 162; facilities 188; giants 168; holocaust 165; issue 78–9, 82, 199–201, 203, 209–11; issues 1, 165; missile capability 34; nonproliferation and disarmament regime 183; nuclear-free status 114; parity 142; patrons 166; planning and training 183; powers 163, 167–8, 173; industry 167; status 105; problem 62, 64; programme 21, 64, 122, 146, 156, 188, 201; realities 169; restraint 165; second-strike capability 30; security concerns 188; sharing arrangements 183; stability 181; states 142, 169, 210; strikes 163; technology 13, 64, 166; tests 64, 167, 170, 202; tests 64, 167, 170, 202; threat 154, 178; triad 162, 181; war 162, 164–5, 169, 173, 180; warheads 164, 166, 169, 181; winter 163

Nuclear arms 162, 164, 166–70, 172–3, 178, 181–3, 186, 191–2, 194; control 162, 169, 172
successes and failures of 169; expenses 181; reduction talks 182
Nuclear conflicts 163; "limited" 163
Nuclear enemy(s) 163; first strike 163
Nuclear missile programme 62, 64, 121; DPRK's 62, 64, 121
Nuclear non-proliferation 1, 4–5, 66, 178, 189, 192; goals of 192
Nuclear proliferation 1, 2, 200, 202–3; negotiations on 2
Nuclear umbrella 167, 178–9, 182–3, 204; Soviet 179
Nuclear war 162, 164–6, 169, 172–3, 180; limited 166, 172; probability of 165
Nuclear warheads 167; functional 167; production of 166
Nuclear weapons 4, 22, 34, 59, 64, 78, 82, 84, 95, 162–74, 178–92, 194, 201–2, 204, 208; arms control treaties 169, 173; bans on creating or using 163; comprehensive ban on 173; delivery systems for 171; deployed 181; development of 170; facilities and materials 167; disclosure of 167; fear of 163; fission and fusion 167; global push to eliminate 162; goal of eliminating 174; international inspections 167; inventories 4, 162; limitations on 167; measures to outlaw 183; nations 167, 169; negotiations to eliminate 171; non-strategic 186; non-use or threat of use of 191; placement of 170–71; policy 169, 188; possible use of 181; power 179; proliferation of 181, 182, 185; research programmes 167; technology 182; test 166; testing of 64; tests 167; used in war 165; use or threat of use 184; prohibition of 184
Nuclear-weapon-capable forces, deployment of 186
Nuclear-weapon-free status 185, 187, 190
Nuclear-weapon-free world 181, 190
Nuclear-weapon-free zones (NWFZ) 183–4; establishment of 184
Nuclear-weapons-free international society 105
Nuclear Weapons Free Zone (NWFZ) 5, 168, 172, 178, 183–7, 189–94; circular 185; development of 184;

establishment of 184; First-generation 183; limited 185; "Second Wave" 190; softer 190–91
Nuclear Weapon State (NWS) 22, 178–9, 181–3, 185, 189, 193–4; *de facto* 182, 189, 192, 194; regional 193; rival 179

Obama, Barack, US President 9, 15, 17–8, 22, 25, 85, 90, 147, 156; liberal hegemony 15; strategic pivot to Asia 18; strategy of 15
Oceania 106
Ochirbat, Punsalmaa, Mongolian President 189
Official Development Direct Investment (ODA) 152
"One Belt and One Road Initiative" (BRI) 92, 98, 222; Abe administration and the 98
"One Belt, One Road" International Cooperation Summit Forum 98
One Belt, One Road policy 143
"One China" policy 14
One Korea Foundation 193
Onon-Baldzh National Park 229
Operation Thunderball 249
Optical internet cables 56
Organisation(s): Buddhist 41; global 32; international 53, 60, 91, 93, 115, 186, 251
Orkhon drainage system 226
Orontes 264
Ota Akihiro 93; visit to Mongolia 93
Otherhood 269
Outer Space Treaty, 1967, 170

P5 181–4, 187, 189–91; joint declaration 187; joint statement 190
Pacific Islands 13, 18
Pacific Ocean 15
Pakistan 92, 108, 142, 162, 165–7, 172–3, 181, 191, 256; nuclear explosives of 162; nuclear tests 167
Palestine, the 264
Panchen Lama 41
Pan-Mongolism 39
Paris Climate Agreement 178
Park, Robert E., 255, 265
Partial Test Ban Treaty, 1963, 170
Pasteur Research Institute of Epidemiology and Microbiology 52
Peace 1, 3–4, 10–12, 14, 22, 24, 47, 53–6, 58, 63, 65, 78, 82, 87, 89, 91, 96–7, 104, 110–11, 120–23, 156, 166, 169, 180, 183, 185, 187–8, 191–2, 200–201, 208, 238, 242, 251–2, 258, 260; cooperation 121; regional 24, 111, 183, 191–2; regional issues of 65; treaty 53–6, 187
Peace and prosperity 10, 87, 91, 110; building of 87; global 110; implementation of 91
Peace and Security of Northeast Asia (PSNA) 186
Peace and stability 4, 47, 97, 104, 120, 123, 201; commitment for 97
Peace-building 121–2, 191–2; initiatives 122
Peace Depot (Japan) 185
Peaceful coexistence 78
Peacekeeping 23, 24, 38, 113, 148, 150, 191, 208; exercise 38; Peacekeeping Operations (PKOs) 38, 113, 191; international 24, 150, 191
Pence, Mike, US Vice President 97, 148
People's Liberation Army (PLA) 112
People-to-people: contacts 94, 105; educational assistance 152; engagement 106; exchanges 77, 145, 152
Peripherality 263–4, 270
Perry, Dr. William J., 164, 165
Personal Protective Equipment (PPE) 52
Peru, hostage crisis in 87
Petroglyphic Complexes of the Mongolian Altai 231
Philippines 14, 18, 86, 92
Piracy 87, 97; problem of 87
Pitakdumrongkit, Dr. Kaewkamol Karen 16
Pivot to Asia 16, 18, 209
Plutonium 167, 201
Poisson, Siméon Denis 164
Poland 155
Policy(ies) 1–5, 9, 12–23, 25, 30–33, 36–9, 47, 50, 53–4, 58–61, 65, 76–7, 79–80, 83–91, 93, 95–9, 103–7, 110, 112–23, 141–5, 147–51, 153–7, 169, 178, 180–81, 186–93, 199, 201, 203, 205–8, 210–11, 219–23, 234, 241, 249, 252; Act East 17, 106, 110; "America First" 3, 12, 15, 18, 25; America First 3, 12, 15, 18, 25; American 38, 186–7; "Arc of Freedom and Prosperity" 87–8, 96; arms control 142; Asian 87, 97, 107, 115, 117; Aso's 96; assistance 145; Central Asian 87; Chinese 25, 39,

298 *Index*

88, 96; containment 88; cooperation 22; democratic trilateral 143; deterrence 181; dialogues 87; diplomatic 123; donor assistance 145; DPRK 20; Japan's 99; economic 77, 104; environmental 223, 234; experimental 155; controversial 142; "Free and Open Indo-Pacific" 4; planning 114; import substitution 104; Indo-Pacific 3, 14, 16, 99, 143, 147; international 114, 142; Japanese 93; language 119; Mongolia's 5, 153, 178, 180, 189; multi-pillar 114; national 86; national security 9, 19, 147; "National Strategy of Engagement and Enlargement" 89; "Neighbourhood First" 106; neutral 187; New Eastern 80; New Northern 58, 208; New Southern 31, 121; no first use pledge 193; non-aligned 187; Northeast Asian 107, 115, 117; nuclear weapons 169, 188; objectionable 30; One Belt, One Road 143; "One China" 14; open ocean 99; "Proactive Contribution to Peace" 86, 91, 95; rebalance 90; rebalancing 156; Russian 88; security 1, 23, 96, 114, 116, 178; self-reliance 79; South Korean 187; strategic 21; tension-reducing 1; third neighbor 38, 113, 144, 148, 150, 180, 207; third neighbourhood 115; trilateral balancing 1; trilateralist 142; Trump Administration's 13; unfriendly 37; Japan's 87; value 96

Political: advantages 191; concessions 31; connections 31; consequences 189; cooperation 65, 86, 141; coordination 51; demands 41; dependence 143; development 220; dialogue 55; discontent 39; gain 189; hidden agenda 191; independence 113; institutions 267; integration 21; interests 50; issues 4, 31; leverage 32; liberalisation 37; multiparty system 36; objectives 191; partnership 52, 104, 115; problems 228; process 62, 64; rapprochement 144; realism 180; regional; mechanisms 190; structures 183; relations 3, 94; rivalries 2, 141; Chinese 41; security 91, 119; sovereignty 22; stability 12, 24, 156, 249; synergy 111; systems 24, 238, 252; transactions 86; will 91, 185, 247

Political-security: coordination 121; nexus 119

Politics 1, 47, 59–60, 65, 104, 106, 200, 220, 255–6, 263; Indian 106; regional 1; world 47, 104

Pollution 219–21, 223, 230, 233, 239, 249, 251–2; environmental 219–20, 223, 230; transboundary transfer of 220

Polycentricity 52

Pompeo, Mike, US Secretary of State 18, 20, 24, 78, 97, 147–8

Port of Vladivostok 58

Ports 48, 61

Poseidon underwater drones 181

Post-Cold War era 14, 88, 90

Poverty 230, 251

Power: American 11, 15, 17; Asian 19, 106, 123; asymmetry 53; balance of 12, 88, 89, 93, 99, 200, 210; big 77; Chinese 30, 38, 40, 85, 99, 111–2, 206; revisionist 111; economic 42, 86; global 15–6, 123, 153; great 30, 65, 77, 82, 84, 103–4, 113, 115, 123, 164, 179–80, 183, 185, 187, 194; middle 4, 36, 103, 122; military 42, 86–7, 89–90, 96–7; national 11, 32; Northeast Asian 120; nuclear 42, 105, 152, 163, 167–8, 170, 173; nuclear-weapon 179; parity 112; projection capability 34; regional 65, 88, 92, 99, 107, 153, 209, 210; revisionist 10; rivalry 3, 179, 194; role of 10; shift 96; small 36, 91; soft 21, 86; structural 119; structure 76, 154; US 86; vacuums 86, 88, 90

Power struggle 1

Power vacuums 86, 88–90

Pragmatism 60

PRC National People's Congress 50

Precious stones 237

Predator 229

Predictability 151, 179, 194

Private sector 12, 87, 95, 98, 106; bilateral government- 106

Privatisation 145

"Proactive Contribution to Peace" policy 86, 91, 95

Production: capacities 61; consumer electronics 59; facilities 49, 193; gas 56, 58; industrial 48; literary 267

Index 299

Propaganda 10
Proportionality 63
Provocations 18, 151
Pukkuksong-3 SLBM 188
Pürevsüren, Lundeg, Mongolian Foreign Minister 146
Putin, Vladimir, Russian President 49–50, 55–8, 60, 62, 64, 143–4, 203, 206, 225; visit to; China 50; Japan 55; Republic of Korea 57

Qing Dynasty 34
Quad Plus 120
Quadrilateral Security Dialogue (Quad 2.0) 106, 119
Quad (US-Japan-India-Australia) 4, 17, 23, 97, 99, 106, 119–21; relationship 17, 99
Quality of life 49, 252

Races 266
Radical changes 76
Radioactive minerals 115
Railways 58, 61
Raisina Dialogue on January 25, 2018, 17
Rajin port 83
Rapid Response Assessment Report (RRAR) 243
Rapprochement 59, 112, 122–3, 143–4, 205; political 144
Rational actor assumption 163–4 .
Rationality 163
Raw materials 56, 79, 263; mineral 56
Reagan, Ronald, US President 142
Realism 10, 180; political 180; principled 10
Realist theory 88
Reciprocity 63
Red Sea 264
Reeves, Jeffrey 40
Reforms 12, 34, 36, 83, 104; economic liberalisation 104; US-led 30
Regional: "activism" 76; affairs 17, 36; alliance 30; associations 53; challenge 142; concerns 21; confidence 186, 191; conflict 90; conflicts 86, 90, 180; cooperation 13, 22, 49, 82–3, 91, 95, 99, 186, 221; democracies 38; development 80, 150; strategies 80; dictators 11; economic; arrangements 31; cooperation 65; development 193; integration 3, 76, 82, 83; leadership 31;
economy 49; energy regime 32; environmental; assessment 226; problems 221; forums 87; governance 16; American 33; governments 33; instability 19; institutions 17, 36, 91–2; integration 21, 65, 92, 99, 142; interests 220; leadership 33; missile defence network 30; multilateral regime 32; nuclear arms race 194; order 15, 33, 85, 89, 208, 211; partnerships 65; peace 24, 111, 183, 191–2; peace and security 24, 183, 191–2; players 16, 47, 121, 199, 209; political; mechanisms 190; structures 183; politics 1; power 65, 88, 92, 107, 209, 210; powers 99, 153; problems 47, 233; construction of 3; projects 87; settlement 62; stability 2, 17, 91, 93, 94, 122, 189; tensions 2, 189; think tanks 184; trade 105, 144; trust-building 180
Regional Comprehensive Economic Partnership (RCEP) 31
Regional conflict zones 90
Regional dialogue 192; 1.5 track 192
Regionalisation 91
Regionalism 85–6, 91–2; European Union (EU)-type 85; in Asia-Pacific 91
Regional multilateral forums 116
Regional Nuclear Weapons-Free Zone Treaties 172
Regional order 85
Regional power 107
Regional security 1, 3, 6, 17, 21, 24, 59, 61–2, 77–9, 85, 91–2, 94, 99, 115, 121, 123, 143, 146, 154, 180, 183, 191–3, 209, 211, 219–20; Mongolian 21
Regional security architecture: China and 92
Regional zones 189, 190
Reischauer, Edwin O., 266
Relations 1–5, 9, 11, 13–25, 31–4, 36–8, 41–2, 47, 49–51, 53–63, 65, 77, 79, 82, 84, 87–8, 91–4, 98–100, 103, 106–12, 114–6, 118–9, 121–3, 141–57, 164, 168, 173, 179–80, 187–91, 194, 199–200, 202–11, 220–22, 224, 228–9, 233, 242, 246, 249, 257, 266, 268; ally 24; balanced 36; bilateral 22–3, 25, 50, 55, 57, 59–62, 91, 93–4, 115, 144–5, 148–53, 157, 188; restoration of 53; Russia and South Korea 57; bilateral

300　Index

alliance 187; China and Japan 92, 100; China and Mongolia 34; China and Russia 36, 49–51, 53–6, 93, 107, 228; China and US 17; commercial 17; constructive 31; deterioration of 92; diplomatic 49, 53, 57, 82, 208; economic 15, 22, 55, 57, 79, 94, 119, 145–6, 148, 156, 224; efficacy of 142; financial 15; foreign 14–5, 21, 23, 36, 180; friendly 23, 36, 37, 59; geographical 4, 155; trilateral 155; good 1, 77, 156, 168, 173, 190–91, 206, 208–9; anomalies in 54; humanitarian 60; India and Japan 106; India and Mongolia 103, 108, 110; strategic nature of 106; India and US 142; inter-Korean 187; international 2, 32, 50, 54, 88, 91, 142, 156, 220, 222; interstate 3; Japan and US 18, 23; military 3, 13, 37, 150; mini-triangular 142; Mongolia and Japanese 152; Mongolia and North Korea 156; Mongolia and Russia 189; Mongolia and Russia 5, 59, 60–61, 189, 199; Mongolia and US 149; Northeast Asia and Russia 3, 49; North Korea and US 187; normalisation of 188; one-of-a-kind 50; political 3, 94; quadrilateral 25; Quad (US-Japan-India-Australia) 4, 17, 99; regional state of 155; Russia and South Korea 57, 59; Russo-Mongol 144; security 15, 18, 114; Sino-Mongol 144; social 249; stabilisation of 63; strategic 111, 151, 187; substantial 38; trade 24, 58, 99, 118, 152, 202, 224; trilateral 25, 143, 145–8, 151, 153–7; trilateralism 4; United States-Japan-Mongolia 4, 141
Religions 143, 155, 260, 262
Religious: affiliations 112; legacy 108
Renewable energy 81
Repression 11
Republic of China (Taiwan) (ROC) 34, 35; ROC government 35
Republic of Korea; *see* Republic of Korea (South Korea) (ROK)
Republic of Korea (South Korea) (ROK) 1, 13, 17–9, 22, 24, 30–31, 34, 47, 49, 57–9, 61–6, 76–9, 81–3, 85, 91, 93, 107, 110, 113–4, 117, 120–23, 143–4, 162–3, 166–9, 182–4, 186–7, 189, 193–4, 199–204, 206–10, 223, 252, 266, 269–70; "Asian Energy Super Ring" 65; international outlook 121
Research Center for Nuclear Weapons Abolition (RECNA) 185; Nagasaki process 185
Reserves 48, 116–7, 124, 221, 230, 232–3; coal 117; cross-border nature 230, 232
Reservoirs 226, 228; cross-border 228
Resilience 87
Resource Centre for Russian-Mongolian cooperation 222
Resources 1–2, 5–6, 10, 18, 41, 48, 82, 85, 87, 108, 116, 119, 142, 145, 166, 169, 200, 202, 220–24, 227, 233, 237–9, 241, 246–7, 249–51, 268; competition 5; cooperation 2; distribution 142; economic 5; energy mineral 1, 6; financial 169; forest 221, 241; labour 48; exploitation of 5, 237; mineral 1, 6; natural 5, 41, 48, 82, 108, 116, 145, 200, 202, 222–4, 227, 233, 237–8, 241, 246, 249–51; scarce 166; technical 169; water 220–21, 223, 268
Rights: human 5, 22, 38, 88, 90, 96, 141, 219, 237; individual 12
Rivalry(ies) 2–3, 5, 112, 120, 141, 179, 184, 194, 200, 206, 210–11; China and Russia 3; China and US 120, 200, 210; economic 141; geostrategic 5; ideological 184; political 2, 141; power 3, 179, 194
Rivers 50, 89, 206–7, 222, 225–30, 232–3; Amur 50, 207, 228–30; Argun 50, 228, 232; Hailar 228; Imalka 227; Mekong 89; project 89; Selenga 222, 225; transboundary 227–8; Uldza 226–7; Ussuri 50, 228, 230
Rivers without Borders 227
Ri Yong Pil 150
Roadmap for Expanded Economic Partnership between the United States of America and Mongolia 148
Rockefeller, David 141
Rockfalls 220
ROK and Russia Joint Statement of 57
ROK-DPRK-Russia cooperation 59
ROK Ministry of Science and Information and Communication 57
Rospotrebnadzor [Federal Service for Supervision of Consumer Protection and Welfare] 52
Rotterdam Convention 251

Rule of law 12, 13, 88, 97, 141, 243; values of 141
Rules-based order 22, 148
Rumsfeld, Donald, Secretary of Defense 24
Russel, Daniel 146
Russia 1–5, 10, 13, 15, 18–9, 21, 24, 31, 34–8, 40, 42, 47–66, 76–7, 80–82, 88, 92–3, 95–6, 99, 103, 107, 113–5, 117, 120–21, 143–6, 148–51, 153–5, 162, 165, 167–73, 181–2, 184, 186–7, 189, 193–4, 199–211, 219, 221–33, 252, 256, 261, 267, 269; annexation of Crimea 42; deterrence policy 181; economic influence in NEA 24; economy 58; exports to; Japan 55; Mongolia 60; South Korea 58; foreign policy 50, 60, 199, 207; foreign trade 51, 56, 58; balance 58; turnover 60; growth rate 48; humanitarian aid 52; imports 51; Japan 55; Mongolia 60; South Korea 58; investment in Mongolia 144; Japan's policy towards 54; leadership 48; market 51; military potential 56; military presence in the South Kuril Islands 57; national priority for 3, 48; NEA policy 65; North Korean conundrum 5; policies 88; policy towards North Korea 5, 199; Russia's policy towards North Korea, success and limitations of 5, 199; security assurances 193; specially protected natural areas (SPNA) 230; success and limitations of policy 5, 199; trade 56, 58, 95; partner 56; turnover 60; US foreign policy towards 88
Russia and South Korea 57–9; bilateral trade 58; cooperation 58–9; joint projects 59; Memorandum of Understanding 57; relations 57, 59; diplomatic 57; trade 58
Russia and US 169, 171
Russia-ASEAN summit 55
Russia-China-Mongolia 5, 62, 219, 221–2, 224–5, 228, 231, 233; cooperation 5, 62, 219; ecological 228; transport systems of 61; trilateral cooperation 62
Russia-China-Mongolia International Protected Area "Dauria" (DIPA) 231
Russia-Mongolia-China Economic Corridor 61
Russian-Chinese Commission 221

Russian Council on International Affairs 64
Russian Far East 3, 47, 49, 56, 62, 65, 203; development of 65
Russian Far Eastern 57–8, 61, 206
Russian Federation 47, 50–52, 54, 57–8, 60, 63, 80, 93, 183, 221–2, 226, 229; foreign policy concept 54; PRC exports to 51
Russian Federation and Mongolia 60, 222, 226; Declaration on the development of strategic partnership 60
Treaty on Friendly Relations and Comprehensive Strategic Partnership 60
Russian Federation and PRC 50, 52, 63, 93
Russian Federation and the ROK 57, ;58
Russian-Korean Forum of Interregional Cooperation 57
Russian-Korean Joint Commission for Economic, Scientific, and Technical Cooperation 57
Russian Ministry of Economic Development 57
Russian Ministry of Health 52
Russian-Mongolian-Chinese trilateral interaction 232
Russian-Mongolian intergovernmental agreement 229
Russian-Mongolian intergovernmental commission 225
Russian-Mongolian Joint Commission on environmental protection 222
Russian-Mongolian UNESCO World Heritage Site 227
Russian SPNAs 230
Russian Trans-Siberian railway 51

S-400 Triumph anti-aircraft missile system (SAM) 52
Sakhalin-Hokkaido gas pipeline 56
Sakhalin Island 54
SALT I, 1972, 171
SALT II., 171
Sam Nunn 164
Samurai bonds 95
Sanctions 20, 32–3, 52, 54–5, 64–5, 82–3, 92, 112–3, 117, 121, 187–9, 199, 201–4, 246; bilateral 187–8; relief from 188; trade 112, 117; UN 64, 121; UNSC-imposed 188

302   Index

Sand storms 223
SARS 76
Saudi Arabia 163
Saylyugem 229
Saylyugemskiy 229
School of International Relations and Public Administration (SIRPA) 154
Schultz, George 164
Science and technology 59–60, 83, 86; innovation in 86
Scientific cooperation 52
Seabed Arms Control Treaty, 1972, 171
Sea lanes 10; Indian Ocean 10; impact on 153; balanced 111
Second Millennium Challenge Compact 148
Security: architecture 2, 4, 6, 17, 61, 65, 88, 92, 99, 111, 123, 143, 210; Asian 92, 157, 187; assurances 168, 182, 184–5, 190, 193; bilateral 23; relations 115; border 111, 115; challenges 1–2, 6, 116, 199; trilateral 148; commitment 90; conventional 104; cooperation 9, 14, 33, 37–8, 94, 97, 116, 121, 146, 192; cultural 119; cyber 111, 115, 151; East Asia's 87; ecological 225; economic 11, 77, 115, 190; energy 2, 32, 65, 81, 105, 115; environment 4, 76, 78, 81, 97, 116; environmental 5, 119, 219, 221, 224, 233, 249–50; global 62, 115, 146, 154, 169, 219–20; guarantees 62–4, 167, 203, 210; homeland 10; ideological 115; issues 13; implications and impacts on 76; independence 85; infrastructure 1; interests 3, 50, 143, 193; international 52, 60, 190; issues 5, 13, 66, 76, 79, 105, 187, 219, 233; mechanisms 4, 23, 85, 122, 183; multilateral 23, 147–8, 179, 200; national 60; non-traditional 76, 116, 124; Northeast Asian 1, 3, 21, 78–9, 95, 120, 150, 157, 187, 191, 192; impact on 153; objectionable 30; partners 16; partnerships 105, 115; policies 1, 23, 96, 114, 116, 178; political 91, 119; regional 1, 3, 6, 17, 21, 24, 59, 61–2, 77–9, 85, 91–2, 94, 99, 115, 121, 123, 143, 146, 154, 180, 183, 191–3, 209, 211, 219–20; relationships 15, 18, 114; requirements 90; shared issues 105; soft 192; strategic 115, 124; construction of 3; strategies 3, 21, 22; traditional 76, 116, 124; trans-regional 219; trilateral 148
Security and prosperity 17, 90, 180
Security partnership, India and Mongolia 113
Seismicity 220
Seko, Hiroshige 55
Selenga HPP 226
Self-defence 36
Self-Defence Force of Japan 94
Self-determination 113–4
Self-interest 114, 144; economic 144
"Self-reliant India" 117
Senkaku Islands 92, 96
Separatism 39; Tibetan 39
Shanghai Cooperation Organisation (SCO) 38–9, 50, 61, 87, 99, 144, 149, 206, 223; Tashkent summit 223; Western perceptions of 39
Shanghai Cooperation Organisation (SCO) summit 61
Shangri-La Dialogue 97
Shanxi 222
Shikotan Islands 54
Shipbuilding 58
Shugaev, Dmitry 52
Shultz, George 142
Shuren hydroelectric power station 226
Siberia 35, 47–8, 54, 80, 206, 227
Siberian Russia 35
Silkhemin Nuruu 229
Silk Road Fund 65
Simon, Count Saint 258
Singapore 14, 16, 18, 55, 62, 78, 87, 91, 105, 117, 151, 188, 193
Singh, Manmohan, Indian Prime Minister 105
Single-state NWFZs (SSNWFZs) 187, 189, 192
Single-state zones 190
Sino-Russian-US 4; strategic competition 4
Six Party Talks (SPT) 21–3, 63–4, 77, 79, 82, 146, 154, 157, 184, 188, 192, 194, 201–05, 209–10; cessation of 157; resumption of 146; stalemate in 146
Sixth Tokyo International Conference on African Development (TICAD VI) 96
Sixth Ulaanbaatar Dialogue on Northeast Asian Security 78
Sklar, Holly 141

Index 303

Slavery 11
Slavic Research Center 88
Small and medium-sized enterprises 56
Smuggling 241–2, 250
Snow leopards 229, 231
Social: challenges 141; cohesion 91; connections 105; consequences 226; development 111, 246; difficulties 77; distance 263; engagement 122; facilities 49; fossils 268; group 264; periphery 264; problems 228; relations 249; ties 54
Socialism 179
Social order 219
Society(ies) 5, 12, 237, 243, 252, 255–6, 259, 261–6, 268–9; "arrested" 5, 255; "fossilized" 5, 255; hunter-gatherer 259; Japanese 266; Jewish 268; marginal 268; Mongolian 37; peripheral 255, 266, 269; primitive 265
Socioeconomic development 47
Soil erosion 219, 222, 230
Soil weathering 222
Sokhondinsky State Natural Biosphere Reserve 229
Solar energy 118
Solar power 124
Solidarity 87
Soni, Dr. Sharad 153
Soong, T.V., 35
SORT 171
South Africa 50, 182
South Asia 17, 25, 142, 162, 173, 190, 231; nuclear arms race 167
South Asian states 98, 105
South China Sea 13, 17, 33, 99, 112; disputed 112; free and open seaways 13
South China Sea maritime region 112
Southeast Asia 15, 32, 36, 85–9, 92, 98, 105–7, 110, 117, 172, 184–5, 239; economic growth in 106; establishment of NWFZs in 184; Islamic fundamentalism in 85; South Korean economic connections with 32
South Korea; see Republic of Korea (South Korea) (ROK); Chinese economic retaliation in 113; economic connections with Southeast Asia 32; economy 166; New Southern Policy 31; New Southern Policy (NSP) 121; policy 187; Russia's exports to 58; Russia's imports from 58; space programme 59; trade relations 58
South Korea and US bilateral alliances 85
South Pacific 172, 184
South Sakhalin Island 53
South-South dialogues 114
Sovereignty 11, 13, 17, 22–3, 36, 41, 83, 123, 150, 190; economic 22; political 22
Soviet Russia 35, 205; military manoeuvres 42; Bloc 36; manipulation 35; proxy 113
Soviet-Mongol army 42
Soviet Union 35, 36, 53–4, 59–60, 89, 166, 168, 170–72, 179, 182, 205, 256; broke up 168; disintegration of 179
Soviet Union and US 170, 171
Space and cyber capabilities 11
Space exploration 110–11
Space programme 59
Special Economic Zone (SEZ) 118
Special Protected Natural Areas (SPNA) 224, 230; Chinese 230; comprehensive network of 230; Russian 230
Spengler, Oswald 255, 257, 259, 266; *Decline of the West* 259
Spiritual: connection 113; links 119; neighbour 107, 124
Spirituality 169
Spratly Islands 97
Sri Lanka 18, 191
SS-NWFZ 190
Stability 2, 4, 6, 12, 16–7, 21, 23–4, 47, 50, 52, 54, 62–3, 76, 78, 90–91, 93–5, 97, 104, 106, 111, 120, 122–3, 142–3, 155–6, 179, 181, 189, 194, 199, 201, 203, 224, 233, 239, 249; alliance 90; economic 95, 233; implications and impacts on 76; international 52; issues 2; military 24; negative impact on 21; nuclear 181; political 12, 24, 156, 249; regional 2, 17, 91, 93–4, 122, 189; strategic 50, 54, 201, 203
Stability and prosperity 94, 97, 106
Stalin 35, 36
State Agency for Financial Services 55
Statecraft 11, 14, 173; Trump's attitude toward 14
Steppe Road Programme 80
Stilwell, General David 150
Stockholm Convention 251

304 *Index*

Stock market 95
Stonequist, E.V., 255–5; Marginal Man, The 265
St. Petersburg International Economic Forum 51
Straits of Malacca 15
Strategic: advantages 3, 76–7; agendas 33; allies 107; autonomy 103, 207; challenges 10; choices 122; competition 4, 11; competitiveness 111; consultative meetings 94; convergence 17; cooperation 157; disadvantages 3, 76–7; environment 13; imagination 4, 104; import 112; intelligence 12; interaction 50; interests 83, 106, 112, 184, 199, 202–3; issues 31; leadership 33; motivations 3, 76; partner 53, 93–4, 204; partners 57; bilateral 94, 205; comprehensive 104, 114, 206; global 104; partnership 23, 38, 50, 59–60, 93–5, 99, 103–4, 110–11, 114–6, 123–4, 149, 151–3, 205, 206–7, 223; partnership agreement 38; patience policy 188; policy 21; relations 111, 116, 151, 187; security 115, 124; sensibilities 34; stability 50, 54, 201, 203; synergy 111; waterways 15
Strategic Arms Limitation Treaty (SALT) 55, 61, 171, 187, 190
Strategic Arms Reduction Treaty (START) 171, 181
Strategic or Policy Summits 142
Strategic Partnership agreement 23
Strategic Partnership in 2019, 23
Strategy(ies) 2–3, 4, 9–10, 12, 14–22, 25, 32, 36–7, 76, 78, 80–81, 92, 97–8, 103–5, 107, 110, 121, 141–4, 147, 151, 153, 155–6, 171, 225, 233, 251–2; America First 15; American 17; Chinese 32, 92; development 80–81; enmeshment 37; Indo-Pacific 4, 16, 18, 21, 25, 97, 147; international 104, 107; 'joined-up' 15; multipronged 20; national 12; negotiation 78; non-alignment 103; Obama's 15; principles of 14; regional development 80; security 3, 21–2; survival 36; trade 17
Submarine-Launched Ballistic Missile (SLBM) 188
Submarines 181–2; nuclear 182
Suga Yoshihide, Japanese Prime Minister 99–100

Suitcase bombs 166
Sumner, William Graham 265
Sunflower Movement 32
Superpowers 1, 2, 84, 142–3, 156, 168–9, 171, 202–3, 205–6; gamesmanship 156
Supply Chain Resilience Initiative (SCRI) 106
Supply chains 118, 241
Surveillance 174, 191
Swaraj, Sushma, India's former External Affairs Minister 111; visit to Mongolia 111
Sweden 155
Syria 42

Tactics 120
Taiwan 14, 21, 23–4, 32–5, 42, 85, 89, 93, 163, 167, 185, 200; defence needs 14; threatening war against 33
Taiwan Relations Act 14
Taiwan (Republic of China) 167
Takizaki Shigeki 150
Tariffs 20
Tashkent summit 61
Tatsujiro Suzuki 185
Tavan Tolgoi 93, 117
Tax fraud 251
Technical: cooperation 52; assistance and training 18, 121
Technological: interaction 112; issues 4
Technology 10–11, 13, 18, 34, 60, 82–3, 86, 108, 118, 166, 170, 182, 224; environmental 224; exports 18; gap 166; nuclear and ballistic missile 13; nuclear weapons 182; transfer 34
Telecommunications 115
Tension(s) 1–3, 23–4, 31, 34, 38, 51, 56, 61, 63, 77, 82, 118–9, 123, 149, 181–3, 185, 189, 210; bilateral 31, 38; China and Russia 51; military 34; North Korea and South Korea 82; regional 2, 189
Terminal High Altitude Area Defence system (THAAD) 30, 182, 203–4
Territorial: claims 32, 57; clause 55; disputes 62; integrity 36, 41, 168, 190; problems 62, 187, 191; water claims 92
Terror 11, 173
Terrorism 12, 87, 97, 105, 115, 149, 250–51
Terrorist group 162, 164; Islamic 162; to acquire two nuclear warheads 164
Terrorists 11, 14, 162, 164, 182, 242, 256;

Index   305

danger of getting ahold of nuclear weapons technology 182; Jihadist 11; threat 14
Thailand 14
The Heads of the Amur 229
Third neighbor policy 148, 150
Third neighbour 36, 38, 113–5, 118, 120, 122, 180
"Third Neighbour" policy 103, 113–5, 122, 144, 207
Third parties 164–5
Threats 5, 11–5, 17–8, 36–7, 39, 42, 53, 56, 61–3, 90, 97, 99–100, 112, 119, 121–2, 147, 154, 162–3, 165, 167, 178, 180, 184, 186, 191, 193–4, 204, 219–20, 226–7, 230, 232, 237, 239, 242, 246–7, 249–51; Chinese 99; common 12; cyber 12; economic 219; elimination of 97; environmental 219, 230; European 165; existential 163; global 18; ideological 42; military 17, 37, 56, 63, 219; mutual 17; nuclear 154, 178; Russian 162; social-environmental 219; terrorist 14; transnational 11
Tiananmen Square Incident 92
Tianjin, port of 40, 41
Tibet 261
Tibetan Buddhism 41
Ties 4, 14, 21, 23, 38, 54, 59–61, 87, 93, 103–8, 110–23, 143, 145–7, 149–50, 152, 154, 157, 199–202, 204–5, 207–11, 227; bilateral 103–4, 107–8, 111, 114, 116, 120–21, 123, 205; cordial 113; cultural 108; diplomatic 105, 108, 121–2, 152; economic 60, 87, 149, 201, 205, 207, 227; progress and momentum in 103; historical 4, 104, 108; reinvigoration of 114; restrictive nature of 108; India and Mongolia 4, 103, 104, 107–8, 111–2, 114, 116; India and ROK 121; institutional 157; military 149; DPRK and Mongolia 122; mutually beneficial 110; trade 60; bilateral 13
Timber 239, 241, 249–51
Tkacik, John 38
Tokyo International Conference on African Development (TICAD) 96
Tomahawk cruise missile 172, 181
Torey Lakes 227
Tourism 56, 58, 81, 118, 222, 224, 230–31; educational 230; sports 222
Tourist infrastructure 222

Toynbee, Arnold 5, 255, 257, 259–63, 266, 268, 270; *A Study of History* 259, 266; concepts of civilisations 263; view of history 266
Track 2 meetings 78
Trade 5, 11, 13, 16–7, 19, 24, 30–32, 40, 51, 54–61, 76–7, 79–80, 82–3, 86–7, 95–7, 99, 105, 108–9, 111–2, 115–8, 120–21, 123–4, 142–4, 147–9, 151–2, 154, 156, 193, 202–3, 206, 224, 237–9, 241–3, 249–50, 252; abuses 11; agenda 13; balance 58; bilateral 13, 30, 56, 58, 80, 95, 105, 109, 116–7, 202; China and Russia 51, 95; competitiveness 118; decline in 58; fair and reciprocal 13; food and medicinal 121; foreign 40, 51, 56, 58, 60, 77; free 40, 51, 58, 77, 79, 87, 97, 206; free flow of 17; gaps 82; global 51, 243; illegal 242–3, 250; improvement of 224; infrastructure 31; international 31; interruptions 120; links 117; Mongolia and Russia 60; multilateral 13; overdependency on 40; regional 105, 144; relations 24, 58, 99, 118, 152, 202, 224; Russia and South Korea 58; Russian 56, 58, 95; sanctions 112, 117; strategies 17; ties 60; turnover 51, 56, 58, 60, 80; wildlife 5, 237
Trade dispute 149
Trade partner 56, 143, 202, 206; options 143
Trade war 76, 111; implications of 76
Trafficking 5, 105, 237–9, 241, 249–51; human 105, 238, 249; minerals 5, 237; timber 241
Transbaikalia 227, 232
Trans-Baikal territory 222, 226, 228
Transboundary biosphere reserve 232
Transboundary special protected natural areas (SPNA) 224
Transit: corridor 2, 80, 95; links 2; routes 95; traffic 61, 144
Transnational criminal organisations 11
Transnational Organized Crime in South East Asia: Evaluation, Growth and Impact 239
Transnational threats 11
Trans Pacific Partnership (TPP) 18, 23, 89
Transparency 151, 154
Transport/Transportation 21, 40, 48, 52, 58, 60–61, 80–81, 143–4, 151, 154–6,

184, 206–7, 224, 239; alternatives 156; connections 144; cooperation 80, 144; hub 80; infrastructure 48, 144, 224; integration 143; systems 61
Trans-Siberian rail system 144
Treaties and agreements 36, 50, 53–6, 60, 82, 108–9, 114, 168–73, 181–84, 187, 190, 246; bilateral alliance 183; intergovernmental 50; international 114, 168, 190, 246; nuclear weapons arms control 169, 173; peace 53–6, 187
Treaty of Amity and Cooperation in Southeast Asia (TAC) 92
Treaty of Bangkok 184
Treaty of Friendship and Cooperation 36
Treaty of Pelindaba 184
Treaty of Rarotonga 184
Treaty of Semipalatinsk 184
Treaty of Tlatelolco 184
Treaty on Friendly Relations and Comprehensive Strategic Partnership 60
Treaty on Friendly Relations and Cooperation 60, 189
Treaty on Good Neighborliness, Friendship, and Cooperation 50
Treaty on the Non-Proliferation of Nuclear Weapons 82, 181
Treaty on the Prohibition of Nuclear Weapons, 2017, 173
Trilateral: alliance 19, 154; approach 19, 155; commission 231; cooperation 59, 62, 65, 143, 148, 157, 221, 224, 228, 233; dialogue 143, 153; environmental interaction 231; foreign ministerial talks 145, 146; groupings 119, 120; interaction 232; investment 224; meetings 61, 80, 94, 146–7, 150–51, 154, 203; partnership 148; relations 143, 145–8, 151, 153–7; US-Japan-Mongolia 145, 153, 155–6; security, multilateral 148; strategic relationship 151; summits 65, 80, 144
Trilateral Commission 141
Trilateral Cooperation Secretariat (TCS) 65
Trilateralism 4, 141–7, 151–7; democratic 4, 141, 143, 145–6, 153–7; forms of 142–3, 157; formula 156; hard-line 142; Japanese views of 151; new 144–5; relationship 4; renovated 142; Sino-Russian-Mongolian version of 157; types of 145
Trilateralism cooperation, integration of 147
Tripartite NWFZ 185
Trump-Battulga meeting 149
Trump, Donald J., US President 2–3, 9–25, 62, 78, 82, 85, 97, 143, 147–50, 154, 156–7, 172, 188, 201, 203; aggressive approach 15; America First policy 3, 12, 15, 18, 25; attitude toward statecraft 14; concession-for-concession approach 20; confrontation style of 15; DPRK policy 20; election of 157; failed diplomacy 20; foreign policy 14, 17, 23; hard-line push for DPRK 20; impeachment of 20; Indo-Pacific policy 16, 143; initiatives 15; National Defense Strategy (NDS) 150; national security; policy 147; strategic principles of 23; strategy 17, 25; North Korea policy 20; policy 15, 85; step-by-step approach 20; urity framework 15
Trump-Kim Singapore summit 18
Trust 17, 22, 65, 76, 78–9, 84, 87, 100, 149, 168, 180, 191, 193, 200, 208; lack of 168
Trust-building 65, 180, 191; regional 180
Trust deficit 17
Tsar Bomba 166
Tsirkon hypersonic cruise missiles 181
Tsogtbaatar, Damdin, Foreign Minister 78, 148; visit to US 148
Tuberculosis 76
Tunka-Khubsgöl cross-border reserve 230
Tunkinsky 230
Turkey 88, 92, 114, 144
Turner, Oliver 15
Two-ness 265
Typhoons 220

Ubsunurskaya hollow 231
Ufa summit 61
Ukraine 42, 182, 200
Ulaanbaatar Declaration 60
Ulaanbaatar Dialogue on Northeast Asia Security (UBD) 21–3, 61, 78, 95, 120, 122–3, 150, 191–2, 208–9
Ulaanbaatar Process (UBP) 192

Ulaanbaatar Railway (UBTZ) 61, 205; modernisation 61
Ultra-nationalism 15
Umebayashi, Dr. Hiromichi 185
Underprivileged group 264
Underwater nuclear drones 181
UNDP 251
Unemployment 38
UNGA Resolution 3472 (XXX) 189
UN General Assembly 146, 172–3
Ungern-Sternberg, Roman von 34
"Unilateral Pacifism" 86
United Kingdom 99, 117, 167, 181, 242, 256
United Nations (UN) 35, 38, 53, 60–61, 64–5, 78, 108, 113, 121, 124, 144, 146, 148–9, 151, 153–4, 167–8, 172–4, 178–9, 184–5, 189, 191, 201–3, 208, 239, 242, 245, 250, 252; sanctions 64, 121; economic 121
United Nations (UN) Advisory Board on Disarmament Matters 185
United Nations (UN) Children's Fund 108
United Nations (UN) Department of Political and Peacebuilding Affairs 78
United Nations (UN) Disarmament Commission (UNDC) 184, 189
United Nations (UN) Economic and Social Commission for Asia Pacific (UNESCAP) 252
United Nations (UN) Educational, Scientific and Cultural Organization (UNESCO) 108, 227, 231–2
United Nations (UN) Environment Programme (UNEP) 242–3, 250–51
United Nations (UN) General Assembly (UNGA) 35, 144, 146, 172–3, 183–4, 187, 189–90, 249
United Nations (UN) High-Level Meeting on Disarmament 185
United Nations (UN) Human Rights Council 148
United Nations (UN) Office on Drugs and Crime (UNODC) 239, 241, 245
United Nations (UN) Security Council (UNSC) 35, 64–5, 108, 151, 153, 179, 187–8, 191, 201–4, 209–11, 250; permanent members of 179
United Nations (UN) Sustainable Development Goals (SDGs) 178

United Sates-Japan-Mongolia trilateral relationship 147
United States-Japan-Mongolia 4, 141, 153; relationship of 4, 141
United States-Japan-Mongolia democratic trilateralism 4, 141
United States-Japan-Mongolia trilateralism: Mongolian views of 153
United States (US) 1, 3–4, 9–25, 30, 33–5, 37–8, 40, 42, 47–8, 52–5, 59, 61–4, 66, 76–9, 82, 85–94, 96–100, 103, 106, 111, 113–4, 117–8, 120–23, 141–57, 162, 165–73, 181–8, 193–4, 199–211, 223, 241–2, 256, 269; 2020 presidential campaign 20, 188; alliance commitments 193; allies and partners 9, 11, 13, 16–7, 97, 141; European 141; Japanese 141; arms sales 186; assistance priorities 148; assistance to Mongolia 148; attitude towards China 100; Biden Administration 24; Bush administration 15, 85; Clinton administration 89–90; commitment in Asia-Pacific region 86; commitment in the Asia-Pacific 86; "critical ally" 147; deployment of its intermediate-range missiles 186; diplomatic and development efforts 12; engagement with the North Korean problem 9; exports 18; technology 18; foreign policy 16; bilateral approach to 16; towards Central Asia 88; towards China 88; towards Russia 88; foreign relations 15; government 30; hegemony 141; immigration system 11; Indo-Pacific policies of 143; Indo-Pacific strategy 16, 97; influence in Asia 33; influence of 33, 89; interests 10, 17; interests and values 10; involvement in Asia 87; leadership 9, 90; military-political alliance 54; military power 86, 90; military strength 11; missile defence system 182; national interests 10; national security 16; National Security Strategy 3, 9; Trump Administration's 3, 9; nuclear weapons 184; in Japan 184; in South Korea 184; Obama administration 15, 17, 22, 25, 90, 147, 156; operations in Afghanistan 90; operations in Iraq 90; policy 14, 59, 89; Central Asia 87; Indo-Pacific 15;

Indo-Pacific national security 9; North Korea 21; Northeast Asia in 18; security 14, 89; Trump Administration's 13; policymaking 10, 23, 25; foreign 23; power 86; priority actions in Indo-Pacific 13; Priority Actions of 13; project scouting, financing, and technical assistance 18; rebalance policy 90; regional involvement 33; retrenchment 156; role 89; in Asian security 92; Ronald Reagan administration 142; Russian threats 162; sanctions on the Chinese Ministry of Defence 52; security policy 14, 89; strategic interest in Asia 106; strategic patience policy 188; strategic policy 21; towards NEA 21; strategy of; national security 3; Trump administration 2–3, 9–19, 21–2, 24–5, 85, 97, 143, 147, 148, 149, 150, 154, 156, 203; withdrawal of its tactical weapons; from the Korean Peninsula 185
United States (US) Agency for International Development (USAID) 242
Université Paris Ouest, Nanterre, France 15
UN Peacekeeping missions 149
Ural-Volga region 48
Urban planning 56
US Army 14, 90; global deployment 90
US Army War College Strategic Studies Institute 14
US Department of Defense 15, 38, 90; Defense Strategic Guidelines 90; "Indo-Pacific Strategy Report" of 2019, 38
US Indo-Pacific Command 24, 38
US-Japan-Mongolia 4, 143, 145–6, 153; trilateral relationship 145, 153, 155–6
US-Japan-Mongolian trilateral relationship 151
US-Japan-Mongolia trilateral 145, 147, 153, 155–6
US-Japan-Mongolia trilateral dialogue 153
US-Japan-Mongolia trilateralism 145, 153–6; importance of 147; US-Japan-ROK trilateral alliance 19
US National Intelligence Strategy of 2019, 9

US National Security Strategy of 2017, 9
US-North Korean summit meeting 188
USSR 36, 49–50, 53, 59, 167, 205; collapse of the 50, 59
Uvs Nuur basin 231
Uyghur independence movement 35
Uzbekistan 116

Vajpayee, Atal Bihari, Prime Minister of India 105, 109
Valdai Discussion Club 64
Values; chains 106, 116; democratic 114; liberal 114; rule of law 141; shared 4, 22, 93, 113, 114, 148, 155; supply chains 118
Vance, Cyrus, Secretary of State 141
Veto power 35, 204
Victor Cha, Korea Chair for the Center for Strategic and International Studies 20
Vietnam 9, 14, 18–9, 49, 78, 87, 89, 92, 97, 117, 149, 165, 193, 242
Vietnam War 89
Violence 11, 37
Voice of America (VOA) 150
Volcker, Paul, Federal Reserve Chief 142

Wallerstein, Immanuel 255, 259, 263
Wang Yi, PRC Foreign Minister 39, 119
War(s) 1–3, 10, 14, 16, 19–20, 22, 25, 30, 33–7, 42, 53–4, 76, 84–6, 88–91, 93, 103–4, 111, 113–4, 141, 144, 151, 162–7, 169, 172–3, 178–80, 183–7, 189, 192, 194, 200–201, 203, 205, 256; conventional 162, 166; fog of 164; nuclear 162, 164–6, 169, 172–3, 180; probability of 164; proxy 163, 166; series of 89; thermonuclear 162–3; two-front 90; zones 165
Washington Post, The 149
Water 97, 153, 219, 221, 226–7; clean 238–9; fresh 219; reservoirs 226; resources 220–21, 223, 268; runoff 228; safety 225; seas and oceans 219; source of 227; supply 225, 238, 243; transboundary 221–2, 226; withdrawal capacities 228
Water basins, preservation of 224
Water bodies 222, 231
Waterways 15; strategic 15
Weaponry 256

Weapon(s) 4–5, 11–2, 18, 20, 22, 34, 51–2, 57, 59, 64, 78, 82, 84, 95, 97, 105, 151, 153, 162–74, 178–94, 201–2, 204, 208; biological 163, 173, 174; chemical 173; destructive 18; modern 57; non-nuclear 22, 172; Russian 52; tactical 182, 185
Weapons of Mass Destruction (WMD) 11–2, 97, 151, 153, 167–8, 179, 189; proliferation of 12, 97
Weather mitigation 239, 243
Weber, Max 264
Weinberger, Caspar 142
Wei Ruan 263; Civilization and Culture 263
Weltanschauungen 270
Western alliance 141
Western Europe 141
Westernization 266
Wetlands 224, 227, 232; protection of 224
White Paper on Developmental Cooperation 2018, 93
Wildlife 5, 237, 239, 242–3, 247, 250–51; poaching 5, 237, 247, 251; poaching and trade 5, 237; trade 5, 237
Williams, Dr. Brad 54
"Wolf warrior" diplomacy 113, 120
Workers 11, 35, 37–8, 41, 83, 202, 208; Chinese 35, 37–8, 41; migrant 37
World Bank 76, 118, 226, 242, 251, 262
World Customs Organization 249
World economy 142; "interdependent" 142
World Health Organization (WHO) 52
World Natural Heritage 227
World Network of Biosphere Reserves 232

World of the Uvs Nuur basin 231
World order 14, 16, 52, 103–4, 116; bipolar 103; free and repressive visions of 14, 16; multipolar 52, 116; pluralistic multi-nodal 104
World Trade Partnership 193
World War II 14, 34, 42, 53–4, 85–6, 89, 91, 163, 165–6, 178, 200, 256; end of 14, 42, 85, 91, 178
World-Wide Fund for Nature (WWF) 232
World Wildlife Fund (WWF) 230, 232
WTO 87
Wuhan 52

Xi Jinping, Chinese President 2, 32–3, 39, 41, 50–51, 65, 99–100, 143–4, 248; "Economic Ring of North-East Asia," 65; visit to; Japan 99; Russia 50
Xinjiang Province 51
Xot-ail 155
Xu Shuzheng, General 34

Yalta Conference 35, 53
Yi Soyeon 59; visited Mongolia 119
"Yoshida Doctrine" 86
Yoshida Shigeru, Japanese Prime Minister 86

Zhang Zhijie 249
Zhih-ben 268
Zionism 269
Zionist movement 268
Zun-Torey Lake 227

Printed in the United States
by Baker & Taylor Publisher Services